Legal Professional Privilege

For Philippa

Legal Professional Privilege

Dr Liz Heffernan
LL.B. (Dublin), LL.M. (Dalhousie), LL.M. and J.S.D. (Chicago)
Senior Lecturer and Fellow, Trinity College Dublin

Bloomsbury Professional

Published by
Bloomsbury Professional
Maxwelton House
41–43 Boltro Road
Haywards Heath
West Sussex
RH16 1BJ

Bloomsbury Professional
The Fitzwilliam Business Centre
26 Upper Pembroke Street
Dublin 2

ISBN 978 184766 733 5

Bloomsbury Professional, an imprint of Bloomsbury Publishing Plc

British Library Cataloguing-in-Publication Data
A catalogue record for this book is available from the British Library

Typeset by Marlex Editorial Services Ltd., Dublin, Ireland
Printed and bound in Great Britain by
Martins the Printers, Berwick-upon-Tweed, Northumberland

Foreword

We live in an age where transparency and openness is valued by society. There are ever increasing demands for access to information and the sources of information. In the world of business and the conduct of our private affairs, the necessity to obtain legal advice is common. Such contact between client and lawyer frequently involves sensitive and confidential information being exchanged. Where litigation is concerned, the lawyer retained may be asked to offer a detailed opinion on the merits of a case. Of necessity, this requires confidentiality so as to enable candid and forthright views to be expressed. In order to be effective, the lawyer and client must be confident that such communications will not be disclosed. In the administration of justice, the exchange of information between parties in dispute has certain limits. One of these is legal professional privilege.

As the author of this most useful work explains:

> "Claims of privilege effectively pit two competing aspects of the public interest in the proper conduct of the administration of justice: first, the full disclosure of information 'which, in the interests of the common good, is desirable for the purpose of ascertaining truth and rendering justice' and, second, the protection from disclosure of confidential communications between the lawyer and client that is essential for the conduct of litigation by 'men skilled in jurisprudence, in the practice of the courts, and in those matters affecting rights and obligations which form the subject of all judicial proceedings'."

The relationship of the lawyer and client is vital to the proper administration of justice. Legal professional privilege seeks to foster and protect this relationship by affording clients the right to consult with their lawyers in confidence, and for those lawyers to advise their clients with candour and free from the concerns that information contained in that advice might be released into the public domain.

This work traces the history of legal professional privilege and the reasons for it, as well as providing a detailed exposition of the law. This textbook deals with interesting and practical topics. Among those is the extent to which a solicitor is protected by legal professional privilege where he advises a client on matters of general business, including matters outside the law. Both civil procedure and criminal procedure is covered and there is a most useful section devoted to the issue of expert evidence in the context of SI 391/1998 and how it affects the communications between lawyers and the expert.

On the criminal side, Dr Heffernan provides an excellent section on the Duty of Disclosure that is on both the prosecution and the defence, and deals with other important issues such as the right of an accused to legal advice at interview and the extent to which the confidentiality of communications between an accused person and his lawyer are protected.

The interface between legal professional privilege and other issues can sometimes be blurred. In this work, the author logically follows up on issues which, if not directly with the ambit of the book's title, are sufficiently connected so as to make them highly relevant. For example, the duty to seek out and preserve evidence, as decided in the *Braddish* case. For this approach, she is to be commended.

This book will be a most welcome addition to the library of practitioners in all areas of the law.

The Hon. Mr. Justice Brian J. McGovern
High Court

23 March 2011

Acknowledgements

The Irish courts recognise evidentiary privileges which further the public interest in fostering certain confidential relationships. This book explores the most prominent of these private privileges, legal professional privilege, which entitles a client to withhold relevant information from disclosure in legal proceedings. The book examines the law and policy underpinning the two principal strands of legal professional privilege: legal advice privilege which protects from disclosure confidential communications between the lawyer and client and litigation privilege which protects information prepared or gathered by the lawyer in preparation for litigation. A range of issues relating to privilege are discussed including the restrictions imposed on privilege by the doctrine of waiver and the application of recognised exceptions. Although the subject of privilege unfolds at the coalface of legal practice, this book has been researched and written from the perspective of the legal academic. While I am conscious of the limitations of academic analysis in this context, it is my hope that the book will be of interest to academics, practitioners and students of the law of evidence alike.

I would like to acknowledge with gratitude the support and assistance of several individuals in the preparation of this book. I am most grateful to the Honorable Mr Justice Brian J McGovern for kindly agreeing to write the foreword. I am indebted to Ms. Sandra Mulvey and the staff at Bloomsbury Professional for their hard work, patience and good cheer throughout the project. My sincere thanks are also due to Ms Tessa Robinson BL for editing the text, Ms Marian Sullivan for typesetting the book and preparing the tables, and Mr Andrew Turner for drafting the index. Several individuals gave generously of their time and expertise and provided invaluable advice and encouragement at various stages. I would like to thank my colleagues at Trinity College Dublin and especially Professor Ivana Bacik BL, Professor Hilary Biehler, Professor William Binchy and Ms Catherine Finnegan. I am also particularly grateful for the help and support of Ms Therese Carrick, Dr Yvonne Daly, Ms Miriam Delahunt BL, Professor Edward J Imwinkelried, Ms Una Ní Raifeartaigh SC and Mr Ray Ryan BL. Finally, very special thanks are due to Conor, Maeve and Rod McAuliffe and to Helen Bradford.

Liz Heffernan
5 April 2011

Contents

Chapter 3 Litigation Privilege

Chapter 4 Without Prejudice Privilege

Chapter 5 Exceptions

Chapter 6 Loss of Privilege

Chapter 9 Criminal Procedure

Chapter 10 Procedural Accommodations: Informer Privilege

Chapter 11 Pre-trial Legal Advice

Table of Cases

A

B

D

E

F

G

I

J

K

L

M

N

O

P

Q

R

T

U

V

W

Z

Table of Statutes

A Ireland

Bunreacht na hÉireann

United Kingdom

International Conventions

Statutory Instruments

Rules of the Superior Courts 1986 (SI 15/1986) (contd)

Other Jurisdictions

Chapter 1

Introduction

LAWYERS AND CLIENTS

[1.01] Ireland is one of the few remaining common law jurisdictions in which the legal profession is divided into two branches, solicitors and barristers. The distinction is largely irrelevant in the present discussion in so far as Irish law recognises that both solicitors and barristers are lawyers for the purposes of privilege. The relationship between the solicitor and the client is particularly significant from the practical standpoint that it is the solicitor whom the client consults in the first instance and, indeed, it is the solicitor who receives instructions directly from the client for the most part. As Byrne and McCutcheon put it:

> 'The solicitor is, therefore, in the frontline of dealing with the public and for most people their only contact with a lawyer is a visit to the office of the family solicitor in order, for example, to deal with legal problems related to the sale of a house (conveyancing) or the drafting of a will.'[1]

The concept of privilege derives from the confidential relationship that is formed between lawyer and client.[2] Whereas the type of 'non-contentious business'[3] to which Byrne and McCutcheon refer often generates confidential communications between lawyer and client which will be protected from disclosure, it is a truism that issues of legal professional privilege more often surface in the context of litigation, in which both solicitors and barristers are engaged.[4] Indeed, the very work of the lawyer, whether solicitor or more

---

1 Byrne and McCutcheon, with Bruton and Coffey, *The Irish Legal System* (5th edn, Bloomsbury Professional, 2009) at para 3.04.

2 On entitlement to legal representation see, eg, *Re Commission to Inquire into Child Abuse* [2002] 3 IR 459; *O'Brien v PIAB* [2005] IEHC 100 (25 January 2005) (MacMenamin J). The lawyer-client relationship may be more complicated where a litigant, such as a child, is deemed to require additional representation from a non-legal source, such as a guardian *ad litem* in family law proceedings.

3 Byrne and McCutcheon, with Bruton and Coffey, *The Irish Legal System* (5th edn, Bloomsbury Professional, 2009) para 3.04.

4 A litigant is entitled to forego legal representation and appear in the proceedings *pro se*: Byrne and McCutcheon, with Bruton and Coffey, *The Irish Legal System* (5th edn, Bloomsbury Professional, 2009) paras 9.04–9.07; and O'Malley, *The Criminal Process* (Thomson Round Hall, 2009) para 8.24. The meaningful enjoyment of the right of access to the courts presupposes the existence of some provision for State-funded legal aid. The statutory foundation for legal aid in criminal proceedings is the Criminal Justice (Legal) Aid Act 1962 as amended. (contd.../)

typically barrister, in preparing for pending or actual litigation is itself protected from disclosure. The subject of privilege affects all legal practitioners, regardless of their qualifications, the particular strand of the profession of which they are members or the nature of their legal practice.

[1.02] The relationship between lawyer and client is fiduciary in character. In the specific context of the solicitor and client, O'Callaghan has described the essential features of the relationship thus:

> 'The universal touchstone of the existence of a fiduciary duty is a relationship of confidence and reliance. The relationship is one which requires the utmost good faith on the part of the solicitor and a full and frank disclosure of all facts in the solicitor's dealings with his client. An obligation is cast on the solicitor to act in the best interests of the client and to avoid any other duty or interest which conflicts with those owed to the client.'[5]

Legal professional privilege seeks to foster and protect these elements of confidentiality and trust that are considered essential to the lawyer–client relationship and by extension the administration of justice.[6]

[1.03] There has been widespread debate in recent years over possible reform of the legal profession. Issues such as the structure of the profession, competitiveness, regulation, access and education have been addressed in a series of investigations and reports[7] that have resulted in limited changes.[8] In

4 (\...contd) See O'Malley, para 8.12 *et seq;* Walsh, *Criminal Procedure* (Thomson Round Hall, 2002) para 11.07 *et seq*; Hogan and Whyte, *JM Kelly: The Irish Constitution* (4th edn, Bloomsbury Professional, 2004) para 6.5.118–6.5.126; and Byrne and McCutcheon, para 9.11 *et seq.* The introduction of provision for legal aid in civil proceedings has been more recent and less expansive. Following the judgment of the European Court of Human Rights in *Airey v Ireland* (1979) 2 EHRR 305, a limited non-statutory scheme for civil legal aid was introduced. However, it was only with the enactment of the Civil Legal Aid Act 1995 that a more substantial, statutory scheme, operated by a Legal Aid Board, was put in place. See Byrne and McCutcheon, paras 9.43–9.48.The tradition among lawyers of undertaking work on a *pro bono* or voluntary basis pre-dated the provision of State-funded legal aid and continues to operate in the current day: Byrne and McCutcheon, para 9.30. A prominent manifestation of the tradition is the Free Legal Advice Centres (FLAC), an independent human rights organisation which has offered free legal services to the public since 1969. See www.flac.ie.

5 O'Callaghan, *The Law on Solicitors in Ireland* (Butterworths, 2000) para 5.01. See also Law Society of Ireland, *A Guide to Professional Conduct of Solicitors in Ireland* (2nd edn, 2002). On the relationship between barrister and client see *Code of Conduct of the Bar of Ireland* (2010) ch 3.

6 *Smurfit Paribas Bank Ltd v AAB Export Finance Ltd* [1990] 1 IR 469, [1990] ILRM 588.

7 Fair Trade Commission, *Report of Study into Restrictive Practices in the Legal Profession* (Stationary Office, 1990); OECD, *Report on Regulatory Reform in Ireland* (OECD, 2001) ch 5; Competition Authority, *Competition in Professional Services: Solicitors and Barristers* (December 2006).

8 Including the establishment of a Legal Services Ombudsman pursuant to the Legal Services Ombudsman Act 2009. For analysis of the debate and reforms, see Byrne and McCutcheon, with Bruton and Coffey, *The Irish Legal System* (5th edn, Bloomsbury Professional, 2009) para 3.05 *et seq.*

contrast, more dramatic reform has been occasioned in the United Kingdom including provision for multi-disciplinary practices in which lawyers and other professionals, such as accountants or estate agents, provide a combination of legal and other professional advice to clients.[9] Clearly a reform of this kind, if eventually introduced,[10] could have profound consequences for the lawyer-client relationship and, by extension, legal professional privilege.[11]

EVIDENTIARY PRIVILEGES

[1.04] It is the starting premise of the law of evidence that in resolving disputes coming before them the trial courts should have at their disposal all relevant evidence. In civil proceedings, this premise is reflected in the rules relating to discovery.[12] As Murphy J observed in *Livingstone v Minister for Justice*:

> 'The principle underlying discovery is that all relevant evidence is not only admissible but is also compellable. Litigants must have an opportunity to be heard to put forward arguments and to place all evidence relative to their claims before the court. Arguments without facts are just as sterile as arguments without legal authority'.[13]

The law recognises a limited range of circumstances in which an individual enjoys a privilege from being compelled to present evidence at trial, whether in the form of testimony, documents or real evidence. In *D v NSPCC,* Lord

---

9 Legal Services Act 2007, Pts 3 and 5, implementing recommendations contained in a report for government by Clementi, *Review of the Regulatory Framework for Legal Services in England and Wales – Final Report* (Department of Constitutional Affairs, December 2004). The Legal Services Board is currently overseeing the final stages of a three-year plan for implementation of the reforms set out in the legislation. See www.legalservicesboard.org.uk (visited 23 January 2011). Corresponding legislation has recently been enacted in relation to Scotland: the Legal Services (Scotland) Act 2010.

10 The Competition Authority, *Competition in Professional Services: Solicitors and Barristers* (2006) did not recommend for the time being that barristers should be permitted to enter into partnership with solicitors or with non-lawyers. It took the view that many of the obstacles cited in relation to possible partnerships between solicitors and non-lawyers were not insuperable (para 5.140). Nevertheless, it conceded that there were issues outside the realm of competition policy which required further exploration (para 5.143). Although the Competition Authority did not refer to legal professional privilege specifically, it noted difficulties caused by conflicting professional standards regarding the confidentiality of client communications (para. 5.140). On a related matter, the Authority recommended that qualified persons other than solicitors should be allowed to practice conveyancing: Competition Authority, paras 4.166–4.172.

11 The UK legislation purports to preserve legal professional privilege so that clients of multidisciplinary practices will enjoy the same entitlement as clients of traditional practices.

12 See **Ch 7**.

13 *Livingstone v Minister for Justice* (2 April 2004, unreported) HC, at p 3.

Denning explained the concept of an evidentiary privilege in the following terms:

> 'When the word 'privilege' is used in law, it is used in a somewhat special sense. It is used to denote a privilege or right to keep things secret – to keep things back from your opponent or from the court – so that they cannot get to know of them: and thereby be hindered in the trial of the case.'[14]

Private Privileges

[1.05] The term 'private privilege' is an umbrella for a miscellany of individual entitlements which are conditioned for the most part by pre-determined rules whether common law or statutory.[15] The Irish courts recognise privileges for certain types of confidential relationship. The most prominent category of private privilege is legal professional privilege, also known as lawyer-client privilege, which comprises two distinct but overlapping strands, legal advice privilege and litigation privilege.[16] The privilege is that of the client: the client alone can waive the privilege and the court will neither order nor permit the lawyer to reveal protected communications.[17]

[1.06] Other types of confidential relationship are also the subject of evidentiary privileges. Sacerdotal privilege safeguards from disclosure communications

---

[14] *D v NSPCC* [1978] AC 171 at 190.

[15] The present discussion draws on Heffernan, Ryan and Imwinkelried, *Evidentiary Foundations: Irish Edition* (Bloomsbury Professional, 2008) para 5.02.

[16] *In re Highgrade Traders Ltd* [1984] BCLC 151 at 161 (*per* Oliver LJ). See *Three Rivers District Council v Bank of England (No 6)* [2004] 3 WLR 1274 at 1313 (*per* Carswell LJ): 'legal professional privilege is a single integral privilege, whose sub-heads are legal advice privilege and litigation privilege'. In England and Wales, a statutory definition of legal professional privilege is provided in the Police and Criminal Evidence Act 1984, s 10:

> (1) Subject to subsection (2) below, in this Act 'items subject to legal privilege' means—
> (a) communications between a professional legal adviser and his client or any person representing his client made in connection with the giving of legal advice to the client;
> (b) communications between a professional legal adviser and his client or any person representing his client or between such an adviser or his client or any such representative and any other person made in connection with or in contemplation of legal proceedings and for the purpose of such proceedings; and
> (c) items enclosed with or referred to in such communications and made—
> (i) in connection with the giving of legal advice; or
> (ii) in connection with or in contemplation of legal proceedings and for the purposes of such proceedings,
>
> when they are in the possession of a person who is entitled to possession of them.
>
> (2) Items held with the intention of furthering a criminal purpose are not items subject to legal privilege.

[17] *Wilson v Rastall* (1792) 4 Term Rep 753, [1775–1802] All ER Rep 597; *R v Derby Magistrates' Court, ex parte B* [1995] 4 All ER 526 at 538; *Three Rivers District Council v Bank of England (No 6)* [2004] 3 WLR 1274 at 1295 (*per* Baroness Hale); *McMullen v Kennedy* [2008] IESC 69 (17 December 2008, unreported) at p 8.

made in confidence by a parishioner to a parish priest in a private consultation.[18] The privilege may not be waived by the parishioner without the consent of the priest.[19] Sacerdotal privilege is unique to the priest–penitent relationship and does not apply by analogy to other counselling contexts.[20] There may be scope to argue for the application of a broader privilege in contemporary society that would embrace other forms of counselling, including marriage counselling, but any such privilege would likely be capable of waiver unilaterally by the persons being counselled.[21] For example, in *ER v JR* the High Court recognised that communications made to a minister of religion who was acting as a marriage counsellor were privileged. Carroll J held that the privilege belonged to the spouses and not the minister and could be waived by mutual consent of the spouses. She reserved the question of whether privilege can arise where the counsellor is not a minister of religion.[22]

[1.07] There is a dearth of Irish case law on other confidential relationships that arguably are worthy of protection by means of comparable privileges. In the United States, for example, a majority of the States, and to some extent the federal courts, have recognised privileges for relationships such as doctor–patient,[23] psychotherapist–patient,[24] accountant–client,[25] and social worker–client.[26] Marital communications are also privileged from disclosure under a vibrant state[27] and federal law tradition.[28] The protection afforded to the institution of marriage by the Irish Constitution[29] arguably includes a privilege

---

18 *Cook v Carroll* [1945] IR 515.

19 *Cook v Carroll* [1945] IR 515 at 519 (per Gavan Duffy J): 'Though there are some reasons common to the cases for the sacerdotal and for the legal privileges, one marked distinction merits notice. As between himself and his attorney, the client is master of the situation, so that, if he thinks fit to waive his privilege, the privilege disappears and the lawyer, his paid servant, cannot set it up. But the priest is not hired, and a parishioner's waiver of privilege should not, as a matter of course, destroy the priest's right to keep his secret ...'.

20 *Johnson v Church of Scientology* (30 April 1999, unreported) HC (Geoghegan J).

21 *Johnson v Church of Scientology* (30 April 1999, unreported) HC (Geoghegan J).

22 *ER v JR* [1981] ILRM 125, 127.

23 See, eg, Rule 503 of the Uniform Rule of Evidence (1999) (reflecting statutes adopted in a majority of the US states) and see generally Broun (ed), *McCormick on Evidence* (6th edn Thomson West, 2006) ch 11. For a Canadian perspective see *Metropolitan life Insurance Co v Frenette* [1992] 1 SCR 647; and *M v Ryan* (1997) 143 DLR 4d 1.

24 See, eg, *Jaffee v Redmond* 518 US 1 (1996).

25 As noted above (see footnotes [9] and [11]), the Legal Services Act 2007 (England and Wales) and the Legal Services Act (Scotland) 2010 allow lawyers to form alternative business structures, including multidisciplinary practices involving non-lawyers, without compromising legal professional privilege.

26 See, eg, *Jaffee v Redmond* 518 US 1 (1996).

27 See, eg, Uniform Rules of Evidence (1999), rule 504.

28 Federal Rule of Evidence 501.

29 Notably by Art 41.3.1°.

in respect of confidential spousal communications.[30] However, the contours of such a privilege have not as yet been drawn by the courts.

THE NATURE OF PRIVATE PRIVILEGE

[1.08] Privileged information comprises one or more confidential communications between properly related parties made during the course of the relationship. Wigmore famously set down four conditions necessary to the establishment of a privilege against the disclosure of communications:

1. The communications must originate in a *confidence* that they will not be disclosed.
2. This element of *confidentiality must be essential* to the full and satisfactory maintenance of the relation between the parties.
3. The *relation* must be one which in the opinion of the community ought to be sedulously *fostered.*
4. The *injury* that would inure to the relation by the disclosure of the communication must be *greater than the benefit* thereby gained for the correct disposal of litigation.[31]

The term 'communication' is broadly defined for the purposes of privilege and extends to matters conveyed orally and in a variety of written forms. Confidentiality entails two elements: physical privacy and an intention on the part of the holder of the privilege to maintain secrecy. Thus, the presence of third parties generally destroys confidentiality,[32] although for practical business reasons this does not apply to support staff such as secretaries. Even if the communication is conveyed in private, privilege will not attach if the holder intended the subsequent disclosure of the communication outside the circle of confidence.[33] The requirement that the communication be made during the course of the relationship necessitates an examination of the purpose of the communication. For example, legal advice privilege applies only where the confidential communication is made in the context of a professional legal relationship and for the purpose of giving or receiving legal advice.[34] The court must be satisfied that the lawyer was acting *as a* lawyer and not in some other capacity.[35]

---

[30] For limited statutory recognition see, eg, Criminal Evidence Act 1992, s 26 and Civil Partnership and Certain Rights and Obligations of Cohabitants Act 2010, s 112.

[31] Wigmore, *Evidence in Trials at Common Law, vol 8* (rev McNaughten, 1961) para 2285 quoted with approval by Gavan Duffy J in *Cook v Carroll* [1945] IR 515 (sacerdotal privilege).

[32] *Fyffes plc v DCC plc* [2005] 1 IR 59.

[33] *Bord na gCon v Murphy* [1970] IR 301.

[34] *Smurfit Paribas Bank Ltd v AAB Export Finance Ltd* [1990] 1 IR 469; *Three Rivers District Council v Governor and Company of the Bank of England (No 6)* [2005] 1 AC 610.

[35] *Buckley v Incorporated Law Society* [1994] 2 IR 44; *Somatra v Sinclair Roche and Temperley* [2001] 1 WLR 2453.

[1.09] If a holder of a privilege satisfies the court that the conditions pertaining to that particular species of privilege have been met, there is a *prima facie* case for privilege. However, as we shall see below, an opposing party may defeat the assertion by showing that the holder has waived the privilege.[36] Waiver may be express or implied and it may be intentional or inadvertent.[37] It may occur during pre-trial correspondence and negotiations between the parties or later during the course of the trial itself. Alternatively, a party may waive privilege by disclosing the privileged communication outside the courtroom to a third party.[38] Not every disclosure to a third party will affect a waiver, however. For example, disclosure to a third party for a limited purpose, unrelated to the proceedings, and on condition of confidentiality, will not lead to the loss of the privilege.[39]

[1.10] A claim of privilege may also be defeated where an opposing party satisfies the court that a recognised exception to the particular privilege applies. Thus a court will not recognise a claim of legal professional privilege where it can be demonstrated that the privilege was used to further crime or fraud or that the privileged information will exonerate an accused or resolve a dispute over a will. Similarly, in proceedings relating to the welfare of a child, privilege may have to yield to disclosure where the judge is satisfied that the information will enable the court to adjudicate in the best interests of the child.[40]

Privilege against Self Incrimination

[1.11] The right not to incriminate oneself holds a special place among the rights of the defence in the Irish criminal justice system, although it is in fact broader and more complex in its scope and application. The right can be traced back into the historical common law and in modern times embodies a series of overlapping protections rooted in the Constitution, international human rights treaties including the European Convention on Human Rights, statute, and the common law. In *R v Director of Serious Fraud, ex parte Smith*, Lord Mustill famously distilled from this corpus of law, the following aspects of the privilege:

> '(1) A general immunity, possessed by all persons and bodies, from being compelled on pain of punishment to answer questions posed by other persons or bodies.
>
> (2) A general immunity, possessed by all persons or bodies, from being compelled on pain of punishment to answer questions the answers to which may incriminate them.

---

[36] See **Ch 6**.

[37] *Guinness Peat Properties Ltd v Fitzroy Robinson* [1987] 1 WLR 1027.

[38] *Fyffes plc v DCC plc* [2005] 1 IR 59.

[39] *Fyffes plc v DCC plc* [2005] 1 IR 59.

[40] For case law examples in relation to each of these exceptions, see **Ch 5**.

(3) A general immunity, possessed by all persons under suspicion of criminal responsibility whilst being interviewed by police officers or others in similar positions of authority, from being compelled on pain of punishment to answer questions of any kind.

(4) A specific immunity, possessed by accused persons undergoing trial, from being compelled to give evidence, and from being compelled to answer questions put to them in the dock.

(5) A specific immunity, possessed by persons who have been charged with a criminal offence, from having questions material to the offence addressed to them by police officers or persons in a similar position of authority.

(6) A specific immunity (at least in certain circumstances, which it is unnecessary to explore), possessed by accused persons undergoing trial, from having adverse comment made on any failure (a) to answer questions before the trial, or (b) to give evidence at trial.'[41]

In the paradigm of the criminal accused, the right not to incriminate oneself encompasses the entitlement not to be compelled, directly or indirectly, to answer questions or produce evidence of an incriminatory nature. The privilege has been developed in this jurisdiction *in tandem* with the constitutional right to silence.[42] As such, it is by no means absolute and, indeed, has been the subject of piecemeal statutory encroachment.[43]

Public Interest Privilege

[1.12] Exceptionally, the State or one of its agents may refuse to surrender information sought in litigation on the ground that disclosure would be contrary to the public interest. All forms of privilege could be said to be rooted in the public interest to a greater or lesser extent. Legal professional privilege, for example, furthers the public interest in the administration of justice because it facilitates the full and frank exchange that is essential to effective legal representation. As its name suggests, 'public interest privilege' evokes the public interest in a more direct and central sense.

Unlike the various private privileges, the application of public interest privilege is not governed by hard and fast rules. In each case, the trial court must engage in a balancing exercise, weighing the public interest in disclosure against the countervailing public interest in confidentiality.

[1.13] The entitlement of the State to resist disclosure of evidence relevant to legal proceedings stretches far back into the common law. It was originally

41 *R v Director of Serious Fraud, ex parte Smith* [1993] AC 1 at 31.

42 Bunreacht na hÉireann, Arts 40.6 and 38.1. See, eg, *Re National Irish Bank Ltd* [1999] 3 IR 145.

43 See, eg, the inference-drawing provisions of the Criminal Justice Act 2007 discussed below in **Ch 11**.

known as 'Crown privilege' or 'executive privilege' and traditionally vested exclusively in the State. Moreover, executive privilege was absolute: the executive branch needed to do no more than assert the privilege and the courts would take at face value the implicit suggestion that disclosure of the material in question would be injurious to the public interest. In *Murphy v Dublin Corporation and the Minister for Local Government*,[44] the Supreme Court broke with the common law tradition and boldly claimed for the courts the power to determine whether relevant evidence should be withheld from disclosure. Walsh J stated:

> 'Under the Constitution the administration of justice is committed solely to the judiciary in the exercise of their powers in the courts set up under the Constitution. Power to compel the attendance of witnesses and the production of evidence is an inherent part of the judicial power of government of the State and is the ultimate safeguard of justice in the State. The proper exercise of the functions of the three powers of government set up under the Constitution, namely, the legislative, the executive and the judicial, is in the public interest. There may be occasions when the different aspects of the public interest 'pull in contrary directions' – to use the words of Lord Morris of Borth-y-Gest in *Conway v Rimmer* [1968] AC 910, 955. If the conflict arises during the exercise of the judicial power then, in my view, it is the judicial power which will decide which public interest shall prevail.'[45]

Walsh J was at pains to stress that it did not follow that the courts would always rule in favour of disclosure. The courts, no less than the other organs of government, were subject to 'the division of powers' which did not give 'paramountcy' to any one of the organs exercising the powers of government over the other.[46] Here, the judicial task was to weigh the competing public interests in favour of and against disclosure with a view to deciding which was the superior interest in the circumstances of the particular case.[47]

[1.14] As a result of *Murphy* and its progeny, the State, like any other holder of privilege, has the burden of asserting the privilege and of persuading the court that it should be upheld in any given case.[48] Where the State asserts the privilege, the courts must weigh the competing public interests, ie, the general interest in disclosure against the particular interest in confidentiality on which the State relies. There is no preference for disclosure over other public interests, such as national security,[49] foreign relations,[50] the prevention and detection of

---

44 *Murphy v Dublin Corporation and the Minister for Local Government* [1972] IR 215.

45 *Murphy v Dublin Corporation and the Minister for Local Government* [1972] IR 215 at 233.

46 *Murphy v Dublin Corporation and the Minister for Local Government* [1972] IR 215 at 234.

47 *Murphy v Dublin Corporation and the Minister for Local Government* [1972] IR 215 at 234.

48 Similarly, public interest privilege may be waived: *McDonald v RTÉ* [2001] 1 IR 355.

49 See, eg, *Gormley v Ireland* [1993] 2 IR 75.

50 See, eg, *Walker v Ireland* [1997] 1 ILRM 363; *Egan v O'Toole* [2005] IESC 53 (29 July 2005).

crime[51] or the proper functioning of the public service.[52] The courts must balance the competing interests on a case-by-case basis.[53] Moreover, there is no class or category of documents that is automatically exempt from production by virtue either of the rank of the person creating the documents or the status of the individual or body intended to use them.[54]

INFORMER PRIVILEGE

[1.15] Historically, the common law protected the identity of police and prison informers from disclosure at trial.[55] This privilege was supported by a twofold justification: the need to protect the lives and safety of informers and the need to safeguard their valued contribution to the prevention and detection of crime. Indeed, the evolution of the privilege has involved its gradual extension from police and prison informers to informers of other public officeholders and entities engaged in law enforcement.[56] For example, the High Court has recognised protection by means of privilege for informers to the Director of Consumer Affairs.[57]

[1.16] Informer privilege is subject to a common law 'innocence-at-stake' exception. The existence and scope of the exception have been the subject of controversy in various parts of the common law world. In principle an Irish court may order disclosure of the informer's identity if disclosure would exonerate an accused. The exception arguably attracts a contemporary constitutional and human rights gloss in so far as Article 38.1 of the Constitution and art 6 of the European Convention on Human Rights (ECHR) guarantee the accused the right to introduce demonstrably exculpatory evidence. However, in *People (DPP) v Kelly*[58] the Supreme Court rejected a challenge to informer privilege in the context of the giving of so-called 'belief evidence' under s 3(2) of the Offences Against the State (Amendment) Act 1972. The court reasoned that the necessary encroachment on the defence's entitlement to cross-examine the garda chief

---

51 See, eg, *Breathnach v Ireland (No 3)* [1993] 2 IR 458; *McDonald v RTÉ* [2001] 1 IR 355; *Traynor v Judge Delahunt* [2008] IEHC 272 (31 July 2008) (McMahon J).

52 See, eg, *Cully v Northern Bank Finance Corp* [1984] ILRM 683; *Incorporated Law Society v Osborne* [1987] ILRM 42; and *Fitzpatrick v Martin* [1988] IR 132.

53 *Ambiorix v Minister for the Environment (No 1)* [1992] 1 IR 277.

54 *Ambiorix v Minister for the Environment (No 1)* [1992] 1 IR 277. On cabinet confidentiality see *Attorney General v Hamilton (No 1)* [1993] 2 IR 250; *O'Brien v Ireland* [1995] 1 ILRM 22; and *Irish Press Publications Ltd v Minister for Enterprise* [2002] 4 IR 110.

55 See **Ch 10**.

56 In England the privilege has been applied to informers of the Gaming Board (*R v Lewes Justices, ex parte Secretary of State for the Home Department* [1973] AC 388) and informers to the National Society for the Prevention of Cruelty to Children (*D v NSPCC* [1978] AC 1).

57 *Director of Consumer Affairs v Sugar Distributors Ltd* [19991] 1 IR 225.

58 *People (DPP) v Kelly* [2006] 3 IR 115.

superintendent witness about the informer did not deprive the accused of a fair trial in that case.

[1.17] Historically the Irish courts were reluctant to extend the cloak of informer privilege to journalists' sources[59] in the absence of a tangible threat to the life or physical integrity of the individuals in question.[60] The traditional view was that journalists were no more exempt than other witnesses from the duty to disclose evidence relevant to a court proceeding. Over time, however, the courts accepted the virtue of preserving the anonymity of journalists' sources and consequently the principle that disclosure should be ordered only where critical to the proceedings and as an evidentiary last resort.[61] Nevertheless, until recently the courts stopped short of endorsing an affirmative entitlement on the part of journalists to protect from disclosure the identity of persons from whom they received information in confidence.

[1.18] The incorporation of the ECHR into Irish law[62] has brought about a sea change in judicial thinking that was manifest in the decision of the Supreme Court in *Mahon Tribunal v Keena and Kennedy.*[63] Press freedom lies at the heart of the guarantee of freedom of expression, contained in art 10 of the ECHR, which constitutes one of the essential foundations of a democratic society.[64] The case law of the European Court references a tension between the various public interests that underpin the potentially applicable rights in this area. It also recognises the invidious position in which journalists may find themselves, forced to choose between a legal duty to disclose information to a court and an ethical duty to preserve the anonymity of a source.[65] In *Mahon Tribunal v Keena and Kennedy*, the Supreme Court embraced the principles prescribed by the Convention and, in so doing, recognised a fledgling privilege with respect to journalists' sources.[66]

THE EMERGENCE OF LEGAL PROFESSIONAL PRIVILEGE

[1.19] In *R v Derby Magistrates' Court, ex parte B*,[67] Lord Taylor CJ traced the history of legal professional privilege from the sixteenth century case of *Berd v Lovelace*, the earliest such case cited in *Holdsworth's History of English Law.*[68]

59 *Re Kevin O'Kelly* (1974) 109 ILTR 97.

60 *Burke v Central Independent Television plc* [1994] 2 IR 61.

61 *People (DPP) v Nevin* [2003] 3 IR 321.

62 European Convention on Human Rights Act 2003.

63 *Mahon Tribunal v Keena and Kennedy* [2009] IESC 64 (unreported, 31 July 2009).

64 *Lingens v Austria* (1986) 8 EHRR 329.

65 *Goodwin v United Kingdom* (1996) 22 EHRR 123.

66 *Mahon Tribunal v Keena and Kennedy* [2009] IESC 64 (unreported, 31 July 2009).

67 *R v Derby Magistrates' Court, ex parte B* [1995] 3 WLR 681, [1995] 4 All ER 526.

68 *Berd v Lovelace* (1577) Cary 62 cited in Lord Taylor's judgment [1995] 3 WLR 681 at 692.

He observed that by the end of the eighteenth century legal professional privilege was 'well on the way to being established on its present basis'.[69] The rationale for the rule and its fundamental tenets were judicially developed over the course of the nineteenth century beginning with the leading cases of *Greenough v Gaskell*[70] and *Bolton v Liverpool Corp*,[71] both decided by Lord Brougham LC at the beginning of 1833.[72]

[1.20] At first the privilege was relatively narrow in scope in so far as it applied only to communications between a client and her lawyer following the commencement of litigation.[73] Over time, the courts extended the privilege in two salient respects: first, its protection reached beyond litigation to other aspects of the lawyer-client relationship; second, in the context of litigation, the privilege was not limited to communications but covered other forms of information. The gradual extension of the cloak of privilege led to the emergence of two distinct yet overlapping strands: legal advice privilege, which protects confidential communications between lawyer and client; and litigation privilege, which protects information gathered or exchanged in connection with court proceedings.[74]

The Rationales for Legal Professional Privilege

[1.21] The successful invocation of any form of privilege undercuts the central tenet of our trial system that a court may compel the disclosure of any relevant evidence; where a privilege is successfully invoked, the public interest in disclosure must yield to a competing public interest in favour of confidentiality. Legal advice privilege facilitates the full and frank communication between a client and her lawyer that is deemed essential to effective legal representation and, by extension, the administration of justice.[75] Similarly, litigation privilege is considered necessary to the proper functioning of the trial process because it

[69] *R v Derby Magistrates' Court, ex parte B* [1995] 3 WLR 681 at 693, [1995] 4 All ER 526 at 538 (citing by way of example *Wilson v Rastall* (1792) 4 Term Rep 753 [1775–1802] All ER Rep 597).

[70] *Greenough v Gaskell* (1833) 1 My & K 98, [1824–34] All ER 767.

[71] *Bolton v Liverpool Corp* (1833) 1 My & K 88, 39 ER 614.

[72] See Hazard Jr, 'An Historical Perspective on the Attorney-Client Privilege' (1978) 66(5) Cal L Rev 1061, 1083–1085 (charting the broadening of privilege by Lord Brougham in these cases).

[73] 'Originally it related only to communications where legal proceedings were in being or in contemplation': *Balabel v Air India* [1988] 1 Ch 317 at 324 (*per* Taylor LJ).

[74] *Anderson v Bank of British Columbia* (1876) 2 Ch D 644; *Wheeler v Le Marchant* (1881) 18 Ch D 675.

[75] *Smurfit Paribas Bank Ltd v AAB Export Finance Ltd* [1990] 1 IR 469; *Miley v Flood* [2001] 2 IR 50.

allows lawyers the freedom to prepare fully for trial.[76] These rationales have been discussed at length in the case law.[77]

Legal Professionals

[1.22] The role of legal professional privilege as an essential prop to the administration of justice in our courts derives from the public interest in providing individuals with access to adequate legal representation in the conduct of their affairs.[78] The cogency of this justification rests on the twin propositions that individuals need the advice of skilled legal professionals to navigate the complexities of the law and that the giving of legal advice requires absolute candour between client and lawyer. In *Greenough v Gaskell*, Lord Brougham LC alluded to the first of these propositions:

> 'The foundation of this rule is not difficult to discover. It is not (as has sometimes been said) on account of any particular importance which the law attributes to the business of legal professors, or any particular disposition to afford them protection ... It is out of regard to the interests of justice, which cannot be upholden, and to the administration of justice, which cannot go on, without the aid of men skilled in jurisprudence, in the practice of the Courts, and in those matters affecting rights and obligations which form the subject of all judicial proceedings. If the privilege did not exist at all, every one would be thrown upon his own legal resources; deprived of all professional assistance, a man would not venture to consult any skilful person, or would only dare to tell his counsellor half his case.'[79]

Candour between Client and Lawyer

[1.23] The notion that legal representation is an essential element in the proper conduct of litigation represents only part of the rationale because standing alone it fails to explain the need to foster and preserve confidentiality between the lawyer and client. A more complete statement of the rationale is found in the famous extract from the judgment of Jessel MR in *Anderson v Bank of British Columbia*:

> 'The object and meaning of the rule is this: that as, by reason of the complexity and difficulty of our law, litigation can only be properly conducted by

---

76 *Gallagher v Stanley* [1998] 2 IR 267.

77 See also Auburn, *Legal Professional Privilege: Law and Theory* (Hart Publishing, 2000) ch 1; Radin, 'The Privilege of Confidential Communication between Lawyer and Client' (1928) 16(6) Cal L Rev 31(4) 487; Peiris, 'Legal Professional Privilege in Commonwealth Law' (1982) 31(4) ICLQ 609.

78 McGrath, *Evidence* (Thomson Round Hall, 2005) at para 10.10, notes that '[l]egal professional privilege began life as a privilege enjoyed by the lawyer based on consideration for his oath and honour' but that this idea was subsequently rejected by the courts in favour of a 'new theory based on the desirability of protecting the inviolability of the lawyer/client relationship' (citing, *inter alia*, *Berd v Lovelace* (1577) Cary 62 and *Wilson v Rastall* (1792) 4 TR 753).

79 *Greenough v Gaskell* (1883) 1 My & K 98 at 103. See also *Grant v Downs* (1976) 135 CLR 674 at 685.

> professional men, it is absolutely necessary that a man, in order to prosecute his rights or to defend himself from an improper claim, should have recourse to the assistance of professional lawyers, and it being so absolutely necessary, it is equally necessary, to use a vulgar phrase, that he should be able to make a clean breast of it to the gentleman whom he consults with a view to the prosecution of his claim, or the substantiating of his defence against the claim of others; that he should be able to place unrestricted and unbounded confidence in the professional agent, and that the communications he so makes to him should be kept secret, unless with his consent (for it is his privilege, and not the privilege of the confidential agent), that he should be enabled properly to conduct his litigation. That is the meaning of the rule'.[80]

This theme is a thread running through the English nineteenth century case law. The courts emphasised the essential role that privilege played in safeguarding the necessary confidence between client and lawyer. As Lord Lyndhurst LC stated in *Holmes v Bradley*,[81] communications between a client and her lawyer should be 'unfettered' in the sense that they should not be restrained by any apprehension that the communications will be divulged and used to the client's prejudice. Indeed, his lordship expressed the view that communications should be privileged 'not merely in the cause then contemplated or depending' but also 'in any subsequent litigation with the same or any other party or parties'.[82] The durability of privilege was encapsulated in the famous phrase of Lindley MR in *Calcraft v Guest:* 'I take it that, as a general rule, one may say once privileged always privileged'.[83]

[1.24] The significance of privilege in safeguarding absolute candour between client and lawyer continues to resonate in the modern English case law. In *R v Derby Magistrates' Court, ex parte B*, Lord Taylor emphasised the imperative of preserving the confidential relation between lawyer and client: '[A] man must be able to consult his lawyer in confidence, since otherwise he might hold back half the truth. The client must be sure that what he tells his lawyer in confidence

---

[80] *Anderson v Bank of British Columbia* (1876) 2 Ch D 644 at 649. For an earlier statement see *Annesley v Earl of Anglesea* (1743) 17 How St Tr 1139 at 1125 *(per* Mounteney B) quoted in McGrath, *Evidence* (Thomson Round Hall, 2005) at para 10.10.

[81] *Holmes v Bradley* (1844) 1 Ph 476, 41 ER 713.

[82] *Holmes v Bradley* (1844) 1 Ph 476 at 480–81, 41 ER 713 at 715. See also *Pearce v Foster* (1885) 15 QBD 114 at 119–120 (*per* Brett MR): 'The reason of the privilege is that there may be that free and confidential communication between solicitor and client which lies at the foundation of the use and service of the solicitor to the client; but, if at any time or under any circumstances such communications are subject to discovery, it is obvious that this freedom of communication will be impaired. The liability of such communications to discovery in a subsequent action would have this effect as well as their liability to discovery in the original action'.

[83] *Calcraft v Guest* [1898] 1 QB 759 at 761, [1895–99] All ER 346 at 348. See also *Hobbs v Hobbs & Cousens* [1959] 3 All ER 827 at 829, [1960] P 112 at 116–117 in which Stevenson J spoke of the 'common sense' basis of privilege in ensuring complete and unqualified confidence in the mind of the client when she consults a legal professional.

will never be revealed without his consent.'[84] In *R (Morgan Grenfell & Co Ltd) v Special Commissioner of Income Tax*,[85] Lord Hoffmann characterised legal professional privilege as a necessary corollary of the right of any person to obtain skilled advice about the law.[86] In a similar vein, the Supreme Court of Canada justified privilege in the following terms in *Jones v Smith:*

> 'Clients seeking advice must be able to speak freely to their lawyers secure in the knowledge that what they say will not be divulged without their consent ... The privilege is essential if sound legal advice is to be given ... Family secrets, company secrets, personal foibles and indiscretions all must on occasion be revealed to the lawyer by the client. Without this privilege clients could never be candid and furnish all the relevant information that must be provided to lawyers if they are to properly advise their clients.'[87]

[1.25] The importance of confidentiality for the lawyer's function of preparing for trial was also a feature in judicial reasoning in the nineteenth century English cases. In *Bolton v Liverpool Corp*,[88] Lord Brougham LC dismissed a bill of discovery in equity seeking inspection of the case that the plaintiff had put to counsel for the purposes of advice:

> 'The very case which he lays before his counsel, to advise upon the evidence, may, and often does, contain the whole of his evidence, and may be, and frequently is, the brief with which that or some other counsel conducts his cause. The principle contended for, that inspection of cases, though not of opinions, may always be obtained as of right, would produce this effect, and neither more nor less, that a party would go into Court to try the cause, and there would be the

84 *R v Derby Magistrates' Court, ex parte B* [1995] 3 WLR 681 at 695.

85 *R (Morgan Grenfell & Co Ltd) v Special Commissioner of Income Tax* [2003] 1 AC 563.

86 *R (Morgan Grenfell & Co Ltd) v Special Commissioner of Income Tax* [2003] 1 AC 563 at 607. Lord Hoffman continued: 'Such advice cannot be effectively obtained unless the client is able to put all the facts before the adviser without fear that they may afterwards be disclosed and used to his prejudice'. See also *Ventouris v Mountain* [2002] 1 WLR 607, 611 (*per* Bingham LJ): 'The doctrine of legal professional privilege is rooted in the public interest, which requires that hopeless and exaggerated claims and unsound and spurious defences be so far as possible discouraged, and civil disputes so far as possible settled without resort to judicial decision. To this end it is necessary that actual and potential litigants, be they claimants or respondents, should be free to unburden themselves without reserve to their legal advisers, and their legal advisers be free to give honest and candid advice on a sound factual basis, without fear that these communications may be relied on by an opposing party if the dispute comes before the court for decision'; *B v Auckland District Law Society* [2003] 2 AC 736 at 757 (*per* Lord Millett): '[A] lawyer must be able to give his client an absolute and unqualified assurance that whatever the client tells him in confidence will never be disclosed without his consent'.

87 *Jones v Smith* [1999] 1 SCR 455 at 474–475.

88 *Bolton v Liverpool Corp* (1833) 1 My & K 88, 39 ER 614; *Balabel v Air-India* [1988] Ch 317, [1988] 2 All ER 246.

original of his brief in his own counsel's bag, and a copy of it in the bag of his adversary's counsel.'[89]

Litigation and General Legal Advice

[1.26] As these quotations suggest, the justification for legal professional privilege was initially linked exclusively to the proper conduct of litigation *per se*. The courts soon recognised that the protection would be insufficient if it was limited to litigation and did not embrace communications across the full gamut of the legal professional relationship.[90] As early as 1833, Lord Brougham LC opined in *Greenough v Gaskell* that the protection afforded by privilege would be 'insufficient' if it were limited to communications connected with legal proceedings; in language which would be echoed by Finlay CJ in the landmark Irish case of *Smurfit Paribas Bank Ltd v AAB Export Finance Ltd*,[91] he noted that all human affairs have a remote connection with litigation 'in so far as every transaction may, by possibility, become the subject of judicial inquiry'.[92] Some 13 years later, in *Carpmael v Powis,* Lord Lyndhurst LC recognised that 'the privilege extends to all communications between a solicitor, as such, and his client, relating to matters within the ordinary scope of a solicitor's duty'.[93]

[1.27] Advocate General Slynn elaborated on the justification for a broad understanding of privilege in *AM & S Europe Ltd v European Commission*:

> '… [The privilege] springs essentially from the basic need of a man in a civilised society to be able to turn to his lawyer for advice and help, and if proceedings begin, for representation; it springs no less from the advantages to a society which evolves complex law reaching into all the business affairs of persons, real and legal, that they should be able to know what they can do under the law, what is forbidden, where they must tread circumspectly, where they run risks.'[94]

---

89 *Bolton v Liverpool Corp* (1833) 1 My & K 88 at 94, 39 ER 614 at 617.

90 *Herring v Clobery* (1842) 1 Ph 91 at 94–5 (*per* Lord Lyndhurst LC); *Pearse v Pearse* (1846) 1 De G & Sm 12 (*per* Knight Bruce VC); *Minter v Priest* [1929] 1 KB 655; *Price Waterhouse v BCCI Holdings (Luxembourg) SA* [1992] BCLC 583 at 588 (*per* Millett J). This development was charted by Finlay CJ in *Smurfit Paribas Bank Ltd v AAB Expert Finance Ltd* [1990] 1 IR 469 at 476–77.

91 *Smurfit Paribas Bank Ltd v AAB Expert Finance Ltd* [1990] 1 IR 469 at 478 (per Finlay CJ): 'Where a person seeks or obtains legal advice there are good reasons to believe that he necessarily enters the area of potential litigation.'

92 *Bolton v Liverpool Corp* (1833) 1 My & K 98 at 102.

93 *Carpmael v Powis* (1846) 1 Ph 687 at 692. See also *Bullivant v AG for Victoria* [1901] AC 196 at 200–201 (*per* Earl of Halsbury LC).

94 *AM & S Europe Ltd v European Commission* [1983] QB 878 at 913 cited with approval by Lord Scott in *Three Rivers District Council v Bank of England (No 6)* [2004] 3 WLR 1274 at 1285 and Kirby J in *Daniels Corp International Pty Ltd v Australian Competition and Consumer Commission* (2002) 192 ALR 561 at 584.

The judgments of the House of Lords in *R v Derby Magistrates' Court, ex parte B*[95] reflect the widely-held judicial view that this justification remains cogent in the present day.[96] Lord Nicholls stated:

> 'The public interest in the efficient working of the legal system requires that people should be able to obtain professional legal advice on their rights and liabilities and obligations. This is desirable for the orderly conduct of everyday affairs. Similarly, people should be able to seek legal advice and assistance in connection with the proper conduct of court proceedings. To this end communications between clients and lawyers must be uninhibited. But, in practice, candour cannot be expected if disclosure of the contents of communications between client and lawyer may be compelled, to a client's prejudice and contrary to his wishes. That is one aspect of the public interest. It takes the form of according to the client a right, or privilege as it is unhelpfully called, to withhold disclosure of the contents of client-lawyer communications. In the ordinary course the client has an interest in asserting this right, in so far as disclosure would or might prejudice him.'[97]

In *Three Rivers District Council v Governor and Company of the Bank of England (No 6)*, Lord Scott remarked that the various authorities on point all have in common the idea that it is necessary in our society that communications between clients and lawyers should be secure against the possibility of scrutiny from others 'whether the police, the executive, business competitors, inquisitive busybodies or anyone else'.[98] In his lordship's opinion, this idea justifies the retention of legal advice privilege in English law 'notwithstanding that as a result cases may sometimes have to be decided in ignorance of relevant probative material'.[99]

---

95 *R v Derby Magistrates' Court, ex parte B* [1995] 3 WLR 681, [1995] 4 All ER 526.

96 *Three Rivers District Council v Governor and Company of the Bank of England (No 6)* [2004] 3 WLR 1274 at 1292 (*per* Lord Rodger): '[T]he public interest justification for the privilege is the same today as it was 350 years ago: it does not change, or need to change, because it is rooted in an aspect of human nature which does not change either. If the advice given by lawyers is to be sound, their clients must make them aware of all the relevant circumstances of the problem. Clients will be reluctant to do so, however, unless they can be sure that what they say about any potentially damaging or embarrassing circumstances will not be revealed later. So it is settled that, in the absence of a waiver by the client, communications between clients and their lawyers for the purpose of obtaining legal advice must be kept confidential and cannot be made the subject of evidence.'

97 *R v Derby Magistrates' Court, ex parte B* [1995] 3 WLR 681 at 698. For Canadian and Australian authority in support, see, eg, *Descoteaux v Mierzwinski* (1982) 141 DLR (3d) 590; *Daniels Corp International Pty Ltd v Australian Competition and Consumer Commission* (2002) 192 ALR 56.

98 *Three Rivers District Council v Governor and Company of the Bank of England (No 6)* [2004] 3 WLR 1274 at 1286.

99 *Three Rivers District Council v Govenor and Company of the Bank of England (No 6)* [2004] 3 WLR 1274 at 1286.

Administration of Justice

[1.28] The emphasis in the case law on the contribution of legal representation to the proper administration of justice underscores that the motivation behind privilege is not the promotion of the client's private interests (though this may appear to be the effect in practice). Claims of privilege effectively pit two competing aspects of the public interest in the proper conduct of the administration of justice: first, the full disclosure of information 'which in the interests of the common good is desirable for the purpose of ascertaining truth and rendering justice'[100] and, second, the protection from disclosure of confidential communications between the lawyer and client that is essential for the conduct of litigation by 'men skilled in jurisprudence, in the practice of the courts, and in those matters affecting rights and obligations which form the subject of all judicial proceedings'.[101] Because the first of these aspects of the public interest constitutes the baseline assumption on which the courts conduct the trial process, the second represents an exception thereto. It follows that privilege must be necessarily limited to what Finlay CJ famously characterised in *Smurfit Paribas Bank Ltd v AAB Expert Finance Ltd* as 'instances which have been identified as securing an objective which in the public interest in the proper conduct of the administration of justice can be said to outweigh the disadvantage arising from the restriction of disclosure of all the facts'.[102]

Questioning the Traditional Rationales

[1.29] This overview of the relevant authorities indicates that the traditional rationales for legal professional privilege continue to influence the courts in the present day. Indeed, it has become customary for courts to re-state the traditional formulations as self-evident truths. In truth, the rhetoric that surrounds legal professional privilege tends to overstate its importance. There is scope to question at least some of the underlying assumptions.

Further consideration of the exact nature of the law's interest in fostering the lawyer-client relationship through the mechanism of privilege is warranted. McGrath seeks to fill a lacuna in the traditional discourse with a succinct account of the specific ways in which legal representation furthers the administration of justice:

> 'First, it can be argued that privilege is crucial to the effective functioning of our adversarial model of justice. This relies heavily on the parties to seek out both the facts and the law that support their case and undermine that of their opponent. The likelihood that the court will reach the right result and justice will be done is intimately tied to the quality of those efforts which are, obviously, likely to be much better if the party is represented by a trained lawyer. ... Secondly, the

[100] *Smurfit Paribas Bank Ltd v AAB Export Finance Ltd* [1990] 1 IR 469 at 477 (*per* Finlay CJ).

[101] *Greenough v Gaskell* (1833) 1 My & K 98 at 103 (*per* Brougham LC).

[102] *Smurfit Paribas Bank Ltd v AAB Export Finance Ltd* [1990] 1 IR 469 at 477.

> representation of the parties by persons with legal training and knowledge is likely to result in more efficient presentation and, hence, disposal of cases. Thirdly, the involvement of a lawyer who is emotionally and financially detached from the underlying dispute aids a realistic appraisal of its prospects of success and its settlement or proper conduct if the matter comes to trial. The foregoing considerations are underpinned and reinforced by the ethical obligations which barristers and solicitors owe to the court, ethical obligations which are not owed by lay clients and which clearly promote the administration of justice.'[103]

These observations imply that the pertinent measure of legal representation in this context resides in its ability to maximise the *effectiveness* of the legal process and thereby to enhance the *quality* of justice that is administered in our courts. Lawyers are not indispensable to the conduct of legal proceedings, a fact that the system itself concedes by virtue of the facility of pro se representation. Nevertheless, in all but the most straightforward of matters, legal professional expertise is a practical precondition to securing the optimum protection of the client's interests. In a system that remains unashamedly adversarial, equal access to legal representation levels the playing field and sharpens the contest. Above all, it holds the promise that the courts will adjudicate the disputes coming before them with the benefit of the most complete explication of the relevant facts, applicable law and party positions.

[1.30] It is intuitive that the ability of lawyers to perform their functions effectively is dependent upon the information at their disposal. The traditional view supposes that absolute candour is a crucial element in the lawyer-client relationship and that privilege is essential to the preservation of that dynamic. It is worthwhile to consider whether these assumptions resonate in contemporary society. How influential is the presence or absence of privilege in a client's decision either to seek legal advice in the first place or, having sought legal advice, to divulge information to her lawyer? Given that privilege is subject to exceptions and the possibility of waiver, it might be suggested that a client who reposes the utmost confidence in the confidentiality of the exchange may be somewhat misguided. For example, a client consulting a lawyer in relation to a family law matter may be surprised to learn that the concept of privilege is far less robust in the quasi-inquisitorial setting of proceedings relating to the welfare of children. At a general level, even if legal professional privilege were a more transparently qualified concept (for example, if it were subject to the judicial balancing of competing public policies on a case-by-case basis) would the perception that confidences might be susceptible to disclosure necessarily have a chilling effect on the lawyer-client relationship? The point that these questions seeks to elicit is not that the traditional assumptions no longer have traction but simply that the proffered justifications for privilege are more debatable than the classic authorities suggest.

---

[103] McGrath, *Evidence* (Thomson Round Hall, 2005) at 10–13 (internal citations omitted).

[1.31] In a similar vein, additional related questions of an institutional flavour remain. Why is it that the giving of legal advice merits the degree of protection associated with legal professional privilege? Tapper has observed:

> 'Perhaps the first point to be made, about which even Lord Brougham [in *Greenough v Gaskell* (1833) 1 My & K 98] was himself somewhat uneasy, is that it is not self-evident why the prosecution of disputes, especially perhaps those which a lawyer's client instigates, is so much more deserving of being fostered than say, the receipt of treatment or psychological counselling which a medical practitioner's patient needs.'[104]

Tapper questions further why the privilege is very strictly confined to lawyers at common law; he notes that 'the justification for that cannot be that otherwise lay people would be bereft of professional advice since it could in many areas be provided by members of other professions such as accountants in relation to taxation, or architects in relation to construction'.[105] Nor does Tapper believe that 'the preference for lawyers' can be explained on the basis of expectations 'since it is dubious whether most members of the public would appreciate that the position of lawyers and accountants or architects is so very different so far as the disclosure of confidential communications is concerned'.[106]

Additional Rationales

[1.32] It is noteworthy that legal professional privilege does not begin and end with confidentiality. The client's interest in asserting and maintaining privilege may stretch beyond the desire to ensure that the information in question is kept confidential. As Smyth J explained in *Shell E & P Ireland Ltd v McGrath (No 2)*, 'the interest of the client in the maintenance of privilege is twofold: (i) the client has an interest in maintaining the confidentiality of the privileged communication; (ii) even if the confidentiality is impaired or lost, the client has an interest in ensuring that the document is not used against him in proceedings'.[107] Thus, even when a privileged communication has been circulated or published, the law may protect the client's interest in ensuring that the communication is not used by an opposing party in proceedings against her.[108]

---

[104] Tapper, 'Prosecution and Privilege' (1996–97) 1 Int'l J Evid & Proof 5 at 12–13.

[105] Tapper, 'Prosecution and Privilege' (1996–97) 1 Int'l J Evid & Proof 5 at 13.

[106] Tapper, 'Prosecution and Privilege' (1996–97) 1 Int'l J Evid & Proof 5 at 13. He continues: 'if anything most people would probably expect communications with their advisers about their private medical and financial affairs to be more resistant to disclosure than those relating to legal disputes'.

[107] *Shell E & P Ireland Ltd v McGrath (No 2)* [2007] 2 IR 574 at 580.

[108] *Shell E & P Ireland Ltd v McGrath (No 2)* [2007] 2 IR 574 at 580. Over 75 years before, Lord Atkin observed in *Minter v Priest* [1930] AC 558 at 566: 'The Privilege claimed is that which covers communications between a solicitor and his client, a privilege the maintenance of which is essential in the best interests of society ...'.

The broader institutional benefits that flow from the privilege were outlined by Baroness Hale in *Three Rivers District Council (No 6)*:

> 'It is in the interests of the whole community that lawyers give their clients sound advice, accurate as to the law and sensible as to their conduct. The client may not always act upon that advice (which will sometimes place the lawyer in professional difficulty, but that is a separate matter) but there is always a chance that he will. And there is little or no chance of the client taking the right or sensible course if the lawyer's advice is inaccurate or unsound because the lawyer has been given an incomplete or inaccurate picture of the client's position.'[109]

Similar sentiments have been expressed in other common law jurisdictions. In *Upjohn Co v United States,* Justice Rehnquist observed that privilege promotes the broad public interest in the observance of law and the administration of justice.[110] Wilson J of the High Court of Australia stated in *Baker v Campbell:*

> 'In fostering the confidential relationship in which legal advice is given and received the common law is serving the ends of justice because it is facilitating the orderly arrangement of the client's affairs as a member of the community.'[111]

The Need to Assert Privilege

[1.33] Legal professional privilege is qualified in notable respects. The privilege belongs to the client[112] and, by its nature, a privilege must be asserted if it is to have effect.[113] A privilege holder may refrain from invoking the privilege, for example through inadvertence or on the basis of a strategic decision that her interests are better served by disclosure. Whatever the reason for the failure to assert, the court will not intervene and recognise the privilege *sua sponte*. Where a claim of privilege is challenged, the privilege holder bears the onus of substantiating her claim.[114]

[1.34] Correlative to the need to assert the privilege is the right of the privilege holder to waive it. Waiver may be deliberate or inadvertent and the privilege may

---

109 *Three Rivers District Council v Governor and Company of the Bank of England (No 6)* [2004] 3 WLR 1274 at 1295–96.

110 *Upjohn Co v United States* (1981) 449 US 383 at 389.

111 *Baker v Campbell* (1983) 153 CLR 52 at 95. See also *Commissioner of Inland Revenue v West-Walker* [1954] NZLR 191 (CA).

112 *Gallagher v Stanley* [1998] 2 IR 267 at 271 *per* O'Flaherty J: 'The privilege does not attach to members of the legal profession. It is a privilege of the client, who can always waive it'. See also *Minter v Priest* [1930] AC 558, 579 (*per* Atkin LJ); *Ventouris v Mountain* [2002] 1 WLR 607; and *Three Rivers District Council v Governor and Company of the Bank of England (No 6)* [2004] 3 WLR 1274 at 1295 (*per* Baroness Hale).

113 *Bula Ltd v Crowley* [1991] 1 IR 220; *Re Freedom of Information Act 1997 as amended; National Maternity Hospital v Information Commissioner* [2007] IEHC 113 (30 March 2007) (Quirke J).

114 *Smurfit Paribas Bank Ltd v AAB Expert Finance Ltd* [1991] 1 IR 469; *Buckley v Bough* (2 July 2001, unreported) HC (Morris J) 4.

be waived in whole or in part. Because privilege is predicated on confidentiality, the presence of a third party during discussions between lawyer and client or the disclosure of a communication to a third party destroys privilege. However, some forms of limited disclosure may escape this general principle, for example disclosure to a third party who shares a common interest or to a third party for a purpose unconnected with the proceedings.[115]

[1.35] Privilege, and the decision whether to invoke or waive it, belongs to the client and not to her lawyer.[116] It follows that the lawyer cannot assert the privilege unless acting on behalf of the client and cannot invoke it once it has been waived by the client. In the conduct of litigation, the lawyer is generally presumed to act with the client's authority.[117] In practical terms, the lawyer has a duty to inform the client as to the existence of the privilege and to assert the privilege on the client's behalf unless otherwise instructed.[118] Similarly, the lawyer is deemed to act on the client's behalf when waiving privilege although there is some dispute across the common law world as to whether inadvertent disclosure by the lawyer has the effect of waiving the privilege.[119]

[1.36] It is vital to appreciate the evidentiary consequences of a valid assertion of privilege. The rules relating to the competence or compellability of a witness may result in the witness being excluded from proceedings entirely. In contrast, privilege does not absolve a party from the need to engage the evidentiary process. Abrahamson, Dwyer and Fitzpatrick emphasise this point in the context of discovery in civil proceedings:

> 'Privilege is not a valid objection to discovery of documents. Rather, it is an objection to production of documents which have been discovered. In other words, even where a document is privileged, the party making discovery is obliged to inform his opponent that the document exists. Privilege will avail him only after that has been done, to prevent his opponent inspecting the document.'[120]

---

[115] *Fyffes plc v DCC plc* [2005] 1 IR 59.

[116] *Gallagher v Stanley* [1998] 2 IR 267 at 271 *per* O'Flaherty J: *McMullen v Carty* (27 January 1998, unreported) SC; *Shell E & P Ireland Ltd v McGrath (No 2)* [2007] 2 IR 574 at 580; *Minter v Priest* [1930] AC 558, 579; *Ventouris v Mountain* [2002] 1 WLR 607, 611. The entitlement of the client to disclose privileged communications if she considers it in her interest to do so has been recognised in EC law: *AM & S Europe Ltd v Commission* Case 155/79 [1982] ECR 1575 at para 28; *Akzo Nobel Chemicals Ltd & Akcros Chemicals Ltd v Commission* Joined Cases T-125/03 & T-253/03 (17 September 2007, unreported) CFI at para 90; *Akzo Nobel Chemicals Ltd and Akcros Chemicals Ltd v European Commission* Case C-550/07P (14 September 2010, unreported), [2010] 5 CMLR 19.

[117] Thanki (ed), *The Law of Privilege* (Oxford University Press, 2006) at para 133.

[118] *McMullen v Carty* (27 January 1998, unreported) SC.

[119] Thanki (ed), *The Law of Privilege* (Oxford University Press, 2006) at para 525 (citing cases).

[120] Abrahamson, Dwyer and Fitzpatrick, *Discovery and Disclosure* (Thomson Round Hall, 2007) at para 34.07.

A person making discovery must swear an affidavit of discovery listing every document to which she has access that falls within the categories ordered or agreed.[121] General assertions over categories of documents or bundles of correspondence will not suffice; the assertion of privilege must be particularised with each document listed individually and briefly described and the corresponding privilege identified.[122]

[1.37] There are a number of procedural options open to a party who wishes to challenge an assertion of privilege. The Rules of Court stipulate that the party should seek production of the documents through service of a notice to produce[123] and, in the event that the documents are not produced, then proceed by way of a motion for inspection.[124] On occasion, the court may itself inspect the documents when deciding whether to recognise the privilege. Exceptionally, it may also be necessary for the court to hear evidence in order to determine whether there is a sufficient factual basis for the assertion.[125]

THE STATUS OF PRIVILEGE

[1.38] The status of privilege has evolved over the centuries. Traditionally classified as a rule of evidence,[126] privilege has assumed a more exalted cast over time. Courts across the common law world have recognised that privilege has a substantive dimension[127] which has been explained by reference to the equitable obligation inherent in confidentiality[128] and the broader matrix of rights to justice.[129]

---

121 See **Ch 7**.

122 *Flynn v Northern Banking* (1898) 32 ILTR 67; *Bula Ltd v Crowley* [1991] 1 IR 220; *Irish Haemophilia Society Ltd v Lindsay* (16 May 2001, unreported) HC (Kelly J).

123 Ord 31, r 15; Ord 32, r 4 CCR; Ord 46A, r 6 DCR.

124 Ord 31, r 18; Ord 32, r 5 CCR.

125 *Minter v Priest* [1929] 1 KB 655 at 668–669; *Duncan v Governor of Portlaoise Prison* [1997] 1 IR 558 at 573–574 (*per* Kelly J.).

126 *Kershaw v Whelan* [1996] 1 WLR 358 at 370 (*per* Ebsworth J).

127 See, eg, the Canadian decisions of *Solosky v Canada* [1980] 1 SCR 821, 105 DLR (3d) 745 and *Descôteaux v Mierzwinski* [1982] 1 SCR 860, 14 DLR (3d) 590, and the South African decision of *Jeeva and Others v Receiver of Revenue, Port Elizabeth and Others* 1995 [2] SA 433 (SE) discussed in Zeffertt, Paizes and Skeen, *The South African Law of Evidence* (Lexis Nexis, 2003) 577. See also Auburn, *Legal Professional Privilege: Law and Theory* (Hart Publishing, 2000) ch 2; Passmore, *Privilege* (2nd edn, xpl publishing, 2006) para 10.26 *et seq;* Andrews, 'Legal Advice Privilege: A Matter of Substance' (2000) 59(1) Camb L J 47.

128 See, eg, *General Mediterranean Holdings SA v Patel* [2000] 1 WLR 272 at 280 *et seq* (*per* Toulson J).

129 See, eg, *United States of America v Philip Morris Inc and Others* [2004] EWCA Civ 330; *Carter v Northmore Hale Davy & Leake* (1995) 183 CLR 121; *Descoteaux v Mierzwinski* (1982) 141 DLR 3d 590; Andrews, 'Legal Advice Privilege: A Matter of Substance' (2000) 59(1) Camb L J 47, 49.

[1.39] In *R v Derby Magistrates' Court, ex parte B*,[130] Lord Taylor famously stated:

> 'The principle which runs through ... [the case law] ... is that a man must be able to consult his lawyer in confidence, since otherwise he might hold back half the truth. The client must be sure that what he tells his lawyer in confidence will never be revealed without his consent. Legal professional privilege is thus much more than an ordinary rule of evidence, limited in its application to the facts of a particular case. It is the fundamental condition on which the administration of justice as a whole rests.'[131]

These sentiments are echoed in judicial statements across the common law world.[132] They disguise a certain tension, however, between the elevated status of privilege and the reality that it may be waived[133] or overridden by various exceptions.[134]

[1.40] In Ireland, the role of privilege in assisting the administration of justice in the courts raises the question of whether it enjoys constitutional protection. In his judgment in the landmark Supreme Court case of *Smurfit Paribas Bank Ltd v AAB Export Finance Ltd*, Finlay CJ stated:

> 'The existence of a privilege or exemption from disclosure for communications made between a person and his lawyer clearly constitutes a potential restriction and diminution of the full disclosure both prior to and during the course of legal proceedings which in the interests of the common good is desirable for the purpose of ascertaining the truth and rendering justice. Such privilege should therefore, in my view, only be granted by the courts in instances which have been identified as securing an objective which in the public interest in the proper conduct of the administration of justice can be said to outweigh the disadvantage arising from the restriction of disclosure of all the facts.'[135]

On the basis of this principle, Finlay CJ concluded that privilege is necessarily limited to information which is closely and proximately linked to the conduct of litigation and the function of administering justice in our courts. Time and again subsequent courts have reiterated these central holdings in *Smurfit Paribas Bank Ltd* when recognising the special contribution that privilege makes to the administration of justice.

---

[130] *R v Derby Magistrates' Court, ex parte B* [1995] 3 WLR 681.

[131] *R v Derby Magistrates' Court, ex parte B* [1995] 3 WLR 681 at 695 (quoted with approval by Kelly J in *Duncan v Governor of Portlaoise Prison* [1997] IR 558 at 575 and in *Miley v Flood* [2001] 1 ILRM 489 at 504).

[132] *Solosky v Canada* (1980) 105 DLR (3d) 745; *Smith v Jones* [1999] 1 SCR 455; *ESSO Australia Resources Ltd v Dawson* [1999] FCA 363, (1999) 162 ALR 79; *Commissioner of Inland Revenue v West-Walker* [1954] NZLR 191.

[133] See **Ch 6**.

[134] See **Ch 5**.

[135] *Smurfit Paribas Bank Ltd v AAB Export Finance Ltd* [1990] 1 IR 469 at 477.

Finlay CJ did not couch his characterisation of privilege in constitutional terms. Arguably, however, his judgment suggests a constitutional dimension. Privilege might be grounded in Article 34 by virtue of its recognised association with the administration of justice. McGrath has suggested that the right to consult with a lawyer in confidence might be protected 'in the civil context by Art. 40.3 as a facet of the right of access to the courts and in the criminal context by the right to legal representation'.[136]

[1.41] Arguably the more recent case of *Martin & Doorley v Legal Aid Board*[137] lends further support for constitutional status. In their submissions before the High Court, the parties assumed that privilege enjoyed the protection of Article 34 of the Constitution. Laffoy J did not squarely address the question, however, her judgment continued in the vein of *Smurfit Paribas Bank Ltd:*

> 'What the judgment of Finlay CJ illustrates is that in this jurisdiction the existence and definition of the parameters of legal professional privilege is predicated on there being a public interest requirement for it in the proper conduct of the administration of justice. It also identifies the nature of such requirement, which is the underlying rationale of the privilege – that the client should not be inhibited in the conduct of litigation or in obtaining legal advice by forced disclosure of communications and advice. Such inhibition might lead to the client not being 'able to make a clean breast of it' or holding 'back half the truth' or even tempt a client's counsel 'to forgo conscientiously investigating his own case' until 'the even of or during the trial' or constitute 'a prohibition upon professional advice and assistance'. It is to obviate such outcomes, which would undermine the proper, fair and efficient administration of justice, that legal professional privilege exists and has been elevated beyond a mere rule of evidence to 'a fundamental condition on which the administration of justice as a whole rests'.' [138]

Statements of this kind fall short of express, unbridled recognition that privilege enjoys constitutional protection. Until such time as the courts are asked to address squarely the constitutional issue, the status of privilege in the Irish legal order will remain somewhat uncertain. The question bears on the authority of the Oireachtas and the courts to uphold privilege on the one hand and to override it on the other.

[1.42] Constitutional considerations aside, privilege also enjoys the protection of the European Convention on Human Rights. In *R v Derby Magistrates' Court, ex parte B*, Lord Taylor recognised that legal professional privilege is a fundamental human right protected by the Convention.[139] This statement echoes

---

136 McGrath, *Evidence* (Thomson Round Hall, 2005) at para 10.109.

137 *Martin & Doorley v Legal Aid Board* [2007] 2 IR 759.

138 *Martin & Doorley v Legal Aid Board* [2007] 2 IR 759 at 775 (internal quotation and citations omitted).

139 *R v Derby Magistrates' Court, ex parte B* [1995] 3 WLR 681 at 696.

the jurisprudence of the European Court of Human Rights, which has located privilege within the protection of the right to privacy under art 8 of the Convention.[140] The Strasbourg organs have also recognised that interference with the confidentiality of the legal professional relationship may infringe the right to a fair trial under art 6.[141] It is important to recall, however, that these rights are not absolute and may be subject to encroachment in exceptional circumstances.

THE ABSOLUTE NATURE OF PRIVILEGE

[1.43] The judgments in *Smurfit Paribas, Martin v Legal Aid Board* and other cases highlight the elevated status that legal professional privilege enjoys in contemporary trial practice. Paradoxically, these cases also make plain that privilege is a qualified concept in Irish law and operates only within the body of legal rules which define and limit the scope of its application. For example, the case law indicates that when a judge determines whether privilege should be recognised or whether a recognised privilege has been waived, she is engaging in the task of applying *a priori* legal rules as opposed to exercising judicial discretion. Provided these rules are met, however, the communication or document in question qualifies for privilege. As Lord Scott observed in *Three Rivers District Council v Governor and Company of the Bank of England (No 6)*, whereas privilege can be waived by the client or overridden by statute, it cannot be displaced by 'some supposedly greater public interest'.[142]

[1.44] The downside of this absolutist approach is that it hampers the ability of the courts to set boundaries to the scope of legal professional privilege. In the same case, Baroness Hale invoked language reminiscent of the judgment of Finlay CJ in *Smurfit Paribas Bank Ltd*:

> 'Legal advice privilege restricts the power of a court to compel the production of what would otherwise be relevant evidence. It may thus impede the proper

---

[140] *Foxley v United Kingdom* (2001) 31 EHRR 25 (ruling that interception of applicant bankrupt's correspondence with his legal advisers violated his right to respect for his correspondence under art 8); *Campbell v United Kingdom* (1993) 15 EHRR 137 at para 46 (recognising in the context of the confidentiality of prisoners' correspondence that any person should be free to consult a lawyer under conditions that favour full and uninhibited discussion).

[141] *Niemitez v Germany* (1993) 16 EHRR 97 (recognising that a search of a lawyer's offices could disproportionately impinge on professional secrecy with repercussions on the administration of justice); *S v Switzerland* (1992) 14 EHRR 670 (ruling that surveillance of communications between custodial detainee and lawyer interfered with detainee's right to prepare his defence).

[142] *Three Rivers District Council v Governor and Company of the Bank of England (No 6)* [2004] 3 WLR 1274 at 1282. At 1283, Lord Scott distinguished the lawyer–client relationship from other confidential relationships such as doctor–patient and accountant–client in so far as only the former attracts this absolute protection. English recognition of the absolute nature of privilege has not been entirely uniform and consistent. For example, in *R v Ataou* [1988] QB 798, the Court of Appeal advocated a balancing exercise as a means of resolving assertions of privilege in criminal proceedings.

administration of justice in the individual case. This makes the communications covered different from most other types of confidential communication, where the need to encourage candour may be just as great.'[143]

Judicial sentiments in this vein reflect concerns over the potentially broad reach of privilege in contemporary trial practice. As such, they strike a marked retreat from the expansive language of the traditional case law authorities discussed above. The signal that seemingly emerges is that the courts will be rigorous in ensuring that privilege, though an ever vibrant concept, is strictly confined within its legal parameters.

RULES VERSUS DISCRETION

[1.45] The domestic and comparative case law reflects an on-going discourse over whether the courts can and should engage directly in the balancing of the competing public interests that underpin assertions of privilege. For example, in *Three Rivers District Council (No 6)*, Lord Carswell opined that determining the bounds of privilege involves striking the proper balance between the opposing imperatives of making the maximum relevant material available to the court and avoiding unfairness to individuals by revealing confidential communications between their lawyers and themselves.[144] Indeed, his lordship characterised the practice that has developed as 'a reconciliation between these principles'.[145]

[1.46] In most common law jurisdictions, this reconciliation is reflected in the legal rules that condition legal professional privilege; when responding to assertions of privilege, it is the function of the trial courts to apply these rules which, in turn, strike the appropriate balance between the competing policy rationales. In this characteristic, legal professional privilege may be distinguished from public interest privilege, formerly known as executive or Crown privilege, which protects from disclosure certain information connected with the operation of government.[146] Public interest privilege is conditioned not by legal rules but by *ad hoc* judicial discretion;[147] the trial judge must engage in an overt balancing exercise, weighing the public interest in disclosure against

143 *Three Rivers District Council v Governor and Company of the Bank of England (No 6)* [2004] 3 WLR 1274 at 1295. Baroness Hale concluded, nevertheless, that 'the privilege is too well established in the common law for its existence to be doubted now'.

144 *Three Rivers District Council v Governor and Company of the Bank of England (No 6)* [2004] 3 WLR 1274 at 1304.

145 *Three Rivers District Council v Governor and Company of the Bank of England (No 6)* [2004] 3 WLR 1274 at 1304.

146 See generally McGrath, *Evidence* (Thomson Round Hall, 2005) ch 10D; Healy, *Irish Laws of Evidence* (Thomson Round Hall, 2004) ch 13; Fennell, *Law of Evidence in Ireland* (3rd edn, Bloomsbury Professional, 2009) at para 8.105 *et seq*.

147 *Murphy v Dublin Corporation and the Minister for Local Government* [1972] IR 215; *Ambiorix Ltd v Minister for the Environment (No1)* [1992] 1 IR 277, [1992] ILRM 209.

some particularised interest in confidentiality, such as national security[148] or the proper functioning of the public service,[149] asserted by the State.

[1.47] It is noteworthy that when considering assertions of legal professional privilege the Canadian courts are not tied by pre-determined rules but rather are permitted to balance the competing public interests in favour of and against privilege on an *ad hoc* basis.[150] In *Smith v Jones*,[151] the Canadian Supreme Court held that legal professional privilege is not absolute and can be set aside in the face of a sufficiently compelling public interest, such as public safety. Jones was charged with the offence of aggravated sexual assault of a prostitute and, in advance of sentencing, his lawyer retained the psychiatrist, Smith, to conduct an assessment of Jones. Based on an interview, Smith formed the opinion that Jones suffered from psychiatric disorders and was a danger to the prostitutes in the area. The defence ultimately decided against using Smith's report at the sentencing hearing and Smith sought a judicial declaration that he was entitled to disclose it to the police and the prosecution. The Supreme Court held that in principle privilege could be overridden in the interests of protecting public safety and sanctioned relatively broad disclosure of Smith's opinion and the material on which it was based.[152]

[1.48] The passage from the judgment of Finlay CJ in *Smurfit Paribas Bank Ltd* quoted above at para **1.40** might be taken to suggest that the Irish courts should balance considerations of confidentiality and disclosure on a case-by-case basis. However, in *Fyffes plc v DCC plc & Others*, Fennelly J discounted this reading of the passage. He emphasised that whether or not documents are privileged is a matter of legal principle and that once privilege is found to exist, there is no judicial discretion to exclude it.[153] He then quoted with approval the statement of Lord Bingham in *Paragon Finance v Freshfields* to the effect that '[s]ave where client and legal adviser have abused their confidential relationship to facilitate

---

[148] *Gormley v Ireland* [1993] 2 IR 75; *Walker v Ireland* [1997] 1 ILRM 363.

[149] *Cully v Northern Bank Finance Corporation* [1984] ILRM 683; *Incorporated Law Society v Osborne* [1987] ILRM 42; *Fitzpatrick v Martin* [1988] IR 132; *Skeffington v Rooney* [1997] 2 ILRM 56.

[150] See generally *Solosky v Canada* [1980] 1 SCR 821, 105 DLR (3d) 745 and *Descôteaux v Mierzwinski* [1982] 1 SCR 860, 14 DLR (3d) 590. See generally Sopinka, Lederman and Bryant, *Law of Evidence in Canada* (Butterworths, 1999 & Supp 2003).

[151] *Smith v Jones* [1999] 1 SCR 455. See Sheldrick, 'Administering public safety: solicitor-client privilege, medical experts and the adversarial process: *Smith v Jones*' (2000) 4 Int'l J Evid & Proof 119. The English Court of Appeal has recognised a similar exception to a doctor's duty of confidentiality: *W v Edgell* [1990] 1 All ER 845.

[152] Sheldrick, 'Administering public safety: solicitor-client privilege, medical experts and the adversarial process: *Smith v Jones*' (2000) 4 Int'l J Evid & Proof 119 at 125 contends that a 'far narrower form of disclosure would have served the interest of safeguarding public safety equally well'.

[153] *Fyffes plc v DCC plc and Others* [2005] 1 IR 59 at 67.

crime or fraud, the protection is absolute unless the client (whose privilege it is) waives it, whether expressly or impliedly'.[154]

[1.49] The absence of a broad discretion was rejected by Finlay CJ in his judgment in *Bula Ltd v Crowley (No 2)*[155] concerning the scope of the exemption from privilege of legal advice obtained to further crime, fraud or conduct injurious to the administration of justice. Finlay CJ dismissed the notion that an exemption should apply where the privilege holder had been accused of conduct that was merely tortious in nature. However, he also dismissed as 'unsound in principle the alternative submission 'that the court should look at the documents and if, as it were, it finds them highly relevant to the issue which appears to arise in the action, should, as a matter of discretion, order their production'.[156]

[1.50] In the seminal decision of *R v Derby Magistrates' Court, ex parte B*,[157] the House of Lords was emphatic in its classification of legal professional privilege as a rule of law as opposed to an exercise of judicial discretion. As noted above, Lord Taylor CJ famously characterised the privilege as 'much more than an ordinary rule of evidence' and as 'a fundamental condition on which the administration of justice as a whole rests'.[158] Lord Nicholls rejected as 'illusory' and 'a veritable will-o'-the wisp' the possibility of a discretionary judicial balancing exercise in this area:

> 'There is no evident stopping place short of the balancing exercise being potentially available in support of all parties in all forms of court proceedings. This highlights the impossibility of the exercise. What is the measure by which judges are to ascribe an appropriate weight, on each side of the scale, to the diverse multitude of different claims, civil and criminal, and other interests of the client on the one hand and the person seeking disclosure on the other hand?'[159]

Lord Nicholls conceded that a court might refuse to recognise privilege where it was satisfied that the client no longer had any interest to protect or, to put it another way, where 'the privilege has become spent'.[160] He cited the example

---

[154] *Paragon Finance v Freshfields* [1999] 1 WLR 1183 at 1188 (cited by Fennelly J in *Fyffes plc v DCC plc and Others* [2005] 1 IR 59 at 67).

[155] *Bula Ltd v Crowley (No 2)* [1994] 2 IR 54, [1994] 1 ILRM 495.

[156] *Bula Ltd v Crowley (No 2)* [1994] 2 IR 54 at 59.

[157] *R v Derby Magistrates' Court, ex parte B* [1995] 3 WLR 681. For critical analysis see Tapper, 'Prosecution and Privilege' (1996–97) 1 Int'l J Evid & Proof 5.

[158] *R v Derby Magistrates' Court, ex parte B* [1995] 3 WLR 681 at 695. See also *Solosky v Canada* [1980] 1 SCR 821, 105 DLR (3d) 745, 760 (legal professional privilege is a 'fundamental civil and legal right').

[159] *R v Derby Magistrates' Court, ex parte B* [1995] 3 WLR 681 at 700. Lord Nicholls [1995] 3 WLR 681 at 699 cited several authorities in support of this conclusion including *Grant v Downs* (1976) 135 CLR 674 at 685 (*per* Stephen, Mason and Murphy JJ): 'As a head of privilege legal professional privilege is so firmly entrenched in the law that it is not to be exorcised by judicial discretion'.

[160] *R v Derby Magistrates' Court, ex parte B* [1995] 3 WLR 681 at 700.

posited by Cross of a scenario in which 'the solicitor for the unsuccessful plaintiff in a civil action takes a statement from a witness who is subsequently prosecuted for perjury, and the prosecution wish to ask the solicitor what the witness said to him'.[161] However, it was Lord Nicholls's view that the availability or non-availability of privilege in circumstances such as these would turn not on a judicial balancing exercise but rather on 'proof that no rational person would regard himself as having any continuing interest in protecting the privilege of confidentiality in the originally privileged material'.[162] Precisely because the law of privilege is grounded in considerations of public interest, it should not be used to protect a client who has no continuing interest in asserting the right and in circumstances where it will seriously prejudice the interests of another.[163]

[1.51] The House of Lords has remained faithful to the absolute tenor of privilege. In *Three Rivers (No 6)*, Lord Scott observed:

> '... if a communication or document qualifies for legal professional privilege, the privilege is absolute. It cannot be overridden by some supposedly greater public interest. It can be waived by the person, the client, entitled to it and it can be overridden by statute but it is otherwise absolute. There is no balancing act that has to be carried out ...'[164]

Thus, the judicial function of determining assertions of privilege involves the application of pre-determined rules rather than the exercise of discretion inherent in the balancing of competing public interests.

OVERRIDING PRIVILEGE

[1.52] The governance of legal professional privilege may not be subject to a general judicial discretion but nevertheless there are other grounds on which a court may override the entitlement.

Legal professional privilege is subject to recognised exceptions.[165] The privilege will not be effective where it is used as an engine for crime, fraud or conduct injurious to the administration of justice.[166] A court may decline to recognise the privilege in the quasi-inquisitorial setting of proceedings relating to the welfare of children where to do so would undermine the paramount consideration of the best interests of the child.[167] Similarly, where an action

---

161 *R v Derby Magistrates' Court, ex parte B* [1995] 3 WLR 681 at 700 quoting from *Cross on Evidence* (5th edn, 1979) at 286. Lord Nicholls also relied on Canadian and New Zealand authority: *R v Dunbar and Logan* (1982) 138 DLR (3d) 221; *R v Craig* [1975] 1 NZLR 597.

162 *R v Derby Magistrates' Court, ex parte B* [1995] 3 WLR 681 at 700.

163 *R v Derby Magistrates' Court, ex parte B* [1995] 3 WLR 681 at 700.

164 *Three Rivers District Council v Governor and Company of the Bank of England (No 6)* [2005] 1 AC 610 at 646 (internal citations omitted).

165 See **Ch 5**.

166 *Murphy v Kirwan* [1993] 3 IR 501, [1994] 1 ILRM 293.

167 *L(T) v L(V)* [1996] IFLR 126.

involves the disposition of the estate of a deceased, the courts have greater leeway to order disclosure on the basis that the proceedings are not *inter partes* in the true sense of the term.[168] The position is less clear-cut in relation to a putative exception to legal professional privilege in criminal proceedings where the innocence of the accused is at stake. Although the House of Lords has set its face against any such exception, the Irish courts have taken a more open approach in the context of informer privilege.[169] It could be argued that Article 38.1 requires the courts to consider the potential impact on the fairness of a trial of the non-disclosure of privileged information. The Irish courts have yet to expressly recognise what might be termed a nascent right on the part of an accused to introduce potentially exculpatory evidence that the prosecution is seeking to withhold on the ground of legal professional privilege.[170]

As noted above, the Supreme Court of Canada has perhaps travelled farthest in dissolving the absolute status of lawyer-client privilege. It has recognised that the privilege can be set aside in exceptional circumstances and, specifically, has carved out a public safety exception thereto.[171]

[1.53] In addition, privilege may be waived by the privilege holder.[172] The concept of waiver is defined in relatively broad terms and embraces scenarios where the privilege is lost inadvertently, such as by dent of unintentional disclosure. Thus, even where the holder asserts privilege with the unbridled intention of protecting the information in question from disclosure in the proceedings, the court may determine subsequently that the privilege has been lost at the holder's own hand.

[1.54] Finally, the common law rules that govern the operation of legal professional privilege may be trumped by statute.[173] The freedom of the Oireachtas to override privilege is curtailed by the protection afforded to individual rights by the Constitution and the European Convention on Human

---

[168] *Crawford v Treacy* [1999] 2 IR 171.

[169] *Ward v Special Criminal Court* [1999] IR 60. But see *People (DPP) v Kelly* [2006] 3 IR 115.

[170] See generally Heffernan and Imwinkelried, 'The Accused's Constitutional Right to Introduce Critical, Demonstrably Reliable, Exculpatory Evidence' (2005) 40 Irish Jurist (ns) 111. The Canadian Supreme Court has recognised that privilege may be overridden by the public interest in enabling the accused to present a full and proper defence. *R v McClure* [2001] 1 SCR 445.

[171] *Smith v Jones* [1999] 1 SCR 455.

[172] See **Ch 6**.

[173] *Fyffes plc v DCC plc* [2005] 1 IR 59 (*per* Fennelly J); Tribunal of Inquiry into Payments to Politicians and Related Matters, Revised Tribunal Dated 24 March 2010 Re Opinion Dated 9 May 1996, para 39 (recognising that the statutory regime for Tribunals of Inquiry preserves rather than trumps privilege). On statutory preservation of legal professional privilege under the Freedom of Information Acts, see *Re Freedom of Information Act 1997 as amended; National Maternity Hospital v Information Commissioner* [2007] IEHC 113 (30 March 2007) (Quirke J). In the South African context see Zeffertt, Paizes and Skeen, *The South African Law of Evidence* (Lexis Nexis, 2003) 577 at 588.

Rights. However, as noted above, the scope of those rights and the extent of the corresponding curtailment in this area have not been delineated with precision. There is a dearth of Irish case law directly on point. Nevertheless, even assuming statutory encroachment is legitimate in principle, the courts are unlikely to infer a statutory intent to sanction disclosure in the absence of 'express words' or 'necessary implication'.[174] Over the years, the scope and application of privilege has been refined by changes in the court rules governing discovery designed to tailor and expedite the procedure.[175] Significant changes include greater specificity in applications for discovery and counterclaims for protection from disclosure on grounds on privilege,[176] and more ample provision for the exchange of expert reports in advance of trial.[177]

PRIVILEGE AND CONFIDENTIALITY

[1.55] Finally, some further explanation is required of the relationship between privilege and the broader concept of confidentiality. Privilege is not synonymous with confidentiality; whereas the latter is a condition of the former, paradoxically it is a broader legal concept.[178] It is customary to distinguish privilege from confidentiality on the ground that the former is an entitlement that may not be displaced by the court if validly asserted whereas the latter is a discretionary bar to disclosure that a trial judge may apply where the balance of justice so requires.[179] Information may have been given, received, prepared or retained in confidence but it does not necessarily follow that the information is privileged.

[1.56] Confidential information that appears to fall within the ambit of professional legal privilege will not be protected if the other conditions of privilege have not been established. During the course of her professional life, a lawyer may be privy to information which the client considers confidential but if the information relates neither to legal advice nor to litigation *per se*, the

174 *R (Morgan Grenfell & Co Ltd) v Special Commissioner of Income Tax* [2003] 1 AC 563; *Bowman v Fels* [2005] 1 WLR 3083; *R (Kelly) v Warley Magistrates' Court* [2007] EWHC 1836 (Admin). See also *Canada (Director of Investigation and Research) v Canadian Railways Ltd* [1972] 3 WWR 547, 26 DLR (3d) 745 (abrogation by legislation must be clear and unambiguous); *Rosenberg v Jaine* [1983] NZLR 1, 12 (a statute cannot abrogate privilege in an indirect way). For discussion of additional New Zealand authorities see Mathieson (ed), *Cross on Evidence* (8th New Zealand edn, Lexis Nexis, 2005) para 10.23.

175 See **Ch 7**.

176 See **Ch 7**.

177 See **Ch 8**.

178 Abrahamson, Dwyer & Fitzpatrick, *Discovery and Disclosure* (Thomson Round Hall, 2007) at para 34.04. See also *Independent Newspapers (Ire) Ltd v Murphy* [2006] IEHC 276 (28 July 2006) (Clarke J).

179 Abrahamson, Dwyer & Fitzpatrick, *Discovery and Disclosure* (Thomson Round Hall, 2007) (citing cases).

information will not be privileged. The lawyer may be ethically bound to respect the confidence but theoretically at least she could be compelled to disclose the information if it were relevant to any legal proceedings. Similarly, confidential legal advice tendered to a party will not be privileged if the information was delivered outside the confines of a professional legal relationship. Even where the various conditions are met, information may be confidential but not privileged if the holder fails to assert the privilege or asserts and subsequently waives the privilege although, in practical terms, waiver not only defeats privilege but also destroys confidentiality. Similarly, a court may be compelled to reject both privilege and confidentiality in exceptional circumstances such as where legal advice is used to further a crime or fraud.

Chapter 2

Legal Advice Privilege

INTRODUCTION

[2.01] Legal advice privilege[1] entitles a client to refuse to disclose, and to have her lawyer refuse to disclose, confidential communications between the two connected with the giving of legal advice.[2] As the holder of the privilege, the client has the onus to establish that the legal conditions characterising the privilege are met. The client must satisfy the court that she and her lawyer exchanged in confidence one or more communications relating to legal advice. The effect of discharging this burden successfully is that privilege is absolute in the sense that the court has no general discretion to override the privilege on the basis of some countervailing public interest.[3] There are some limited exceptions to the privilege[4] and, of course, the client may subsequently waive the privilege.[5] Nevertheless, the judicial function of determining assertions of privilege involves the application of *a priori* rules rather than the exercise of a discretionary balancing of competing public interests.[6]

SCOPE

[2.02] The communications which are protected by legal advice privilege may relate to litigation but they need not be so related; it is sufficient that the communications were exchanged in the context of the professional legal relationship.[7] This principle was recognised as far back as the late nineteenth

---

1 See generally Passmore, *Privilege* (2nd edn, xpl publishing, 2006) ch 2; Thanki (ed), *The Law of Privilege* (Oxford University Press, 2006) ch 2; Matthews and Malek, *Disclosure* (Sweet & Maxwell, 2001) para 9.009 *et seq;* McGrath, *Evidence* (Thomson Round Hall, 2005) pp 524–536; Healy, *Irish Laws of Evidence* (Thomson Round Hall, 2004) Ch 13.II.

2 *Smurfit Paribas Bank Ltd v AAB Export Finance Ltd* [1990] 1 IR 469, [1990] ILRM 588; *Society for the Protection of Unborn Children (Ireland) Ltd v Grogan* [1992] 2 IR 471; *Miley v Flood* [2001] 2 IR 50, [2001] 1 ILRM 489.

3 *R v Derby Magistrates' Court, ex parte B* [1995] 1 4 All ER 526; *Three Rivers District Council v Governor and Company of Bank of England (No 6)* [2004] 3 WLR 1274, [2005] 1 AC 610.

4 See **CH 5**.

5 See **CH 6**.

6 See Andrews, 'Legal Advice Privilege: A Matter of Substance' (2000) 59(1) Camb L J 47.

7 For the purposes of privilege, litigation extends to proceedings in foreign jurisdictions. Keane, *The Modern Law of Evidence* (7th edn, Oxford University Press, 2008) p 610 (citing *Re Duncan* [1968] P 306 and *IBM Corpn v Phoenix International (Computers) Ltd* [1995] 1 All ER 413).

century and is reflected in this statement by Lord Brougham LC in *Greenough v Gaskell:*

> '[I]t does not appear that the protection is qualified by any reference to proceedings pending or in contemplation. If touching matters that come within the ordinary scope of professional employment, [lawyers] receive a communication in their professional capacity, either from a client, or on his account, and for his benefit in the transaction of his business, or, which amounts to the same thing, it they commit to paper, in the course of their employment on his behalf, matters which they know only through their professional relation to the client, they are not only justified in withholding such matters, but bound to withhold them, and will not be compelled to disclose the information or produce the papers in any Court of law or equity, either as party or as witness.'[8]

The contemporary case law remains faithful to the broad proposition that legal advice privilege reaches beyond the context of pending or contemplated litigation.[9] Indeed, with the emergence of two distinct doctrinal strands within legal professional privilege, litigation privilege has become the principal vehicle for the assertion of privilege once litigation is anticipated or in train. Legal advice privilege is typically associated with the giving and receiving of legal counsel in the generic sense; the paradigm in the present day is a scenario in which the client and lawyer communicate about a matter which is not yet related to litigation in any tangible sense or, indeed, which is unlikely ever to form the basis of legal proceedings. However, it is important to grasp that where legal advice is sought or received in connection with litigation, it is covered by both strands of privilege, legal advice privilege and litigation privilege.[10] Consequently, if the conditions of one strand are not made out, a successful claim of privilege remains a possibility under the other strand.

[2.03] Perhaps mindful of the need to temper the inhibitive effect of a burgeoning doctrine of privilege on the important pre-trial practice of disclosure, the Irish courts impose an exacting standard on the eligibility for legal advice privilege of matters coming within what Lord Brougham LC termed in *Greenough v Gaskell* 'the ordinary scope of professional employment'. Not every fact or communication received by a lawyer in her professional capacity will be protected. In his landmark judgment in *Smurfit*

8 *Greenough v Gaskell* (1883) 1 My & K 98 at 101.

9 See, eg, *Three Rivers District Council v Governor and Company of Bank of England (No 6)* [2004] 3 WLR 1274 at 1283 *per* Lord Scott: '... legal advice privilege is frequently sought or given in connection with current or contemplated litigation. But it may equally well be sought or given in circumstances and for purposes that have nothing to do with litigation'.

10 McGrath, *Evidence* (Thomson Round Hall, 2005) at para.10.08, suggests that confidential communications between client and lawyer regarding actual or anticipated litigation are perhaps best viewed as protected by legal advice privilege alone, and litigation privilege confined to third party communications (communications between either the lawyer or the client and a third party) and the lawyer's work product.

Paribas Bank Ltd v AAB Export Finance Ltd, Finlay CJ drew the line at legal advice, as opposed to the more amorphous concept of legal assistance, on the premise that only the former supposes a close and proximate link to the conduct of litigation and the function of administering justice in the courts.

> 'Where a person seeks or obtains legal advice there are good reasons to believe that he necessarily enters the area of potential litigation. The necessity to obtain legal advice would in broad terms appear to envisage the possibility of a legal challenge or query as to the correctness or effectiveness of some step which a person is contemplating. Whether such query or challenge develops or not, it is clear that a person is then entering the area of possible litigation.'[11]

DURATION

[2.04] Legal advice privilege is not subject to any temporal limitation. It subsists for the duration of the legal professional relationship and indeed continues to operate after the relationship has ceased for all other purposes.[12] Because the privilege belongs to the client, it clearly survives the death of the lawyer. However, as a general rule it also survives the death of the client and vests in her successors in title.[13]

[2.05] The longevity of legal advice privilege is encapsulated in the famous phrase of Lindley MR in *Calcraft v Guest*,[14] 'once privileged, always privileged,' which was quoted with approval by the High Court in *Quinlivan v Tuohy*.[15] The permanency of privilege is considered an essential prop to effective legal representation because it provides the client with the assurance that she can communicate freely and candidly without fear that the information will be disclosed on some unforeseen occasion in the future.[16]

ESSENTIAL FEATURES: *THREE RIVERS DISTRICT COUNCIL (NO 6)*

[2.06] In 2004, the House of Lords delivered a landmark decision on legal professional privilege in the case of *Three Rivers District Council v Governor and Company of the Bank of England (No 6)*.[17] The Lords considered several specific aspects of the privilege which are discussed in this chapter and the next.

---

[11] *Smurfit Paribas Bank Ltd v AAB Export Finance Ltd* [1990] 1 IR 469 at 478.

[12] *Bell v Smith* [1968] SCR 664, 68 DLR (2d) 571.

[13] *Bullivant v AG for Victoria* [1901] AC 196; *R v Malloy* [1997] 2 Cr App R 283. See also *Swidlerand Berlin v United States* No 97-1192 (USSC) (1998); *Estate Bilden v Sarif* (1933) CPD 275; *Euroshipping Corp of Monrovia v Minister for Agricultural Econonics and Marketing and Others* (1979) (1) SA 637 (C) discussed in Zeffertt, Paizes and Skeen, *The South African Law of Evidence* (Lexis Nexis, 2003) p 584.

[14] *Calcraft v Guest* [1898] 1 QB 759.

[15] *Quinlivan v Tuohy* (29 July 1992, unreported) HC (Barron J).

[16] *Porter v Scott* [1979] NI 6.

[17] *Three Rivers District Council v Governor and Company of the Bank of England (No 6)* [2004] 3 WLR 1274, [2005] 1 AC 610.

In a lengthy judgment, Lord Scott summarised the essential features of legal advice privilege. Although English and Irish law diverge in some respects, the following extract from his judgment is generally instructive from an Irish perspective:

> 'First, legal advice privilege arises out of a relationship of confidence between lawyer and client. Unless the communication or document for which privilege is sought is a confidential one, there can be no question of legal advice privilege arising. The confidential character of the communication or document is not by itself enough to enable privilege to be claimed but is an essential requirement.
>
> Second, if a communication or document qualifies for legal professional privilege, the privilege is absolute. It cannot be overridden by some supposedly greater public interest. It can be waived by the person, the client, entitled to it and it can be overridden by statute, but it is otherwise absolute. There is no balancing exercise to be carried out ... legal professional privilege, if it is attracted by a particular communication between lawyer and client or attaches to a particular document, cannot be set aside on the ground that some other higher public interest requires that to be done.
>
> Third, legal advice privilege gives the person entitled to it the right to decline to disclose or to allow to be disclosed the confidential communication or document in question. There has been some debate as to whether this right is a procedural right or a substantive right. In my respectful opinion the debate is sterile. Legal advice privilege is both. It may be used in legal proceedings to justify the refusal to answer certain questions or to produce for inspection certain documents. Its characterisation as procedural or substantive neither adds to nor detracts from its features.
>
> Fourth, legal advice privilege has an undoubted relationship with litigation privilege. Legal advice is frequently sought or given in connection with current or contemplated litigation. But it may equally well be sought or given in circumstances and for purposes that have nothing to do with litigation. ...'.[18]

LEGAL CONDITIONS

[2.07] Legal advice privilege protects from disclosure confidential communications passing between a client and her lawyer in the context of a professional legal relationship and for the purposes of receiving or giving legal advice. The individual or entity seeking to invoke the privilege bears the burden of establishing these five essential conditions: (1) a communication (2) conveyed in confidence (3) between a lawyer and her client (4) during a professional legal relationship (5) for the purpose of receiving or giving legal advice.

---

18 *Three Rivers District Council v Governor and Company of the Bank of England (No 6)* [2004] 3 WLR 1274 at 1282–1283, [2005] 1 AC 610 at 646–647 (internal citations omitted).

By virtue of the fact that privilege cuts across the law's fundamental policy in favour of disclosure, the courts tend to interpret these conditions restrictively.[19] The conditions also reflect the pragmatic function performed by trial courts when sifting through information that may potentially constitute evidence at trial. In making determinations in relation to discovery and disclosure, the courts are anxious to resist blanket assertions of privilege and, at the same time, safeguard genuine claims.

(1) Communication

[2.08] The term 'communication' is broadly defined for the purposes of privilege and covers a range of information conveyed orally and in a variety of written or electronic forms. Where a client consults her lawyer in person or by telephone, the conversation between the two comprises one or more communications for this purpose. Similarly, lawyers and clients routinely communicate by means of correspondence such as letter, fax and email. Privilege will extend to material which may not lend itself to the characterisation of communication in the conventional sense.[20] Notes of meetings or discussions compiled by the lawyer provide an apt illustration.

Whatever the mode of communication, the underlying purpose must relate to the giving or receiving of legal advice. Indeed, the nexus between the matter communicated and the provision of legal advice is a defining characteristic of legal advice privilege.[21] Documents passing between the client and lawyer for purposes other than the giving or receiving of legal advice are not protected.

[2.09] What is the position where information is communicated by one party to the professional legal relationship but the communication is not received by the other party? In *Three Rivers District Council v Governor and Company of the Bank of England (No 5)*, Lord Longmore expressed the view that 'a document which was intended to be a communication between client and solicitor was still privileged even if not in fact communicated'.[22]

Communications and Related Documents

[2.10] What if the documents neither request, convey nor record legal advice but are nevertheless relevant to the giving or receiving of legal advice in some secondary sense? The concept of a 'communication' is construed liberally in the further sense that material which forms part of the process of communicating may be protected even where the connection with legal advice is not express or clear on the face of the material. In considering this question, the courts will examine the purpose for which the communication was made having regard to the totality of the circumstances as opposed to focusing solely on the form of

---

[19] *Smurfit Paribas Bank Ltd v AAB Export Finance Ltd* [1990] 1 IR 469 at 477 (*per* Finlay CJ).

[20] *Mayor and Corporation of Bristol v Cox* (1884) 26 Ch D 678.

[21] *Miley v Flood* [2001] 2 IR 50, [2001] 1 ILRM 489.

[22] *Three Rivers District Council v Governor and Company of the Bank of England (No 5)* [2003] QB 1556 at 1575 (CA).

communication or the information contained therein. For example, a document conveyed by the client to the lawyer may be protected where it is incidental to the giving of instructions.[23]

[2.11] Particular difficulties arise where communications which would appear to qualify for privilege are intrinsically linked to other forms of information. Whereas the courts will take the pragmatic step of distinguishing protected from unprotected material thereby limiting the application of privilege and the corresponding restriction on disclosure, instances may arise in which severance is not possible or desirable.

[2.12] Documents that record communications between lawyers and clients, such as notes or memoranda of oral conversations[24] or documents that reproduce or incorporate legal advice previously given[25] are obvious examples. Records of this kind will be protected, assuming the other conditions of legal advice privilege are met, but generally only to the extent that they contain communications. Thus, in *R v Manchester Crown Court, ex parte Rogers*,[26] details on a solicitor's attendance note recording information other than matters passing between the client and lawyer were held not to attract privilege. Similar considerations would pertain to a solicitor's bill of costs unless it contained the substance of communications that are privileged.[27]

[2.13] During the course of a consultation, a client may furnish her lawyer with one or more documents relevant to the matter on which legal advice is sought. Whether the document in question is a privileged communication depends upon the purpose for which the document was created. Because protected communications are firmly grounded in the exchange between lawyer and client, it follows that privilege will extend to a document prepared by the client for the purpose of obtaining legal advice.[28]

---

23 Passmore, *Privilege* (2nd edn, xpl publishing, 2006) at 78 observes that the convenient shorthand of regarding documents as privileged 'is strictly inaccurate and occasionally confusing' because 'it is the purpose for which the communication contained within or evidenced by the document is made that determines whether or not privilege attaches'. In this regard, it is necessary to identify the original purpose of the communication which may not be the same as the purpose for which the document was communicated between the client and lawyer.

24 *Hurstridge Finance Ltd v Lismore Homes Ltd* (15 February 1991, unreported) HC (Costello J).

25 Abrahamson, Dwyer and Fitzpatrick, *Discovery and Disclosure* (Thomson Round Hall, 2007) para 35.14.

26 *R v Manchester Crown Court, ex parte Rogers* [1999] 1 WLR 832.

27 *Ainsworth v Wilding* [1900] 2 Ch 315; *Grant v Southwestern and County Properties Ltd* [1975] Ch 185.

28 *Re Murray Consultants Ltd (formerly Sage Consultants Ltd) and Nocrumb Ltd (formerly Murray Consultants Ltd), Horgan v Murray and Milton* [1999] 1 ILRM 257. O'Sullivan J stated that if any doubt existed as to whether a document had been prepared for the purpose of taking legal advice, then he would read the document himself and make a specific ruling in relation to it.

[2.14] In contrast, the law will not protect from disclosure a so-called 'pre-existing document', ie, a document created for some other purpose prior to the client seeking legal advice.[29] In *Tromso Sparebank v Beirne*,[30] Costello J applied the principle to copies of pre-existing documents sought for purposes of litigation:

> 'Legal professional privilege primarily exists so that a litigant can have recourse to his legal advisers in circumstances which enable him to have complete confidence that the communications made to him and from him will be kept secret. It is well established that this privilege extends to documents which come into existence after litigation is commenced, either for the purpose of obtaining or giving legal advice ... But I cannot see that the protection of the interests of a litigant requires the privilege to be extended to copies of documents which came into existence prior to the contemplation of litigation, documents which are themselves not privileged and which the other side could probably inspect as a result of a third party discovery order and which they could have produced at the trial pursuant to a *subpoena duces tecum*.'[31]

Privilege will generally encompass information gleaned by the lawyer and incorporated into the advice tendered to the client. Here too, how far a court is willing to go in upholding a claim of privilege may depend upon whether the information is self standing or is so woven into the legal advice as to form an intrinsic part. Drawing on English experience, Keane surmises that where a communication includes information that the lawyer received from a third party and conveys to the client, 'the whole communication will be privileged'.[32]

Facts Distinguished from Communications

[2.15] The courts have imposed other limitations on the concept of communication for purposes of legal advice privilege. Legal advice privilege applies only to matters *communicated* between the client and lawyer and not to every fact that may come to the lawyer's attention during the course of the legal professional relationship.[33] The distinction between facts communicated and facts ascertained has a common sense footing in the reality that legal representation may require the lawyer to engage in a range of tasks over and above direct consultation with the client.

---

29 See McGrath, *Evidence* (Thomson Round Hall, 2005) para 10.20.

30 *Tromso Sparebank v Beirne* [1989] ILRM 257 (internal citation omitted).

31 *Tromso Sparebank v Beirne* [1989] ILRM 257 at 261–262. In contrast, letters between the plaintiff bank and its legal advisers that came into existence for the purpose of advising the plaintiff bank in relation to the subject of the litigation were privileged even though litigation had not been contemplated at the time when the documents came into existence: *Tromso Sparebank v Beirne* [1989] ILRM 257 at 262. See also *Dunnes Stores Ltd v Smyth* (24 July 1995, unreported) HC (Costello P).

32 Keane, *The Modern Law of Evidence* (7th edn, Oxford University Press, 2008) at 612 (citing *Re Sarah C Getty Trust* [1985] QB 956).

33 *Dwyer v Collins* (1852) 7 Exch 639 at 646.

[2.16] Some divergence of opinion is apparent among the traditional authorities on the scope of legal advice privilege in this regard. The concept of protected communication sketched by Lord Brougham in *Greenough v Gaskell*[34] was broad, arguably in keeping with his vision of the role played by privilege in the administration of justice. Having reviewed cases in which privilege had been refused, Lord Brougham stated:

> 'In all such cases, it is plain that the attorney is not called upon to disclose matters which he can be said to have learned by communication with his client or on his client's behalf, matters which were so committed to him in his capacity of attorney, *and matters which in that capacity alone he had come to know*.'[35]

[2.17] This formula suggests an expansive understanding of privilege, stretching beyond matters strictly communicated and encompassing many facts observed or ascertained by the lawyer. In other nineteenth century cases, such as *Manser v Dix*,[36] privilege was upheld partly owing to the impossibility of ordering discovery of matters touching on the arena of legal advice without disclosing the advice itself. The case involved a suit to set aside the sale by the plaintiff of certain leasehold hereditaments. Page Wood VC recognised that certain documents in the hands of one of the defendants were privileged from production, namely, the draft agreement as approved by counsel and the opinion of counsel on alterations in the draft. At issue was the possible disclosure of the instructions given by that defendant to counsel in relation to the preparation of the initial draft. The Vice Chancellor could 'scarcely conceive any case more calling for protection at the hands of the Court'. He continued:

> 'To say that these instructions are not privileged would be a refinement which I cannot make in a case of this description. If I were to order these instructions to be produced I should go the whole length of deciding that, in every case between vendor and purchaser, if the purchaser raises a difficulty upon the title, he might be entitled to say that eighteen to twenty years before, when the same property was offered for sale, the person then selling had certain consultations with his solicitor or counsel, there being then no dispute, and as soon as the contract was concluded he sent instructions for a conveyance to his counsel, and that the purchaser in every such case would be entitled to see those documents. If that be the rule, I do not see how to prevent the enormous injustice of enabling every purchaser to obtain production and discovery of all objections to the title, and everything that has passed between the vendor and his solicitors with reference to the title.'[37]

[2.18] The same thread of reasoning ran through the judgments in *Lyell v Kennedy (No 2)*[38] in which the House of Lords refused to compel a client to

34 *Greenough v Gaskell* (1833) 1 My & K 98, 39 ER 618.

35 *Greenough v Gaskell* (1833) 1 My & K 98 at 104–105 (emphasis added).

36 *Manser v Dix* (1855) 1 K & J 451, 69 ER 536.

37 *Manser v Dix* (1855) 1 K & J 451 at 459–460.

38 *Lyell v Kennedy (No 2)* (1883) 9 App Cas 81.

answer interrogatories regarding matters of which the client claimed to have no knowledge other than information derived from privileged communications he received from his solicitors. Lord Bramwell captured the sentiment of the Lords when he stated: 'It appears to me, therefore, upon the reason and principle of the thing, that a man ought not to be called upon to state what his belief is, founded upon information, which information is privileged, and which he is not bound to disclose'.[39]

[2.19] Thanki discerns in the traditional case law a distinction between the position of the client and that of her lawyer. In the case of the client, the confinement of privilege to communications (as opposed to the underlying facts that might be referenced therein) ensured that the client could not 'hide information relevant to a dispute by communicating it to his lawyer'.[40] Thus, as Page Wood VC conceded in *Manser v Dix*, a client could be forced to testify about relevant matters stopping short of privileged communications.[41] In contrast, as the above authorities indicate, it seems that historically the lawyer could resist giving evidence on wider grounds.[42]

[2.20] Nevertheless, rather than sweeping the totality of the information gleaned in the context of the legal professional relationship within the folds of privilege, some nineteenth century courts narrowed their focus to the client's interest in protecting information *communicated* to the lawyer and the lawyer's *communicated* responses thereto.[43] Thus, in *Dwyer v Collins*,[44] it was held that in an action on a bill of exchange a lawyer could be asked to produce a bill given to him by the client. Parke B stated:

> 'The relation of attorney and client prevents the former from disclosing any communication made to him in the ordinary course of his employment, and on the faith of the confidence which the client reposes in his legal adviser. But the privilege does not extend to matters of fact which the attorney knows by any other means than confidential communication with his client, though, if he had not been employed as attorney, he probably would not have known them.'[45]

Similarly, where a document is produced in court, a lawyer could be required to give evidence about the state of the document on a previous occasion on which

---

39 *Lyell v Kennedy (No 2)* (1883) 9 App Cas 81 at 93.

40 Thanki (ed), *The Law of Privilege* (Oxford University Press, 2006) para 2.53.

41 *Manser v Dix* (1855) 1 K & J 451 at 454–55.

42 Thanki (ed), *The Law of Privilege* (Oxford University Press, 2006) at para 2.53 (quoting Bray, *The Principles and Practice of Discovery* (1885) 358, 429).

43 In *Sawyer v Birchmore* (1835) 3 My & K 572, 40 ER 218, Pepys MR recognised that a solicitor as witness was 'bound to answer questions seeking information as to matters of fact, as distinguished from matters of confidential communication'. (1835) 3 My & K 572 at 578. See McGrath, *Evidence* (Thomson Round Hall, 2005) para 10.21.

44 *Dwyer v Collins* (1853) 7 Exch 639, 155 ER 11054.

45 *Dwyer v Collins* (1852) 7 Exch 639 at 646. See also *Sawyer v Birchmore* (1835) 3 My & K 572, 40 ER 218 (solicitor bound to produce letters).

he had seen it.[46] Earlier authority also supported the view that a lawyer could be called to prove his client's handwriting.[47]

Client Identity

[2.21] The principle that legal advice privilege does not extend to facts that a lawyer ascertained or could have ascertained independent of communications with her client is entrenched in the contemporary case law. The proposition that factual information of this kind may extend to the very identity of the client was tested in the High Court in *Miley v Flood.*[48] The case arose out of the investigation by the Tribunal of Inquiry into Certain Planning Matters and Payments into allegations that monies had been paid to politicians in order to secure the rezoning of lands owned by a UK registered company. The applicant solicitor, who was a partner in the law firm that represented the company, was summonsed before the Tribunal and asked to disclose the identity of the individuals within the company who had instructed him. The applicant refused to do so arguing that client identity constitutes confidential, privileged information. The matter came before the High Court by way of an application for judicial review of the ruling of the respondent chairman of the Tribunal that privilege does not extend to client identity.

[2.22] Kelly J quoted at length from the judgment of Finlay CJ in *Smurfit Paribas Bank Ltd v AAB Export Finance Ltd*[49] and detailed the conditions cited therein for the assertion of legal advice privilege including the condition that privilege is limited to communications and, within that realm, specifically to communications seeking or containing legal advice.[50] Having observed that there was no Irish authority on the specific issue of client identity, Kelly J conducted an extensive review of authorities from various common law jurisdictions. He concluded that the applicant was not entitled as a matter of Irish law to assert privilege over the identity of the persons who had provided him with instructions on behalf of the company.[51]

---

46 *Brown v Foster* (1857) 1 H & N 736, 156 ER 1397.

47 *Hurd and Another v Moring* (1824) 1 Car & P 372, 171 ER 1236. This view was confirmed in *Dwyer v Collins* (1853) 7 Exch 639, 646.

48 *Miley v Flood* [2001] 2 IR 50, [2001] 1 ILRM 489. See McGrath, 'Legal Professional Privilege: The Identity of a Client' (March 2001) Bar Rev 268; Dee, 'Privileged Background' (Oct 2001) Law Soc Gaz 20.

49 *Smurfit Paribas Bank Ltd v AAB Export Finance Ltd* [1990] 1 IR 469.

50 *Miley v Flood* [2001] 1 ILRM 489 at 508.

51 *Miley v Flood* [2001] 1 ILRM 489 at 517–518. Kelly J observed that the position might be different where the naming of the client would incriminate or where the identity of the client was so bound up with the nature of the advice sought that to reveal the client's identity would have the effect of revealing the advice. However, there was no evidence to suggest that either of these eventualities would occur in this case.

Communications with Third Parties

[2.23] Because legal advice privilege is grounded in the confidential exchange between client and lawyer, it does not extend to communications between either the client or the lawyer and a third party.[52] For example, in *Hurstridge Finance Ltd v Lismore Homes Ltd*, Costello J held that privilege did not attach to notes of meetings held between lawyers and third parties.[53] This limitation, which applies even when the communication with the third party concerns a matter upon which the client has sought legal advice, is a characteristic that distinguishes legal advice privilege from litigation privilege.[54]

Of course, in contemporary practice, aspects of the legal professional relationship are often conducted through intermediaries such as legal secretaries or apprentice solicitors. Indeed, even where a particular professional legal relationship is habitually conducted by means of direct communication, occasions may arise in which the client and lawyer need to communicate indirectly through representatives. The courts tend to take a pragmatic approach influenced by conventional practices. A communication made to an agent of the lawyer, such as an associate, is generally protected; similarly, a communication made to an agent of the client is protected provided that the client has cloaked the agent with the necessary authority to receive legal advice on the client's behalf.[55]

(2) Confidentiality

[2.24] A second pre-requisite to an assertion of legal advice privilege is proof that the communication passed between the client and lawyer in confidence.[56] In *Three Rivers District Council v Governor & Company of Bank of England (No 6)*, Lord Scott LJ explained the significance of the element of confidentiality:

> '... legal advice privilege arises out of a relationship of confidence between lawyer and client. Unless the communication or document for which privilege is sought is a confidential one, there can be no question of legal advice privilege

---

[52] *Bord na gCon v Murphy* [1970] IR 301.

[53] *Hurstridge Finance Ltd v Lismore Homes Ltd* (15 February 1991, unreported) HC.

[54] *Three Rivers District Council v Governor & Company of Bank of England (No 6)* [2004] 3 WLR 1274, 1283, [2005] 1 AC 610, 646.

[55] *Wheeler v Le Marchant* (1881) 17 Ch D 675, 682; *Anderson v Bank of British Columbia* (1876) 2 Ch D 644, 649; *Minter v Priest* [1930] AC 558. For an Antipodean perspective see *C-C Bottlers Ltd v Lion Nathan Ltd* [1993] 2 NZLR 445. See also Matthews and Malek, *Disclosure* (Sweet & Maxwell, 2001) para 9.014 (citing cases).

[56] See generally Tapper, 'Privilege and Confidence' (1972) 35 MLR 83; Heydon, 'Legal Professional Privilege and Third Parties' (1974) 37 MLR 601.

> arising. The confidential character of the communication or document is not by itself enough to enable privilege to be claimed but it is an essential requirement.[57]

Confidentiality assumes the existence of two elements: the passing of communications in private and an intention on the part of the privilege holder to maintain secrecy. Whether a communication is made in confidence is largely a question of fact which turns upon the circumstances surrounding the exchange[58] including 'a consideration of any precautions taken to preserve the confidentiality of the communication'.[59]

Third Parties

[2.25] The presence of a third party at a consultation between the lawyer and client defeats the claim of confidence.[60] Exceptionally, where the third party is attending to protect the interests of the client, the predicate confidentiality may be deemed to exist. For example, the presence of a relative may not disturb the confidentiality of an exchange between an elderly client and her lawyer assuming that the legal advice does not touch upon the relative's own interests.[61] The New Zealand Court of Appeal has held that a third party who overhears a confidential communication should not be permitted to testify about the communication unless the client waives privilege.[62]

Lawyers frequently correspond with third parties in the course of representing their clients. Correspondence of this kind is not privileged either because the substantive content does not constitute legal advice *per se*[63] or because the publication to the third party of any legal advice referenced in the correspondence undermines the condition of confidence.[64] Here again, the presence of the third party inherently negates the necessary condition that the parties intended the communication to be confidential.

---

57 *Three Rivers District Council v Governor & Company of Bank of England (No 6)* [2003] 3 WLR 1274 at 1282, [2005] 1 AC 610 at 646. See also *Bank of Lisbon and South Africa Ltd v Tandrien Beleggings (Pty) Ltd and Others (No 2)* 1983 (2) SA 626 (W) at 629G *per* Van Dijkhorst J: '[t]he basis of privilege is confidentiality. When confidence ceases, privilege ceases'.

58 *Minter v Priest* [1930] AC 558.

59 McGrath, *Evidence* (Thomson Round Hall, 2005) at para10.23. In *Kennedy v Law Society of Ireland & Others,* (20 January 1998, unreported) SC at 6 Murphy J rejected the Law Society's assertion of privilege over documentation passing between it and a firm of accountants, *inter alia*, on the grounds that it was not confidential to the Society and that copies of much of it had been furnished to the other side.

60 Abrahamson, Dwyer and Fitzpatrick, *Discovery and Disclosure* (Thomson Round Hall, 2007) para. 35.27.

61 *R v Dunbar* (1982) 138 DLR (3d) 221 at 224.

62 *R v Uljee* [1982] 1 NZLR 561.

63 *Buckley v Incorporated Law Society* [1994] 2 IR 44.

64 *Murphy v Kirwan* [1993] 3 IR 501.

[2.26] This point was explored by the Supreme Court in *Bord na gCon v Murphy.*[65] The complainants, a statutory body empowered to mount prosecutions under the Greyhound Industry Act 1958, wrote to the defendant asking him to respond to allegations that he had committed certain offences under the Act. The defendant was subsequently convicted and, at the hearing of his appeal, the complainants sought to adduce as evidence the reply to the complainant's initial letter which had been written by a solicitor on the defendant's behalf. On a case stated, the Supreme Court rejected the defendant's assertion that the reply was privileged because it incorporated protected communications between the defendant and his solicitor. Walsh J stated:

> 'The protection which extends to communications between a solicitor and client depends upon the confidential character of the communication and, if a client has instructed a solicitor to write a particular letter to another party, namely, the complainants in this case, it is quite clear that the content of that letter or the fact that the writing of it was directed by the client is not, and was not intended to be, a confidential communication. Therefore, it would not be a breach of privilege to require the solicitor to answer the question of whether or not he had been instructed to write the documents in question and of whether or not he had been instructed to make the statements therein contained – whether they be admissions, confessions or otherwise.'[66]

Technological Developments

[2.27] The advent of new technologies such as facsimile, email and mobile telephone text, has transformed the manner in which individuals communicate. Questions surround the security of these forms of media and whether they permit communication in confidence. For example, if a client transmits a letter to a lawyer by fax or sends a message by email, can the communication be said to be confidential for the purposes of legal advice privilege?

[2.28] There appears to be an absence of authority on point. It is suggested that a court faced with a question of this kind should adopt a common sense approach, adapting the traditional test to the contemporary setting. This would involve an assessment of two factors (one subjective and the other objective) in the particular circumstances of the case: first, did the party or parties intend the communication to be confidential; and, second, was the communication sent and

---

65 *Bord na gCon v Murphy* [1970] IR 301.

66 The judgment of Ó Dálaigh CJ, in *Bord na gCon v Murphy* [1970] IR 301 at 312, echoes the point: 'Privilege for what? Privilege attaches to confidential communications between solicitor and client. Here by hypothesis the client's statement was made to the solicitor not in confidence but specifically and expressly for disclosure to the Bord …'. See also *Fraser v Sutherland* (1851) 2 Gr 442 (Ch) (communications to solicitor intended to be put and actually put to client's creditors were not privileged); *Buckley v Incorporated Law Society* [1994] 2 IR 44 (correspondence between a solicitor and the Incorporated Law Society and correspondence between the solicitor and other third parties not privileged).

received in conditions of privacy? The assessment might well turn on the issue of whether and to what extent the communication could be accessed by third parties. If determinations about the confidentiality of communications are based largely on the intentions of the client and lawyer,[67] the courts are likely to lean in favour of recognising privilege provided the expectation of privacy is not unreasonable in the circumstances. For example, a client may reasonably expect that an email sent to a lawyer at her individual email address will be received in confidence. However, the same expectation may not reasonably apply where the email was copied to third parties or was sent to a general law firm address.

(3) Communications between the Client and Lawyer

[2.29] A third condition is that the communication is exclusive to the bilateral relationship between the client and her lawyer. Simply put, legal advice privilege does not extend to communications involving third parties. This condition is encapsulated to an extent in the condition of confidentiality. However, it warrants separate treatment not least because the absence of third parties is a defining characteristic of legal advice privilege that distinguishes it from litigation privilege.

[2.30] As noted above, the law is pragmatic in its recognition that both clients and lawyers may act through the agency of third parties. Jessel MR stated in *Anderson v Bank of British Columbia*:

> '[The rule] goes not merely to a communication made to the professional agent himself by the client directly, it goes to all communications made by the client to the solicitor through intermediary agents, and he is not bound to write letters through the post, or to go himself personally to see the solicitor; he may employ a third person to write the letter, or he may send the letters through a messenger, or he may give a verbal message to a messenger, and ask him to deliver it to the solicitor, with a view to his prosecuting his claim, or of substantiating his defence.'[68]

Communications exchanged with an agent of the lawyer, such as a legal partner or associate, are generally protected but communications exchanged with an agent of the client are protected only if the client has cloaked the agent with the necessary authority to receive legal advice on the client's behalf.[69]

---

67 As commentators such as Abrahamson, Dwyer and Fitzpatrick suggest, *Discovery and Disclosure* (Thomson Round Hall, 2007) para 35.28.

68 *Anderson v Bank of British Columbia* (1876) 2 Ch D 644 at 649–650.

69 *Wheeler v Le Marchant* (1881) 17 Ch D 675. See generally, Passmore, *Privilege* (2nd edn, xpl publishing, 2006) ch 4; 'Agents' Reports and the Attorney-Client Privilege' (1954) 21(4) U of Chicago L Rev 752. The presence of an interpreter does not destroy privilege: Abrahamson, Dwyer and Fitzpatrick, *Discovery and Disclosure* (Thomson Round Hall, 2007) para. 35.27, n 60 (citing *R (Bozkurt) v Thames Magistrates' Court* [2002] RTR 15, 18).

Corporate Clients

[2.31] The decision of the English Court of Appeal in *Three Rivers District Council v Governor and Company of the Bank of England (No 5)*[70] has complicated traditional English legal thinking on communications between corporate clients and legal advisers.[71] This was just one aspect of legal professional privilege raised and debated in this protracted litigation. In the wake of the collapse of Bank of Credit and Commerce International SA (BCCI), liquidators and creditors instituted proceedings against the Bank of England for misfeasance in public office in respect of the Bank's supervision of BCCI. The conduct of the Bank had already been the subject of a public inquiry chaired by Lord Bingham. In the legal proceedings, the claimants sought disclosure of documents which had been prepared by the Bank's employees for the purpose of being passed to lawyers who were advising the Bank in its dealings with the inquiry.

The trial judge dismissed the application for discovery on the basis that the Bank was entitled to assert legal advice privilege over the documents in question, but the liquidators and creditors appealed successfully to the Court of Appeal.[72] The court accepted the claimants' argument that legal advice privilege extends only to communications between solicitor and client and held that privilege does not protect preparatory materials drawn up by employees even where those materials were prepared at the solicitor's request and for the purpose of being shown to the solicitor. The effect of the court's holding is that information provided to solicitors by an employee is no different from information provided by an independent third party.[73] On the facts presented, the only documents for which privilege could be claimed were communications between the lawyers and select officers and employees of the Bank who had been specifically appointed to deal with issues relating to the inquiry. These particular officers and employees were 'the client' for the purposes of privilege as opposed to any single titular officer of the Bank including the governor.[74]

[2.32] This aspect of the judgment of the Court of Appeal generated considerable controversy. When the case was appealed to the House of Lords, the Attorney General, the Law Society and the Bar Council intervened by way

---

70 *Three Rivers District Council v Governor and Company of the Bank of England (No 5)* [2003] QB 1556.

71 See Spencer, 'Corporate Privilege – Shrinking the Zone of Silence' (2007) 3(2) JCPP 12; Loughrey, 'Legal Advice Privilege and the Corporate Client' (2005) 9 E & P 183; Passmore, *Privilege* (2nd edn, xpl publishing, 2006) para 4.008 *et seq.*

72 *Three Rivers District Council v Governor and Company of the Bank of England (No 5)* [2003] QB 1556.

73 *Three Rivers District Council v Governor and Company of the Bank of England (No 5)* [2003] QB 1556 at 1574 (*per* Longmore LJ).

74 *Three Rivers District Council v Governor and Company of the Bank of England (No 5)* [2003] QB 1556 at 1581.

of written submissions inviting the Lords to reverse the Court of Appeal's position.[75] These submissions emphasised the concern that the Court of Appeal may have overstepped the mark in holding that communications between a lawyer and the client's employees should be treated as communications between the lawyer and third parties for the purposes of privilege.[76] The traditional English view was that legal advice privilege protected not only direct communications between the client and lawyer but also communications made through an intermediate agent of either.[77] The interveners before the House of Lords in *Three Rivers (No 6)* emphasised that the implications of the holding of the Court of Appeal were particularly profound for corporate clients who must necessarily communicate through officers or employees.[78]

This important issue fell outside the narrow terms of the appeal[79] and the Lords decided against issuing any *obiter dicta* on point. Lord Scott cited several reasons for declining to express a view including the fact that the judgment of the Court of Appeal would continue to constitute binding precedent.[80] Thus, the position in English law appears to be that a client's employees are considered third parties for the purposes of privilege with the consequence that their communications with the client's lawyers are not generally protected unless the corporation specifically cloaks them with the authority to act as its agent for purposes of seeking legal advice.

[2.33] Keane has criticised the 'designation' approach in *Three Rivers* as overly restrictive while noting that the dominant purpose test may suffer from the opposite taint of excessive breadth.[81] He suggests that '[t]he answer may be to adopt the test used in the United States, which limits the corporate client to those who play a substantial role in deciding and directing the corporation's response to the legal advice given'.[82]

---

75 *Three Rivers District Council v Governor and Company of the Bank of England (No 6)* [2004] 3 WLR 1274 at 1281, [2005] 1 AC 610 at 645.

76 *Three Rivers District Council v Governor and Company of the Bank of England (No 6)* [2004] 3 WLR 1274 at 1282, [2005] 1 AC 610 at 645.

77 *Price Waterhouse v BCCI Holdings (Luxembourg) SA* [1992] BCLC 583 at 588 (*per* Millett J).

78 *Three Rivers District Council v Governor and Company of the Bank of England (No 6)* [2004] 3 WLR 1274 at 1282, [2005] 1 AC 610 at 645.

79 *Three Rivers District Council v Governor and Company of the Bank of England (No 6)* [2004] 3 WLR 1274 at 1282, [2005] 1 AC 610 at 645.

80 *Three Rivers District Council v Governor and Company of the Bank of England (No 6)* [2004] 3 WLR 1274 at 1290, [2005] 1 AC 610 at 653–654.

81 Keane, *The Modern Law of Evidence* (7th edn, Oxford University Press, 2008) at 612. See also Loughrey, 'Legal advice privilege and the corporate client' (2005) 9 E & P 183.

82 Keane, *The Modern Law of Evidence* (7th edn, Oxford University Press, 2008) (citing *Upjohn Co v United States* 499 US 383, 101 S Ct 677 (1981) at 684). See also Spencer, 'Corporate Privilege – Shrinking the Zone of Silence' (2007) 3(2) JCPP 12; Loughrey, 'Legal advice privilege and the corporate client' (2005) 9 E & P 183.

[2.34] Other issues may arise in relation to corporate clients.[83] In *Ochre Ridge Ltd v Cork Bonded Warehouses Ltd & Another*,[84] the High Court upheld the entitlement of a corporate client to assert privilege over documents that came into existence 'before the company itself came into existence, as a shelf company for the purposes of entering a contract'.[85] Lavan J stated:

> 'The fact that the communications relate to a phase prior to the incorporation of the plaintiff itself, Ochre Ridge Limited, is irrelevant so long as the communications form part of a spectrum of legal advice between legal advisor and client. It would be illogical to claim that a company could not claim privilege over documents relating to a pre-incorporation phase as no claim of privilege could ever be possible as to this period then and would deny the benefit of privilege to a vast array of proceedings'.[86]

Joint and Common Interests

[2.35] Mathieson has distinguished joint and common interest privileges in the following terms:

> 'A joint interest privilege arises where two or more persons are jointly concerned in obtaining the privileged communication. The clearest example is that of a joint retainer but something less is sufficient, provided that the privileged communication concerns the joint interests of the parties at the time of the communication.
>
> ...
>
> A common interest privilege arises where there has been a disclosure of privileged material to another person with a common interest at the time of the disclosure. The common interest must be the subject matter of the communications in respect of which the claim is made. The two interests must be either identical or so closely related as to make it in appropriate to treat parties claiming privilege separately.'[87]

What is the position where a solicitor is instructed by two clients in relation to a matter in which the clients are jointly interested? The position adopted by the English Court of Appeal is that communications between the solicitor and one of the clients will not be privileged as against the other client but they will be

---

83 See generally Higgins, 'Legal Advice Privilege and Its Relevance to Corporations' (2010) 73(3) MLR 371; Higgins, 'Corporate Abuse of Legal Professional Privilege' (2008) 27(3) CJQ 377.

84 *Ochre Ridge Ltd v Cork Bonded Warehouses Ltd & Another* (13 July 2004, unreported) HC (Lavan J).

85 *Ochre Ridge Ltd v Cork Bonded Warehouses Ltd & Another* (13 July 2004, unreported) HC (Lavan J) at p 11.

86 *Ochre Ridge Ltd v Cork Bonded Warehouses Ltd & Another* (13 July 2004, unreported) HC (Lavan J).

87 Mathieson (ed), *Cross on Evidence* (8th New Zealand edn, (Lexis Nexis, 2005) para 10.22.

protected from disclosure to any third party.[88] In other words, the clients and the solicitor are located within a circle of confidence from which third parties are excluded. Consequently, the clients are deemed to have a shared interest and occupy a common position for the purposes of privilege.

[2.36] The scenario of two clients sharing the services of a single solicitor is just one of a broad range of examples in which privilege is defined as embracing a joint interest. As Lavan J observed in *Ochre Ridge Ltd v Cork Bonded Warehouses Ltd & Another*, 'privilege may be claimed by one not strictly a client of the legal advisor if he has an interest in common with such a client'.[89]

The English courts have developed an extensive jurisprudence in relation to common interest privilege.[90] The issue has a particular resonance in circumstances where a party is resisting a claim that she waived privilege by arguing that she disclosed the privileged communication not to a third party but to a party with whom she shared a common interest.[91]

(4) The Legal Professional Relationship

[2.37] A fourth condition of legal advice privilege is that the communication is made in the context of a professional legal relationship. The paradigm of legal advice privilege is a scenario in which a client establishes a relationship with a particular lawyer and routinely turns to that lawyer for advice relating to the panoply of legal issues that she encounters during her lifetime. The reality is that individuals may consult not one but several different lawyers and furthermore that advice may be sought *ad hoc* and at short notice. For purposes of privilege, the professional legal relationship need not pre-date the seeking of advice; the relationship will be deemed to exist provided the client communicated with the lawyer with the intention of establishing the relationship.[92]

---

[88] *Buttes Gas and Oil Co v Hammer (No 3)* [1981] QB 223 (joint parties to a conveyancing transaction).

[89] *Ochre Ridge Ltd v Cork Bonded Warehouses Ltd & Another* (13 July 2004, unreported) HC (Lavan J) at p 12 (citing cases).

[90] See, eg, *Buttes Gas and Oil Co v Hammer (No 3)* [1981] QB 223 (joint parties to a conveyancing transaction); *Re Konigsberg (a bankrupt)* [1989] 3 All ER 289 (conveyancing transaction). The same principle applies to the relationship between insurers and an insured (*Guinness Peat Properties Ltd v Fitzroy Robinson Partnership (a firm)* [1987] 2 All ER 716) and to the beneficiaries of an estate and the estate's executors (*Ontario (Attorney General) v Ballard Estate* (1994) 119 DLR (4th) 750 (Ont Gen Div)) but not to the relationship between a trade union and its member (*Jones v Great Central Rly Co* [1910] AC 4) nor the relationship between company directors and shareholders (*CAS (Nominees) Ltd v Nottingham Forest plc* [2001] 1 All ER 954). Even where the joint interest exists, a conflict of interest between the clients may have the effect of breaking the circle of confidence: *TSB Bank plc v Robert Irving & Burns (a firm)* [2000] 2 All ER 826.

[91] See **Ch 6**.

[92] *Minter v Priest* (1833) [1930] AC 558.

In teasing out the concept of a legal professional relationship, the courts have focused on two distinct requirements: first, the person with whom the client communicates must be a lawyer and, second, the lawyer must be acting in her professional capacity at the time of the communication.

Lawyer

[2.38] Turning to the first of these requirements, the term 'lawyer' is broadly defined. It includes solicitors and barristers qualified to practice in Ireland[93] and it also extends to lawyers admitted to practice in foreign jurisdictions.[94]
Privilege presupposes that the lawyer has the necessary qualifications to act as such. Thus, an apprentice solicitor or a legal secretary is not a lawyer for the purposes of legal advice privilege. Similarly, the traditional view at common law is that professionals other than lawyers who may advise on legal subjects, such as architects or accountants, generally fall outside the scope of the privilege.[95] In *New Victoria Hospital v Ryan*,[96] the English Employment Appeal Tribunal rejected a claim of privilege over correspondence between the defendant employers and a firm of personnel consultants relating to the dismissal of the plaintiff employee. Tucker J explained the motivation behind the restriction:

> '... [I]n our opinion the privilege should be strictly confined to legal advisers such as solicitors and counsel, who are professionally qualified, who are members of professional bodies, who are subject to the rules and etiquette of their professions, and who owe a duty to the court. This is a clearly defined and easily identifiable qualification for the attachment of privilege. To extend the privilege to unqualified advisers such as personnel consultants is in our opinion unnecessary and undesirable'.[97]

Malek and Matthews identify a significant exception: 'To the extent that the non-lawyer professional seeks or receives counsel's advice or drafts and transmits instructions from and advice to the lay client, he can be said to be acting as the lay client's agent, and the communications may be privileged within the rule'.[98]

[2.39] In a noteworthy development, the UK Legal Services Act 2007 makes provision for the legal profession to engage in alternative business structures including multidisciplinary practices in which lawyers and other professionals,

---

93 *Dunnes Stores Ltd v Smyth* (24 July 1995, unreported) HC (Costello J).

94 *Re Duncan* [1968] P 306; *Great Atlantic Insurance Co v Home Insurance Co* [1981] 1 All ER 529; *IBM Corp v Phoenix International (Computers) Ltd* [1995] 1 All ER 413.

95 *Chantrey Martin v Martin* [1953] 2 QB 286; *New Victoria Hospital v Ryan* [1993] ICR 201; *Wilden Pump Engineering Co v Fusfeld* [1985] FSR 159. See Pogue, 'Evidence: Privilege, Extension of Attorney-Client Privilege to Administrative Practitioners' (1953) 51 Mich L Rev 601.

96 *New Victoria Hospital v Ryan* [1993] ICR 201.

97 *New Victoria Hospital v Ryan* [1993] ICR 201 at 203–204.

98 Malek and Matthews, *Disclosure* (Sweet & Maxwell, 2001) at para 9.019.

such as accountants or estate agents, provide a combination of legal and other professional advice to clients.[99] The legislation purports to preserve legal professional privilege so that clients of multidisciplinary practices will enjoy the same entitlement as clients of traditional law practices. The Legal Services Board is currently overseeing the final stages of a three-year plan for implementation of the reforms set out in the legislation.[100]

[2.40] Communications between a client and an individual whose licence to practice law has been revoked by the governing professional body are generally not protected. However, recognising the need to protect a client acting in good faith, the courts will uphold the privilege if the client reasonably believed that the individual was fit to practice at the material time.[101]

[2.41] Communications made before the lawyer was employed are not generally protected.[102] However, privilege may come into play before the employment relationship has been formalised; it is sufficient that the client consulted the lawyer with a view to obtaining legal advice. Viscount Dunedin alluded to this scenario in *Minter v Priest*:

> 'Now, if a man goes to a solicitor, as a solicitor, to consult and does consult him, though the end of the interview may lead to the conclusion that he does not engage him as his solicitor or expect that he should act as his solicitor, nevertheless the interview is held as a privileged occasion.'[103]

The Court of Appeal cited as justification for this liberal approach the need to encourage free and open exchange between individuals in need of legal advice and potential legal representatives.[104]

Communications made after the lawyer's employment has ceased are not privileged.[105] However, the cessation of the lawyer's employment has no retrospective effect; communications made during the course of the lawyer-client relationship remain privileged even after the lawyer has ceased to act.

In-House Lawyers

[2.42] The status of in-house lawyers for the purposes of privilege has generated controversy in recent years. Within the structure of government, the tendering of

---

99 Legal Services Act 2007, Pts 3 and 5; Legal Services (Scotland) Act 2010.

100 See www.legalservicesboard.org.uk (visited 30 March 2011).

101 *Calley v Richards* (1854) 19 Beav. 401.

102 *Greenoughv Gaskell* (1883) 1 My & K 98.

103 *Minter v Priest* (1930) AC 558 at 573. The principle was endorsed by the other Lordships including Lord Atkin, *Minter v Priest* (1930) AC 558 at 584–585. For an Irish case in which a solicitor who was consulted by a custodial detainee but not retained and subsequently gave evidence see *People (DPP) v Buck* [2002] 2 IR 268.

104 *Minter v Priest* (1930) AC 558. See also VP, 'Evidence: Witness, Privilege, Attorney and Client' (1932) 21(1) Cal L Rev 67.

105 *Greenough v Gaskell* (1883) 1 My & K 98 at 104 (*per* Lord Brougham LC).

legal advice by key legal officeholders has been held to attract privilege. In *Duncan v Governor of Portlaoise (No 2)*,[106] the Supreme Court recognised that legal advice privilege extends to the Attorney General in her role as legal advisor to the government. Similarly, communications between members of An Garda Síochána and the Director of Public Prosecutions are protected by legal professional privilege.[107]

[2.43] In *Geraghty v Minister for Local Government*,[108] the principle of protection was applied to the permanent legal advisers to a government department. Griffin J endorsed the proposition expounded by the English Court of Appeal in *Crompton Ltd v Customs and Excise Commissioners (No 2)*[109] that 'there can be no difference between the position of a full-time salaried legal adviser employed by a government department, a local authority, an industrial concern or any single employer, and the position of a legal adviser who practises his profession independently and is rewarded for his services by fees'.[110]

[2.44] In the private sector, the position of in-house lawyers can be precarious, depending on whether they are classified as employees or legal advisers. Although the common law has tended to include communications with in-house lawyers within the cloak of protection,[111] the opposite position prevails in EC competition law. In *AM & S Europe Ltd v Commission*,[112] the Court of Justice considered a challenge to the powers of the Commission to order production of business records for the purposes of investigating possible infringements of the EC rules on competition.

The applicant, an undertaking based in the UK, submitted that legal professional privilege was a principle common to all the member states and that it applied by extension in Community law. It followed that the Commission was restrained in any investigation from seeking production of written communications between in-house counsel and client where the undertaking

---

106 *Duncan v Governor of Portlaoise (No 2)* [1998] 1 IR 433. See also *Society for the Protection of Unborn Children (Ireland) Ltd v Grogan* [1992] 2 IR 471.

107 *DPP v Nevin* (13 December 2001, unreported) CCA; *Corbett v DPP* [1999] 2 IR 179 at 186–187; *Breathnach v Ireland (No 3)* [1993] 2 IR 458 at 471; *Goodridge v Chief Constable of Hampshire* [1999] 1 WLR 1558.

108 *Geraghty v Minister for Local Government* [1975] IR 300.

109 *Crompton Ltd v Customs and Excise Commissioners (No 2)* [1972] 2 QB 102, [1974] AC 415.

110 *Geraghty v Minister for Local Government* [1975] IR 300 at 312.

111 *Somatra v Sinclair Roche and Temperley* [2001] 1 WLR 2453; *Re Director of Investigation and Research and Shell Canada Ltd* (1975) 55 DLR (3d) 713; *Attorney General for Northern Territory v Kearney* (1985) 158 CLR 500 (HC); *Van den Heever v Die Meester en andere* (1997) [3] SA 102 (T); Mohamed v *President of the Republic of South African and Others* (2001) (2) SA 1145 (C). On in-house lawyers see generally Passmore, *Privilege* (2nd edn, xpl publishing, 2006) para 4.041 *et seq*.

112 *AM & S Europe Ltd v Commission* [1982] ECR 1575 (judgment of 19 May 1982).

asserted privilege and took reasonable steps to demonstrate that the protection was properly claimed.

[2.45] The Court of Justice noted that although the principle of legal professional privilege was generally recognised within the Community, there were considerable differences in the nature and degree of protection afforded by the various national legal systems. It identified two conditions common to the laws of the member states:

> '... on the one hand, such communications are made for the purposes and in the interests of the client's rights of defence and, on the other hand, they emanate from independent lawyers, that is to say, lawyers who are not bound to the client by a relationship of employment.'[113]

The court characterised this second condition as a natural emanation of the association between the giving of legal advice and the administration of justice in general and the servicing of the client's needs in particular.[114] While the protection afforded to communications between client and lawyer must apply 'without distinction to any lawyer entitled to practise his profession in one of the member states and regardless of the member state in which the client lives,'[115] such protection could not be extended beyond the limits outlined.[116] In summary, a lawyer who was an employee of the client was not 'an independent lawyer' for the purposes of legal professional privilege.[117]

[2.46] This position was confirmed by the recent decision of the Grand Chamber of the Court of Justice in *Akzo Nobel Chemicals Ltd v European Commission.*[118] The question of the status of in-house lawyers for the purposes of privilege arose again in the context of the Commission's enforcement of EC competition law.[119] The proceedings originated in the Commission's launch in 2003 of an investigation into possible anti-competitive practices by the applicants Akzo Nobel Chemicals Ltd and Akcros Chemicals Ltd. Materials seized by Commission officials during a dawn raid of the applicants' premises

---

113 *AM & S Europe Ltd v Commission* [1982] ECR 1575 at para 21.

114 *AM & S Europe Ltd v Commission* [1982] ECR 1575 at para 24.

115 *AM & S Europe Ltd v Commission* [1982] ECR 1575 at para 25.

116 *AM & S Europe Ltd v Commission* [1982] ECR 1575 at para 26.

117 *AM & S Europe Ltd v Commission* [1982] ECR 1575 at para 27.

118 *Akzo Nobel Chemicals Ltd and Akcros Chemicals Lts v European Commission* Case C-550/07P (14 September 2010), [2010] 5 CMLR 19. See generally, Norton Rose, 'Under Privileged' (September, 2010) http://www.nortonrose.com/knowledge/publications/2010; Piper, 'Akzo Nobel: No Privilege for In-House Lawyers under EU Competition Law' (16 September 2010) http://www.dlapiper.com; Fry, 'Akzo Nobel: In-House Counsel the Underprivileged in EU Competition Law' (28 September 2010) http://www.williamfry.ie/publication-article; Heineman, 'European Rejection of Attorney-Client Privilege for Inside Lawyers', The Harvard Law School Forum on Corporate Governance and Financial Regulation (2 October 2010) http://blogs.law.harvard.edu/corpgov.

119 Pursuant to Regulation No 17 of 6 February 1962 ([1959–62] OJ 87).

in the UK included two emails exchanged between a general manager at Akcros and an in-house lawyer at Akzo Nobel's internal legal department. The in-house lawyer was a member of the Netherlands Bar and Akzo's coordinator for competition law. The applicants asserted privilege over the emails but the Commission rejected the assertion and placed copies of the emails in a general file with other non-privileged documentation.[120]

[2.47] The applicants appealed unsuccessfully to the Court of First Instance (now known as the General Court).[121] The General Court recalled that, in *AM & S,* the Court of Justice had defined the concept of an independent lawyer in essentially negative terms; rather than emphasising qualifications or membership of a profession, the court had identified the existence of an employment relationship between the client and lawyer as an insurmountable bar to the invocation of privilege. The General Court took the view that privilege attaches only where the lawyer tenders legal advice 'in full independence'; this presupposes in turn that the lawyer 'structurally, hierarchically and functionally, is a third party in relation to the undertaking receiving that advice'.[122] Thus, the General Court held that the email correspondence at issue in the proceedings was not protected by legal professional privilege.

[2.48] An appeal to the Court of Justice was anxiously anticipated as an opportunity to establish parity between internal and external lawyers for purposes of privilege in EC competition law. Several interveners before the court, including the Irish and UK Governments and various international legal professional organisations, argued that the time was ripe for change. Nevertheless, in April 2010, Advocate General Kokott delivered an opinion which adhered strictly to the line in *AM & S v Commission*[123] and some six months later, the Court of Justice itself followed suit.

[2.49] Before the court, the applicants and a number of the interveners disputed the General Court's interpretation of the judgment in *AM & S v Commission.* They rejected the proposition that by virtue of her status as an employee of the client an in-house lawyer could not satisfy the criterion of independence. An in-house lawyer enrolled in a bar or law society was subject to rules of professional ethics and discipline which rendered her equally independent as an external lawyer. Indeed, in the case of Akzo's in-house lawyer, his contract with the

120 Correspondence ensued between the applicants and the Commission which culminated in the Commission's final decision on point, Decision C (2003) 1533 of 8 May 2003.

121 *Akzo Nobel Chemicals Ltd and Akcros Chemical Ltd v Commission* Joined cases T-125/03 & T-253/03 (17 September 2007), [2007] OJ C 269/43.

122 *Akzo Nobel Chemicals Ltd and Akcros Chemical Ltd v Commission* Joined cases T-125/03 & T-253/03 (17 September 2007), [2007] OJ C 269/43, at para 168.

123 *Akzo Nobel Chemicals Ltd and Akcros Chemicals Ltd v Commission* Case C-550/07P (29 April 2010) (Opinion of Advocate General Kokott) [2010] 5 CMLR 19.

applicant company incorporated a commitment on the company's part to respect his freedom to perform his functions independently.[124]

The Court of Justice, however, rejected this position:

> '[T]he requirement of independence means the absence of any employment relationship between the lawyer and his client, so that legal professional privilege does not cover exchanges within a company or group with in-house lawyers.'[125]

The court cited with approval Advocate General Kokott's opinion that the concept of independence should be determined not only positively, that is 'by reference to professional ethical obligations,' but also negatively, 'by the absence of an employment relationship'. The court continued:

> 'An in-house lawyer, despite his enrolment with a Bar or Law Society and the professional ethical obligations to which he is, as a result subject, does not enjoy the same degree of independence from his employer as a lawyer working in an external law firm does in relation to his client. Consequently, an in-house lawyer is less able to deal effectively with any conflicts between his professional obligations and the aims of his client.[126]

It was the court's view that the existence of an employment relationship necessarily compromised the lawyer's independence.[127] Moreover, the 'close ties' between the lawyer and her employer were reinforced where, as here, the lawyer carried out other tasks within the company.[128] The combination of her 'economic dependence' and 'close ties' with her employer led to the inescapable consequence that the in-house lawyer was not professionally independent to the same degree as an external lawyer.[129]

[2.50] The ruling of the Court of Justice in *Akzo Nobel* underscores the significance of the distinction between internal and external legal advice. The decision sends a clear message to undertakings operating within the reach of the EC competition regime that communications will be protected from disclosure only where they are exchanged with outside counsel. In the immediate term, the decision may have the consequent effect of rendering companies more reliant on

---

124 *Akzo Nobel Chemicals Ltd v European Commission* Case C-550/07P (14 September 2010), [2010] 5 CMLR 19 paras 32–35. The applicants argued further that membership of the Netherlands Bar in particular provides additional guarantees of independence for the in-house lawyer (para 36).

125 *Akzo Nobel Chemicals Ltd v European Commission* Case C-550/07P (14 September 2010), para 44, [2010] 5 CMLR 19.

126 *Akzo Nobel Chemicals Ltd v European Commission* Case C-550/07P (14 September 2010), para 45, [2010] 5 CMLR 19.

127 *Akzo Nobel Chemicals Ltd v European Commission* Case C-550/07P (14 September 2010), para 47, [2010] 5 CMLR 19.

128 *Akzo Nobel Chemicals Ltd v European Commission* Case C-550/07P (14 September 2010), para 48, [2010] 5 CMLR 19.

129 *Akzo Nobel Chemicals Ltd v European Commission* Case C-550/07P (14 September 2010), para 49, [2010] 5 CMLR 19.

external lawyers than had previously been the case (thereby increasing the cost of legal advice) and corporate officers more cautious in their communications with in-house lawyers. The situation is further complicated by the fact that undertakings are subject to the governance of national competition arrangements alongside the EC regime. Whether communications exchanged with an in-house lawyer are privileged or susceptible to disclosure may depend on whether an investigation is being conducted by the Commission or a particular national authority.[130]

The precedential effect of the *Akzo Nobel* decision is limited in the sense that it is technically confined to the field of EC competition law. However, the decision may have a spill-over effect should the issue of privilege surface in other areas of EC law. It is significant in this regard that the principle on which the decision rests was enunciated in sufficiently broad and general terms that it could potentially apply to any scenario involving an in-house lawyer regardless of the kind of legal work the lawyer performs or the nature of the European legal proceedings in which the issue arises.

Legal Aid Board Solicitors

[2.51] In *Martin & Doorley v Legal Aid Board*,[131] Laffoy J held that the position of a solicitor employed by the Legal Aid Board to represent a legally aided client is *sui generis* for the purposes of privilege. She construed s 32(2) of the Civil Legal Aid Act 1995 as imposing an obligation on a solicitor, employed by the Board to represent a legally aided client, to provide information that would be otherwise protected by privilege to assist the Board in carrying out its statutory mandate.[132] The Oireachtas clearly intended to extend the umbrella of privilege from the client and her solicitor to cover the Board and such authorised persons.[133] Consequently, the privilege was not lost by disclosure to such persons in confidence for this limited purpose.[134] Laffoy J did concede that the legally aided client and her solicitor operate on a different footing from the conditions that prevail in the ordinary legal professional relationship:

> 'The difference is that a solicitor in private practice is the ultimate arbiter of the range of persons to whom confidential client information may be disclosed. In reality, even in the ordinary relationship, of necessity confidential information may be disclosed to a wide range of people, from the secretary photocopying the client's statement for inclusion in counsel's brief, to the cost accountant

[130] In dismissing an alternative ground of appeal, namely that refusing to apply legal professional privilege to the email correspondence violated the principle of equal treatment, the court noted the wide disparity in the practice of the member states on point: *Akzo Nobel Chemicals Ltd v European Commission* Case C-550/07P (14 September 2010), [2010] 5 CMLR 19, paras 71–72.

[131] *Martin & Doorley v Legal Aid Board* [2007] 2 IR 759.

[132] *Martin & Doorley v Legal Aid Board* [2007] 2 IR 759 at 771–772.

[133] *Martin & Doorley v Legal Aid Board* [2007] 2 IR 759 at 777.

[134] *Martin & Doorley v Legal Aid Board* [2007] 2 IR 759 at 779.

> considering the case file in the context of drawing a bill of costs. In the case of solicitors employed by [the Board], the ultimate decision as to who will see confidential information rests with [the Board] when it determines to avail of the power conferred by subs. (2) of s.32.'[135]

Acting in a Professional Legal Capacity

[2.52] In addition to establishing that she communicated with a lawyer, properly qualified as such, the client seeking to assert privilege must also establish that the lawyer was consulted in her professional capacity. This condition stretches far back into the historical common law. In *Bramwell v Lucas*, Abbott CJ did not doubt that the privilege is confined to 'communications to the attorney in his character as attorney'.[136] He observed that 'where the communication might have been made by any other person as well as an attorney, and where the character or office of attorney has not been called into action,' the communication is in principle outside the realm of protection.[137] Consequently, the fact that a communication is exchanged between lawyer and client does not afford the protection of privilege.[138] Lord Buckmaster echoed the sentiment in *Minter v Priest*:

> 'The relationship of solicitor and client being once established, it is not a necessary conclusion that whatever conversation ensued was protected from disclosure. The conversation to secure this privilege must be such as, within a very wide and generous ambit of interpretation, must be fairly referable to the relationship, but outside that boundary the mere fact that a person speaking is a solicitor, and the person to whom he speaks is his client affords no protection'.[139]

For the purposes of privilege it may be necessary to distinguish between various statements made within the course of a lawyer-client consultation. In his judgment in the same case, Lord Atkin observed that whereas client and solicitor may meet for the purpose of legal advice and exchange protected communications, privilege would not cover statements made at the same meeting for some other purpose.[140]

Personal Relationship

[2.53] Difficulties may arise where the client and lawyer share a personal as well as a professional relationship. The traditional view is that communications are not protected where advice was sought or given 'as a friend' or where the matter

[135] *Martin & Doorley v Legal Aid Board* [2007] 2 IR 759 at 779.

[136] *Bramwell v Lucas* (1824) 2 B & C 745 at 749.

[137] *Bramwell v Lucas* (1824) 2 B & C 745 at 749.

[138] *Smith Bird v Blower* [1939] 2 All ER 406.

[139] *Minter v Priest* [1930] AC 558 at 568.

[140] *Minter v Priest* [1930] AC 558 at 581.

disclosed did not relate to the professional relationship.[141] In *Smith v Daniell*,[142] a legal opinion obtained by the plaintiff from the ex-Chancellor, Lord Westbury, was not privileged because it was clear that it had been given out of friendship as opposed to professional duty. The issue arose in a suit to set aside an award made by a company committee of which the defendant was the chairman. The plaintiff had sought a number of legal opinions as to whether the committee had been properly constituted. In the case of Lord Westbury, there was evidence that the opinion was private and not intended to be used in the proceedings. Bacon VC stated:

> 'Then as to the case laid before Lord Westbury, I cannot consider it in any other light than as a statement made by the Plaintiff to a friend of his. Lord Westbury's great qualifications are not in question; but that it was not a professional communication is clear on the face of it. Lord Westbury did not, when he expressed an opinion, express it in discharge of any professional duty. The old rule was that, unless the communication was made strictly in a professional capacity, the privilege could not attach ...'[143]

Legal and Business Adviser

[2.54] A more pressing concern in modern commercial practice is the position of a lawyer who combines the functions of legal adviser and business adviser. In *Somatra Ltd v Sinclair Roche and Temperlay*,[144] the plaintiff company sued the defendant firm of solicitors for damages arising out of the defendant's allegedly negligent representation of the plaintiff in litigation related to the sinking of the plaintiff's ship. The defendants claimed legal professional privilege over certain communications between the firm's managing partner and the other partners concerning negotiations conducted by the managing partner with a view to settling the suit. Whereas the defendants contended that the managing partner was effectively acting as in-house counsel, exercising professional skill and judgment as a solicitor on behalf of the firm, the plaintiff submitted that the position was no different to that of the managing partner of a firm of accountants, for whom no question of a claim of privilege could arise. Clarke LJ rejected this analogy on the ground that the managing partner was in fact a lawyer and thus in a position to give legal advice to the partnership. The reality was that the managing partner had been wearing both hats at the same time (acting as the firm's managing partner, and in that capacity trying to settle the claim, and as a lawyer, giving legal advice to the partnership). Although acknowledging that this was a borderline case, the court was willing on balance to uphold the claim of privilege.[145]

---

141 *Greenough v Gaskell* (1883) 1 My & K 98 at 104 (*per* Lord Brougham LC).

142 *Smith v Daniell* (1887) LR 18 Eq 649.

143 *Smith v Daniell* (1887) LR 18 Eq 649 at 654.

144 *Somatra Ltd v Sinclair Roche and Temperlay* [2000] 1 WLR 2453.

145 *Somatra Ltd v Sinclair Roche and Temperlay* [2000] 1 WLR 2453 at 2467.

Other Scenarios

[2.55] In contemporary Irish society, there are many entities, whether statutory or non-statutory, which perform functions associated with the operation of the law in its myriad forms. These functions often include engagement with members of the public and in some instances extend to the giving of confidential advice. Nevertheless, the courts have distinguished scenarios of this kind with the classic lawyer-client relationship. In *Buckley v Incorporated Law Society*,[146] the High Court was asked to resolve a dispute over discovery of documents relating to complaints which members of the public had made to the defendant concerning a particular solicitor. In rejecting the submission that the correspondence between the complainants and the defendant was protected from disclosure, Costello J recalled the policy underpinning privilege:

> 'The law of evidence protects from disclosure on the grounds of privilege communications between a solicitor and his client. This privilege, legal professional privilege, is founded on the impossibility of conducting legal business without professional assistance and on the necessity, in order to render that assistance effectual, of securing full and unreserved intercourse between the two. It follows therefore that in respect of letters of complaint written by a complainant to the defendant and subsequent correspondence between the defendant and the complainants no legal professional privilege arises as the complainants were not consulting the defendant as a legal adviser.'[147]

This statement reflects the traditional view that the giving of legal advice is not privileged unless proffered within the confines of the classic lawyer-client relationship.

(5) Legal Advice

[2.56] The final condition attaching to legal advice privilege is the important qualification that the communication must have been made for the purposes of the giving or receiving of legal advice.[148] Keane notes that the term 'does not mean advice given by a lawyer without more, but advice about legal rights and liabilities'.[149] Drawing on the decision of the English Court of Appeal in *Balabel v Air-India*,[150] he refers to the 'continuum of communications' that typically passes between a client and her solicitor in relation to a transaction or matter and states that 'where information is passed between them as part of that continuum,

---

[146] *Buckley v Incorporated Law Society* [1994] 2 IR 44.

[147] *Buckley v Incorporated Law Society* [1994] 2 IR 44 at 47–48.

[148] *Kennedy v Law Society & Others* (20 January 1999, unreported) SC at 6 (*per* Murphy J) (privilege does not attach to documentation which does not disclose any form of legal advice); *Buckley v Bough* (2 July 2001, unreported) HC (Morris J) at 5: 'What is privileged is the communication. The communication only attracts privilege if it seeks or contains legal advice. The communication of other information is not protected in Irish law'.

[149] Keane, *The Modern Law of Evidence* (7th edn, Oxford University Press, 2008) at 613.

[150] *Balabel v Air-India* [1988] Ch 317.

the aim being to keep both informed so that legal advice may be sought and given as required, privilege will attach'.[151]

[2.57] The condition of legal advice reflects a tension in the law of privilege between the need to balance the public interest in favour of the disclosure of relevant evidence with the competing public interest in maintaining the confidentiality of the lawyer-client relationship. Conscious that the gradual expansion of legal professional privilege has led to a corresponding diminution in the principle of disclosure, the courts have strictly enforced the limitation that the communication passing between the client and her lawyer must be made for the purpose of receiving or giving legal advice. Although the giving of legal advice constitutes the central function of the legal professional, a lawyer performs a range of other more functional tasks in the course of representing her clients. By extension, not every communication that passes between a client and her lawyer contains legal advice.

[2.58] The development of the case law on legal advice has been influenced by the evolving role of the legal professional in society.[152] In previous centuries, lawyers fulfilled functions which they would not pursue today; many lawyers acted as 'men of business' conducting work undertaken in the modern day by insurance agents, estate agents, money lenders and others.[153] The diversity of activities in which lawyers engaged complicated the task of determining the scope and application of legal advice privilege. The task of the legal professional in the modern day presents challenges of its own not least because the core function of advising on legal matters has become increasingly complex, technical and specialised. The significant influence that legal issues exert over the conduct of business and private affairs and the heightened profile of legal professionals in society have been cited as justifications for restricting privilege.[154] Nevertheless, in the words of Lord Rodger in *Three Rivers District Council (No 6)*: 'In relation to legal advice privilege what matters today remains the same as what mattered in the past: whether the lawyers are being asked qua lawyers to provide legal advice'.[155]

---

[151] Keane, *The Modern Law of Evidence* (7th edn, Oxford University Press, 2008) at 613.

[152] See, eg, Radin, 'The Privilege of Confidential Communication between Lawyer and Client' (1928) 16(6) Cal L Rev 487; Hazard, 'An Historical Perspective on the Attorney-Client Privilege' (1978) 66(5) 1061.

[153] *Three Rivers District Council v Bank of England (No 6)* [2004] 3 WLR 1274 at 1294, [2005] 1 AC 610 at 657 (*per* Lord Rodger).

[154] *Balabel v Air India* [1988] Ch 317 at 331–332 (*per* Taylor LJ). But see *Nederlandse Reassurantie Groep Holding NV v Bacon & Woodrow (a firm)* [1995] 1 All ER 976 in which the Court of Appeal adopted a flexible stance with respect to transactions calling for both legal and commercial advice.

[155] *Three Rivers District Council v Bank of England (No 6)* [2004] 3 WLR 1274 at 1294, [2005] 1 AC 610 at 657.

[2.59] In Ireland, the Supreme Court fashioned a significant gloss on the scope of legal advice privilege in *Smurfit Paribas Bank Ltd v AAB Export Finance Ltd.*[156] The High Court proceedings concerned a floating charge that the defendant company had secured over the assets of a third party. During the course of discovery, the defendant claimed privilege over correspondence and instructions that it had exchanged with its solicitors in relation to the charge. The defendant neither sought nor received any legal advice in the correspondence although the defendant's instructions enabled the solicitors to draft the necessary documentation in relation to the charge. Costello J held that the correspondence was not privileged because it did not contain any legal advice but rather dealt exclusively with the drafting of the documentation.

[2.60] In upholding this position on appeal, Finlay CJ emphasised the need for rigorous scrutiny of assertions of privilege:

> 'The existence of a privilege or exemption from disclosure for communications made between a person and his lawyer clearly constitutes a potential restriction and diminution of the full disclosure both prior to and during the course of legal proceedings which in the interests of the common good is desirable for the purpose of ascertaining the truth and rendering justice. Such privilege should, therefore, in my view, only be granted by the courts in instances which have been identified as securing an objective which in the public interest in the proper conduct of the administration of justice can be said to outweigh the disadvantage arising from the restriction of disclosure of all the facts.'[157]

Finlay CJ stated that the expansion of legal advice privilege from cases of actual or contemplated litigation to cases of communications seeking legal advice could be justified only on the basis of a close and proximate link to the conduct of litigation and the function of administering justice in the courts. He explained that nexus in the following way:

> 'Where a person seeks or obtains legal advice there are good reasons to believe that he necessarily enters the area of potential litigation. The necessity to obtain legal advice would in broad terms appear to envisage the possibility of a legal challenge or query as to the correctness or effectiveness of some step which a person is contemplating. Whether such query or challenge develops or not, it is clear that a person is then entering the area of possible litigation'.[158]

---

[156] *Smurfit Paribas Bank Ltd v AAB Export Finance Ltd* [1990] 1 IR 469.

[157] *Smurfit Paribas Bank Ltd v AAB Export Finance Ltd* [1990] 1 IR 469 at 477. For similar sentiments concerning the desirability of setting boundaries over the scope of legal advice privilege see the judgment of Baroness Hale in *Three Rivers District Council v Bank of England (No 6)* [2004] 3 WLR 1274 at 1295, [2005] 1 AC 610 at 659.

[158] *Smurfit Paribas Bank Ltd v AAB Export Finance Ltd* [1990] 1 IR 469 at 478. This aspect of the judgment appears frequently in the subsequent case law. See, eg, *Fitzpatrick & Others v Ireland & Others* (18 February 1999, unreported) HC (Laffoy J); *Ochre Ridge Ltd v Cork Bonded Warehouses Ltd & Another* (13 July 2004, unreported) HC (Lavan J) pp 3–4.

The learned chief justice drew a distinction between communications seeking legal advice, which are privileged because they are sufficiently close and proximate to the conduct of litigation, and communications seeking simple legal assistance which are not:

> 'There are many tasks carried out by a lawyer for his client and properly within the legal sphere, other than the giving of advice, which could not be said to contain any real relationship with the area of potential litigation. For such communications there does not appear to me to be any sufficient public interest or feature of the common good to be secured or protected which could justify an exemption from disclosure.'[159]

[2.61] In his judgment in *Smurfit Paribas*, Finlay CJ did not provide practical examples of the purely functional tasks that epitomise legal assistance. However, in a separate judgment, McCarthy J stated:

> 'In the instant case, the fundamental issue arises from the contrasting demands – candour by the client to his solicitor and the public interest in the true resolution of litigation. In my view communication of fact leading to the drafting of legal documents and requests for the preparation of such, albeit made to a solicitor, unless and until the same results in the provision of legal advice, is not privileged from disclosure.'[160]

Presumably legal assistance would also include such tasks as the witnessing of a signature or the lodging of documents.

[2.62] In *Three Rivers District Council (No 6)*, the Court of Appeal questioned the wisdom of legal advice privilege attaching to matters such as the conveyance of real property or the drawing up of a will.[161] However, the House of Lords favoured a more liberal construction of legal advice that would potentially embrace communications relating to matters of this kind. Lord Rodger stated:

> 'A client's financial or tax position, or the financial or tax position of members of his family, may well be relevant to the way in which he asks his solicitor to structure a property transaction. Or else, for example, the client may have private worries about his son's ability to fend for himself which explain why he conveys

---

159 *Miley v Flood* [2001] ILRM 489; *Buckley v Bough* (2 July 2001, unreported) HC (Morris J); *Ochre Ridge Ltd v Cork Bonded Warehouses Ltd & Another* (13 July 2004, unreported) HC (Lavan J).

160 *Smurfit Paribas Bank Ltd v AAB Export Finance Ltd* [1990] 1 IR 469 at 480.

161 *Three Rivers District Council v Bank of England (No 6)* [2004] QB 916, 935 (*per* Lord Phillips MR). In *Ochre Ridge Ltd v Cork Bonded Warehouses Ltd & Another* (13 July 2004, unreported) HC, Lavan J observed that legal advice does not extend to 'business matters nor to conveyancing documents' but that 'correspondence associated with a conveyance for the purpose of seeking or giving legal advice' would be protected. He cited in support Cannon and Neligan, *Evidence* (Roundhall, 2002) p 260 but noted that the authors had relied in turn on *Balabel v Air India* [1988] Ch 317, the relevance of which had been limited by the Supreme Court's more restrictive interpretation of legal advice privilege in *Smurfit Paribas Bank Ltd*.

> a more legitimate interest in keeping such matters private. The case for confidentiality is, if anything, even more obvious when it comes to the preparation of a will. Rightly or wrongly, the provisions are often shaped by past relationships, indiscretions, experiences, impressions and mistakes, as well as by jealousies, slights, animosities and affections, which the testator would not wish to have revealed but which he must nevertheless explain if the solicitor is to carry out his wishes. Divulging the provisions during the testator's lifetime or disclosing the reasons for them after the testator's death could often cause incalculable harm and misery. The public interest lies in minimising the risk of that happening.'[162]

[2.63] The fact that communications between a client and her lawyer relate to a seemingly functional matter does not preclude the possibility that legal advice has been given or received. The case of *Miley v Flood*[163] demonstrates this point. The applicant, a solicitor, represented a company in proceedings before the Tribunal of Inquiry into Certain Planning Matters and Payments. When asked to disclose the identity of the individuals within the company who had instructed him, the applicant refused on the ground that client identity constitutes confidential, privileged information. Kelly J held that privilege did not extend beyond confidential communications seeking or containing legal advice to collateral facts such as the identity of the client. Nevertheless, the learned judge attached the important caveat that client identity would warrant protection where it was so bound up with the nature of the advice sought that to reveal the identity would have the effect of disclosing the advice.[164]

[2.64] The reality that each case must be assessed on its facts was illustrated by the earlier case of *Hurstridge Finance Ltd v Lismore Homes Ltd.*[165] Costello J accepted an assertion of privilege over communications between the controller of a company and the company's solicitors relating to the drafting of certain agreements. Having considered the surrounding circumstances and the documents themselves, the learned judge was satisfied that the controller had consulted the solicitors with a view to receiving legal advice and not merely to secure the drafting of the documents.

[2.65] In *Ochre Ridge Ltd v Cork Bonded Warehouses Ltd & Another*, Lavan J observed that 'the ostensible simplicity of the distinction between 'legal advice' privilege and 'legal assistance' privilege belies the difficulty of this distinction'

[162] *Three Rivers District Council v Bank of England (No 6)* [2004] 3 WLR 1274 at 1293, [2005] 1 AC 610 at 656.

[163] *Miley v Flood* [2001] 2 IR 50, [2001] 1 ILRM 489.

[164] *Miley v Flood* [2001] 2 IR 50 at 81. The issue of client identity may involve other considerations not raised in *Miley v Flood.* For example, in a corporate or governmental context it may be difficult to identify 'the client' to whose communications privilege should attach. *Three Rivers District Council v Bank of England (No 6)* [2004] 3 WLR 1274 at 1296, [2005] 1 AC 610 at 659 (*per* Baroness Hale).

[165] *Hurstridge Finance Ltd v Lismore Homes Ltd* (15 February 1991, unreported) HC (Costello J).

and suggested that the task of determining the circumstances in which privilege applies must be approached 'with some caution'.[166] In upholding an assertion of privilege over most of the documentation at issue in the proceedings before him, Lavan J applied a 'dominant purpose' test.[167] Indeed, in summarising the principles governing legal advice privilege, Lavan J stated:

> 'The dominant purpose of the communications must be the seeking or giving of legal advice. While most of the Irish cases or textbook writers do not employ the terminology of a 'dominant purpose' as to the test for legal advice privilege (it more usually being associated with 'litigation' privilege, not the subject of discussion here), it is useful in determining the scope of 'legal advice' and appears to form part of the test in the English authorities.'[168]

[2.66] Whether the requirements for legal advice privilege include a 'dominant purpose' element remains open to question.[169] The concept of the dominant purpose of legal advice sits uneasily with authority which recognises that the legal advice tendered by lawyers may be inextricably linked to broader advice of a non-legal nature.[170] Whereas, as Lavan suggests, the test might assist in determining the scope of privilege in some instances, its inclusion in the context of legal advice (as opposed to litigation privilege) is a potential source of confusion. The respective strands of privilege are characterised by significant differences in terms of purpose, context and conditions. As the case law relating to litigation privilege illustrates, the dominant purpose sets a high bar which might not be appropriate for legal advice privilege. The test might also prove impractical not least because judicial probing of the motivation of the client could itself trespass on the confidentiality of the lawyer-client relationship which privilege is designed to protect.

Finally, on the subject of legal assistance as opposed to legal advice, it is instructive to recall the observation of Kelly J in *Miley v Flood* that hybrid communications will be protected from disclosure in their entirety where it is not is possible to parcel out those aspects dealing exclusively with legal advice.

Presentational Advice

[2.67] Aside from the five conditions pertaining to legal advice privilege discussed above, other issues relating to the scope of the privilege have surfaced

166 *Ochre Ridge Ltd v Cork Bonded Warehouses Ltd* (13 July 2004, unreported) HC pp 5–6.

167 *Ochre Ridge Ltd v Cork Bonded Warehouses Ltd* (13 July 2004, unreported) HC p 12.

168 *Ochre Ridge Ltd v Cork Bonded Warehouses Ltd* (13 July 2004, unreported) HC at p 3 (citing *Three Rivers District Council v Governor and Company of the Bank of England (No 5)* [2003] QB 1556).

169 See, eg, *United States of America v Philip Morris Inc and Others* [2004] EWCA Civ 330. For insightful commentary on this aspect of *Ochre Ridge Ltd*, see Abrahamson, Dwyer and Fitzpatrick, *Discovery and Disclosure* (Thomson Round Hall, 2007) para 35.36.

170 See, eg, *Miley v Flood* [2001] 2 IR 50, [2001] 1 ILRM 489 (hybrid communications will be protected from disclosure where it is not possible to parcel out the aspects dealing specifically with legal advice).

occasionally in the case law. In *Three Rivers District Council v Bank of England (No 6)*,[171] the House of Lords considered the specific question of whether legal advice privilege extends to communications seeking or giving legal advice in relation to the presentation of information to a public inquiry.[172]

As noted above, the case had its origins in the collapse of the Bank of Credit and Commerce International SA (BCCI) in 1991.[173] BCCI's liabilities far exceeded its assets and its depositors and shareholders stood to lose their deposits and investments. The Bank of England was charged by statute with the supervision of banks and financial institutions carrying on business in the UK. Shortly after the collapse of BCCI, the Government established an independent inquiry, chaired by Lord Bingham, into the Bank's supervision of BCCI. The Bank appointed three officials to deal with all communications with the inquiry and these officials, together with other Bank personnel appointed to assist, became known as the Bank's Bingham Inquiry Unit (BIU). The law firm Freshfields was retained by the Bank to advise generally on all the Bank's dealings with the inquiry and Freshfields in turn retained counsel for that purpose. Freshfields and counsel gave advice as to the Bank's communications with the inquiry as well as the preparation and presentation of the Bank's submissions and evidence.

[2.68] Following the publication of the Bingham Inquiry Report, liquidators and creditors of BCCI brought an action against the Bank for misfeasance in public office in respect of its supervision of BCCI prior to its collapse. The claimants sought disclosure of a substantial number of documents that had been prepared by the Bank's employees for the purpose of transmission to Freshfields. The trial judge dismissed the application for discovery on the basis that the Bank was entitled to assert legal advice privilege over the documents in question:

> 'In my judgment an internal confidential document, not being a communication with a third party, which was produced or brought into existence with the dominant purpose that it or its contents be used to obtain legal advice is privileged from production.'[174]

The liquidators and creditors appealed successfully to the Court of Appeal.[175] The court accepted the claimants' argument that legal advice privilege extends only to communications between solicitor and client; it does not protect

---

[171] *Three Rivers District Council v Bank of England (No 6)* [2004] 3 WLR 1274, [2005] 1 AC 610.

[172] In *Ahern v Judge Mahon and Others* [2008] IEHC 118 (8 May 2008, unreported) (Kelly J), the High Court addressed a similar issue under the rubric of litigation privilege.

[173] This summary of the complicated factual and procedural history of the case is drawn principally from the judgment of Lord Scott.

[174] *Three Rivers District Council v Governor and Company of the Bank of England (No 5)* [2002] EWHC 2730 (*per* Tomlinson J) quoted by Scott LJ in *Three Rivers District Council v Governor and Company of the Bank of England (No 6)* [2004] 3 WLR 1274 at 1279, [2005] 1 AC 610 at 642. Scott LJ at 1278–1279, [2005] 1 AC 610 at 642 explained the reason that the Bank asserted legal advice as opposed to litigation privilege: (contd.../)

preparatory materials drawn up by employees even where those materials were prepared at the solicitor's request and for the purpose of being shown to the solicitor. For the purposes of privilege, the court took the view that information provided to solicitors by an employee is essentially no different from information provided by an independent third party.[176] It followed that the only documents for which privilege could be claimed were communications between the BIU and Freshfields seeking or giving legal advice. For the purposes of privilege, the BUI alone was to be regarded as Freshfield's client rather than any single officer or employee within the Bank including the Governor.[177]

[2.69] An issue debated before the Court of Appeal was whether material prepared for a so-called 'presentational purpose' (ie, putting relevant factual material before the inquiry in a positive light so as to minimise possible criticism of the Bank) attracted legal advice privilege. The court appeared to take the view that it did not.[178]

The Bank's petition to the House of Lords for leave to appeal against the Court of Appeal's order was dismissed and the Bank then began the task of disclosing documents pursuant to the order. However, a dispute ensued between the parties regarding the scope of the order and led to a further discovery application by the claimants. The trial judge read the Court of Appeal's judgment (overturning his own previous decision) as drawing a firm distinction between legal advice sought or given for presentational purposes, which did not attract legal advice privilege, and legal advice sought or given as to the client's legal rights and obligations, which was protected. The trial judge held that the Bank could withhold from disclosure only those communications between the BUI and Freshfields that had passed for the purpose of seeking or obtaining advice concerning the Bank's rights and obligations.[179]

---

[174] (\...contd) 'In *In re L (A Minor) (Police Investigation: Privilege)* [1997] AC 16, 26 Lord Jauncey of Tullichettle described litigation privilege as 'essentially a creature of adversarial proceedings' and held that the privilege could not be claimed in order to protect from disclosure a report prepared for use in non-adversarial proceedings. Lord Lloyd of Berwick and Lord Steyn, at pp 30 and 37, expressed their agreement. The Bingham Inquiry could not have been described as adversarial. It was, as inquiries invariably are, an inquisitorial proceeding. It was no doubt with *In re L* in mind that the Bank did not claim that the documents of which disclosure was being sought were entitled to litigation privilege'.

[175] *Three Rivers District Council v Governor and Company of the Bank of England (No 5)* [2003] QB 1556.

[176] *Three Rivers District Council v Governor and Company of the Bank of England (No 5)* [2003] QB 1556 at 1574. See discussion para **2.29** *et seq*.

[177] *Three Rivers District Council v Governor and Company of the Bank of England (No 5)* [2003] QB 1556 at 1581.

[178] *Three Rivers District Council v Governor and Company of the Bank of England (No 5)* [2003] QB 1556 at 1582–1583.

[179] [2003] EWHC 2565 (Comm), summarised by Scott LJ at *Three Rivers District Council v Bank of England (No 6)* [2004] 3 WLR 1274 at 1281, [2005] 1 AC 610 at 644–645.

On appeal by the Bank, the Court of Appeal held that legal advice privilege is limited to communications passing between the client and lawyer seeking or giving advice as to legal rights or liabilities. Dismissing the appeal, the court held that advice as to how the Bank should present its case to the inquiry was not protected by privilege.[180]

[2.70] The House of Lords unanimously upheld a further appeal brought by the Bank. The issue before the Lords was the narrow one of whether the communications between the BUI and Freshfields or counsel relating to the inquiry (so-called 'presentional advice') were protected by legal advice privilege.

Lord Scott criticised the Court of Appeal for failing to afford legal advice privilege 'a scope that reflects the policy reasons that justify its presence in our law'.[181] He pointed out that whereas the authorities on which the Court of Appeal founded its approach were all concerned with private law rights and obligations, legal advice privilege must also extend to advice and assistance in relation to public law rights, liabilitics and obligations.[182] The impossibility of a principled exclusion from legal advice privilege of communications relating to public law rights, liabilities and obligations was sufficient, in Lord Scott's view, to dispose of the issue on appeal. He continued:

> 'Every public inquiry conducts its proceedings and expresses its conclusions under the shadow of judicial review. The inquiry's procedures may be judicially reviewed if they are perceived to be unfair. The inquiry's conclusions may be judicially reviewed if they are thought to be unsustainable in light of the evidence the inquiry has received. Presentational advice or assistance given by lawyers to parties whose conduct may be the subject of criticism by the inquiry is advice or assistance that may serve to avoid the need to invoke public law remedies. It would be – or should be – readily accepted that, once an inquiry's conclusions have been reached and communicated to the sponsors of the inquiry, advice from lawyers to someone criticised as to whether a public law remedy might be available to quash the critical conclusions would be advice that qualified for legal advice privilege. It makes no sense at all, in my opinion, to withhold the protection of that privilege from presentational advice given by the lawyers for the purpose of preventing that criticism from being made in the first place.'[183]

---

[180] *Three Rivers District Council v Governor and Company of the Bank of England (No 6)* [2004] QB 916 at 934.

[181] *Three Rivers District Council v Governor and Company of the Bank of England (No 6)* [2004] 3 WLR 1274 at 1286, [2005] 1 AC 610 at 650. See also the judgment of Lord Brown [2004] 3 WLR 1274 at 1320, [2005] 1 AC 610 at 682–683.

[182] *Three Rivers District Council v Governor and Company of the Bank of England (No 6)* [2004] 3 WLR 1274 at 1287, [2005] 1 AC 610 at 650.

[183] *Three Rivers District Council v Governor and Company of the Bank of England (No 6)* [2004] 3 WLR 1274 at 1287, [2005] 1 AC 610 at 650–651.

This quotation suggests that that the flaw in the reasoning of the Court of Appeal lay not in its emphasis on the client's rights, liabilities and obligations but rather in the exclusivity of its focus on private law rights, liabilities and obligations. In itself, the holding of the House of Lords in *Three Rivers District Council (No 6)* that presentational advice comes within the remit of protection sheds only limited light on the scope of legal advice privilege. Given the many and varied nature of communications between a client and her lawyer, how can a trial court determine with precision those matters that are protected and those that are not? Specifically, how close a connection is required between the advice sought or tendered and the client's legal rights, liabilities and obligations? Although presentational privilege may have posited a relatively straightforward case for the Lords, what of other, borderline cases where the answer is more elusive?

[2.71] Interestingly, Lord Rodger cast privilege in even broader terms than Lord Scott, recognising that protected advice may potentially extend beyond the conventional understanding of public law or private law rights and obligations.[184] He pointed out that the privilege applies to advice on criminal law matters 'which it may not always be easy to characterise as relating, strictly speaking, to rights and obligations of the client'.[185] Similarly, by way of example, communications relating to the legal position of some person other than the client and communications concerning the potential repercussions of a course of action contemplated by the client's adult child would also be protected.[186]

[2.72] Lord Brown adopted an equally liberal stance on the application of privilege to presentational advice. In his view privilege would attach to communications concerning the presentation of a case for any formal inquiry 'whether concerned with public or private law issues, whether adversarial or inquisitorial in form, whether held in public or in private, whether or not directly affecting [the client's] rights or liabilities'.[187] The assistance that a lawyer lent to a client in this presentational setting was precisely the sort of professional service for which lawyers are ordinarily employed.[188] Furthermore, it was a setting that implicated the underlying justification for privilege, namely the need for candour on the part of the client in order to render the lawyer's service

[184] *Three Rivers District Council v Governor and Company of the Bank of England (No 6)* [2004] 3 WLR 1274 at 1293, [2005] 1 AC 610 at 656.

[185] *Three Rivers District Council v Governor and Company of the Bank of England (No 6)* [2004] 3 WLR 1274 at 1293, [2005] 1 AC 610 at 656.

[186] *Three Rivers District Council v Governor and Company of the Bank of England (No 6)* [2004] 3 WLR 1274 at 1293, [2005] 1 AC 610 at 656.

[187] *Three Rivers District Council v Governor and Company of the Bank of Bank of England (No 6)* [2004] 3 WLR 1274 at 1319, [2005] 1 AC 610 at 683.

[188] *Three Rivers District Council v Governor and Company of the Bank of Bank of England (No 6)* [2004] 3 WLR 1274 at 1319, [2005] 1 AC 610 at 683.

effective.[189] In Lord Brown's view it was simply not practical to distinguish between the different interests of persons appearing before tribunals, be they persons whose reputation was clearly at stake or persons who had instructed lawyers with a view to making the best presentation of their case at an inquiry.[190]

[2.73] Lord Carswell took note of the unquestionable increase in the breadth of work commonly carried out by lawyers and the marked proliferation in the number and variety of tribunals other than courts of law.[191] Given the serious consequences that may flow from findings of inquiries, his lordship opined that it may be of considerable importance to persons or bodies affected that their case be put as effectively as possible.[192] Lord Carswell did not believe that the Bank should be deprived of the protection of privilege simply because it did not stand in the shoes of an individual whose conduct was called into question and whose reputation was at risk in a public inquiry; the Bank's interests might differ but it did not follow that they should be disregarded.[193] His lordship continued:

> 'The work of advising a client on the most suitable approach to adopt, assembling material for presentation of his case and taking statements which set out relevant material in an orderly fashion and omit the irrelevant is to my mind the classic exercise of one of the lawyer's skills. I can see no valid reason why that should cease to be so because the forum is an inquiry or other tribunal which is not a court of law, provided that the advice is given in a legal context ...'[194]

Indeed, Lord Carswell pointed out that the availability of competent legal advice will materially assist an inquiry by reducing irrelevance and encouraging the making of proper admissions.[195]

[2.74] When discussing the scope of legal advice for the purposes of privilege, several of the Lords quoted with approval the requirement of a 'relevant legal context' propounded by Lord Taylor in the Court of Appeal in *Balabel v Air India*:

---

[189] *Three Rivers District Council v Governor and Company of the Bank of Bank of England (No 6)* [2004] 3 WLR 1274 at 1319, [2005] 1 AC 610 at 683.

[190] *Three Rivers District Council v Governor and Company of the Bank of Bank of England (No 6)* [2004] 3 WLR 1274 at 1320, [2005] 1 AC 610 at 684 (citing the example of developers and objectors at a planning inquiry).

[191] *Three Rivers District Council v Governor and Company of the Bank of Bank of England (No 6)* [2004] 3 WLR 1274 at 1317, [2005] 1 AC 610 at 681.

[192] *Three Rivers District Council v Governor and Company of the Bank of Bank of England (No 6)* [2004] 3 WLR 1274 at 1317, [2005] 1 AC 610 at 681.

[193] *Three Rivers District Council v Governor and Company of the Bank of Bank of England (No 6)* [2004] 3 WLR 1274 at 1317, [2005] 1 AC 610 at 681.

[194] *Three Rivers District Council v Governor and Company of the Bank of England (No 6)* [2004] 3 WLR 1274 at 1318, [2005] 1 AC 610 at 681.

[195] *Three Rivers District Council v Governor and Company of the Bank of England (No 6)* [2004] 3 WLR 1274 at 1318, [2005] 1 AC 610 at 681 (quoting from the Chairman's Note on Lawyers of 5 November 1998 delivered by Lord Phillips in connection with the BSE tribunal).

> 'legal advice is not confined to telling the client the law; it must include advice as to what should prudently and sensibly be done in the relevant legal context.'[196]

Lord Rodger engaged in a straightforward application of this principle to the facts. The Bingham Inquiry had been established to investigate the Bank's supervision of BCCI under the Banking Acts with the consequence that the Banking Acts formed the relevant legal context.[197] When the BIU consulted Freshfields, and through them counsel, about the presentation of the Bank's evidence to the inquiry, it was seeking their comments and assistance as lawyers professing expertise in the field.[198]

[2.75] On the concept of relevant legal context, Lord Scott offered the following guidance to trial judges:

> 'If a solicitor becomes the client's 'man of business', and some solicitors do, responsible for advising the client on all matters of business, including investment policy, finance policy and other business matters, the advice may lack a relevant legal context. There is, in my opinion, no way of avoiding difficulty in deciding marginal cases whether the seeking of advice from or the giving of advice by lawyers does or does not take place in a relevant legal context so as to attract legal advice privilege. In cases of doubt the judge called upon to make the decision should ask whether the advice relates to the rights, liabilities, obligations or remedies of the client either under private law or under public law. If it does not then, in my opinion, legal advice privilege would not apply. If it does then, in my opinion, the judge should ask himself whether the communication falls within the policy underlying the justification for legal advice privilege in our law. Is the occasion on which the communication takes place and is the purpose for which it takes places such as to make it reasonable to expect the privilege to apply? The criterion must, in my opinion, be an objective one.'[199]

---

196 *Balabel v Air India* [1988] Ch 317 at 330 quoted by Lord Scott *Three Rivers District Council v Governor and Company of the Bank of England (No 6)* [2004] 3 WLR 1274 at 1289, by Lord Rodger at 1294, by Baroness Hale at 1296 and by Lord Carswell at 1316.

197 *Three Rivers District Council v Governor and Company of the Bank of England (No 6)* [2004] 3 WLR 1274 at 1294, [2005] 1 AC 610 at 658.

198 *Three Rivers District Council v Governor and Company of the Bank of England (No 6)* [2004] 3 WLR 1274 at 1295, [2005] 1 AC 610 at 658. Lord Rodger continued: 'Either expressly or impliedly, the BIU was asking them to put on legal spectacles when reading, considering and commenting on the drafts. In other words it was asking them to consider, as lawyers, how the Bank's evidence could be most effectively presented to Bingham LJ, given that he was inquiring into the Bank's discharge of their legal responsibilities under the Banking Acts. ... What matters is that the BIU was instructing the lawyers in Freshfields to carry out a function which necessarily involved the use of their legal skills if it was to be performed properly.'

199 *Three Rivers District Council v Bank of England (No 6)* [2004] 3 WLR 1274 at 1288, [2005] 1 AC 610 at 651.

Chapter 3

Litigation Privilege

INTRODUCTION

[3.01] Consulting with a client in confidence is just one of the many tasks that a lawyer undertakes when preparing for and conducting litigation on that client's behalf. By virtue of its limited scope, legal advice privilege is ill-equipped to protect from disclosure the panoply of confidential information generated by litigation. Whereas legal advice privilege extends to confidential communications between client and lawyer made for the purpose of receiving or giving legal advice, by its nature it does not cover other information associated with the trial process.

Litigation privilege[1] fills this lacuna by protecting from disclosure two forms of information created with legal proceedings in mind. The privilege was first developed to protect communications between either a client or her lawyer and a third party, such as a potential witness or an expert.[2] It subsequently evolved to embrace other material generated by the lawyer during the course of proceedings and known colloquially as the lawyer's 'work product'. This material includes a range of documents such as draft pleadings, legal submissions and lawyer's notes. By protecting from disclosure the lawyer's preparations for trial, litigation privilege responds to the inherently adversarial nature of legal proceedings. As Justice Jackson stated in the US Supreme Court case of *Hickman v Taylor*: 'Discovery was hardly intended to enable a learned profession to perform its functions either without wits or on wits borrowed from the adversary'.[3]

[3.02] In civil proceedings, the issue of litigation privilege typically arises during the course of discovery. One party seeks discovery of a document and the

---

1 See generally, Passmore, *Privilege* (2nd edn, xpl publishing, 2006) chs 3–5; Thanki (ed), *The Law of Privilege* (Oxford University Press, 2006) ch 3; Matthews and Malek, *Disclosure* (Sweet & Maxwell, 2001) para 9.028 *et seq.;* McGrath, *Evidence* (Thomson Round Hall, 2005) pp 536–548; Abrahamson, Dwyer & Fitzpatrick, *Discovery and Disclosure* (Thomson Round Hall, 2007) ch 35; Dee, *Discovery* (2004) ch 6.

2 *Anderson v Bank of Columbia* (1876) 2 Ch D 644; *Southwark and Vauxhall Water Co v Quick* (1878) 3 QBD 315; *Wheeler v Le Marchant* (1881) 17 Ch D 675. The development of litigation privilege was discussed by Kelly J in *Ahern v Judge Mahon and Others* [2008] IEHC 118 (8 May 2008) (Kelly J).

3 *Hickman v Taylor* 329 US 495, 516 (1947).

other party responds by asserting privilege. In *M'Mahon v Gt Northern Ry Co*,[4] Palles LCB stated the position thus:

> 'Two general propositions as to privilege in such cases may be laid down, and the only difficulty is where to draw the line dividing the two. In the first place information of a litigant in reference to the cause of action is *prima facie* discoverable, and, consequently, if the litigant has a number of servants their written statements to him in reference to the cause of action ought *prima facie* to be produced. On the other hand, there is the right of the party with reference to his legal adviser that professional communications passing between them, or documents prepared for the purpose of being submitted to a legal adviser, are privileged.'[5]

As this quotation implies, there is an inherent tension in the law relating to litigation privilege. On the one hand, the privilege benefits both sides in the adversarial process by providing lawyers with the scope to prepare fully and freely for trial. On the other hand, courts are anxious to ensure that the cloak of privilege is not abused by parties who seek to hide relevant documentary evidence within its folds.[6]

RATIONALES FOR LITIGATION PRIVILEGE

[3.03] Litigation privilege preserves the adversarial character of the common law trial process by allowing lawyers to prepare for trial without having to disclose their pre-trial preparations to the other side.[7] Traditionally the privilege was rationalised in part by the reality that by disclosing pre-trial preparations, including the exchange of information with third parties, a party runs the risk of revealing confidential communications passing between her and her lawyer. In other words, legal advice privilege would be undermined if disclosure swept so broadly as to embrace confidential instructions given and the legal advice received as part and parcel of pre-trial preparations.

Confidentiality

[3.04] In *Woori Bank & Hanvit LSP Finance Ltd v KDB Ireland Ltd*,[8] Finlay Geoghegan J quoted from the judgment of Jessel MR in *Anderson v Bank of*

---

4 *M'Mahon v Gt Northern Ry Co* (1906) 40 ILTR 172.

5 *M'Mahon v Gt Northern Ry Co* (1906) 40 ILTR 172 at 173.

6 *Wheeler v Le Marchant* (1881) 17 Ch D 675; *Waugh v British Railways Board* [1980] AC 521. In *Irish Haemophilia Society v Judge Lindsay and Blood Transfusion Board* (16 May 2001, unreported) HC Kelly J stated at p 11: 'Care must be taken to ensure that the privilege is not abused on the one hand and on the other that the requirements for its assertion are not such as to in effect dilute or destroy it'.

7 *Waugh v British Railways Board* [1980] AC 521 at 531; *Lee v SW Thames Regional Health Authority* [1985] 1 WLR 845.

8 *Woori Bank & Hanvit LSP Finance Ltd v KDB Ireland Ltd* [2005] IEHC 451 (21 December 2005).

British Columbia when discussing confidentiality as an essential element of litigation privilege. She observed:

> 'The purpose and effect of a claim to legal professional privilege in a litigation context is to preserve as confidential to the party to the litigation, as against the other party, confidential communications either with its lawyers or third parties.'[9]

It is debatable of course, whether lawyer-client communications are so intricately entwined with other preparations for trial that the two cannot be severed. Whereas there may be particular instances where the public interest in preserving the confidentiality of the legal professional relationship would be threatened, standing alone it is arguably too slim a reed on which to rest such a broad, general policy against disclosure.

[3.05] Nevertheless, classic cases such as *Anderson v Bank of British Columbia*[10] indicate that the courts viewed the protection of communications with third parties as a natural outgrowth of the confidential relationship between lawyer and client. Jessel MR stated:

> 'The solicitor requires further information, and says, I will obtain it from a third person. That is confidential. It is obtained by him as solicitor for the purpose of the litigation, and it must be protected upon the same ground, otherwise it would be dangerous, if not impossible, to employ a solicitor. You cannot ask him what the information he obtained was. It may be information simply for the purpose of knowing whether he ought to defend or prosecute the action, but it may be also obtained in the shape of collecting evidence for the purpose of such prosecution or defence. All that, therefore, is privileged.'[11]

The need to preserve the confidentiality of third party communications is a thread in the fabric of protection which the law affords to pre-trial preparations. It is said to enhance the quality of legal representation, for example by allowing lawyers to reduce much of their work product to writing without fear that it could be disclosed to the other side on demand.[12]

The Adversarial Process

[3.06] An additional rationale for litigation privilege derives from its association with the adversarial process and, specifically, the gathering of evidence by

---

9 *Woori Bank & Hanvit LSP Finance Ltd v KDB Ireland Ltd* [2005] IEHC 451 (21 December 2005) at 24. Elsewhere in her judgment, Finlay Geoghegan J stated: 'The objectives relevant to communications between a client and third parties appear to be the ability of a party to litigation to prepare its case in the adversarial system without disclosure to the opposing party and also the necessity for a party to litigation to obtain full and frank statements from potential witnesses' (at p 23).

10 *Anderson v Bank of British Columbia* (1876) 2 Ch D 644.

11 *Anderson v Bank of British Columbia* (1876) 2 Ch D 644 at 649. See also *Wheeler v Le Marchant* (1881) 17 ChD 675 at 682; *Kennedy v Lyell* (1883) 23 Ch 387 at 404.

12 McGrath, *Evidence* (Thomson Round Hall, 2005) at para 10.34 (quoting from the judgment of Murphy J in *Hickman v Taylor* 329 US 495, 510–511 (1947)).

litigants which is a fundamental characteristic of our adversarial system of trial. In *Three Rivers District Council v Governor and Company of the Bank of England (No 6)*,[13] Lord Rodger stated:

> 'Litigation privilege relates to communications at the stage when litigation is pending or in contemplation. It is based on the idea that legal proceedings take the form of a contest in which each of the opposing parties assembles his own body of evidence and uses it to try to defeat the other, with the judge or jury determining the winner. In such a system each party should be free to prepare his case as fully as possible without the risk that his opponent will be able to recover the material generated by his preparations.'[14]

By affording the parties freedom to prepare for trial in private, litigation privilege furthers the aim of a creating a fair and level playing field for the adversarial contest. Optimising the conditions in which the parties gather evidence and prepare for trial is thought to maximise the strengths of the system, improving the likelihood of settlement, enhancing the presentation of the parties' respective cases at trial and safeguarding decision-making by judges and juries.

LIMITING PRIVILEGE

[3.07] The broad brush with which these rationales for litigation privilege have been painted has generated some measure of controversy. In *Three Rivers District Council v Bank of England (No 6)*,[15] Lord Scott observed *obiter dicta* that whereas the need to afford litigation privilege to the seeking or giving of legal advice for purposes of actual or contemplated litigation is easy to understand, the same cannot be said of 'documents or communications which although having the requisite connection with litigation neither constitute nor disclose the seeking or giving of legal advice'.[16] His lordship cited communications between litigant and third parties as an 'obvious example'.[17]

In England, debate about the extent of litigation privilege is necessarily influenced by a limited but discernible shift towards a more inquisitorial approach in certain types of legal proceeding. *In re L (A Minor) (Police Investigation: Privilege)*,[18] the House of Lords restricted litigation privilege to

[13] *Three Rivers District Council v Governor and Company of the Bank of England (No 6)* [2004] 3 WLR 1274, [2005] 1 AC 610.

[14] *Three Rivers District Council v Governor and Company of the Bank of England (No 6)* [2004] 3 WLR 1274 at 1291, [2005] 1 AC 610 at 654–655.

[15] *Three Rivers District Council v Governor and Company of the Bank of England (No 6)* [2004] 3 WLR 1274, [2005] 1 AC 610.

[16] *Three Rivers District Council v Governor and Company of the Bank of England (No 6)* [2004] 3 WLR 1274 at 1284, [2005] 1 AC 610 at 647.

[17] *Three Rivers District Council v Governor and Company of the Bank of England (No 6)* [2004] 3 WLR 1274, [2005] 1 AC 610.

[18] *In re L (A Minor) (Police Investigation: Privilege)* [1997] AC 16.

communications or documents connected with *adversarial* proceedings strictly defined. It is noteworthy that in *Three Rivers District Council v Bank of England (No 6)*,[19] Lord Scott took the view that civil litigation conducted pursuant to the English Civil Procedure Rules is in many respects no longer quintessentially adversarial. Linking these two developments, Lord Scott suggested that the decision in *In re L* warrants a new look at the justification for litigation privilege.[20]

[3.08] In an Irish setting, inquisitorial constraints on privilege are confined to proceedings concerning the welfare of children and, even here, take the form of a flexible limitation as opposed to a watertight exception.[21] The Commercial Court has introduced certain procedural innovations in the vein of the English reforms but, in general, civil proceedings in this jurisdiction remain firmly adversarial in character. Thus, there has been no corresponding call for the revisiting of the policy underpinning litigation privilege.

Nevertheless, McGrath observed in 2005 that 'in recent times, the courts have begun to question whether the application of litigation privilege actually advances the administration of justice'.[22] He discerned from the decision of the Supreme Court in *Gallagher v Stanley*,[23] discussed below, 'dissatisfaction on the part of the Court with the imperialist tendencies of litigation privilege in the hands of parties who wish to withhold probative material from disclosure'.[24] Whereas there has been no substantial rolling back of litigation privilege in the intervening period, the contemporary case law reflects a firm judicial hand in reviewing and resolving claims for protection from disclosure. In general, the courts recognise the need for detailed critical analysis of the asserted grounds for privilege in the particular factual context presented. Moreover, in civil proceedings it is important to recall that litigation privilege has evolved within the framework of the court rules on discovery which have placed increasing emphasis on structure and specificity in applications for orders of discovery and counterclaims for exemption from production and inspection on grounds of privilege.[25]

---

19 *Three Rivers District Council v Governor and Company of the Bank of England (No 6)* [2004] 3 WLR 1274, [2005] 1 AC 610.

20 *Three Rivers District Council v Governor and Company of the Bank of England (No 6)* [2004] 3 WLR 1274, [2005] 1 AC 610.

21 See **Ch 5**. The courts adopt an analogous stance when applying an exception in the context of testamentary dispositions.

22 McGrath, *Evidence* (Thomson Round Hall, 2005) at para 10.35.

23 *Gallagher v Stanley* [1998] 2 IR 267.

24 McGrath, *Evidence* (Thomson Round Hall, 2005) at 10.35.

25 See **Ch 7**.

Relationship between Legal Advice Privilege and Litigation Privilege

[3.09] In *Three Rivers District Council v Governor and Company of the Bank of England (No 6)*[26] Lord Scott explained the interaction between legal advice privilege and litigation privilege. He stated:

> '[L]egal advice privilege has an undoubted relationship with litigation privilege. Legal advice is frequently sought or given in connection with current or contemplated litigation. But it may equally well be sought or given in circumstances and for purposes that have nothing to do with litigation. If it is sought or given in connection with litigation, then the advice would fall into both of the two categories. But it is long settled that a connection with litigation is not a necessary condition for privilege to be attracted. On the other hand it has been held that litigation privilege can extend to communications between a lawyer or the lawyer's client and a third party or to any document brought into existence for the dominant purpose of being used in litigation. The connection between legal advice sought or given and the affording of privilege to the communication has thereby been cut.'[27]

Legal professional privilege was described by Lord Carswell in the same case as 'a single integral privilege, whose sub-heads are legal advice privilege and litigation privilege'.[28] As developed by English courts in the nineteenth century, legal professional privilege was initially limited to the context of litigation and, indeed, litigation remains at its core in the present day. There is an overlap between legal advice privilege and litigation privilege in so far as the latter embraces communications between the lawyer and client sought or provided in the context of legal proceedings. In the past, courts have generally tended to downplay the distinction between the two.[29]

[3.10] To some extent, the interaction between the two species of privilege is a matter of common sense. There are situations in which the assistance of a legal professional is sought only at the cusp of litigation. The client may have been sued or may anticipate suit; alternatively the client may wish to proceed against another party. When proceedings are so clearly in the contemplation of client and lawyer, communications passing between them concerning the underlying legal dispute will necessarily be protected by litigation privilege. Legal advice sought or given in connection with pending or anticipated litigation potentially

---

26 *Three Rivers District Council v Governor and Company of the Bank of England (No 6)* [2004] 3 WLR 1274, [2005] 1 AC 610.

27 *Three Rivers District Council v Governor and Company of the Bank of England (No 6)* [2004] 3 WLR 1274 at 1283, [2005] 1 AC 610 at 646–647.

28 *Three Rivers District Council v Governor and Company of the Bank of England (No 6)* [2004] 3 WLR 1274 at 1313, [2005] 1 AC 610 at 677.

29 *Waugh v British Railways Board* [1980] AC 521 at 541–542 (per Lord Edmund-Davies). See also *United States of America v Philip Morris Inc and Others* [2004] EWCA Civ 330; *R (Kelly) v Warley Magistrates' Court* [2008] 1 WLR 2001.

falls within both strands of privilege but it tends to be asserted by parties and accepted more readily by courts as protected by litigation privilege. It is not that legal advice privilege is extinguished or subsumed within litigation privilege; in practical terms legal advice privilege remains a valid but dormant option. Indeed, there may be strategic or other reasons that encourage a party to claim legal advice privilege over its litigation counterpart.

[3.11] The strategy of the Bank of England in *Three Rivers District Council v Govenor and Company of the Bank of England (No 6)*[30] illustrates the point. The prior holding of a majority of the House of Lords in *In re L (A Minor) (Police Investigation: Privilege)*[31] that litigation privilege was limited to adversarial proceedings was thought to explain the Bank's decision to successfully assert legal advice privilege in relation to communications passing between the Bank and its lawyers in relation to a public inquiry that had been established to investigate the Bank's supervision of the collapsed BCCI.[32]

In *Fitzpatrick & Others v Ireland & Others*,[33] the defendants sought to resist disclosure of certain documents on the grounds of legal advice and litigation privilege. The plaintiffs argued that privilege could not be claimed as being made in contemplation of the proceedings. However, Laffoy J rejected the suggestion that documents generated in advance of litigation could not be privileged as contrary to the statement of Finlay CJ in *Smurfit Paribas Ltd v AAB Export Finance Ltd* that '[w]here a person seeks or obtains legal advice, there are good reasons to believe that he necessarily enters the area of potential litigation'.[34] This case underscores the potential role that legal advice privilege may play in supplementing a claim of litigation privilege where the privilege holder has difficulty establishing that the proceedings were sufficiently proximate for purposes of litigation privilege. Of course in circumstances of overlap such as these, legal advice privilege will only protect communications between the client and lawyer (and not communications with third parties or other aspects of the lawyer's work product).

Communications relating to matters peripheral to the litigation may fall outside litigation privilege strictly defined but nevertheless qualify for legal advice privilege. But it is generally a truism that litigation privilege takes precedence over legal advice privilege as soon as litigation appears on the horizon.[35]

---

30 *Three Rivers District Council v Governor and Company of the Bank of England (No 6)* [2004] 3 WLR 1274, [2005] 1 AC 610.

31 *In re L (A Minor) (Police Investigation: Privilege)* [1997] AC 16.

32 *Three Rivers District Council v Governor and Company of the Bank of England (No 6)* [2004] 3 WLR 1274 at 1278, [2005] 1 AC 610 at 642 (*per* Scott LJ).

33 *Fitzpatrick & Others v Ireland & Others* (18 February 1999, unreported) HC (Laffoy J).

34 *Smurfit Paribas Ltd v AAB Export Finance Ltd* [1990] 1 IR 469 at 478.

35 McGrath, *Evidence* (Thomson Round Hall, 2005) at para 10.08, identifies some uncertainty over the relationship between two sub-categories of legal professional privilege and, in particular, over (contd.../)

CONFIDENTIALITY

[3.12] Confidentiality is an essential element in litigation privilege although its contours may not map precisely the nature and scope of the concept as it applies to legal advice privilege. In the context of litigation privilege, Keane has observed that confidentiality 'enables lawyers to encourage strong cases and discourage weak ones, which is in the interests of the state'.[36]

[3.13] The issue of whether litigation privilege extends to non-confidential communications gathered in preparation for trial was considered by the High Court in *Woori Bank & Hanvit LSP Finance Ltd v KDB Ireland Ltd.*[37] The defendant sought discovery of transcripts of telephone conversations between employees or agents of the plaintiff bank and third parties. The plaintiff conceded that the conversations had not been confidential but argued that privilege attached nevertheless because the conversations had been conducted for the purpose of evidence-gathering for litigation.[38] Finlay Geoghegan J concluded that confidentiality of communication between the client and third parties is a prerequisite to a successful claim of privilege in a litigation context. She observed:

> 'The objectives relevant to communications between a client and third parties appear to be the ability of a party to litigation to prepare its case in the adversarial system without disclosure to the opposing party and also the necessity for a party to litigation to obtain full and frank statements from potential witnesses. Whether one considers litigation privilege to be a subcategory of legal professional privilege or a separate heading does not matter. Regardless of which it is, it is also clear from the authorities ... that at the core of the litigation privilege is the privilege attaching to confidential communications between a party to litigation and his lawyers.'[39]

Having recalled the admonition of Finlay CJ in *Smurfit Paribas Bank Ltd v AAB Expert Finance Ltd*[40] against unprincipled extensions in the application of privilege, Finlay Geoghegan J noted that rendering confidential to the party

---

35 (\...contd) 'whether communications between a client and his or her legal adviser regarding litigation in being or anticipated are protected only by legal advice privilege'. He concludes that 'the better view is that such communications are more properly protected by legal advice privilege alone and that litigation privilege should be regarded as applied to third party communications and work product only'.

36 Keane, *The Modern Law of Evidence* (7th edn, Oxford University Press, 2008) at 611 (citing the judgment of Bingham LJ in *Ventouris v Mountain* [1991] 1 WLR 607 at 611).

37 *Woori Bank & Hanvit LSP Finance Ltd v KDB Ireland Ltd* [2005] IEHC 451 (21 December 2005) (Finlay Geoghegan J).

38 *Woori Bank & Hanvit LSP Finance Ltd v KDB Ireland Ltd* [2005] IEHC 451 (21 December 2005) (Finlay Geoghegan J) p 19.

39 *Woori Bank & Hanvit LSP Finance Ltd v KDB Ireland Ltd* [2005] IEHC 451 (21 December 2005) (Finlay Geoghegan J) p 23.

40 *Smurfit Paribas Bank Ltd v AAB Expert Finance Ltd* [1990] 1 IR 469 at 476.

claiming privilege 'communications either with its lawyer or third parties which are not already confidential to it' did not appear to form part of the general principle underpinning litigation privilege. She drew support for this view from the approach of the Supreme Court in *Fyffes plc v DCC plc*.[41] In that case the Supreme Court held that limited disclosure of privileged material to a third party for a particular purpose not directly connected to the litigation will not result in the privilege being lost. However, as Finlay Geoghegan J observed in *Woori Bank*, that steps had been taken to preserve confidentiality was 'a material fact in the conclusions of the Court [in *Fyffes*] that privilege had not been lost'.[42] She continued: 'If there is no necessity in the first place for a communication with a third party to be confidential then there could be no need to preserve confidentiality'.[43]

PROCEEDINGS FOR PURPOSES OF PRIVILEGE

[3.14] Litigation privilege protects from disclosure information gathered or exchanged when legal proceedings are pending or anticipated. As we have seen, the House of Lords has set boundaries to litigation privilege by limiting its reach to adversarial proceedings.[44] The approach of the Irish judiciary is arguably more flexible: privilege is presumptively applicable in all types of proceeding but trial judges retain a discretion to favour disclosure in the particular circumstances of inquisitorial settings such as testimonial proceedings[45] and proceedings relating to the welfare of children.[46] These categories of cases are sometimes classified as exceptions to legal professional privilege.

[3.15] The application of litigation privilege to proceedings of tribunals of inquiry was affirmed by a divisional sitting of the High Court in *Ahern v Judge Mahon & Others*.[47] The proceedings arose out of the investigation of the

---

41 *Fyffes plc v DCC plc* [2005] 1 IR 59.

42 *Woori Bank & Hanvit LSP Finance Ltd v KDB Ireland Ltd* [2005] IEHC 451 (21 December 2005) (Finlay Geoghegan J) at p 25.

43 *Woori Bank & Hanvit LSP Finance Ltd v KDB Ireland Ltd* [2005] IEHC 451 (21 December 2005) (Finlay Geoghegan J) a p 25. Finlay Geoghegan J did not consider it necessary to decide whether a 'materials for evidence' privilege exists in Irish law separate and distinct from legal professional privilege. This suggestion had been advanced by the plaintiffs relying on Matthews and Malek, *Disclosure* (Sweet & Maxwell, 2001) ch 9 who had traced it in turn to Bray, *Principles and Practice of Discovery* (1885) p 407.

44 *In re L (A Minor) (Police Investigation: Privilege)* [1997] AC 16; *Three Rivers District Council v Governor and Company of the Bank of England (No 6)* [2004] 3 WLR 1274 at 1312, [2005] 1 AC 610 at 675 (*per* Carswell LJ recognising as one of the conditions of litigation privilege that 'the litigation must be adversarial, not investigative or inquisitorial').

45 *Crawford v Treacy* [1999] 2 IR 171.

46 *L(T) v L(V)* [1996] IFLR 126.

47 *Ahern v Judge Mahon & Others* [2008] IEHC 118 (8 May 2008) (Divisional High Court). The Australian Federal Court has held that proceedings before a Royal Commission are not strictly adversarial and do not provide an appropriate context for claims of privilege: (contd.../)

Tribunal of Inquiry into Certain Planning Matters and Payments into the financial affairs of former Taoiseach Mr Bertie Ahern in the early 1990s. At issue before the Divisional High Court was, *inter alia*, the issue of Mr Ahern's entitlement to claim privilege in respect of communications between his legal advisors and an expert retained by him for the purpose of the tribunal's proceedings. Having referred to Irish and English authorities on point, the court determined that legal professional privilege extends to documents generated in connection with the instruction and retention of an expert witness provided that they are prepared for the purpose of litigation. It followed that all of the 150 documents that were the subject of the claim of litigation privilege in the present proceedings would attract such privilege were Mr Ahern involved in litigation properly so-called.

[3.16] Kelly J characterised the question before the court as whether Mr Ahern could invoke the privilege as a person whose affairs were under examination by the tribunal. It was the tribunal's contention that Mr Ahern's status was more akin to a witness than a party and consequently that he was not entitled to claim privilege under the Tribunals of Inquiry (Evidence) Act 1921. However, the court took the opposite position: as a person whose conduct was under examination by the tribunal, Mr Ahern was entitled to the fundamental constitutional rights identified by the Supreme Court in *Re Haughey.*[48] Those rights, grounded in Article 40.3, included the right to one's good name, the right to fair procedures and the right to natural and constitutional justice. Kelly J expressed the conclusion of the court thus:

> 'It would, in my view, be anomalous and make little sense if a person to whom *Re Haughey* rights applies could not assert an entitlement to Litigation Privilege. A person appearing before a tribunal of inquiry and to whom *Re Haughey* rights applies is to be regarded as being in the same position as a party to High Court litigation and not a mere witness from the point of view of Legal Professional Privilege.'[49]

The court based its judgment on the Constitution primarily but expressed the belief that its determination was supported by decisions in other jurisdictions that lack corresponding protections.[50]

---

47 (\...contd) *AWB Ltd v Cole* (2006) 152 FCR 382. But in New Zealand, privilege has been held to apply in a range of judicial and administrative proceedings involving compulsory disclosure. See Mathieson, *Cross on Evidence* (8th New Zealand edn, Lexis Nexis, 2005) para 10.24 (discussing cases).

48 *Re Haughey* [1971] IR 217.

49 *Ahern v Judge Mahon & Others* [2008] IEHC 118 (8 May 2008) (Divisional High Court).

50 See also Tribunal of Inquiry into Payments to Politicians and Related Matters, Revised Tribunal Ruling Dated 24 March 2010 Re Opinion Dated 9 May 1996, para 36 *et seq*.

THE DURATION OF LITIGATION PRIVILEGE

[3.17] It is well settled that legal advice privilege is not tempered by any time limit; it persists beyond the cessation of the client-lawyer relationship and, indeed, survives the death of either the client or the lawyer.[51] In contrast, there has been some uncertainty over the duration of litigation privilege. On the one hand, the temporal reach of this strand of privilege is clearly constrained by its nexus to particular proceedings. On the other hand, there is precedent to suggest that privilege may continue for the purpose of subsequent related proceedings.[52] Given its direct relationship with legal proceedings, litigation privilege generally subsists for the duration of those proceedings and is extinguished when they come to a close. Documents or communications protected from disclosure in the course of particular proceedings do not necessarily remain privileged for all purposes and all time.[53]

[3.18] This general proposition may give rise to difficulty where the subject matter of the proceedings is litigated in subsequent, additional suits. In *Bord na Mona v Sisk*,[54] Costello J followed the principle enunciated by Parker LJ in *The Aegis Blaze*:[55]

> 'Unless the party claiming privilege or his successor is a party to the subsequent action, no question of a claim to privilege will arise … If, however, the party claiming privilege in the second action is the person entitled to privilege in the first action, but there is no connection of subject matter whatsoever, it is most improbable that the question will arise, for in such circumstances the document will not be relevant and will not therefore be disclosable, and there will therefore be no question of production. If, however, there is sufficient connection for the document to be relevant, then it is, in my view, right that the party entitled to the privilege should be able to assert it in the second action … The rule has been stated time and time again over a very long period …'[56]

The proceedings before the High Court in *Bord na Mona v Sisk* concerned a dispute over a contract for the construction of office buildings. The dispute had been referred to arbitration which had led, in turn, to proceedings in England to enforce the arbitral award. The plaintiff resisted discovery of documents in its possession in relation to the English proceedings on the ground that they were privileged. Costello J held that the plaintiff was entitled to assert privilege in the

51 *Bullivant v AG for Victoria* [1901] AC 196.

52 *McMullen v Kennedy* [2008] IESC 69 (17 December 2008) p 8.

53 *Re Proceeds of Crime Act 1996: MFM v PW* [2001] 3 IR 462; *Porter v Scott* [1979] NI 6; *Blank v Canada (Minister of Justice)* [2006] 2 SCR 319.

54 *Bord na Mona v Sisk* [1990] 1 IR 85.

55 *The Aegis Blaze* [1986] 1 Lloyd's Rep 203.

56 *The Aegis Blaze* [1986] 1 Lloyd's Rep 203 at 209–210.

present action because it had been party to the earlier action and the documents were relevant to both actions.[57]

[3.19] The principle was extended in *Quinlivan v Tuohy*[58] to a scenario in which the nexus in terms of subject matter between the two proceedings was more remote. The plaintiff sought damages for personal injuries arising out of a road traffic accident. The plaintiff had suffered similar injuries in a previous road traffic accident that had been the subject of separate proceedings. The defendants in the present proceedings sought discovery of two medical reports prepared in anticipation of the earlier proceedings. The medical reports were relevant to the later proceedings in so far as they held the promise of shedding light on the plaintiff's medical condition at the time of the second accident. It was clear that the plaintiff had been entitled to assert privilege over the reports in the context of the earlier proceedings. Barron J held that the reports remained privileged for the purpose of the later proceedings.[59]

[3.20] In reaching this conclusion in *Quinlivan*, Barron J relied on both *Bord na Mona v Sisk*[60] and *The Aegis Blaze*,[61] although arguably the court's approach was more liberal than these and other authorities would support. Writing shortly after the decision in *Quinlivan*, Conlon argued that in cases of this kind the protection afforded to medical reports by legal professional privilege should not be allowed to subsist beyond the particular litigation for which they were prepared.[62] This change, he contended, would bring about greater fairness, openness and equality in the conduct of proceedings.[63] This immediate issue has been overtaken to a limited extent by changes in the discovery rules designed to promote greater transparency and expedition in the use of medical reports in personal injuries actions.[64] Nevertheless, the wisdom of extending litigation privilege beyond the immediate proceedings or closely related actions remains debatable, particularly given the inherent differences between this strand of privilege and its legal advice counterpart.[65]

---

57 *Bord na Mona v Sisk* [1990] 1 IR 85.

58 *Quinlivan v Tuohy* (29 July 1992, unreported) HC (Barron J).

59 *Quinlivan v Tuohy* (29 July 1992, unreported) HC (Barron J) at p 4.

60 *Bord na Mona v Sisk* [1990] I R 85.

61 *The Aegis Blaze* [1986] 1 Lloyds Rep 203.

62 Conlon, 'Once Privileged, Always Privileged: *Quinlivan v Tuohy*' (1995) ILT 56 at 57.

63 Conlon, 'Once Privileged, Always Privileged: *Quinlivan v Tuohy*' (1995) ILT 56 at 58 (quoting Jacob, *The Fabric of English Civil Justice* (1987) at p 94).

64 Rules of the Superior Courts (Disclosure of Reports and Statements) 1988 (SI 391/1998). See **Ch 8**. For similar provisions in the commercial law context see Rules of the Superior Courts (Commercial Proceedings) 2004 (SI 2/2004); Rules of the Superior Courts (Competition Proceedings) 2005 (SI 130/2005).

65 See, eg, McGrath, *Evidence* (Thomson Round Hall, 2005) at para.10.89 (concluding that 'litigation privilege should only apply to communications in the proceedings for which they came into being unless the identity of the parties and the subject matter of the proceedings are the same'). (contd.../)

SCOPE OF THE INFORMATION PROTECTED

[3.21] Litigation privilege covers a very broad range of information gathered, prepared or communicated under the shadow of litigation.[66] It protects communications between the client and her legal team (solicitors and barristers) and communications between members of the legal team.[67] Privilege also attaches to information compiled by a legal professional in connection with legal proceedings, known colloquially as the lawyer's 'work product'.

Third Parties

[3.22] Communicating with third parties is an important aspect of preparing for and conducting trial proceedings. The need for solicitors to obtain information relating to pending or anticipated litigation was recognised by the common law courts in the nineteenth century. In *Anderson v Bank of British Columbia*, Jessel MR stated:

> '... the solicitor's acts must be protected for the use of the client. The solicitor requires further information, and says, I will obtain it from a third person. That is confidential. It is obtained by him as solicitor for the purpose of the litigation, and it must be protected upon the same ground, otherwise it would be dangerous, if not impossible, to employ a solicitor. You cannot ask him what the information he obtained was. It may be information simply for the purpose of knowing whether he ought to defend or prosecute the action, but it may be also obtained in the shape of collecting evidence for the purpose of such prosecution or defence. All that, therefore, is privileged.'[68]

Where a party intends to call a witness to testify at trial, the existence and identity of the witness must be disclosed but other information pertaining to the witness and her testimony will be protected by privilege,[69] subject to any disclosure obligations imposed on a party by the relevant rules of court.[70]

---

65 (\...contd) But see *Croke v Waterford Crystal Ltd* [2009] IEHC 158 (31 March 2009) (Birmingham J). The Canadian Supreme Court has held that litigation privilege does not endure beyond the proceedings in which it was formed and any related proceedings: *Blank v Canada (Minister of Justice)* [2006] 2 SCR 319. See Ives and Pitel, 'Filling in the blanks for litigation privilege: *Blank v Canada (Minister of Justice)*' (2007) 11 Int'l J Evid & Proof 49; Goudkamp, 'Litigation privilege: transient or timeless? *Blank v Canada (Minister of Justice)*' (2007) 11 Int'l J Evid & Proof 322.

66 *Three Rivers District Council v Governor and Company of the Bank of England (No 6)* [2004] 3 WLR 1274 at 1297, [2005] 1 AC 610 at 660. See generally, Thanki (ed), *The Law of Privilege* (Oxford University Press, 2006) para 3.11 *et seq*.

67 In *McMullen v Clancy* (3 November 1999, unreported) HC, McGuinness J made an *obiter dicta* comment at p 3 to the effect that she had had read just one document in a 'booklet of documents which appeared on the face of it to be a Brief to Counsel' because, *inter alia*, she considered the remaining documents to be covered by legal professional privilege.

68 *Anderson v Bank of British Columbia* (1876) 2 Ch D 644 at 649–650.

69 *R (Kelly) v Warley Magistrates' Court* [2008] 1 WLR 2001.

70 See **Chs 7** and **9**. See generally Passmore, *Privilege* (2nd edn, xpl publishing, 2006) para 3.177 *et seq*.

[3.23] Traditionally, litigation privilege played an important role in protecting from disclosure consultations between lawyers and experts in the preparation and conduct of legal proceedings.[71] Changes in the rules of court governing discovery in civil proceedings[72] and statutory and case law developments in relation to disclosure in criminal proceedings[73] have narrowed the scope of privilege in this regard. A party must disclose the identity of any expert witnesses whom she intends to call to give evidence and in some instances the documents on which the expert's opinion will be based. In certain types of proceedings, such as personal injuries actions, the party must exchange expert reports with the other parties in advance of trial.[74] These restrictions do not apply to an expert whom the party engages in a purely advisory capacity and whose opinions will not be presented as evidence at trial.[75] In other situations, the practical protection afforded by privilege is limited to consultations between the client or more typically her lawyers and the expert witness.[76]

Pre-Existing Documents

[3.24] Litigation is characterised by voluminous documentation gathered, procured and produced in connection with the preparation of a claim or response thereto. Almost invariably questions arise from time to time over the nature and range of documentation that is cloaked within the folds of privilege. Documents *prepared* by the client in connection with anticipated litigation or for the purpose of obtaining legal advice are protected.[77] Similarly, privilege extends to documents *created* or *procured* by the lawyer in preparation for litigation. But what is the position in relation to documents that came into existence before

---

71 See generally Pattenden, 'Litigation privilege and expert opinion evidence' (2000) 4 In't J Evid & Proof 213; Passmore, *Privilege* (2nd edn, xpl publishing, 2006) para 3.109 *et seq;* Thanki (ed), *The Law of Privilege* (Oxford University Press, 2006) para 3.97 *et seq.*

72 See **Chs 7** and **8**.

73 See **Ch 9**.

74 See **Ch 8**.

75 *Fyffes plc v DCC plc* [2005] 1 IR 59. The English Civil Procedure Rules, Part 35, have formalised this distinction between so-called adversarial experts and advisory experts.

76 In *Smith v Jones* [1999] 1 SCR 455, the Canadian Supreme Court held that the lawyer-client privilege can be set aside in favour of a compelling public interest. Specifically, the court recognised the entitlement of a psychiatrist, who had conducted an assessment of a criminal defendant in preparation for sentencing, to disclose his report to the police and prosecution where he had formed the view that the individual was a threat to public safety and the defence had decided not to use the report in the sentencing proceedings. See Sheldrick, 'Administering public safety: solicitor-client privilege, medical experts and the adversarial process: *Smith v Jones*' (2000) 4 Int'l J Evid & Proof 119.

77 *Re Murray Consultants Ltd (formerly Sage Consultants Ltd) and Nocrumb Ltd (formerly Murray Consultants Ltd), Horgan v Murray and Milton* [1999] 1 ILRM 257. O'Sullivan J stated that if any doubt existed as to whether a document had been prepared for the purpose of taking legal advice, then he would read the document himself and make a specific ruling in relation to it.

litigation was a prospect and that come into the hands of the lawyer from either the client or some other source?

[3.25] In general, privilege does not attach to pre-existing documents, ie, documents created for some purpose other than litigation.[78] This principle was discussed by the English Court of Appeal in *Ventouris v Mountain*[79] which arose out of a dispute over discovery during the course of an action for recovery under a marine insurance policy. The defendant, as representative of the underwriters, asserted privilege over documents that had been in existence before the litigation and that his solicitor had acquired for use in the proceedings. The defendant rested his entitlement on the premise that privilege covers *any* original document obtained by a party for the purposes of the litigation regardless of when the document came into existence or the purpose for which it was created. The Court of Appeal, however, eschewed such a broad construction of litigation privilege. Bingham LJ reasoned that whereas the courts must not encroach on the rights of a litigant to procure legal advice and prepare properly for trial, it was hard to see how these rights were threatened if a party was obliged to produce an original pre-existing document that she had obtained from a third party – after all, the third party could herself be compelled to produce the document at trial.[80]

[3.26] The fact that a pre-existing document is obtained by the client or lawyer and then used in connection with litigation does not lend it the veneer of a contemporaneous preparation for trial that would attract privilege. Thus, the English courts have held that a document sent by a client to a solicitor or sent by a solicitor to a third party 'enjoys no greater protection in the hands of the solicitor or third party than it had in the hands of the client'.[81]

Copies and Verbatim Records

[3.27] Questions arise from time to time about the status of records or copies of documents for the purposes of privilege. In *Tromso Sparebank v Beirne*,[82] Costello J applied the general principle governing pre-existing documents to copies of same. The plaintiff Norwegian bank instituted proceedings to recover damages arising out of the defendants' failure to honour promissory notes issued to one of the bank's customers. The claim involved allegations of fraud and/or negligent misrepresentation on the part of the fourth defendant, the Northern Bank Ltd. The latter sought discovery of various materials including

---

78 See McGrath, *Evidence* (Thomson Round Hall, 2005) para 10.20; Passmore, *Privilege* (2nd edn, xpl publishing, 2006) ch 5.

79 *Ventouris v Mountain* [1991] 1 WLR 607.

80 *Ventouris v Mountain* [1991] 1 WLR 607 at 612.

81 Keane, *The Modern Law of Evidence* (7th edn, Oxford University Press, 2008) at 620 (discussing *R v Justice of the Peace for Peterborouogh, ex p Hicks* [1977] 1 WLR 1371 and *R v King* [1983] 1 WLR 411).

82 *Tromso Sparebank v Beirne* [1989] ILRM 257.

copies of documents that the plaintiff had obtained from its customer for the purpose of supplying them to its legal advisers in connection with the proceedings. Noting that there had been some conflict in the governing English authorities, Costello J concluded that privilege should not lie:

> 'I see no reason why legal professional privilege should apply to the copy documents with which this case is concerned. Legal professional privilege primarily exists so that a litigant can have recourse to his legal advisers in circumstances which enable him to have complete confidence that the communications made to him and from him will be kept secret. It is well established that this privilege extends to documents which come into existence after litigation is commenced, either for the purpose of obtaining or giving legal advice. But I cannot see that the protection of the interests of a litigant requires the privilege to be extended to copies of documents which came into existence prior to the contemplation of litigation, documents which are themselves not privileged and which the other side could probably inspect as a result of a third party discovery and which they could have produced at the trial pursuant to a *subpoena duces tecum*.'[83]

In contrast, letters between the plaintiff bank and its legal advisers, which came into existence for the very purpose of advising the plaintiff bank in relation to the subject of the litigation, were privileged even though litigation had not been contemplated at the time.[84]

[3.28] As Costello J acknowledged in *Tromso Sparebank*, the English case law on copy documents was inconsistent, for a time, the waters surrounding the principle that pre-existing documents are not privileged being muddied by fine distinctions based on the authorship of the copies. In a series of cases, the English courts grappled with the issue of whether privilege vests in copies of pre-existing documents where the copies have been made by solicitors.[85] The prevailing view, it seems, is that 'if a document is not privileged when a party receives it, a copy of the document does not become so because a solicitor makes the copy for litigious purposes'.[86] To this has been added the limited gloss that very exceptionally where a selection of unprivileged documents in the hands of a third party has been assembled and copied by a solicitor, the copies may be privileged if and in so far as they convey the trend of the solicitor's advice to her client.[87]

---

[83] *Tromso Sparebank v Beirne* [1989] ILRM 257 at 261–262 (internal citation omitted).

[84] *Tromso Sparebank v Beirne* [1989] ILRM 257 at 262. See also *Dunnes Stores Ltd v Smyth* (24 July 1995, unreported) HC (Costello P).

[85] See, eg, *Buttes Gas and Oil Co v Hammer (No 3)* [1981] QB 223; *Dubai Bank Ltd v Galadari* [1990] Ch 98; Zuckerman, 'Legal Professional Privilege and the Ascertainment of Truth' (1990) 53(3) MLR 381. But see also *O'Sullivan v Herdmans Ltd* [1986] NI 214.

[86] *Ventouris v Mountain* [1991] 1 WLR 607 at 619 (*per* Bingham LJ).

[87] *Sumitomo Corpn v Credit Lyonnais Rouse Ltd* [2002] 1 WLR 479, 494–498 (recognising this limited exception derived from *Lyell v Kennedy (No 3)* (1884) 27 Ch D 1 but declining to apply it in the instant case).

[3.29] The status of records of communications was considered by Finlay Geoghegan J in *Woori Bank & Hanvit LSP Finance Ltd v KDB Ireland Ltd*:[88]

> 'It appears to me that it is necessary to distinguish a document which is a verbatim record (either in electronic or typewritten format) of a communication between a party to litigation and a third party from a document which has been prepared by or on behalf of the plaintiff for the purpose of litigation. Whilst it might be said that the only reason for which the particular communications have been recorded is that litigation is contemplated, it does not appear to me that this means that the recording should be treated as a document created for the purposes of litigation and to which the dominant purpose test ... is applied'.[89]

Thus, the record does not constitute an independent communication for purposes of privilege and is protected only in so far as the communication it records is itself privileged.[90] The learned judge went on to hold that privilege did not attach to transcripts of non-confidential telephone conversations between employees or agents of the plaintiff Woori Bank and third parties.

[3.30] The same approach governs translations of documents. In *Sumitomo Corpn v Credit Lyonnais Rouse Ltd*,[91] the English Court of Appeal held that for the purposes of privilege there is no principled distinction between a translation of an unprivileged document in the control of a party claiming privilege and a copy of such a document. Parker LJ said of copies and translations alike:

> 'Each derives solely from the original document, and each is directed at reproducing the sense of, and the information contained in, the original document as exactly and precisely as is reasonably practicable. Neither the process of copying nor the process of translation involves the addition of anything to or the subtraction of anything from the sense of the original document or the information contained in it. In particular, neither process in itself introduces any element of confidentiality which does not or did not exist in the original document. The fact that, unlike a copy, a translation is not a 'replica' of the original document ... does not seem to us to be a relevant distinction for present purposes'.[92]

---

88 *Woori Bank & Hanvit LSP Finance Ltd v KDB Ireland Ltd* [2005] IEHC 451 (21 December 2005).

89 *Woori Bank & Hanvit LSP Finance Ltd v KDB Ireland Ltd* [2005] IEHC 451 (21 December 2005) at 20.

90 *Woori Bank & Hanvit LSP Finance Ltd v KDB Ireland Ltd* [2005] IEHC 451 (21 December 2005) pp 20–21 (relying on *Telebooth Pty Ltd v Telstra Corporation Ltd* [1994] 1 BR 337 and *MFW v PW* [2001] 3 IR 462). In *Buckley v Bough* (2 July 2001, unreported) HC (Morris J), legal professional privilege was held not to attach to a transcript of a hearing before a medical fitness to practice committee.

91 *Sumitomo Corpn v Credit Lyonnais Rouse Ltd* [2002] 1 WLR 479.

92 *Sumitomo Corpn v Credit Lyonnais Rouse Ltd* [2002] 1 WLR 479 at 491.

Information Exchanged with an Adverse Party

[3.31] At various stages during the trial process, the opposing parties are required to communicate with each other and exchange information. The bulk of these duties arises during the course of discovery in civil proceedings and disclosure in criminal proceedings and is the subject of a panoply of procedural rules. An issue relating to privilege typically arises where one party seeks disclosure of an item of evidence in another party's possession or control and the other party resists on the ground that the evidence is protected by a particular privilege.

[3.32] Common sense suggests that privilege should not extend to information exchanged with an opposing party; were this not so, the very rationale for protecting the information from disclosure would be turned on its head. Privilege serves the function of enabling the client and her lawyer to keep their pre-trial preparations secret from any adverse party. But where the information has been provided by the adverse party herself, the underlying purpose is clearly defeated. As Hutton LCJ observed in *McKay v McKay*, 'there is no need to keep the information secret from the opposing party because he already knows of it'.[93]

[3.33] The principle is not watertight, however, and its application may depend upon whether the adverse party was the original source of the information. In *McKay v McKay*, for example, the respondent's claim of privilege lacked traction because the very information had emanated from the appellant. The plaintiff sought damages for personal injuries sustained while he was unloading hay, in the course of his employment, from a vehicle under the management and control of the appellant. The appellant was insured by the third party respondent and, during the course of the proceedings, sought discovery of statements he had made to the respondent's inspectors together with the inspector's report. As noted above, the Court of Appeal held that privilege cannot apply where the adverse party has herself supplied the information and is therefore aware of it. The court was satisfied that, in the present case, the respondent had not asserted privilege with a view to keeping the statements secret from the appellant but rather for the tactical purpose of being equipped to undermine the appellant's evidence in the event that it deviated from the previous statements in any material way.

[3.34] In contrast, courts have taken a more benign view of claims of privilege in cases where a party has inadvertently disclosed protected information to an adverse party. Notwithstanding the reality that the adverse party has had sight of privileged information and is therefore aware of its content, the privilege holder

[93] *McKay v McKay* [1988] NI 611 at 617.

may seek to prevent the adverse party from making use of that information in the proceedings.[94]

[3.35] The decision in *McKay* hints at a judicial concern that privilege should not be a means by which a party gains an unfair advantage at trial. *Tobakin v Dublin Southern Districts Tramways Co*, decided several decades earlier, illustrates the point.[95] The plaintiff, who was a marksman, brought an action seeking damages for injuries sustained in an accident which he attributed to the negligence of the defendants. In the wake of the accident, an agent of the defendants procured a statement from the defendant about the cause of the accident which the agent reduced to writing and the plaintiff signed. In a passage resonant of the imperative of safeguarding fair procedures, Gibson J rejected the suggestion that the document was exempt from discovery:

> 'Are the defendants at liberty to say that they will not allow the plaintiff to see this document so signed, on the ground that it is a privileged communication which they got from him for the purposes of litigation? Stated in that bald form the proposition is repugnant to common sense. ... My view of the question is that the plaintiff has got an interest in the paper as well as the defendants. He is to be bound by it; and if he is not to see it, he may be taken by surprise at the trial. This document, to which they have bound him by his signature, is one in which he has got an interest: it is his document so far as his signature is attached to it.
>
> The defendants cannot claim exemption from discovery simply by stating that they extracted it from the plaintiff for the purposes of their own defence.'[96]

[3.36] Particular difficulties can arise where information is exchanged with an adverse party with a view to the settlement of an action. This issue is typically addressed under the rubric of without prejudice privilege. Occasionally, however, settlement is classified as a facet of the broader purpose of litigation and, specifically, as an effort to avoid litigation by dent of compromise. In *Re Murray Consultants Ltd and Nocrumb Ltd: Horgan v Murray*,[97] the High Court was asked to adjudicate on a number of claims of privilege raised during discovery in the context of a shareholder's claim of corporate oppression under s 205 of the Companies Act 1963. One such claim related to documents concerning the value of shares which the petitioner obtained during the course of settlement negotiations; another related to a document drafted by the petitioner during settlement negotiations with the intention of handing it over to the respondents. O'Sullivan J recognised privilege on both counts. Noting that there was no clear authority on point, he reasoned that the first documents were privileged in principle because 'the policy of the courts is to encourage

---

94 *Shell E & P Ireland Ltd v McGrath (No 2)* [2007] 2 IR 574; *Guinness Peat Properties Ltd v Fitzroy Robinson* [1987] 1 WLR 1027. See **Ch 6**.

95 *Tobakin v Dublin Southern Districts Tramways Co* [1905] 2 IR 58.

96 *Tobakin v Dublin Southern Districts Tramways Co* [1905] 2 IR 58 at 60–61.

97 *Re Murray Consultants Ltd and Nocrumb Ltd: Horgan v Murray* [1999] ILRM 257.

settlement' and 'the purposes of litigation include attempting to compromise it'.[98] In relation to the second claim, O'Sullivan J was satisfied that a party who intended to hand over a document at the time of drafting was entitled to change her mind in the event that the settlement negotiations 'went sour'. Again, the underlying rationale was that the document came into existence for a general litigious purpose, namely, the specific objective of settling the action.[99]

Lawyer's Notes

[3.37] There was some authority at common law for the proposition that a lawyer's shorthand notes of proceedings in an action were privileged in that suit and, indeed, any subsequent suit arising out of the same subject matter.[100] The stance was later reversed in favour of the proposition that a transcript of proceedings held in public and any copy thereof cannot be privileged regardless of the fact that these documents may have been procured in anticipation of future litigation.[101]

[3.38] In *MFM v PW*,[102] the High Court affirmed that transcripts or solicitors' notes of proceedings and evidence are a matter of record and not privileged in the action in which they are taken or any subsequent action.[103] However, the position was less clear-cut where the notes combined a record of proceedings and/or evidence with entries made by the solicitor for the purpose of litigation. Finnegan J took the view that the notes are privileged in so far as they contain material designed to assist the client in the prosecution of the action.[104] In giving effect to these principles, the traditional practice of the courts has been to allow production of the notes with the privileged parts covered up.[105] Hence, the learned judge directed partial disclosure of the note at issue in the proceedings and indicated that he would examine the note with a view to determining the extent to which it should be covered up.[106]

---

98 *Re Murray Consultants Ltd and Nocrumb Ltd: Horgan v Murray* [1999] ILRM 257 at 260.

99 *Re Murray Consultants Ltd and Nocrumb Ltd: Horgan v Murray* [1999] ILRM 257 at 260. O'Sullivan J concluded that notes made by the petitioner himself for the purpose of taking legal advice in the proceedings fell 'unambiguously' within the protection of privilege. [1999] ILRM 257 at 261.

100 *Nordon v Defries* (1882) 8 QBD 508.

101 *Lambert v Home* [1914] 3 KB 86.

102 *MFM v PW* [2001] 3 IR 462.

103 *MFM v PW* [2001] 3 IR 462 at 467.

104 *MFM v PW* [2001] 3 IR 462 at 467.

105 *MFM v PW* [2001] 3 IR 462 at 466–467.

106 *MFM v PW* [2001] 3 IR 462 at 467–468.

CONDITIONS SURROUNDING LITIGATION PRIVILEGE

[3.39] Given the potentially broad application of litigation privilege, the law imposes two restrictions both of which relate to the relationship between the litigation and the item of evidence over which privilege is asserted. The first restriction is temporal: the proceedings must have been reasonably apprehended, if not actually underway, at the time the evidence was created or procured.[107] The second restriction pertains to the motivation behind the decision to create or procure the material over which privilege is sought: preparation for litigation must have been the dominant underlying purpose.[108] These conditions which qualify litigation privilege are discussed in detail below.

THE PROXIMITY OF LITIGATION

[3.40] Litigation privilege is broader than legal advice privilege in terms of its substantive scope: it is not limited to communications but covers a wide range of other information. Nevertheless, in terms of its temporal reach, litigation privilege is more limited than legal advice privilege because it presupposes a tangible link to litigation.[109]

The privilege clearly applies where legal proceedings have formally commenced.[110] Beyond this, however, the courts have failed to devise a precise formula for defining the point at which privilege comes into play. The traditional authorities seemed to suggest that, if not actually commenced, litigation had to be objectively certain or at least very probable.[111] However, in *Wheeler v Le Marchant*, some of the Lords were satisfied that the privilege could be predicated on a more subjective yardstick, namely, that litigation was contemplated.[112]

---

[107] *Silver Hill Duckling Ltd v Minister for Agriculture* [1987] IR 289; *M'Mahon v Gt Northern Ry Co* (1906) 40 ILTR 172.

[108] *Gallagher v Stanley* [1998] 2 IR 267; *M'Mahon v Gt Northern Ry Co* (1906) 40 ILTR 172.

[109] See generally, Passmore, *Privilege* (2nd edn, xpl publishing, 2006) para 3.064 *et seq*; Thanki (ed), *The Law of Privilege* (Oxford University Press, 2006) para 3.47 *et seq*.

[110] *Wheeler v Le Marchant* (1881) 17 ChD 675 at 681 (*per* Jessel MR); *M'Mahon v Great Northern Railway Co* (1906) 40 ILTR 172; *Gamble v Garda Síochána Complaints Board* [2004] IEHC 364 (17 November 2004) at p 1 (*per* Finnegan J): 'In relation to the two documents in respect of which privilege is claimed ... each post dates the institution of these proceedings and came into existence with a view to defending same. They are entitled to legal professional privilege.'

[111] *Fenner v London & South Eastern Railway Co* (1872) LR 7 QB 767; *Collins v London General Omnibus Co* (1893) 68 LTNS 831; *Rushbrooke v O'Sullivan* [1926] IR 500.

[112] *Wheeler v Le Marchant* (1881) 17 Ch D 675 at 683 and 685 (*per* Brett LJ and Cotton LJ, respectively). See also *Kerry County Council v Liverpool Salvage Association* (1903) 38 ILTR 7.

[3.41] In modern times, the English courts have applied the general test of whether objectively speaking the litigation was reasonably proximate at the time the information was created or procured.[113] An example is *Crompton Business Machines Ltd v Customs and Excise Commissioners (No 2)*,[114] in which Viscount Dilhorne stated that 'legal professional privilege cannot be claimed for documents which come into existence prior to the date when litigation can reasonably be anticipated'.[115] In that case, the defendant commissioners asserted privilege over investigations of the plaintiffs' financial affairs on the ground that they had been prepared in anticipation of arbitration. The plaintiffs contended that arbitration could not have been reasonably anticipated at the time the investigations were conducted because the parties were statutorily obliged to complete a negotiation process prior to recourse to arbitration. The House of Lords took the view that ordinarily arbitration could not be regarded as apprehended or threatened until the commissioners had made their assessment and put it formally to the taxpayer as a preliminary step en route to arbitration. However, the Lords upheld the claim of privilege in this particular case because the plaintiffs had made clear from the outset that they were seeking to have the matter referred to arbitration. The plaintiffs had written, challenging the rate of the annual purchase tax and requesting that the letter be treated as a request for arbitration. On receipt of the letter, the commissioners were entitled 'reasonably to anticipate litigation'.[116]

[3.42] This standard for determining the necessary connection between the gathering of information and the application of litigation privilege has influenced the reasoning of the Irish courts. An early case is *M'Mahon v Gt Northern Ry Co*.[117] The plaintiff, a servant of the defendant company, brought an action in relation to injuries he sustained when his foot was caught by an unprotected points rod. He brought a motion for liberty to inspect certain reports that had been compiled by porters employed by the defendant and that contained notes of evidence collected from onlookers. An issue before the court was whether the reports were privileged given that they had been compiled before the defendant had been notified by the plaintiff of threatened legal proceedings. Palles LBC was satisfied that the assertion of privilege would have been 'plainly

[113] Keane, *The Modern Law of Evidence* (7th edn, Oxford University Press, 2008) at p 615, states: 'The test is whether litigation was reasonably in prospect, which will not be satisfied if there is only a possibility of litigation, even if a distinct possibility, or a general apprehension of future litigation'.

[114] *Crompton Business Machines Ltd v Customs and Excise Commissioners (No 2)* [1974] AC 405.

[115] *Crompton Business Machines Ltd v Customs and Excise Commissioners (No 2)* [1974] AC 405 at 421.

[116] *Crompton Business Machines Ltd v Customs and Excise Commissioners (No 2)* [1974] AC 405 at 421. See also *United States of America v Philip Morris Inc and Others* [2004] EWCA Civ 330.

[117] *M'Mahon v Gt Northern Ry Co* (1906) 40 ILTR 172.

sufficient' if litigation had actually been commenced and that legal authority supported the application of the same principle where, as here, there was 'a reasonable anticipation of future litigation'.[118]

[3.43] In *Silver Hill Duckling Ltd v Minister for Agriculture*,[119] the plaintiffs sued the Minister for compensation for the slaughter of their flock of ducks in the wake of an outbreak of bird flu. The Minister refused discovery of a number of documents on the ground that they had been generated by lawyers for the purpose of advising him and his officers in relation to a possible claim by the plaintiffs. O'Hanlon J stated:

> 'Having considered the relevant authorities, I am of the opinion that once litigation is apprehended or threatened, a party to such litigation is entitled to prepare his case, whether by means of communications passing between him and his legal advisers, or by means of communications passing between him and third parties, and to do so under the cloak of privilege.'[120]

O'Hanlon J cited the decision of the House of Lords in *Crompton Amusement Machines Ltd*[121] but indicated nevertheless that he would have been more inclined to favour the stance adopted by the Court of Appeal:

> '... that once it was apparent to both sides that they were not going to reach agreement and that the ultimate recourse to arbitration was well-nigh inevitable, then a situation had arisen where litigation between the parties could fairly be regarded as apprehended or threatened.'[122]

In *Silver Hill Duckling Ltd*, the point of inevitability was reached when it became clear that the disparity between the amount of compensation the plaintiff was seeking and the amount the Minister was offering was so wide that the claim could only be resolved by litigation.[123]

[3.44] The standard of 'well-nigh' inevitability represents a potentially significant qualification of the concept of 'reasonable anticipation' elucidated in *Alfred Crompton Amusement Machines Ltd*. However, O'Hanlon J did not appear to be offering the 'well-nigh' inevitability standard as an alternative or substitute for the 'reasonable anticipation' yardstick. The general standard set by the learned judge for the application of litigation privilege was whether litigation was apprehended or threatened; a situation in which recourse to litigation is well-nigh inevitable was seemingly cited as a specific instance in which the standard was met. This interpretation of the judgment is supported by

118 *M'Mahon v Gt Northern Ry Co* (1906) 40 ILTR 172 at 173.

119 *Silver Hill Duckling Ltd v Minister for Agriculture* [1987] IR 289.

120 *Silver Hill Duckling Ltd v Minister for Agriculture* [1987] IR 289 at 292.

121 *Crompton Amusement Machines Ltd v Customs and Excise Commissioners (No 2)* [1974] AC 405.

122 *Silver Hill Duckling Ltd v Minister for Agriculture* [1987] IR 289 at 292.

123 *Silver Hill Duckling Ltd v Minister for Agriculture* [1987] IR 289 at 292.

a common sense reading of the relevant terms: whereas there are situations in which litigation is apprehended or threatened but not necessarily inevitable, the converse does not hold true.

[3.45] The uncertainty generated by the 'well-nigh' standard in *Silver Hill Duckling* persisted in a second case on point, *PJ Carrigan Ltd v Norwich Union Fire Society Ltd,* decided by O'Hanlon J some five years later. Following the destruction of their premises by fire, the plaintiffs notified the defendants of their intention to submit an insurance claim. The defendants harboured doubts about the validity of the claim and commissioned a firm of loss adjustors to explore the likely cause of the fire. O'Hanlon J was satisfied that the report had been obtained in contemplation of litigation; even at that early stage in the processing of the claim, the defendants had in mind the possibility that they would repudiate liability under the policy and thereby force the plaintiffs to litigate their claims. Thus, the advice of the loss adjustors was sought not merely on the quantum of financial loss but also on the veracity of the claim itself.

The exceptional factual circumstances of the case – the suspicions harboured by the defendants from the outset – clearly influenced the result. Indeed, a plausible implication of O'Hanlon J's ruling is that the mere compiling of reports in connection with the routine processing of claims would not be privileged.

Although O'Hanlon J purported to apply *Silver Hill Duckling*, the threshold of apprehended or threatened litigation clearly fell far short of well-nigh inevitability in *PJ Carrigan*. The defendants were undoubtedly acting in contemplation of litigation but, at the same time, litigation was no more than a possibility at the time the report was commissioned.[124]

[3.46] The subsequent case of *Irish Press Publications Ltd v Minister for Enterprise*[125] lends grist to this mill. Carroll J rejected the suggestion that litigation privilege attached to a document that had been procured at a time when litigation was at most a possibility. In the wake of an investigation conducted by the Competition Authority into the newspaper industry, the plaintiffs sued the defendants for damages for libel, negligence and wrongful interference with their constitutional right to good name arising out of a statement made by the then Minister for Enterprise. The defendants asserted privilege over various documents including a note prepared by a civil servant for the Minister following publication of the Competition Authority's report. Carroll J held that the claim of privilege did not meet the *Silver Hill Duckling*

---

[124] Abrahamson, Dwyer and Fitzpatrick, *Discovery and Disclosure* (Thomson Round Hall, 2007) at para. 35.48, suggest that in this regard *PJ Carrigan Ltd v Norwich Union Fire Society Ltd* [1987] IR 618 should be regarded as confined to its facts.

[125] *Irish Press Publications Ltd v Minister for Enterprise* [2002] 4 IR 110.

test because litigation was mentioned in the document as only one possible option.[126]

[3.47] There is ample contemporary English authority supporting the proposition that a mere possibility of litigation is not sufficient to ground litigation privilege. For example, in *United States of America v Philip Morris Inc*,[127] the Court of Appeal rejected the suggestion that privilege would extend to information or communications gathered or exchanged in general apprehension of future litigation. The judgment of Brooke LJ embraces a 'real likelihood' of litigation as the appropriate standard while at the same time conceding that the issue of when litigation privilege comes into play is not susceptible to bright-line definition:

> 'In the present case it is quite clear that the judge correctly considered that a 'mere possibility' of litigation did not suffice. He was also correct to conclude that the fact that there was 'a distinct possibility that sooner or later someone might make a claim' was insufficient. So was 'a general apprehension of future litigation'. He repeated three times that the appropriate test was that litigation must have been reasonably in prospect. The expression 'real likelihood' seems to have been used as a counterpoise to 'a mere possibility', and I do not consider that any more can properly be read into this phrase. The judge was certainly not saying that there must have been a greater than 50% chance of litigation.'[128]

In Ireland, the holding in *Silver Hill Duckling Ltd* influenced the subsequent case of *Power City Ltd v Monahan*[129] in which the High Court considered again the issue of when litigation can be reasonably apprehended for the purposes of litigation privilege. The plaintiff's claim arose out of the alleged theft of a consignment of electronic/hi-fi equipment while in the custody of the defendants during transportation from the UK to Ireland. The defendants were notified on 6 October 1992 that the plaintiff was holding them fully liable for all losses arising out of the theft. The issue before the court was whether privilege attached to various documents which came into existence after that date. Kinlen J held that litigation privilege stretched back to 6 October 1992, the point at which the defendants were notified of the plaintiff's assertion of liability.[130]

[3.48] The Supreme Court has not had occasion to address squarely the issue of the proximity of litigation for purposes of privilege. In *Gallagher v Stanley,*

126 *Irish Press Publications Ltd v Minister for Enterprise* [2002] 4 IR 110 at 114.

127 *United States of America v Philip Morris Inc* [2004] EWCA Civ 220.

128 *United States of America v Philip Morris Inc* [2004] EWCA Civ 220 at para 68 (Chadwick and Scott Baker LJJ concurring).

129 *Power City Ltd v Monahan* (14 October 1996, unreported) HC (Kinlen J).

130 *Power City Ltd v Monahan* (14 October 1996, unreported) HC (Kinlen J) at p 9. Dee, *Discovery* (2004) at para 6.04, infers from the judgment that notification marked the point at which 'the judge felt that matters were in issue between the parties'.

O'Flaherty J considered it 'essential' that litigation should be 'reasonably apprehended at the least' before a claim of privilege can be upheld.[131]

The Underlying Purpose: The Dominant Purpose Test

[3.49] Litigation privilege protects from disclosure information generated for the specific purpose of conducting legal proceedings. Given its underlying rationale, the privilege is not designed to protect information that was generated for some other purpose but that may have the incidental effect of assisting preparations for litigation. Courts across the common law world have grappled with the vexed question of when the procuring of information is sufficiently closely connected to litigation to justify the application of privilege. For example, a report compiled in the aftermath of an accident at a place of work may be used by the employer's lawyers when defending a legal claim brought by an injured employee. But can the report be said to have been prepared in connection with litigation if it also serves other purposes, such as fulfilling the employer's statutory obligation to notify a government authority of work-related accidents or assisting the employer in improving company policy on accident prevention? As Palles LCB stated in *M'Mahon v Gt Northern Ry Co*, 'the governing motive is what regulates the question whether a particular document is privileged'.[132]

[3.50] The prevailing approach, known as the dominant purpose test;[133] was adopted by the House of Lords in the landmark case of *Waugh v British Railways Board.*[134] The plaintiff's suit arose out of the death of her husband, a British Rail employee who had been killed in an accident at work. During the course of discovery, the plaintiff sought the disclosure of an accident report that had been drawn up by the defendant two days after the accident. The House of Lords held that privilege could not attach unless the dominant purpose for which a report of this kind had been prepared was its submission to a legal adviser for use in anticipated or pending litigation. Lord Wilberforce was particularly influenced by the evidential value of the report:

> 'It is clear that the due administration of justice strongly requires disclosure and production of this report: it was contemporary; it contained statements by witnesses on the spot; it would be not merely relevant evidence, but almost certainly the best evidence as to the cause of the accident.'[135]

---

[131] *Gallagher v Stanley* [1998] 2 IR 267 at 272.

[132] *M'Mahon v Gt Northern Ry Co* (1906) 40 ILTR 172 at 173 (citing *Collins v London General Omnibus Co*, 68 LT 831 and *Woolley v North London Ry Co*, LR 4 CP 604).

[133] See generally, Passmore, *Privilege* (2nd edn, xpl publishing, 2006) para 3.025 *et seq;* Thanki (ed), *The Law of Privilege* (Oxford University Press, 2006) para 3.68 *et seq*.

[134] *Waugh v British Railways Board* [1980] AC 521.

[135] *Waugh v British Railways Board* [1980] AC 521 at 531–532.

The dominant purpose test struck an appropriate balance between the need to furnish the court with this sort of relevant evidence and the need to allow the parties adequate freedom to prepare for trial. Lord Wilberforce continued:

> 'It appears to me that unless the purpose of the submission to the legal adviser in view of litigation is at least the dominant purpose for which the relevant document was prepared, the reasons which require privilege to be extended to it cannot apply. On the other hand to hold that the purpose ... must be the sole purpose would, apart from difficulties of proof, in my opinion, be too strict a requirement, and would confine the privilege too narrowly ...'[136]

Applying the test to the facts at hand, the Lords concluded that whereas litigation constituted one of the purposes for which this particular report was generated, it was not the dominant purpose. An equally important purpose was to inform British Rail of the cause of the accident so that steps could be taken to avoid a recurrence. As such, the report was not only relevant evidence but arguably the best evidence as to the cause of the accident.

[3.51] Subsequent case law has made plain that the onus of establishing that litigation was the sole or dominant purpose behind the creation of the document rests on the party asserting the privilege.[137]

The dominant purpose test fashioned in *Waugh* represented a departure from the traditional common law approach whereby the courts upheld claims of privilege where preparation for litigation was merely one of the purposes behind the creation of documents and, indeed, perhaps no more than a secondary purpose.[138] The test has been endorsed in several common law countries. In Australia, the traditional position was the diametric opposite of the English equivalent in so far as the courts favoured disclosure of documents unless apprehended litigation was the sole motivation behind their creation.[139] However, this stance has since given way to the more flexible standard of the dominant purpose.[140]

---

[136] *Waugh v British Railways Board* [1980] AC 521 at 533.

[137] See, eg, *Woori Bank & Hanvit LSP Finance Ltd v KDB Ireland Ltd* [2005] IEHC 451 (21 December 2005) (Finlay Geoghegan J); *Downey v Murray* [1988] NI 600.

[138] For subsequent application of the test see, eg, *Re Highgrade Traders Ltd* [1984] BCLC 151; *Price Waterhouse v BCCI Holdings (Luxembourg) SA* [1992] BCLC 583; *Hellenic Mutual risks Assoc'n (Bermuda) Ltd v Harrison: The 'Sagheera'* [1997] 1 Lloyd's Rep 160.

[139] *Grant v Downs* (1976) 135 CLR 674; *Southern Cross Airlines Holdings Ltd v Arthur Andersen & Co* [1999] FCA 786.

[140] *Esso Australia Resources Ltd v Commissioner of Taxation* (1999) 201 CLR 49. The dominant purpose test was embraced by the New Zealand courts in the 1980s. See, eg, *Guardian Royal Exchange Co v Stuart* [1985] 1 NZLR 596; *General Accident Fire & Life Assurance Corp Ltd v Elite Apparel Ltd* [1987] 1 NZLR 129; *Carlton Cranes Ltd v Consolidated Hotels Ltd* [1988] 2 NZLR 555.

The Dominant Purpose Test in Ireland

[3.52] The dominant purpose test was adopted by the High Court in *Silver Hill Duckling Ltd v Minister for Agriculture.*[141] Having determined that the defendants' entitlement to claim legal professional privilege arose at the point at which litigation could fairly be regarded by the defendants as apprehended or threatened,[142] O'Hanlon J turned to the issue of the scope of privilege. Referring to *Waugh v British Railways Board*, he concluded that the protection from disclosure could extend not only to communications passing between the Minister for Agriculture and his legal advisers but also to any documents that came into existence for the dominant purpose of preparing for litigation then apprehended or threatened.[143]

[3.53] The case of *PJ Carrigan Ltd v Norwich Union Fire Society Ltd*,[144] discussed above, originated in an insurance claim that the plaintiff policyholder sent to the defendant insurers after the plaintiff's premises had been destroyed by fire. The defendants were suspicious of the claim and commissioned a report from a firm of loss adjusters. In subsequent proceedings for the recovery of thc plaintiff's loss, the defendants asserted privilege over the report. Applying the test set down in *Waugh* and accepted in *Silver Hill Duckling*, O'Hanlon J assessed the situation thus:

> '... I am satisfied on the evidence which has been adduced on behalf of the defendants in this case that the possibility of repudiating liability under the policy was a very real factor in their thinking from the time the claim to be indemnified was made by the plaintiffs, and that when commissioning a report from [the firm of loss adjusters], they were concerned to obtain not merely an evaluation of the claim in terms of financial loss, but also whatever expert advice could be given as to the circumstances in which the fire broke out. They already viewed the claim with some suspicion and wished to know whether any evidence available at the scene of the fire suggested that their suspicions were well-founded. In other words, they were, even at that early stage, contemplating the possibility of a showdown with the plaintiffs, in which they, the defendants, might well decide to repudiate liability under the policy, and the plaintiffs in turn would then have to decide whether they were prepared to embark on litigation to enforce their claims under the policy.'[145]

O' Hanlon J concluded that while litigation was not threatened at the time the report was commissioned it was apprehended in the thinking of the defendants

---

[141] *Silver Hill Duckling Ltd v Minister for Agriculture* [1987] IR 289 (O'Hanlon J).

[142] *Silver Hill Duckling Ltd v Minister for Agriculture* [1987] IR 289 at 292–293. See para **3.43**.

[143] *Silver Hill Duckling Ltd v Minister for Agriculture* [1987] IR 289 at 294.

[144] *PJ Carrigan Ltd v Norwich Union Fire Society Ltd* [1987] IR 618.

[145] *PJ Carrigan Ltd v Norwich Union Fire Society Ltd* [1987] IR 618 at 620.

and that this apprehension constituted a dominant purpose in looking for the report. The document was thus privileged.[146]

[3.54] The application of the dominant purpose test to reports compiled in the wake of accidents was raised again in the High Court in *Davis v St Michael's House.*[147] The accident at issue in the proceedings arose when the plaintiff fell at the school at which she was a pupil and suffered an injury to her left femur. Lynch J recognised the entitlement of the defendants to assert privilege over an accident report, witness statements and other documents on the ground that the information in question had been prepared for the dominant purpose of use in litigation. Lynch J concluded that 'the only purpose of such statements and reports can be to ensure that there is an accurate record of what happened from as many persons who may know something about it as possible' so that in the event of a claim the parties and individuals concerned could be properly prepared.[148]

[3.55] The dominant purpose test was subsequently endorsed by the Supreme Court in *Gallagher v Stanley.*[149] The infant plaintiff brought proceedings against various defendants seeking damages for injuries allegedly suffered as a result of medical negligence at the time of his birth. During the course of discovery, the defendant hospital in which the plaintiff had been born asserted privilege over certain statements made to the matron by nurses on duty at the material time. The Supreme Court applied the dominant purpose test. Lynch J expressly adopted the reasoning in *Waugh.* He stated:

> 'People as often as not act from mixed motives or for a number of reasons, rather than one single motive or reason. Therefore to require that the sole reason for obtaining the statements the subject matter of this appeal should have been the anticipation or contemplation of litigation is to set too high a test before privilege can arise. The true test is that the anticipation and/or contemplation of litigation should have been the dominant motive or reason.'[150]

On the facts of the case, the Supreme Court rejected the hospital's contention that the statements had been requested by the matron on the morning after the birth with litigation in mind. O'Flaherty J stated:

> 'I find it impossible to hold that the sole purpose which motivated the matron in having the nurses provide these statements was in regard to possible litigation. I think that the matron would have had in the forefront of her considerations, as well as the possibility of litigation, that she should be in a position to account for

[146] *PJ Carrigan Ltd v Norwich Union Fire Society Ltd* [1987] IR 618 at 620.

[147] *Davis v St Michael's House* (25 November 1993, unreported) HC (Lynch J).

[148] *Davis v St Michael's House* (25 November 1993, unreported) HC at p 5. See also *Re Freedom of Information Act 1997 as amended; National Maternity Hospital v Information Commissioner* [2007] IEHC 113 (30 March 2007) (Quirke J).

[149] *Gallagher v Stanley* [1998] 2 IR 267.

[150] *Gallagher v Stanley* [1998] 2 IR 267 at 273–274.

> how the hospital was run, as far as her domain was concerned, and how the staff under her control had conducted themselves in regard to what must have been a quite traumatic occurrence on the night in question. As a matter of professional standards and decorum, as well as for the proper management and running of a hospital, it seems to me that a matron would, in such a situation as this, require this information. She would require of her nurses that they give a factual account of the course of events where there has been an untoward occurrence with serious consequences.'[151]

[3.56] The dominant purpose test was applied in a commercial context in *Woori Bank & Hanvit LSP Finance Ltd v KDB Ireland Ltd.*[152] The proceedings centred on a series of agreements concluded in October 2000 between the first plaintiff, a Korean bank, the second plaintiff, a company incorporated in Ireland, the defendant, an Irish company and provider of financial services, and others. The agreements permitted the defendant to make investments on behalf of the second plaintiff and, in July 2002, the defendant arranged for the second plaintiff to enter a loan agreement with a Japanese company, AEL Corporation. A dispute arose between the parties regarding the validity of that loan agreement and, more broadly, the extent of the plaintiffs' contractual and other rights.

[3.57] The defendant sought disclosure of three categories of documents over which the plaintiffs asserted legal professional privilege. The first category comprised redacted portions of two internal reports of Woori Bank that the plaintiffs contended had been created for the dominant purpose of the present litigation. The circumstances surrounding the transactions at issue in the proceedings had been investigated by the Board of Inspection and Audit (BAI) and the Financial Supervisory Service (FSS) in Korea. In relation to the first of the disputed documents, Finlay Geoghegan J held that the plaintiffs had failed to discharge their burden of establishing that, as a matter of probability, litigation was the dominant purpose behind its creation; while litigation had been contemplated, an 'equal purpose' was the creation of a report for management or corporate governance purposes of the Bank's position in relation to the BAI investigation and the AEL loan transaction.[153] A similar result was reached in relation to the second document. Here Finlay Geoghegan J held that at a minimum an equal purpose behind the creation of the document was the furnishing to FSS of information relating to the transactions at issue.[154]

---

151 *Gallagher v Stanley* [1998] 2 IR 267 at 272–273.

152 *Woori Bank & Hanvit LSP Finance Ltd v KDB Ireland Ltd* [2005] IEHC 451 (21 December 2005) (Finlay Geoghegan J).

153 *Woori Bank & Hanvit LSP Finance Ltd v KDB Ireland Ltd* [2005] IEHC 451 (21 December 2005) at p 11. The learned judge based her determination on two affidavits sworn by a representative of Woori Bank, as well as 'the file on which the document was placed and the nature of the document itself'.

154 *Woori Bank & Hanvit LSP Finance Ltd v KDB Ireland Ltd* [2005] IEHC 451 (21 December 2005) pp 11–12.

[3.58] In *Hansfield Developments & Others v Irish Asphalt Ltd & Others*,[155] the plaintiff builders brought proceedings against defendant providers of infill claiming that the defendants' product contained excessively high levels of pyrite that had caused defects in houses constructed by the plaintiffs. The defendants sought non-party discovery of certain documents in the possession of HomeBond, a national agency that operated a scheme designed to protect the rights of house purchasers. The documents comprised correspondence and written communications between the plaintiffs and HomeBond. McGovern J stated:

> 'Having read the documents, it seems to me that they are substantially concerned with how the pyrite issue should be addressed and investigated. Undoubtedly, they deal with issues such as how to address defects in houses arising out of this problem, but the communications are not specific to any litigation although they could be said to be of relevance to the apprehended claims.'[156]

The learned judge concluded that the documents were not created with the dominant purpose of preparing for litigation; if litigation was a purpose, it was secondary or equal to another purpose such as 'the working out between HomeBond and the plaintiffs as to how they should address and investigate the issue of pyrite involvement in the housing defects generally'.[157]

Intent

[3.59] It is interesting to note that when applying the dominant purpose test the courts consider the motivation of the person who sought or procured the information rather than that of the person who provided the information. Thus, in *Gallagher v Stanley*,[158] it was the motivation of the matron rather than the nurses that occupied the attention of the court. In fact, there is earlier Irish authority to the effect that the means by which the information comes to the attention of the solicitor is not significant provided that the motivation behind the gathering and communication of the information is its use in litigation. In *M'Mahon v Gt Northern Ry Co* (1906) 40 ILTR 172 at 173, Palles LCB observed that 'if that which is procured by the solicitor is privileged, it is equally privileged if volunteered to the solicitor for the purpose of being used as evidence'. In his view this showed that 'the governing motive is what regulates the question whether a particular document is privileged'.

---

155 *Hansfield Developments & Others v Irish Asphalt Ltd & Others* [2009] IEHC 90 (17 February 2009) (McGovern J).

156 *Hansfield Developments & Others v Irish Asphalt Ltd & Others* [2009] IEHC 90 (17 February 2009) at p 6.

157 *Hansfield Developments & Others v Irish Asphalt Ltd & Others* [2009] IEHC 90 (17 February 2009) at p 6. For additional examples of judicial application of the dominant purpose test see *Power City Ltd v Monahan Trading* (14 October 1996, unreported) HC (Kinlen J) p 9; *McKay v McKay* [1988] NI 611.

158 *Gallagher v Stanley* [1998] 2 IR 267.

[3.60] The approach in *Gallagher v Stanley* is consistent with the English case law. In *Guinness Peat Properties Ltd v Fitzroy Robinson Partnership*,[159] the Court of Appeal held that the dominant purpose of a communication had to be assessed objectively having regard not only to the intentions of the author but also to the motivation of the person who had procured the communication. At issue was the potential application of privilege to a letter and attachments that the defendant firm of architects had sent to their insurers relating to a claim by the plaintiff building developers. The defendants conceded that their purpose in sending the letter was to comply with a condition in the insurance policy which required immediate notification to the insurers of a claim of this kind. However, the Court of Appeal focused on the motivation of the insurers who had procured the communication through the requirement of immediate written notification of the claim. The court held that the letter and attachments were privileged because the intention of the insurers had been to gather the necessary documentation for submission to their lawyers for advice in relation to the claim.[160]

[3.61] The extract from O'Flaherty J's judgment in *Gallagher v Stanley* quoted above at para **3.55** indicates that the courts engage in an objective assessment of the motivation behind the preparation of the report or statement.[161] This aspect of the dominant purpose test has proved controversial. The trial court effectively second-guesses the motivation of the author or procurer of the report and possibly reaches an assessment that contradicts her stated intention. This conundrum has prompted the criticism that the dominant purpose test is 'strongly influenced by policy and lends itself to manipulation by the courts to achieve a desired result'.[162] The judicial enquiry is necessarily constrained by

[159] *Guinness Peat Properties Ltd v Fitzroy Robinson Partnership* [1987] 1 WLR 1027.

[160] The court recognised that in circumstances such as these the insurers are the real defendants for all practical purposes. The defendants and the insurers shared a common interest in the proceedings and were represented by the same legal team. It followed that communications within the circle of confidence (which comprised the lawyers, the defendants and the insured) were privileged as against any other parties. See also *Buttes Gas and Oil Co v Hammer (No 3)* [1981] QB 223.

[161] This point was echoed by Barron J in *Gallagher v Stanley* [1998] 2 IR 267, 274–275. It seems on all fours with the English approach as encapsulated in the following quotation from Keane, *The Modern Law of Evidence* (7th edn, Oxford University Press, 2008) at 616: 'Although application of the dominant purpose test can give rise to difficulty, in many cases of accident investigation it will be possible to conclude that the major purpose was the prevention of recurrence. The courts will not be deterred from reaching such a conclusion, where appropriate, even if those under whose direction the report was prepared depose that its dominant purpose was submission to solicitors in anticipation of litigation and the report itself refers only to that purpose' (citing *Lask v Gloucester Health Authority* (1985) 2 PN 96 and discussing *Neilson v Laugharne* [1981] QB 736 and *Re Highgrade Traders Ltd* [1984] BCLC 151).

[162] McGrath, *Evidence* (Thomson Round Hall, 2005) at para 10.47 (discussing the example of *Mark v Flexibox Ltd* [1988] NI 58).

the facts presented in each individual case:[163] in some instances the intentions of the persons procuring the communication in question may be difficult to discern; in others the communication may not have been procured by any person, as for example where the compilation of a report is required by law.[164] It may be useful in such instances to fall back on the general guidance issued by the Court of Appeal in *Guinness Peat Properties Ltd*, namely that the dominant purpose of a communication should be determined on an objective reading of the entirety of the evidence.[165] This common sense approach was echoed in the judgment of Finlay Geoghegan J in *Woori Bank:*

> 'I accept the submission that the decision of the Supreme Court in *Gallagher v Stanley* means that the purpose of the document is a matter for objective determination by the court in all the circumstances and does not depend on the motivation of the person who caused the document to be created. Further that the court should not make a finding that the dominant purpose of a document is litigation based upon a bald assertion, even on affidavit, of such motivation or intention of the creator of the document.'[166]

Consequences of Judicial Decisions Relating to Privilege

[3.62] The effect of a judicial determination not to recognise privilege may vary depending upon the facts of the particular case. The unsuccessful proponent of the privilege may reverse course and opt to actively deploy the information in the proceedings, for example by adducing it as evidence or using it as a means to prepare for settlement or trial. The kernel of denial of privilege is a prohibition on the proponent hiding the information from the other party or parties to the proceedings. By denying the assertion of privilege, the court is essentially affording all parties equal access to the information for the purposes of the proceedings. O'Flaherty J articulated the implication against the backdrop of the facts in *Gallagher v Stanley*:

> 'Both principles, full disclosure on the one hand and legal professional privilege on the other, are there to advance the cause of justice. Sometimes they may be on a collision course, but not, I think, here. This is not like a case where a client is expected to deal with his lawyer with the utmost disclosure so that his case will be properly presented. It is rather a case where both sides are entitled to know what exactly happened before and at the birth of the infant. After all the nurses are the mother and the child's nurses as well as being hospital employees. I

---

163 Abrahamson, Dwyer & Fitzpatrick, *Discovery and Disclosure* (Thomson Round Hall, 2007) at para 35.49 (comparing *Gallagher v Stanley* [1998] 2 IR 267 with *Re Highgrade Traders Ltd* [1984] BCLC 151 (CA)).

164 *Re Barings plc* [1998] 1 All ER 673.

165 *Guinness Peat Properties Ltd v Fitzroy Robinson Partnership* [1987] 1 WLR 1027 at 1036 (*per* Slade LJ).

166 *Woori Bank & Hanvit LSP Finance Ltd v KDB Ireland Ltd* [2005] IEHC 451 at p 4 (internal citation omitted).

> believe it is likely to help the course of the trial if these documents are made available to the plaintiff's advisers now and I do not see that the principle of legal professional privilege suffers in any way.'[167]

These observations underscore the importance of confidentiality as a characteristic of pre-trial preparation. They suggest that the courts will refuse to sanction the withholding of relevant information unless satisfied that it is necessary to protect those aspects of pre-trial preparation that warrant confidentiality. For example, had the nurses' statements at issue in *Gallagher v Stanley* been made directly to the hospital's legal advisers, arguably they may have come within the realm of protected information.

[3.63] The result in *Gallagher v Stanley* reflects the relatively limited scope for successful assertions of privilege under the dominant purpose test. Whereas the spectre of litigation may encourage individuals and corporate actors to gather information in the wake of a tortious event or contractual dispute, this may not be sufficient to protect the information from disclosure. In order for privilege to attach, the party must be in a position at a future point to show that litigation was the dominant purpose behind the gathering of information and, by implication, that any other objective motivations were less influential at best.

[3.64] The case of *Irish Press Publications Ltd v Minister for Enterprise and Employment*[168] reflects the close relationship that exists between the temporal requirement and the dominant purpose requirement for the purposes of litigation privilege. As noted above, the plaintiffs sought damages for libel and related claims arising out of a public statement made by the defendant Minister in response to a Competition Authority investigation into the newspaper industry. The High Court rejected the defendant's claim of privilege over a note prepared by a civil servant outlining the options open to the defendant following publication of the Competition Authority report. Carroll J held that the document met neither the temporal requirement set out in *Silver Hill Duckling Ltd v Minister for Agriculture*[169] nor the dominant purpose test:

> 'The document, in my opinion fails both tests. Litigation was mentioned only in the context of a possible option for the first defendant and the document was not prepared with the dominant purpose of preparing for litigation.'[170]

167 *Gallagher v Stanley* [1998] 2 IR 267 at 273.

168 *Irish Press Publications Ltd v Minister for Enterprise and Employment* [2002] 4 IR 110.

169 *Silver Hill Duckling Ltd v Minister for Agriculture* [1987] IR 289.

170 *Irish Press Publications Ltd v Minister for Enterprise and Employment* [2002] 4 IR 100 at 114.

Chapter 4

Without Prejudice Privilege

INTRODUCTION

[4.01] *Inter partes* communications made in furtherance of the settlement of civil proceedings[1] are protected by a distinct form of privilege known as 'without prejudice privilege'.[2] It renders inadmissible as proof in pending or subsequent litigation any statements or admissions made in a genuine attempt to reach a settlement.[3] The privileged information may be conveyed in written correspondence or stated in the course of face-to-face negotiations. It may apply even before litigation has formally commenced.[4] However, the privilege presupposes the existence of a genuine dispute.[5] The protection against the information being offered in evidence applies to the instant proceedings[6] and, in addition, to any subsequent litigation connected with the same subject matter, whether between the same or different parties.[7] Without prejudice is 'the joint privilege of both parties' and as such may be waived only by mutual consent.[8]

[4.02] From the standpoint of policy, without prejudice privilege promotes the settlement of disputes without recourse to full blown litigation.[9] The settlement of proceedings is a significant objective of the administration of justice and in practice the majority of cases filed in the Irish courts are resolved in this

---

1 The concept does not apply to criminal proceedings. *R v Hayes* [2005] 1 Cr App R 557.

2 See generally Passmore, *Privilege* (2nd edn, xpl publishing, 2006) ch 10; B Thanki (ed), *The Law of Privilege* (Oxford University Press, 2006) ch 7; Matthews and Malek, *Disclosure* (Sweet & Maxwell, 2001) para 9.108 *et seq*.; Abrahamson, Dwyer and Fitzpatrick, *Discovery and Disclosure* (Thomson Round Hall, 2007) ch 36; McGrath, 'Without Prejudice Privilege' (2001) 5 Int'l J Evid & Proof 213.

3 *Rush & Tompkins Ltd v Greater London Council* [1989] AC 1280 (HL); *Cutts v Head* [1984] Ch 290; *Walker v Wilsher* (1889) 23 QBD 335. For a perspective on protecting documents procured during settlement negotiations under the rubric of litigation privilege see *In Re Murray Consultants Ltd and Nocrumb Ltd: Horgan v Murray* [1999] 1 ILRM 257.

4 *Barnetson v Framlongton Group Ltd* [2007] 3 All ER 1054.

5 *Bradford & Bingley plc v Rashid* [2006] 4 All ER 705 (HL).

6 It may be asserted at any stage in the proceedings whether before or during the trial itself: Keane, *The Modern Law of Evidence* (7th edn, Oxford University Press, 2008) p 633 (citing cases).

7 Keane, *The Modern Law of Evidence* (7th edn, Oxford University Press, 2008) at 633.

8 Keane, *The Modern Law of Evidence* (7th edn, Oxford University Press, 2008) at 633.

9 This is often referred to as the 'public policy' aspect of without prejudice privilege. See, eg, Passmore, *Privilege* (2nd edn, xpl publishing, 2006) paras 10.007–10.008.

manner. Without prejudice privilege allows litigants the freedom to communicate freely without fear that anything said in pursuit of a settlement will be used against them in the proceedings in the event that the negotiations break down.[10] In particular, the privilege allows a party to shield from the trier of fact any admissions made during the course of negotiations and the nature and amount of any offers to settle. Public policy aside, it has been suggested that the secrecy of *inter partes* negotiations may be enforced as a matter of contract, the parties having embarked on this course on the understanding that the contents of their discussions will not be used to the prejudice of either party.[11]

Multiple Parties

[4.03] Civil litigation frequently involves multiple parties and at any time in the proceedings settlement negotiations may be conducted between some but not all of those parties. What is the effect of without prejudice on those parties who were not privy to the negotiations? The general rule is that communications made in furtherance of settlement may not be disclosed to any other party; in other words, the privilege operates for all purposes and against all parties to the proceedings.[12] However, the case law evinces departures from the general rule.

[4.04] *Gnitrow Ltd v Cape plc*[13] originated in a claim brought by the employees of the plaintiff shipyard operator seeking damages for injuries caused by exposure to asbestos. The plaintiff reached a settlement with the employees and then sought a contribution from two independent contractors that were implicated in the employees' claim. The plaintiff's insurance company reached an agreement with one of the independent contractors and the plaintiff instituted contribution proceedings against the defendant, the other independent contractor. The Court of Appeal granted the defendant's application for disclosure of the agreement between the plaintiff's insurance company and the first independent contractor on the basis that it was relevant to determining the defendant's potential contribution to the employees' damages. Pill LJ was careful to emphasise the exceptional circumstances of case at hand. In order to ensure that the plaintiff was not overcompensated for its expenditure, the trial

---

10 *Moorview Developments Ltd v First Active plc* [2009] 2 IR 788 at 819 *per* Clarke J: 'It is clear that without prejudice privilege stems from the need to permit parties to negotiate in a frank manner with a view to encouraging the resolution of potential litigation'; *Greencore Group Plc & Others v Murphy* [1995] 3 IR 520 (*per* Keane J); *Ryan v Connolly* [2001] 1 IR 627, [2002] 2 ILRM 174 (*per* Keane CJ); *Muller v Linsley & Mortimer* (1994) TLR 635, [1996] PNLR 74; *Rush & Tompkins Ltd v Greater London Council* [1989] AC 1280.

11 Abrahamson, Dwyer and Fitzpatrick, *Discovery and Disclosure* (Thomson Round Hall, 2007), at para 36.04, characterise the concept of an implied agreement between the parties as a second justification for the privilege after the primary justification of encouraging the settlement of disputes.

12 *Rush & Tompkins Ltd v Greater London Council* [1989] AC 1280.

13 *Gnitrow Ltd v Cape plc* [2000] 3 All ER 763.

judge needed to know the size of the sum contributed by the first independent contractor. The objective of a just apportionment of responsibility between the three parties necessarily took precedence over the conventional justifications for without prejudice privilege.

THE SETTLEMENT CONTEXT

[4.05] The operation of without prejudice privilege is subject to certain conditions. The communication over which privilege is asserted must have been made in the specific context of the negotiation of a settlement.[14] Communications that relate to the dispute in general or to aspects of the proceedings that have no immediate bearing on attempts to settle the dispute will not be protected. Moreover, even within the realm of settlement, the courts will insist that the communication was made in a *bona fide* attempt to settle the dispute.[15] Thus, not everything stated during the course of settlement negotiations will be protected.

[4.06] In *Greencore Group plc & Others v Murphy and Others*, Keane J drew a distinction between admissions as to matters in the past, which would be protected by privilege, and statements as to future conduct, which would not:

> 'Since the primary object of the rule is to ensure that a party is not embarrassed by having admissions made by him solely for the purpose of settlement negotiations subsequently used to his detriment in litigation, it is obvious that statements which related solely to his future conduct and could not be regarded as admissions made as part of an offer of settlement would not necessarily be protected from disclosure.'[16]

The English authorities evince some difference of opinion over the scope of the privilege. Some judicial statements imply that the protection from disclosure is limited to 'admissions' made in the course of negotiations; other dicta, occasionally within the same judgments, support a broader understanding of the privilege as encompassing virtually anything said during the settlement process.[17] In *Unilever plc v Proctor & Gamble Co*,[18] the Court of Appeal recognised that a liberal interpretation of the scope of the privilege constituted a functional necessity. Walker LJ commented that '... to dissect out identifiable

---

[14] *Buckinghamshire County Council v Moran* [1990] Ch 623; *Kooltrade Ltd v XTS Ltd* [2001] FSR 158. Thanki (ed), *The Law of Privilege* (Oxford University Press, 2006) para 7.07, lends the term 'negotiations' a broad reading in this context: 'the rule is not limited to negotiations aimed at resolving the legal issues between the parties' but rather applies to 'any negotiations aimed at avoiding or reducing the scope of litigation, irrespective of whether they directly address or seek to resolve the relevant legal issues'.

[15] *Rush & Tompkins Ltd v Greater London Council* [1989] AC 1280.

[16] *Greencore Group plc & Others v Murphy* [1995] 3 IR 520 at 526.

[17] *Rush & Tompkins Ltd v Greater London Council* [1989] AC 1280; *Cutts v Head* [1984] Ch 290.

[18] *Unilever plc v Proctor & Gamble Co* [2000] 1 WLR 2436.

admissions and withhold protection from the rest of without prejudice communications ... would not only create huge practical difficulties but would be contrary to the underlying objective of giving protection to the parties ...'.[19]

[4.07] In Ireland, the judgment of Clarke J in *Moorview Developments Ltd v First Active plc*[20] endorses a correspondingly broad understanding of the scope of without prejudice privilege. Clarke J declared himself satisfied that 'it is unnecessary, in the context of negotiations which seek to resolve existing or potential litigation, for a party asserting privilege to identify that admissions against interest had been made in the course of those negotiations'.[21] On the facts before him in that case, the learned judge concluded that all of the negotiations between the parties leading to settlement arrangements were privileged.[22] *Moorview Developments Ltd* is also authority for the widely recognised, common sense proposition that once a settlement is reached between the parties, the settlement agreement is itself admissible in evidence.[23]

INTENT

[4.08] A second, related condition is that the communication must have been made with the intention that the contents would not be disclosed to the prejudice of either party. Given its subjective tenor, this condition may be difficult to establish. It is directed in part at the exclusion from the scope of privilege of so-called 'open offers' which are made for tactical reasons rather than in a genuine attempt to settle the dispute. The party asserting the privilege will be expected to produce evidence of a concerted effort to resolve the differences between the parties.[24] Given these realities, judicial analysis in this area tends to be fact intensive.

[4.09] The label 'without prejudice', commonly affixed to settlement correspondence, is frequently cited as evidence of the necessary intent; it is said to reflect an understanding among the participants that the contents of any negotiations will not be used by one party to the prejudice of the other party in the underlying proceedings. Although the label is usually taken as an indication

19 *Unilever plc v Proctor & Gamble Co* [2000] 1 WLR 2436 at 2448–2449.

20 *Moorview Developments Ltd v First Active plc* [2009] 2 IR 788.

21 *Moorview Developments Ltd v First Active plc* [2009] 2 IR 788 at 820.

22 *Moorview Developments Ltd v First Active plc* [2009] 2 IR 788 at 820.

23 *Moorview Developments Ltd v First Active plc* [2009] 2 IR 788 at 820. See also *Quinlivan v Tuohy and Curtin* (29 July 1992, unreported) HC (Barron J). On the admissibility of evidence as to whether an agreement had in fact been reached see also *County Council of Meath v Irish Shell Ltd* [2006] IEHC 391 (6 December 2006) (Lavan J).

24 *Cheddar Valley Engineering Ltd v Chaddlewood Homes Ltd* [1992] 1 WLR 820.

that the communication was made in furtherance of settlement, the courts have emphasised that it is not conclusive of the existence of privilege.[25]

[4.10] In *Christie v Odeon (Ireland) Ltd*,[26] the plaintiff sued her employer seeking damages for injuries sustained in an accident at work. Her action was statute barred but she submitted that she had a reasonable justification for delay in that the parties had been engaged in settlement negotiations. The plaintiff sought to rely on certain correspondence between the defendants' insurers and the plaintiff's solicitor that was marked 'without prejudice'. The Supreme Court held that the mere existence of such correspondence was insufficient to support the suggestion of settlement negotiations. Kingsmill Moore J stated:

> 'It may be conceded that the most apt and most proper use of the words 'without prejudice' is to protect negotiations for settlement, but it would be to close one's eyes to all experience of the way correspondence is conducted between solicitors to suggest that all or even the majority of letters so headed have to do with attempts at settlement of the case. The use of those words has unfortunately become quite indiscriminate in legal correspondence. Hardly a case comes before the Courts in which there is not a series of letters unconnected with settlements but bearing this heading.'[27]

In the present case, the plaintiff had adduced no evidence, other than two letters marked 'without prejudice', that any thoughts of settlement were entertained.

[4.11] In *Ryan v Connolly*,[28] the Supreme Court reinforced the point that the presence of the label 'without prejudice' does not automatically render the document in question privileged. In any case where privilege is claimed and that claim is challenged, the court is entitled to look at the document in order to determine the veracity of the claim. The factual matrix of the case was similar to *Christie*. It originated in a road traffic accident and concerned the affect on legal proceedings of settlement negotiations between the parties. The defendants claimed that the plaintiff's claim was statute barred. In reply, the plaintiff contended that the defendants were estopped from relying on the statute because they had used settlement negotiations to induce the plaintiff to delay instituting

---

25 *Greencore Group Plc & Others v Murphy* [1995] 3 IR 520 in which Keane J recognised that while privilege is usually asserted by the practice of marking the relevant correspondence or documents 'without prejudice' the application of the rule is not necessarily dependent on the use of those words. See also *South Shropshire District Council v Amos* [1987] 1 All ER 340 (CA); *Dixon Stores Group Ltd v Thames Television plc* [1993] 1 All ER 349; *Prudential Assurance Co Ltd v Prudential Insurance Co of America* [2002] EWHC 2809 (Ch D). In *Hansfield Developments & Others v Irish Asphalt Ltd & Others* [2009] IEHC 90 (17 February 2009), McGovern J held at p 4 that privilege attached to a document that was stated to be 'strictly without prejudice' and that related to the settlement of a dispute the terms of which were confidential between the parties.

26 *Christie v Odeon (Ireland) Ltd* (1958) 92 ILTR 106.

27 *Christie v Odeon (Ireland) Ltd* (1958) 92 ILTR 106 at 109.

28 *Ryan v Connolly* [2001] 1 IR 627, [2002] 2 ILRM 174.

proceedings. In a passage with faint echoes of his judgment in *Greencore,* Keane CJ stated:

> 'Thus, where a party invites the court to look at 'without prejudice' correspondence, not for the purpose of holding his opponent to admissions made in the course of negotiations, but simply in order to demonstrate why a particular course had been taken, the public policy considerations may not be relevant. It would be unthinkable that the attachment of the 'without prejudice' label to a letter which expressly and unequivocally stated that no point under the Statute of Limitations would be taken if the initiation of proceedings was deferred pending negotiations, would oblige a court to decide, if the issue arose, that no action of the defendant had induced the plaintiff to refrain from issuing proceedings.'[29]

EXCEPTIONS

[4.12] Without prejudice privilege occupies a less exalted place in the trial process than legal professional privilege, a reality that is manifest in a series of recognised exceptions.[30] In *Rush & Tompkins Ltd v Greater London Council*, Lord Griffiths opined that the privilege may be pierced and without prejudice material disclosed 'for a variety of reasons when the justice of the case requires it'.[31] In *Moorview Developments Ltd v First Active plc*, Clarke J declared: 'The overriding principle is that a very heavy weight indeed needs to be attached to without prejudice privilege'.[32] Consequently, 'the only circumstances' where evidence of without prejudice communications can be admitted is where 'it can be clearly shown that greater damage to the interests of justice would be affected by non-admission than by disclosure'.[33]

[4.13] Certainly, the existence of recognised exceptions grounded in the public interest does not translate into a general judicial discretion to admit without prejudice statements.[34] The principal exceptions[35] arise where there is a dispute over the existence or terms of a settlement,[36] where one party has allegedly

[29] *Ryan v Connolly* [2001] 1 IR 627 at 632.

[30] *Unilever plc v Proctor & Gamble Co* [2000] 1 WLR 2436.

[31] *Rush & Tompkins Ltd v Greater London Council* [1989] AC 1280 at 1300.

[32] *Moorview Developments Ltd v First Active plc* [2009] 2 IR 788 at 820.

[33] *Moorview Developments Ltd v First Active plc* [2009] 2 IR 788 at 820 (quoting from McGrath, *Evidence* (Thomson Round Hall, 2005) at para 10.128).

[34] Passmore, *Privilege* (2nd edn, xpl publishing, 2006) para 10.052.

[35] For a detailed discussion of the individual exceptions see Passmore, *Privilege* (2nd edn, xpl publishing, 2006) ch 10(4).

[36] *Moorview Developments Ltd v First Active plc* [2009] 2 IR 788 at 820 *per* Clarke J: '[T]he whole purpose behind the privilege is to encourage negotiation and settlement of litigation. That purpose would hardly be achieved if parties were precluded from leading evidence as to, at least, aspects of the negotiations, in circumstances where it was contended that the negotiations had achieved the desired end of settling the litigation'; *County Council for the County of Meath v Irish Shell Ltd* [2006] IEHC 391 (6 December 2006) (Lavan J); *Tomlin v Standard Telephones and Cables Ltd* [1969] 1 WLR 1378.

engaged in perjury, blackmail or other improper conduct,[37] where the existence of without prejudice communications may be relevant to an issue of estoppel[38] or delay,[39] and where a party has signed a *Calderbank* letter on the issue of costs.[40]

WAIVER

[4.14] The existence of without prejudice privilege presupposes a mutual understanding between the parties. The courts will examine the correspondence between the parties in its entirety in order to assess whether there has been a meeting of minds as to the nature of their exchange. If a letter is dispatched marked 'without prejudice' then any reply will be assumed to have been sent on the same basis unless there is a clear indication to the contrary. The mutuality inherent in the privilege is also evident in the principle that the parties may jointly waive their right to non-disclosure.[41]

[4.15] Whereas without prejudice privilege cannot be created by one party acting alone, the courts have recognised that exceptionally it can be destroyed unilaterally. Where a party puts the subject matter of the privilege directly in issue, the effect is akin to waiver, and the material will be available to both parties for use in the proceedings.[42] The courts will now allow a party to cherry-pick from among privileged material; once the veil of privilege is pierced, any protected information becomes ripe for disclosure. Lord Clarke emphasised this point in *Somatra Ltd v Sinclair Roche and Temperley*:

> 'Fairness requires that where a party deploys privileged or without prejudice material as part of its case at trial the other party should be entitled ... to rely upon the other without prejudice material which came into existence as part of the same without prejudice process.'[43]

As noted above, the existence of multiple parties complicates the litigation and raises the spectre of unfairness between negotiating parties and the other parties to the dispute. In *Rush & Tompkins Ltd v Greater London Council*, Lord Griffiths cited the instance of one party to multi-party litigation assuming 'an

---

37 *Unilever plc v Proctor & Gamble Co* [2000] 1 WLR 2436; *SIB Ltd v Fincken* [2004] 1 All ER 1125. This exception extends to threats of improper conduct. See, eg, *Greenwood v Fitts* (1961) 29 DLR (2d) 260.

38 *Ryan v Connolly* [2001] 1 IR 627, [2002] 2 ILRM 174.

39 *Walker v Wilsher* (1889) 23 QBD 335.

40 *Cutts v Head* [1984] 1 Ch 290. Although without prejudice communications are generally protected from disclosure in an application for costs, in *Calderbank v Calderbank* [1975] 3 All ER 333, the court sanctioned reference to a without prejudice letter containing an offer to settle where the author had entered a reservation acknowledging the right to make the reference.

41 *Blow v Norfolk County Council* [1967] 1 WLR 1280.

42 *Muller v Linsley & Mortimer* (1994) TLR 635, [1996] PNLR 74; Thanki (ed), *The Law of Privilege* (Oxford University Press, 2006) paras 7.35–7.36.

43 *Somatra Ltd v Sinclair Roche and Temperley* [2000] 1 WLR 2453 at 2463 (CA).

unreasonably intransigent attitude' to settlement as justification for protecting from disclosure genuine negotiations conducted by other parties.[44]

Application of Privilege

[4.16] It is important to appreciate the practical implications of without prejudice privilege. It is designed, first and foremost, to shield admissions made by one party during the course of settlement negotiations from use as evidence by the other party in the proceedings. The privilege does not envelope in a cloak of confidentiality statements made in negotiations, it merely precludes the other side from offering those statements as proof at trial.

[4.17] For example, during negotiations to settle an action for personal injuries arising out of a road traffic accident, a defendant may implicitly concede certain facts in dispute, such as the fact that she was speeding or that it was raining at the time of the accident. If the negotiations fail to lead to a settlement, the plaintiff is at liberty to contest all relevant factual matters including the defendant's speed or the prevailing weather conditions. The effect of the privilege is to restrain the plaintiff from offering as proof the concessions made by the defendant during the course of negotiations. The statements made in negotiations are inadmissible and the plaintiff must produce independent evidence to support its version of the facts. This point should not be overstated, however. The case law reflects an inherent tension between the practical imperative of facilitating discovery and to need to ensure respect for the sanctity of genuine attempts at settlement.

Procedure

[4.18] The procedural steps that assist the courts in locating the common ground between these competing objectives were discussed by Keane J in *Greencore Group Plc & Others v Murphy.*[45] As in the ordinary course of discovery, the party must include in her affidavit of discovery all the documents relevant to the issues in the proceedings that are in her possession, power or procurement. However, the other party is not entitled to the production for inspection of any documents contained in the affidavit in respect of which a claim of privilege is properly made. In other words, the documents must be discovered even though they may be privileged from production and inspection. In any case where the privilege is claimed and that claim is challenged, the court is entitled to look at the documentation in order to determine whether privilege attaches.[46] Keane J noted that, on inspection by the courts, documents that *prima facie* are protected by without prejudice privilege may turn out not to be so protected. But before a

[44] *Rush & Tompkins Ltd v Greater London Council* [1989] AC 1280 at 1350.

[45] *Greencore Group Plc & Others v Murphy* [1995] 3 IR 520.

[46] See also *Ryan v Connolly* [2001] 1 IR 627, [2002] 2 ILRM 174.

court can properly determine whether particular statements are protected or not, the parties must first complete the procedural steps outlined above. It is only when the relevant documents are discovered, privilege is claimed against production, and the claim is challenged, that the court can then resolve the issue of the admissibility of the documents.[47]

[47] *Ryan v Connolly* [2001] 1 IR 627, [2002] 2 ILRM 174. On the facts of the *Greencore* case, Keane J concluded that it would be premature for him to determine the admissibility of the documents at issue given that these various procedural steps had not been undertaken.

Chapter 5

Exceptions

INTRODUCTION

[5.01] Legal professional privilege has general application across the full breadth of the criminal and civil law. However, an assertion of privilege may be defeated where the opposing party establishes that the information in question comes within one of a series of acknowledged exceptions. Various common law courts have recognised specific, limited circumstances in which the benefits of disclosure outweigh the potentially chilling effect on the lawyer-client relationship. The existence of these exceptions and the scope of their application have been the subject of controversy.[1]

[5.02] Historically, the courts have been reluctant to encroach on the sanctity of the lawyer-client relationship for fear that any diminution in protection from disclosure would undermine the client's confidence in her lawyer. In *R v Derby Magistrates' Court, ex parte B*,[2] the House of Lords famously extolled the absolute nature of legal professional privilege and rejected the notion of exceptions thereto.

[5.03] The Irish courts have been less emphatic in their endorsement of privilege. While recognising the imperative of protecting the lawyer-client relationship, they have acknowledged the cost that privilege exacts on the general principle of disclosure. Whereas in *R v Derby Magistrates' Court, ex parte B* the House of Lords characterised privilege as a right, qualified in only very limited respects, the Irish courts have tended to couch privilege in the language of public policy. The evolving Irish approach is epitomised in this frequently quoted passage from the judgment of Finlay CJ in *Smurfit Paribas Bank Ltd v AAB Export Finance Ltd*:

> 'The existence of a privilege from disclosure for communications made between a person and his lawyer clearly constitutes a potential restriction and diminution of the full disclosure both prior to and during the course of legal proceedings which in the interests of the common good is desirable for the purpose of ascertaining the truth and rendering justice. Such privilege should, therefore, in my view, only be granted by the courts in instances which have been identified as securing an objective which in the public interest in the proper conduct of the

1 The principal exceptions are discussed below. For a more complete list see Matthews and Malek, *Disclosure* (Sweet & Maxwell, 2001) para 9.056 *et seq.*

2 *R v Derby Magistrates' Court, ex parte B* [1995] 3 WLR 681, [1995] 4 All ER 526.

administration of justice can be said to outweigh the disadvantage arising from the restriction of disclosure of all the facts'.[3]

The posture of privilege in Finlay CJ's assessment of the law is informative; his comments indicate that privilege constitutes an exception to the controlling benchmark of disclosure and must be applied restrictively as such. Although the learned chief justice was not advocating that claims of privilege be determined on the basis of an open-ended balancing test (in which the courts would weigh the public interest in disclosure against the public interest in the confidentiality of the lawyer-client relationship on a case-by-case basis), nevertheless his judgment emphasises the judicial imperative of confining privilege to its proper context through close supervision of the various conditions that limit its application.[4] These sentiments must surely influence the manner in which the courts approach the question of exceptions to legal professional privilege; they imply that exceptions will be countenanced where supported by a recognised public interest imperative.[5] At the same time, it is important to dismiss any supposition that the courts have licence to whittle down the protection afforded to the legal professional relationship in an *ad hoc* piecemeal fashion. The purpose of ensuring candour on the part of the client would be undermined if the possibility of trial judges recognising exceptions to privilege could not be predicted. Consequently, categories of exception have emerged and developed as the common law has progressed, each of them reflecting a countervailing public interest in favour of disclosure.

[5.04] The categories of exception are not closed and some jurisdictions have adopted a more liberal approach to overriding privilege than others. In Canada, the lawyer-client privilege is by no means absolute and may be set aside in the face of a sufficiently compelling public interest. In *Smith v Jones*,[6] the Canadian Supreme Court carved out a public safety exception to privilege. Jones was charged with the offence of aggravated sexual assault of a prostitute and, in advance of sentencing, his lawyer retained the psychiatrist, Smith, to conduct an assessment of Jones. Based on an interview, Smith formed the opinion that Jones suffered from psychiatric disorders and was a danger to prostitutes in the

---

3 *Smurfit Paribas Bank Ltd v AAB Export Finance Ltd* [1990] 1 IR 469 at 477. See also *Gallagher v Stanley* [1998] 2 IR 267 at 271 (*per* O'Flaherty J).

4 Such as the condition discussed in *Smurfit Paribas Bank Ltd v AAB Export Finance Ltd* [1990] 1 IR 469 itself that the protected communications relate to the giving or receiving of legal advice as opposed to assistance.

5 McGrath, *Evidence* (Thomson Round Hall, 2005) at 10.58, suggests that 'exceptions should be made to legal professional privilege where the balance of public interest in disclosure clearly outweighs that in the maintenance of privilege'.

6 *Smith v Jones* [1999] 1 SCR 455. See Sheldrick, 'Administering public safety: solicitor-client privilege, medical experts and the adversarial process: *Smith v Jones*' (2000) 4 Int'l J Evid & Proof 119. The English Court of Appeal has recognised a similar exception to a doctor's duty of confidentiality: *W v Edgell* [1990] 1 All ER 845.

area. The defence ultimately decided against using Smith's report at the sentencing hearing and Smith sought a judicial declaration that he was entitled to disclose it to the police and the prosecution. The Supreme Court held that in principle privilege could be overridden in the interests of protecting public safety and sanctioned relatively broad disclosure of Smith's opinion and the material on which it was based.[7]

STATUTE

[5.05] Before examining the categories of judge-made exception to legal professional privilege, some mention should be made of the role of statute in tempering its application and effect. Privilege is a common law construct and may be overridden by statute[8] subject to the important caveat that the Oireachtas must not encroach on the protection afforded to privilege by the Constitution and the European Convention on Human Rights. However, the scope of those rights and the extent of the corresponding curtailment remain matters of uncertainty.

[5.06] Statutes often purport to copper-fasten lawyer-client privilege as opposed to overriding it. A relatively recent example may be found in the Criminal Justice (Surveillance) Act 2009. The Act places on a statutory footing the power of the Garda Síochána, the Defence Forces and the Revenue Commissioners to conduct surveillance[9] and provides for the admission in evidence at trial of the informational fruits of that surveillance.[10] As a pre-condition to the conduct of surveillance, the authorities must secure a valid authorisation or approval,[11] generally from a judge of the District Court. Section 5, which sets out the various conditions governing judicial authorisation and re-authorisation, includes in subsection (4) the following pertinent qualification:

---

7 Sheldrick, 'Administering public safety: solicitor-client privilege, medical experts and the adversarial process: *Smith v Jones*' (2000) 4 Int'l J Evid & Proof 119 at 125 contends that a 'far narrower form of disclosure would have served the interest of safeguarding public safety equally well'.

8 *Fyffes plc v DCC plc* [2005] 1 IR 59 (*per* Fennelly J).

9 The term 'surveillance' is defined in s 1 as '(a) monitoring, observing, listening to or making a recording of a particular person or group of persons or their movements, activities and communications or (b) monitoring or making a recording of places or things, by or with the assistance of surveillance devices'. The same section provides a somewhat circular definition of 'surveillance device' as 'an apparatus designed or adapted for use in surveillance'. However, the section expressly excludes from the ambit of the Act three devices which are significant from a practical standpoint: a CCTV; a camera used to take photographs in a public place; and a night-vision apparatus 'to the extent to which it is not used to make a recording of any person who, or place or thing that, is being monitored or observed'.

10 Separate provision is made for the use of tracking devices, ie, surveillance devices that are used 'only for the purpose of providing information regarding the location of a person, vehicle or thing': ss 1 and 8.

11 Section 3.

> 'The judge shall not issue an authorisation if he or she is satisfied that the surveillance being sought to be authorised is likely to relate primarily to communications protected by privilege'.

No further guidance is provided regarding the nature of the privilege statutorily protected and the extent of that protection. A common sense reading would suggest that the subsection embraces legal professional privilege; indeed, the reference to 'communications' supports an argument that its principal import is to ensure respect for the inviolability of lawyer-client communications. Nevertheless, the protection itself is couched in ambiguous and uncertain terms. On what basis might a judge decide that the proposed surveillance is 'likely' to relate 'primarily' to communications protected by privilege? The importance of this point is underscored by the statutory stipulation that the application for an authorisation shall be made *ex parte* and heard 'otherwise than in public'.[12] In the absence of a conventional adversarial setting, the information on which the judge bases her determination may be limited to information which she elicits *sua sponte* from the applicant authorities. The support that the subsection potentially lends to legal professional privilege is significantly undercut by these practical realities.

Crime, Fraud and Conduct Injurious to the Administration of Justice

[5.07] The courts have consistently recognised that privilege may be lost if used as a cloak to conceal and further crime or fraud[13] or conduct injurious to the administration of justice.[14] The contribution of privilege to the effective administration of justice would be wholly undermined if privilege could be used to service unlawful conduct. As Stephen LJ stated in *R v Cox and Railton*:

> 'The reason on which the rule is said to rest cannot include the case of communications criminal in themselves or intended to further any criminal purpose, for the protection of such communications cannot possibly be otherwise than injurious to the interests of justice and to those of the administration of justice.'[15]

[5.08] The historical view was that criminal or fraudulent communications did not come within the definition of privilege because crime or fraud could not qualify as matters protected by professional confidence.[16] To put it another way, criminal or fraudulent communications were necessarily outside the ambit of the legal professional relationship. It followed that crime or fraud was not an

12 Section 5(1)(a).

13 *Fyffes plc v DCC plc* [2005] 1 IR 59.

14 *Murphy v Kirwan* [1993] 3 IR 501.

15 *R v Cox and Railton* (1884) 14 QBD 153.

16 *Follott v Jeffereys* (1850) 1 Sim NS 3; *Russell v Jackson* (1851) 9 Hare 387.

exception in the true sense; in the absence of a lawyer-client relationship no privilege could arise in the first place. This positivist approach has been criticised by Auburn as placing 'technical niceties above the clear and simple reality of the situation'.[17] In a detailed critique of the traditional rationale, he argues that the crime–fraud exception rests not 'on some immutable view of the scope of the professional relationship' but rather on 'a flexible balancing' of competing public policy concerns.[18]

[5.09] The crime–fraud exception is perhaps the best known of the exceptions to legal professional privilege and has been widely recognised across the common law world.[19] The exception has been acknowledged as applying to both legal advice privilege and litigation privilege.[20] It may be invoked at any stage in civil or criminal proceedings at which the disclosure of otherwise privileged material may be compelled or contested.[21]

Crime

[5.10] Historically, the exception was limited in notable respects. At common law, it applied to the use of legal advice to further crime as opposed to other forms of misconduct.[22] In addition, it was limited to situations in which a client communicated with a lawyer for the specific purpose of obtaining advice that would assist in achieving those criminal ends.[23]

[5.11] *R v Cox and Railton*[24] arose out of a prosecution for conspiracy to defraud a judgment creditor. The defendants were partners who consulted a solicitor about the execution by Railton of a bill of sale over the partnership's assets in favour of Cox. The prosecution alleged that the bill of sale was fraudulent and designed to prevent the execution of a judgment that had been obtained against Railton in a libel action. The Court for Crown Cases Reserved upheld the

---

17 Auburn, *Legal Professional Privilege: Law and Theory* (Hart Publishing, 2000) at p 160.

18 Auburn, *Legal Professional Privilege: Law and Theory* (Hart Publishing, 2000) at p 172. Some contemporary cases support this public policy rationale. See, eg, *Banque Keyser Ullmann SA v Skandia (UK) Insurance Co Ltd* [1986] 1 Lloyd's Rep 336, 338; *Barclays Bank v Eustice* [1995] 4 All ER 511, 523.

19 See, eg, *Solosky v Canada* [1980] 1 SCR 821, *Descôteaux v Mierzwinski* [1982] 1 SCR 860; *Clark v United States* 289 US 1 (1933), *United States v Zolin* 491 US 554 (1989); *Keep Brothers v Birch and Bradshaw* [1928] NZLR 260.

20 *Kuwait Airways Corp v Iraqi Airways Co (No 6)* [2005] 1 WLR 2734, 2746; *R (Hallinan Blackburn Gittings & Nott (a firm)) v Middlesex Guildhall Crown Court* [2005] 1 WLR 766.

21 Passmore, *Privilege* (2nd edn, xpl publishing, 2006) para 8.013.

22 *R v Cox and Railton* (1884) 14 QBD 153; *Russell v Jackson* (1851) 9 Hare 387. See *Francis & Francis (a firm) v Central Criminal Court* [1988] 3 All ER 775 (HL); *R v Crown Court at Northampton, ex parte DPP* (1991) 93 Cr App R 376; *R v Leeds Magistrates' Court, ex parte Dumbleton* [1993] Crim LR 866.

23 Newbold, 'The Crime-Fraud Exception to Legal Professional Privilege' (1990) 53 MLR 472 at 475.

24 *R v Cox and Railton* (1884) 14 QBD 153.

entitlement of the prosecution to call the solicitor to testify at the defendants' trial about his communications with the defendants.

The comparative case law is replete with examples of other forms of criminal conduct that have triggered the application of the exception such as disposing of the proceedings of drug trafficking,[25] unlawfully trading,[26] bribing a juror,[27] and transferring assets prior to bankruptcy.[28]

[5.12] The solicitor in *R v Cox and Railton* had been ignorant of the criminal purpose that had motivated the defendants to consult him. The court famously held that the exception applies regardless of whether the lawyer is aware of the criminal or fraudulent purpose for which the legal advice is being sought.[29] Thus at common law it is the client's intention to further crime that provides the trigger for the application of the exception. The exception thus has the effect of liberating the lawyer to give evidence against her client where it transpires that the client sought advice for a criminal or fraudulent purpose.[30]

[5.13] In England, however, there has been some muddying of the water over the question of intent. The crime exception has a statutory basis in s 10(2) of the Police and Criminal Evidence Act 1984 which states that 'items held with the intention of furthering a criminal purpose are not items subject to legal privilege'.[31] In *Francis & Francis (a firm) v Central Criminal Court*,[32] the House of Lords construed s 10(2) to mean that privilege was lost where documents were held with the intention of furthering a criminal purpose regardless of whether the intention was that of the person holding the documents, invariably the solicitor, or any other person, such as the client or possibly a third party. In this case the client was not the person whom the police suspected of criminal activity but rather a relative of that person; indeed, the client was seemingly unaware of the alleged criminality. Nevertheless, the House of Lords held that

---

25 *R v Central Criminal Court, ex parte Francis & Francis (a firm)* [1989] 1 AC 346.

26 *Butler v Board of Trade* [1971] Ch 680.

27 *Matter of Doe* 551 F 2d 899 (2d Cir 1977).

28 *United States v Ballard* 779 F 2d 287 (5d Cir 1986).

29 *R v Cox and Railton* (1884) 14 QBD 153. See also *R v Central Criminal Court, ex parte Francis & Francis* [1989] AC 346; *Kuwait Airways Corp v Iraqi Airways Co (No 6)* [2005] 1 WLR 2734, 2739 (*per* Longmore LJ). However, privilege may attach if the lawyer is not a party to the misconduct and upon learning of the intended course of action warns the client of the legal consequences: *Butler v Board of Trade* [1971] Ch 680.

30 Newbold, 'The Crime-Fraud Exception to Legal Professional Privilege' (1990) 53 MLR 472 at 475: 'Thus, it must be assumed that where the lawyer is acting bona fide, he or she will be quite willing to provide to the appropriate executive authority evidence of client communications which were made in furtherance of crime or fraud provided that the authority makes out a prima facie case against the client'.

31 Police and Criminal Evidence Act 1984, Pt II.

32 *Francis & Francis (a firm) v Central Criminal Court* [1988] 3 All ER 775.

the solicitors' files were 'items' ordinarily subject to privilege but excluded from protection by virtue of s 10(2).[33]

Fraud

[5.14] Over time the exception to legal professional privilege evolved to embrace forms of wrongdoing short of criminal misconduct. The initial, substantial broadening of the principle occurred over a century ago and concerned instances of fraud. In *Williams v Quebrada Railway, Land and Copper Co Ltd,* Kekewich J stated:

> '... where there is anything of an underhand nature or approaching to fraud, especially in commercial matters where there should be the veriest good faith, the whole transaction should be ripped up and disclosed in all its nakedness to the light of the court.'[34]

[5.15] In *Ventouris v Mountain*, Bingham LJ famously spoke of the vibrancy of privilege 'in the absence of iniquity'.[35] This phrase suggests a flexible, broad-brush approach to the notion of misconduct. Indeed, the concept of fraud for the purposes of the exemption has been defined liberally to include a wide range of deceitful and dishonest conduct.[36] For example, in *Barclays Bank plc v Eustice,* privilege was held to be lost where the privilege holder entered into transactions that were below value in order to prejudice the interests of a creditor.[37] In *Gamlen Chemical Co (UK) Ltd v Rochem Ltd,*[38] a conspiracy involving a breach of the duties of fidelity and confidentiality in employment was deemed sufficiently egregious to trigger the application of the exception. At the same time, mindful of the exalted place legal professional privilege occupies in the common law tradition, the English courts will not rush to cast privilege aside. As Schiemann LJ explained in *Gamlen Chemical Co:*

---

[33] The police suspected that the client's relative had laundered the proceeds of drug trafficking by giving sums of money to members of his family, including the client, for the purchase of properties. The police secured an order requiring the solicitors to produce all files in their possession relating to the conveyance to which the client was a party. The House of Lords held that it was enough for purposes of the exception that the conveyancing documents were intended by the relative, a third party, to be used to further the criminal purpose of laundering the proceeds of drug trafficking. For critical analysis of the case see Newbold, 'The Crime-Fraud Exception to Legal Professional Privilege' (1990) 53 MLR 472 at 777–84; Passmore, *Privilege* (2nd edn, xpl publishing, 2006) para 8.006–8.009.

[34] *Williams v Quebrada Railway, Land and Copper Co Ltd* [1895] 2 Ch 751 at 755. See also *Bullivant v Attorney General for Victoria* [1901] AC 196.

[35] *Ventouris v Mountain* [1991] 1 WLR 607 at 611.

[36] *Crescent Farm Sports v Sterling Offices* [1972] Ch 553 at 565 (*per* Goff J): 'I agree that fraud in this connection is not limited to the tort of deceit, and includes all forms of fraud and dishonesty, such as fraudulent breach of trust, fraudulent conspiracy, trickery and sham contrivances'.

[37] *Barclays Bank plc v Eustice* [1995] 1 WLR 1238 (CA).

[38] *Gamlen Chemical Co (UK) Ltd v Rochem Ltd* [1983] RPC 1 (7 December, 1979, unreported) CA (Civ).

'[T]he court must in every case, of course, be satisfied that what is prima facie proved really is dishonest, and not merely disreputable or a failure to maintain good ethical standards, and bear in mind that legal professional privilege is a necessary thing and is not lightly to be overthrown, but on the other hand, the interests of victims of fraud must not be overlooked. Each case depends on its own facts.'[39]

[5.16] *Dubai Aluminium Co Ltd v Al Alawi* centred on a dispute between the plaintiff company, which operated an aluminium smelter in Dubai, and the defendant employee over the latter's conduct as a sales manager during the period 1984 to 1993. The plaintiff instituted proceedings against the defendant, among others, asserting claims for money had and received, damages for breach of his employment contract and the recovery of secret commissions. The defendant sought the discharge of *Anton Piller* and *Mareva* orders that the plaintiff had obtained against him and claimed in support that the plaintiff had conducted an unlawful investigation of his finances. The defendant sought discovery of the fruits of that investigation and the plaintiff responded by asserting legal professional privilege. The case raised an issue of first impression, namely, whether the documents in question were relevant to criminal, fraudulent or otherwise iniquitous acts or purposes so as to fall outside the protection of privilege.

[5.17] The specific charge levelled by the defendant was that when investigating the defendant's finances, agents of the plaintiff had acted in contravention of English data protection legislation and Swiss banking laws. Rix J ordered disclosure[40] over the plaintiff's objection that this would stretch the exception to legal professional privilege too far:

'[I]t seems to me that criminal or fraudulent conduct for the purposes of acquiring evidence in or for litigation cannot properly escape the consequence that any documents generated by or reporting on such conduct and which are relevant to the issues in the case are discoverable and fall outside the legitimate area of legal professional privilege. It is not as though there are not legitimate avenues which can be sought with the aid of the court to investigate (for instance) banking documents. ... In such circumstances, it does not seem to me to be too great an intrusion on legal professional privilege to require that documentation such as in question in this case should be disclosed. Otherwise the position would be that the party employing the criminal or fraudulent agent would have it

39 *Gamlen Chemical Co (UK) Ltd v Rochem Ltd* [1983] RPC 1 (7 December, 1979, unreported) CA (Civ), quoted in *Dubai Aluminium Co Ltd v Al Alawi* [1999] 1 WLR 1964 at 1967 (*per* Rix J).

40 Rix J recognised that the extent of disclosure required raised a difficult question that could only be resolved on 'a case-by-case basis, and even a document by document basis': *Dubai Aluminium Co Ltd v Al Alawi* [1999] 1 WLR 1964 at 1970. Upon the giving of certain undertakings and cross-undertakings, the defendant was given unconditional leave to defend the first claim, the plaintiffs withdrew the other claims, and the *Anton Piller* and *Mareva* orders were discharged.

entirely within his own power to decide which of the criminally or fraudulently acquired information he was willing to rely on and disclose and which he was not. Where such a party will be asking the court to make inferences from such material, it is only fair that such material should be seen as a whole.'[41]

[5.18] The courts have distinguished between various legal consultative contexts with a view to identifying the nature of legal advice that will trigger the application of the exception. Privilege will clearly be lost where documents have been generated in the course of or in furtherance of a fraud.[42] Similarly, communications with a solicitor will not be protected where the client consults the solicitor 'in order to learn how to plan, execute, or stifle an actual fraud'.[43] Criminal or fraudulent conduct undertaken for the purposes of litigation is tainted in the same way.[44] However, the law does not seek to inhibit lawyers in 'the entirely legitimate professional business' of advising clients on their past and future conduct.[45] Thus, privilege presumptively attaches to communications with a solicitor about an intended course of action 'in order to be advised whether it is legitimate or not' or to the laying before a solicitor of 'the facts relating to a charge of fraud ... with the object of being advised about the best way to meet it'.[46] Pressing the exception too far would have the undesirable effect of dissuading persons facing allegations of fraud from seeking legal advice.[47]

Conduct Injurious to the Administration of Justice

[5.19] In the present day, the exception has been applied to conduct injurious to the administration of justice. In the landmark case of *Murphy v Kirwan*,[48] the Supreme Court held that a party defending a claim that he had abused the process of the court by instituting frivolous and vexatious proceedings was not entitled to resist discovery of legal advice obtained in relation to those proceedings. Finlay CJ stated:

[41] *Dubai Aluminium Co Ltd v Al Alawi* [1999] 1 WLR 1964 at 1969.

[42] *O'Rourke v Darbishire* [1920] AC 581, 613 (*per* Sumner LJ); *Kuwait Airways Corp v Iraqi Airways Co (No 6)* [2005] 1 WLR 2734, 2739 (*per* Longmore LJ).

[43] *O'Rourke v Darbishire* [1920] AC 581, 613 (*per* Sumner LJ). See also *Kuwait Airways Corp v Iraqi Airways Co (No 6)* [2005] 1 WLR 2734, 2739 (*per* Longmore LJ). Dennis notes that a purpose to defraud may be easier to infer 'where a client seeks advice on how to structure a transaction yet to be carried out than if he seeks advice on the effect of what has already been done': Dennis, *The Law of Evidence* (4th edn, Sweet & Maxwell, 2010) para 10.14 (citing *Barclays Bank plc v Eustice* [1995] 4 All ER 511).

[44] *Chandler v Church* (1987) 137 NLJ 451; *Dubai Aluminium Co Ltd v Al Alawi* [1999] 1 WLR 1964.

[45] *Dubai Aluminium Co Ltd v Al Alawi* [1999] 1 WLR 1964 at 1970 (*per* Rix J).

[46] *O'Rourke v Darbishire* [1920] AC 581 at 613 (*per* Sumner J).

[47] *Buttes Gas and Oil Co v Hammer (No 3)* [1981] QB 223.

[48] *Murphy v Kirwan* [1993] 3 IR 501, [1994] 1 ILRM 293.

> '... the essence of the matter is that professional privilege cannot and must not be applied so as to be injurious to the interests of justice and to those in the administration of justice where persons have been guilty of conduct of moral turpitude or of dishonest conduct, even though it may not be fraud.
>
> Nothing could be more injurious to the administration of justice nor to the interests of justice than that a person should falsely and maliciously bring an action, and should abuse for an ulterior or improper purpose the processes of the court.'[49]

[5.20] This general principle was applied more recently in *McMullen v Kennedy*.[50] The case involved 'a long running saga of litigation involving the plaintiff and a number of other parties including two firms of solicitors and a barrister (since deceased)'.[51] It originated in an unsuccessful action for professional negligence brought by the plaintiff against his former solicitors regarding the settlement of litigation to which he had been a party. The senior counsel who had acted for the plaintiff in the settlement testified on behalf of the solicitors in the negligence action. The defendant in the present proceedings acted for the former solicitors in their defence of the negligence claim. The essence of the plaintiff's claim was that the defendant improperly influenced the outcome of the negligence action by encouraging the senior counsel to assume responsibility for the error in the settlement. The Supreme Court recognised that allegations of this kind, involving dishonesty or moral turpitude, fell broadly within the exception. Macken J stated:

> 'Here the allegation on its face is clearly a very serious one indeed, made against an officer of the court and allegedly constituting an attempt to persuade a counsel to give evidence, in order to 'buy off' a possible or likely claim against that very counsel, falling into the category of moral turpitude, if it were true. It would in my view be injurious to the interests of justice to permit legal professional privilege to be applied in such circumstances, so as to prevent proper disclosure. That said, however, it is only in such unusual circumstances that I am prepared to make an exceptional order, which in ordinary course would not be made, having regard to the importance attaching to the principle of legal professional privilege'.[52]

[5.21] At the same time, the court signalled that it was not in favour of blanket disclosure to the plaintiff of all the documents sought and in which privilege might vest. The correct approach, in Macken J's view, was for the court to view the documents in question and determine whether they included information relevant to the proceedings which should be disclosed. It would then be necessary for the court to take the appropriate steps to permit the putative

49 *Murphy v Kirwan* [1993] 3 IR 501 at 511.

50 *McMullen v Kennedy* [2008] IESC 69 (17 December 2008).

51 *McMullen v Kennedy* [2008] IESC 69 (17 December 2008) at p 8 (*per* Fennelly J).

52 *McMullen v Kennedy* [2008] IESC 69 (17 December 2008) pp 4–5.

privilege holder to be heard.[53] Fennelly J dissented from the decision to order disclosure, subject even to the procedural conditions outlined by Macken J, because in his view the appellant had not produced any evidence to support his underlying contention. However, on the broad and general proposition that privilege cannot be used as a cloak for crime, fraud or moral turpitude, Fennelly J was in agreement with the majority. He stated that he had 'no difficulty' in accepting that an agreement or conspiracy to procure the giving of false evidence along the lines alleged would be 'illegal' and that 'legal professional privilege cannot conceivably be used to prevent an affected party from having access to documents tending to prove its existence'.[54]

Tortious Conduct

[5.22] Whereas the history of the crime–fraud exception has been one of gradual, continuous extension, the courts have drawn a line at conduct injurious to the administration of justice. *Murphy v Kirwan* represents a high water mark in the application of the exception in the Irish jurisprudence in that subsequent cases evince a less expansionist approach.

[5.23] In *Bula Ltd v Crowley (No 2)*,[55] the plaintiff company brought proceedings against the defendant for negligence in carrying out his duties as receiver to the plaintiff. The plaintiff sought discovery of documents containing legal advice obtained by the defendant contending that the nature of the defendant's conduct rendered such documents exempt from privilege. Finlay CJ noted that the exemption, though expanded over time, had been limited to conduct that contained an element of fraud, dishonesty or moral turpitude. He distinguished the scenario in *Murphy v Kirwan*, which involved an allegation of a malicious prosecution, from the present case, where the allegation was one of merely tortious conduct:

> 'The contention made in this case that such an exception should be extended to any case where it was proved that the nature of the legal advice obtained by a party was clearly relevant to an issue as to the commission of a tort would be inconsistent with the principles which I have set out. It would be a massive undermining, in my view, of the important confidence in relation to communications between lawyers and their clients which is a fundamental part of our system of justice and is considered in all the authorities to be a major contributor to the proper administration of justice.'[56]

Notwithstanding the confidence with which Finlay CJ distinguished *Murphy v Kirwan*, questions remain concerning the precise scope of the crime-fraud exception. Part of the difficulty stems from judicial use of the term 'moral

---

53 *McMullen v Kennedy* [2008] IESC 69 (17 December 2008) p 5.

54 *McMullen v Kennedy* [2008] IESC 69 (17 December 2008) p 9.

55 *Bula Ltd v Crowley (No 2)* [1994] 2 IR 54, [1994] 1 ILRM 495.

56 *Bula Ltd v Crowley (No 2)* [1994] 2 IR 54 at 59. See also *Crescent Farm Sports v Sterling Offices* [1972] Ch 533 (exception not applied to a claim for interference with contractual relations).

turpitude' which is not defined for purposes of the exception.[57] The case law indicates that conduct involving an element of moral turpitude comes within the exception but that tortious conduct does not. But does the classification of conduct as tortious necessarily preclude the possibility that it contained an element of moral turpitude?

[5.24] In *Shell E & P Ireland Ltd v McGrath (No 2)*,[58] the plaintiff sought an injunction restraining the defendants from using in the proceedings a solicitor's attendance docket that had been inadvertently disclosed. The underlying litigation involved Shell's application for the attachment and committal of the five defendants for breach of an injunction restraining them from interfering with the installation of a natural gas pipeline at Rossport, County Mayo. The defendants disputed the plaintiff's entitlement to assert privilege over the attendance docket contending that the plaintiff had been guilty of abuse of process and moral turpitude in maintaining the attachment and committal proceedings. The claim was that the plaintiff was using the proceedings to exert pressure on the defendants so as to stifle debate and protest over the pipeline project. It was alleged that the plaintiff had taken a strategic decision to create a sense of urgency before the court regarding access to the lands. Relying on *Murphy v Kirwan*,[59] the defendants argued that, given this reprehensible conduct on the part of the plaintiff, the application of privilege in the instant case would be injurious to the interests of justice.

[5.25] Smyth J rejected the defendants' claim on the law and the facts. He considered that the legal position was governed by *Bula Ltd v Crowley (No 2)*,[60] which made clear that the exemption is restricted to conduct which contains an element of fraud, dishonesty or moral turpitude and does not extend to allegations of tortious conduct. Here the defendants' plea in tort for malicious prosecution was expressly excluded from the principle in *Murphy v Kirwan* by *Bula Ltd v Crowley (No 2)*.[61] In addition, Smyth J determined that the attendance docket did not support the defendants' version of the facts. He rejected the suggestion of a strategic decision to create a contrived urgency and declared himself satisfied that 'at all material times the plaintiff wished to enter onto the lands along the length of the pipeline but, as determined by other judges, this aspiration was frustrated or interrupted or impeded or inhibited by the proceedings and actions of the defendants in different ways and at different times'.[62]

57 *In Re Estate of Treacy, deceased; Crawford v Treacy* [1999] 2 IR 171 at 177. O'Sullivan J recognised *obiter* that legal advice rendered to enable a deceased to defeat the legal entitlement of his wife would be sufficiently tainted with moral turpitude to trigger the exception.

58 *Shell E & P Ireland Ltd v McGrath (No 2)* [2007] 2 IR 574.

59 *Murphy v Kirwan* [1993] 3 IR 501.

60 *Bula Ltd v Crowley (No 2)* [1994] 2 IR 54.

61 *Shell E & P Ireland Ltd v McGrath (No 2)* [2007] 2 IR 574 at 583.

62 *Shell E & P Ireland Ltd v McGrath (No 2)* [2007] 2 IR 574 at 584.

In terms of the classification of the conduct in *Shell* (and returning to the question raised above), Smyth J applied the assumption of Finlay CJ in *Bula Ltd v Crowley (No 2)* that conduct which is pleaded as tortious does not contain the element of moral turpitude that would bring it within the exception. Having determined that the plaintiff's conduct did not involve an element of moral turpitude, he was not required to consider how the court might resolve a scenario in which conduct might qualify as both.

Standard of Proof

[5.26] A court asked to adjudicate on a claim that legal professional privilege should be cast aside on the basis of the crime–fraud exception is placed in an invidious situation. At the time the claim is made, criminal or fraudulent conduct is generally alleged but has not been established. If the court insists on proof of wrongdoing, the onus placed on the claimant may be so high that disclosure becomes a practical impossibility. On the other hand, a liberal approach to disclosure would substantially undercut the protection afforded by legal professional privilege.[63] The displacement of privilege is undoubtedly an exceptional occurrence. Beyond this, however, the courts have struggled to identify the strength of the case that the claimant must make in order to satisfy the court that privilege should give way.

[5.27] In *Murphy v Kirwan*,[64] Egan J alluded to the standard of proof that must be met by a party seeking to defeat an assertion of privilege by invoking the crime–fraud exception. He stated: 'The rule does not apply merely because fraud is alleged in the action. There must be some *prima facie* evidence that the allegation has a foundation in fact'.[65] Egan J cited with approval the determination of the House of Lords in *O'Rourke v Darbishire*[66] that the person alleging fraud must show to the satisfaction of the court good grounds for saying that *prima facie* a state of things exists which, if not displaced at the trial, will support a charge of fraud. Indeed, subsequent English cases have emphasised that a very strong *prima facie* case of fraud is required in order to invoke the exception.[67] However, the need for each case to be judged on its own facts has also weighed heavily with the courts.[68]

---

63 Passmore, *Privilege* (2nd edn, xpl publishing, 2006) para 8.053 (discussing cases).

64 *Murphy v Kirwan* [1993] 3 IR 501, [1994] 1 ILRM 293.

65 *Murphy v Kirwan* [1993] 3 IR 501 at 514. See also *Derby & Co Ltd v Weldon (No 7)* [1990] 1 WLR 1156; *Barclays Bank plc v Eustice* [1995] 1 WLR 1238.

66 *O'Rourke v Darbishire* [1920] AC 581.

67 *Bankers Trust Co v Shapira* [1980] 1 WLR 1274; *Buttes Gas and Oil Co v Hammer (No 3)* [1981] QB 223; *Kuwait Airways Corp v Iraqi Airways Co (No 6)* [2005] 1 WLR 2734.

68 *Derby & Co v Weldon (No 7)* [1990] 1 WLR 1156, 1173 *(per* Vinelott J): 'There is a continuous spectrum and it is impossible to, as it were, calibrate or express in any simple formula the strength of the case that the plaintiff must show'.

[5.28] These observations lend support to the approach of Fennelly J in his dissenting judgment in *McMullen v Kennedy*.[69] The plaintiff's case rested on the contention that the defendant solicitor had been involved in an agreement or conspiracy to procure false testimony. The three members of the Supreme Court[70] agreed that by its nature this context came within the substantive scope of the exception. However, whereas the majority were willing to permit a form of conditional disclosure, Fennelly J voted to dismiss the appeal on the ground that the plaintiff had come 'nowhere close' to establishing the underlying contention.[71]

INNOCENCE AT STAKE

[5.29] In criminal proceedings, there is some dispute over whether an assertion of privilege may be maintained where the defence seek disclosure of the privileged communication in order to establish the innocence of the accused.[72]

The traditional position at common law was that no privilege attached to information in the possession of a party that would assist the defence of the accused. Caulfield J stated in *R v Barton*:

> 'If there are documents in the possession or control of a solicitor which, on production, help to further the defence of an accused man, then in my judgment no privilege attaches. I cannot conceive that our law would permit a solicitor or other person to screen from a jury information which, if disclosed to the jury, would perhaps enable a man to either establish his innocence or to resist an allegation made by the Crown.'[73]

Caulfield J's decision was one of first impression based not on authority but rather on his conception of the rules of natural justice.[74] However, in *R v Ataou*[75] his approach found favour with the English Court of Appeal which purported to set down a two-step test: first, the judge must inquire whether the client continues to have any recognisable interest in asserting privilege; and, second, if so, whether his interest outweighs the public interest in the disclosure of all relevant and admissible evidence to the defence in criminal proceedings.[76] This principle marked a break with the common law tradition which has long emphasised that privilege is subject to rules rather than a discretionary balancing exercise.

---

69 *McMullen v Kennedy* [2008] IESC 69 (17 December 2008).

70 Fennelly, Kearns and Macken JJ.

71 *McMullen v Kennedy* [2008] IESC 69 (17 December 2008) at p 10.

72 See generally Auburn, *Legal Professional Privilege: Law and Theory* (Hart Publishing, 2000), ch 9.

73 *R v Barton* [1973] 1 WLR 115 at 118. *See also R v Ataou* [1988] 2 All ER 321; *R v Craig* [1975] 1 NZLR 597; *R v Dunbar and Logan* (1982) 138 DLR (3d) 221.

74 *R v Barton* [1973] 1 WLR 115 at 118.

75 *R v Ataou* [1988] 2 All ER 321, [1988] QB 798.

76 *R v Ataou* [1988] 2 All ER 321 at 326, [1988] QB 798 at 807 (*per* French J).

[5.30] A dramatically different stance was adopted by the House of Lords in *R v Derby Magistrates' Court, ex parte B.*[77] The appellant was charged with the murder of a girl but was acquitted at trial. After his arrest he confessed to the crime but later changed his account and sought to cast blame on his stepfather. His stepfather was subsequently charged with the murder and the appellant was called as a prosecution witness. Counsel for the stepfather sought to cross-examine the accused on the instructions he had given his solicitor in relation to his own trial. The appellant asserted privilege and the prosecution sought an order directing the solicitor to produce the information.

[5.31] On appeal, the House of Lords refused to order the witness or his solicitor to hand over the evidence in question. Lord Taylor famously quipped:

> 'Legal professional privilege is thus much more than an ordinary rule of evidence limited in its application to the facts of a particular case. It is a fundamental condition on which the administration of justice as a whole rests.'[78]

Lord Taylor distinguished legal professional privilege from public interest immunity and rejected the suggestion that the former is subject to any form of balancing exercise.[79] He emphasised that any restriction on the absolute character of privilege would necessarily threaten its fundamental purpose:

> '[O]nce any exception to the general rule is allowed, the client's confidence is necessarily lost. The solicitor, instead of being able to tell his client that anything which the client might say would never in any circumstances be revealed without his consent, would have to qualify his assurance. He would have to tell the client that his confidence might be broken if in some future case the court were to hold that he no longer had 'any recognisable interest' in asserting his privilege. One can see at once that the purpose of the privilege would thereby be undermined.'[80]

Lord Lloyd concurred in this characterisation of the governing legal principle. He clarified the reason for rejecting a balancing exercise: it was not because of any inherent difficulty in the exercise *per se* but rather the status of legal professional privilege as the predominant public interest. He observed: 'A balancing exercise is not required in individual cases, because the balance must always come down in favour of upholding the privilege, unless, of course, the privilege is waived'.[81]

---

77 *R v Derby Magistrates' Court, ex parte B* [1995] 3 WLR 681, [1995] 4 All ER 526.

78 *R v Derby Magistrates' Court, ex parte B* [1995] 3 WLR 681 at 695, [1995] 4 All ER 526 at 540–541.

79 *R v Derby Magistrates' Court, ex parte B* [1995] 3 WLR 681 at 696, [1995] 4 All ER 526 at 541.

80 *R v Derby Magistrates' Court, ex parte B* [1995] 3 WLR 681 at 696, [1995] 4 All ER 526 at 541.

81 *R v Derby Magistrates' Court, ex parte B* [1995] 3 WLR 681 at 697, [1995] 4 All ER 526 at 542.

[5.32] The approach of the House of Lord has not found universal favour.[82] Whereas it resonated with the courts in Australia,[83] the Canadian courts have been generally more receptive to the disclosure of evidence that would assist the accused.[84] In *R v McClure*,[85] the Canadian Supreme Court held that privilege may be overridden in the face of the compelling public interest in enabling an accused to present a full and proper defence. Similarly, in the United States, the Sixth Amendment's due process clause[86] has operated as a springboard for a right on the part of the defence to introduce demonstrably reliable exculpatory evidence.[87]

[5.33] It is not clear how the Irish courts would resolve a conflict between legal professional privilege and innocence at stake. In the context of informer privilege, as a facet of public interest immunity, the need to avoid convicting innocent persons has been cited as a relevant factor in balancing the competing public interests in confidentiality and disclosure.[88] However, in *People (DPP) v Kelly*,[89] the Supreme Court upheld the entitlement of a prosecution witness, a senior garda officer, to protect the anonymity of his informer notwithstanding the limitation it necessarily imposed on the defence's right to cross-examination. The witness had been presenting so-called 'belief evidence' pursuant to s 3(2) of the Offences Against the State (Amendment) Act 1972. On a trial for the offence of membership of an illegal organisation,[90] the subsection permits a garda officer not below the rank of chief superintendent to testify as to her belief that the accused was a member at the material time. It is noteworthy that in deciding to uphold the claim to informer privilege over the accused's right to introduce potentially exculpatory evidence, the Supreme Court was influenced, *inter alia*, by the special setting of the Offences Against the State regime. Whether a more flexible judicial approach would prevail in a proceeding involving an ordinary offence remains an open question. The ever increasing

---

82 For a critique of the decision see Tapper, 'Prosecution and Privilege' (1996–97) 1 Int'l J Evid & Proof 5.

83 *Carter v Managing Partner, Northmore Hale Davy &Leake* (1995) 129 ALR 593, 183 CLR 129. For critical analysis see Auburn, *Legal Professional Privilege: Law and Theory* (Hart Publishing, 2000) pp 188–191. The decision in *Carter* was subsequently overturned Australian Evidence Act 1995, s 123. Dennis, *The Law of Evidence* (4th edn, Sweet & Maxwell, 2010) para 10.26.

84 McGrath, *Evidence* (Thomson Round Hall, 2005) at para 10.84; Auburn, *Legal Professional Privilege: Law and Theory* (Hart Publishing, 2000) pp 185–86 (discussing cases).

85 *R v McClure* [2001] 1 SCR 445.

86 Applied to the States via the Fourteenth Amendment.

87 See Heffernan and Imwinkelried, 'The Accused's Constitutional Right to Introduce Critical, Demonstrably Reliable, Exculpatory Evidence' (2005) 40 Irish Jurist (ns) 111.

88 *Director of Consumer Affairs v Sugar Distributors* [1991] 1 IR 225; *Ward v Special Criminal Court* [1998] 2 ILRM 493. See **Ch 10**.

89 *People (DPP) v Kelly* [2006] 3 IR 115.

90 Under the Offences Against the State Act 1939, s 21.

influence of the case law of the European Court of Human Rights may be a factor in the future development of the law in this area. The right of an accused person to evidence necessary for the conduct of her defence may take precedence over the right of another person, such as the appellant in *R v Derby Magistrates,* to protection for her lawyer-client communications.[91]

Also unresolved is the question whether informer privilege constitutes a special case or whether the courts should adopt a uniform approach across all species of privilege.

TESTAMENTARY DISPOSITIONS

[5.34] Privilege generally survives the death of the client and continues to exist for the benefit of the client's successors in title. However, some courts have recognised an exception in the case of disputes over testamentary dispositions. The justification for piercing privilege is twofold. First, the deceased client has no interest to be protected other than ensuring that her intentions are carried out with the consequence that lifting privilege will have no chilling effect on the lawyer-client relationship. In other words, the rationales for privilege do not apply.[92] The second justification is that probate proceedings are more inquisitorial than adversarial in nature.

Lord Scarman elaborated on these policy rationales in the case *In re estate of Fuld deceased:*

> '... there can be in a probate case an apparent clash or conflict between the right of the court to know everything that its witness knows or has said about execution, and the right of a party to claim privilege for communications passing between that witness and himself or his solicitor for the purpose of collecting evidence for the hearing. If there be such a conflict, I have no doubt that it must be resolved in favour of the court. Strictly, however, there is no such conflict because the court in its inquisitorial capacity is seeking the truth as to its execution. The parties upon the issue of execution are assisting the court in its search for the truth. It seems to me, therefore, that if the court comes to the conclusion that the truth can only be discovered by asking a witness to produce earlier statements that he may have made in writing concerning execution, then the court is entitled to insist on seeing those statements ...'[93]

[5.35] In *Re Estate of Treacy, deceased; Crawford v Treacy,*[94] the plaintiff executors of an estate brought an application for directions. The first defendant claimed to be married to the deceased and was so named in his will but there

---

[91] Dennis, *The Law of Evidence* (4th edn, Sweet & Maxwell, 2010) para 10.26 points out that the only Convention right which the stepfather could invoke would be a qualified right to privacy under art 8. Dennis also presents the broader argument that, since there seems little chance that the English courts will reconsider their stance, Parliament should intervene.

[92] *Russell v Jackson* (1851) 9 Hare 387.

[93] *In re estate of Fuld deceased* [1965] P 405 at 410.

[94] *Re Estate of Treacy, deceased; Crawford v Treacy* [1999] 2 IR 171.

was a dispute as to whether the two were in fact married at the date of his death. The defendants sought discovery of documents relating to the preparation of the will and over which the plaintiffs asserted privilege.

O'Sullivan J accepted the special place occupied by proceedings concerning testamentary dispositions on the landscape of privilege and disclosure. However, he distinguished the present case from the English authorities of *Russell v Jackson*[95] and *In re estate of Fuld deceased*.[96] Whereas justice clearly required the production of the documents or evidence in those cases, the same could not be said of present case. The documents sought by the first defendant related to advice but the facts upon which that advice was given would be available independently to the court. In the circumstances, O'Sullivan J was not convinced that the truth could only be discovered by ordering disclosure of the documents in question. In this sense, the interests of justice did not necessitate disclosure.[97]

Proceedings Relating to Children

[5.36] Proceedings affecting the welfare of children depart from the strict adversarial model in several respects. One noteworthy example is that the courts may be more flexible in their application of the rules of evidence.

In *In re L (A Minor) (Police Investigation: Privilege)*,[98] a majority of the House of Lords held that care proceedings under Part IV of the Children Act 1989 were 'investigative' rather than adversarial in nature with the consequence that litigation privilege was excluded.[99] The proceedings in this case concerned a child of drug addicts who became sick after ingesting a quantity of methadone. The mother contended that the child had consumed the drug by accident whereas the police suspected that it had been administered to the child deliberately. At issue in the care proceedings was the possible disclosure to the police of a pathologist's report that had been commissioned by the mother but that undermined her version of events. By a majority of three to two, the House of Lords rejected the mother's claim that the report was protected from disclosure by litigation privilege.

[5.37] The majority approved *Oxfordshire County Council v M*[100] in which the Court of Appeal held that in care proceedings the trial judge has the authority to 'override' litigation privilege and order the production of an expert report. Lord

---

95 *Russell v Jackson* (1851) 9 Hare 387.

96 *In re estate of Fuld deceased* [1965] P 405.

97 *Re Estate of Treacy, deceased; Crawford v Treacy* [1999] 2 IR 171 at 177.

98 *In re L (A Minor) (Police Investigation: Privilege)* [1997] AC 16, [1996] 2 All ER 78. See McEwan, 'The Uncertain Status of Privilege in Children Act Cases: Re L' (1996–97) 1 Int'l J Evid & Proof 80; Dennis, *The Law of Evidence* (4th edn, Sweet & Maxwell, 2010) para 10.35.

99 Lords Mustill and Nicholls dissenting.

100 *Oxfordshire County Council v M* [1994] 2 All ER 269, [1994] 2 WLR 393.

Jauncey in *re L* drew a sharp distinction between an adversarial proceeding, in which litigation privilege played an important part, and a non-adversarial proceeding such as care proceedings relating to the welfare of a child.[101] However, he eschewed the notion that privilege is 'overridden' in such circumstances and preferred the view that it is prevented by the 1989 Act from arising in the first place.[102]

[5.38] The same terrain had been traversed in the Irish case of *L(T) v L(V)*[103] in which McGuinness J reached the same conclusion that in principle the veil of legal professional privilege could be pierced in certain proceedings concerning the welfare of children. The applicant wife brought proceedings against the respondent husband seeking a decree of judicial separation and orders of custody, maintenance and division of family property. The respondent objected to discovery of notes contained in his diary on the ground of legal professional privilege. Matrimonial litigants are frequently advised to keep notes of events affecting the parties and the children for the purpose of instructing their lawyers in preparation for trial. McGuinness J accepted that the respondent's diary fell within this practice and consequently would be protected by privilege in the normal way. The issue before the court was whether disclosure should trump privilege where the document in question contains information relevant to the welfare of the children.

[5.39] The case predated the decision of the House of Lords in *In re L* but McGuinness J gleaned from the pre-existing English authorities[104] the important principle that proceedings concerning the welfare of children are not fully adversarial in nature but rather cast the court in an inquisitorial role. She took the view that this principle could be applied in this jurisdiction to cases governed by s 3 of the Guardianship of Infants Act 1964. The Irish courts have a statutory duty in such cases – buttressed by the constitutional right of the child to have her welfare protected by the court – to seek to achieve a result which accords with the best interests of the child. McGuinness J adopted the English approach that the court has the power to override legal professional privilege 'in suitable circumstances where the welfare of a child is in issue'.[105]

[5.40] It is important to note certain caveats that McGuinness J entered to her determination of this guiding principle. The English cases to which she referred dealt with medical and expert reports which are the type of material that would normally require to be disclosed in this context. She cautioned that the same considerations do not necessarily apply to other matters normally protected by privilege. The learned judge continued:

---

[101] *In re L (A Minor) (Police Investigation: Privilege)* [1997] AC 16 at 24–25.

[102] *In re L (A Minor) (Police Investigation: Privilege)* [1997] AC 16 at 27.

[103] *L(T) v L(V)* [1996] IFLR 126.

[104] Including *Oxfordshire County Council v M* [1994] 2 All ER 269, [1994] 2 WLR 393.

[105] *L(T) v L(V)* [1996] IFLR 126 at 136.

> 'In each case the desirability of disclosure must on the facts of the case be weighed against the desirability of maintaining the privilege and a decision taken in the light of the interest of the child concerned.'[106]

This is a particularly illuminating passage because it emphasises the distinct approach required by the court when considering confidentiality versus disclosure in the quasi-inquisitorial setting of proceedings concerning the welfare of children. Whereas in other contexts, the courts have stressed that assertions of privilege should be resolved by the application of pre-determined legal rules, proceedings concerning the welfare of children seem to require the courts to engage in a balancing exercise.

[5.41] A further implication is that proceedings concerning the welfare of children do not constitute a blanket exemption to legal professional privilege and that the issue must be addressed on a case-by-case basis. Indeed, the terms in which McGuinness J cast this exemption from privilege are also worthy of note. She accepted that the power to override privilege in such cases should be exercised only rarely when the court is satisfied that it is necessary.[107] Indeed, this limitation was reflected in the result reached on the facts of the case: having reviewed the respondent's diary, McGuinness J held that its nature was not such that the interests of the children required that it be disclosed by way of discovery.[108]

---

[106] *L(T) v L(V)* [1996] IFLR 126 at 137.

[107] Citing the judgment of Johnston J in *Re A (Minors: Disclosure of Material)* [1991] 2 FLR 473. This point was emphasised by Lord Steyn in *Oxfordshire County Council v M* [1994] 2 WLR 393 at 403, [1994] 2 All ER 269 at 282.

[108] *L(T) v L(V)* [1996] IFLR 126 at 137.

Chapter 6

Loss of Privilege

INTRODUCTION

[6.01] A *prima facie* case of privilege is established where the privilege holder discharges her burden of satisfying the court that the conditions pertaining to the privilege have been met. The holder of a privilege, although confident that she is entitled to resist disclosure as a matter of law, may decide to waive the privilege for strategic or other reasons.[1] Alternatively, an opposing party may defeat an assertion of privilege by establishing that the holder has waived the privilege. Waiver may be deliberate or inadvertent, express or implied, and the privilege may be waived in whole or in part.[2] It may occur at any stage in the trial process: during pre-trial correspondence or negotiations between the party or during the course of the trial itself.[3] Moreover, it may take place even after the privilege has been asserted and recognised by the court.

Once adopted, however, the act of waiver is irreversible; if a client has waived the privilege 'he cannot then reassert it'.[4] Moreover, because a party is not permitted to edit her evidence, a client who seeks to disclose select elements of a privileged communication runs the risk of being compelled to reveal the communication in its entirety.[5] The compromise options that may be open to a

1 On loss of privilege see generally Auburn, *Legal Professional Privilege: Law and Theory* (Hart Publishing, 2000) chs 10–12; Passmore, *Privilege* (2nd edn, xpl publishing, 2006) ch 7; Thanki (ed), *The Law of Privilege* (Oxford University Press, 2006) ch 5; Matthews and Malek, *Disclosure* (Sweet & Maxwell, 2001) ch 10; McGrath, *Evidence* (Thomson Round Hall, 2005) para 10.91 *et seq*; Healy, *Irish Laws of Evidence* (Thomson Round Hall, 2004) ch 13.II. For other comparative perspectives see, eg, Mathieson (ed), *Cross on Evidence* (8th New Zealand edn, Lexis Nexis, 2005) para 10.29 *et seq*.; Zeffertt, Paizes and Skeen, *The South African Law of Evidence* (Lexis Nexis, 2003) ch 17.

2 *Guinness Peat Properties Ltd v Fitzroy Robinson* [1987] 1 WLR 1027, [1987] 2 All ER 716; *Fyffes plc v DCC plc* [2005] 1 IR 59.

3 *Hannigan v DPP* [2001] 1 IR 378.

4 Keane, *Modern Law of Evidence* (7th edn, Oxford University Press, 2008) at p 630.

5 Keane, *Modern Law of Evidence* (7th edn, Oxford University Press, 2008) at p 631 (citing *Great Atlantic Insurance Co v Home Insurance Co* [1981] 1 WLR 529 and *George Doland Ltd v Blackburn, Robson, Coates & Co* [1972] 1 WLR 1338).

court in cases of this kind include permitting the production of documents in part[6] and permitting production in redacted form.[7]

[6.02] Despite the wide range of circumstances in which waiver may occur, courts tend to approach loss of privilege with a degree of caution, bearing in mind the special place that privilege holds in the administration of justice.[8] When deciding whether privilege has been lost in a particular case, the courts will be influenced to some extent by considerations of fairness between the parties.[9] However, the Supreme Court has emphasised that waiver, like the privilege it abrogates, is governed by pre-determined rules as opposed to a discretionary balancing of competing interests.[10]

Inadvertent Disclosure

[6.03] In *Guinness Peat Properties Ltd v Fitzroy Robinson*,[11] the plaintiff building developers brought an action for breach of contract and negligence against the defendant architects. During the course of discovery, the defendants inadvertently disclosed a letter that they had sent to their insurers prior to the commencement of proceedings and over which they had intended to assert privilege. The inadvertent disclosure came to the defendants' attention when they received a copy of the report of the plaintiffs' expert witness which referred to the correspondence. The defendants persuaded the court that the letter was privileged and that it had remained privileged at all times. The plaintiffs appealed against an order restraining them from making further use of the letter and requiring the return of all copies thereof.

[6.04] Slade LJ stated the relevant principles broadly as follows. First, where solicitors for one party to litigation have mistakenly included in the list of discoverable documents an item over which they could have asserted privilege, the court will ordinarily permit them to amend the list at any time before inspection of the item has taken place. Second, once the other party has inspected the document, it is generally too late for the party asserting privilege to correct the mistake by applying for injunctive relief. Third, the court retains

6 Production in part may not be a realistic solution in some instances. For example, in *Great Atlantic Insurance Co v Home Insurance Co and Others* [1981] 1 WLR 529, the Court of Appeal held that a memorandum which dealt with a single subject matter was not capable of being divided into separate and distinct memoranda with the consequence that the memorandum had effectively been waived in full.

7 *Brennan and Others v Sunderland City Council and Others* [2009] ICR 479.

8 *Fyffes plc v DCC plc* [2005] 1 IR 59 (*per* Fennelly J citing *Lillicrap & Another v Nalder & Son (A Firm) & Another* [1993] 1 WLR 94).

9 *Fyffes plc v DCC plc* [2005] 1 IR 59; *Redfern Ltd v O'Mahony* [2009] IESC 18 (4 March 2009).

10 *Fyffes plc v DCC plc* [2005] 1 IR 59; *Redfern Ltd v O'Mahony* [2009] IESC 18 (4 March 2009).

11 *Guinness Peat Properties Ltd v Fitzroy Robinson* [1987] 1 WLR 1027, [1987] 2 All ER 716.

an equitable power to intervene where the other party (a) has procured inspection of the item by fraud or (b) on inspection, realises that she has been permitted to see the item only by reason of an obvious mistake.[12]

[6.05] On this last point, Slade LJ expressed the personal view that the court should ordinarily intervene 'unless the case is one where the injunction can properly be refused on the general principles affecting the grant of a discretionary remedy, for example, on the ground of inordinate delay'.[13] In the present case, the plaintiffs' solicitors must have realised that the letter had been disclosed by mistake. Although no doubt acting in what they conceived to be the best interests of their clients, the plaintiffs' solicitors were 'in all circumstances seeking to take advantage of what they must have known was an obvious error'. Slade LJ concluded that it had been proper for the court to intervene to protect the defendants who had moved promptly to seek relief as soon as they became aware of what had occurred.[14]

[6.06] The reasoning in *Guinness Peat* represents an outgrowth of a longstanding principle that where one party to legal proceedings has obtained privileged information by trick the privilege holder may secure injunctive relief to prevent the deployment of the material in the proceedings.[15] Subsequent decisions have shed further light the approach the courts should take when deciding whether disclosure is attributable to an obvious mistake. In essence, the privilege holder has the burden of establishing on the balance of probabilities that the mistake would have been obvious to a reasonable solicitor.[16] Thus, the test is an objective one although the subjective circumstances of the particular case may also bear on the determination.[17]

[6.07] The consequences of inadvertent disclosure were debated before the High Court in *Shell E & P Ireland Ltd v McGrath (No 2)*.[18] The underlying litigation involved Shell's application for the attachment and committal of the five defendants for breach of an injunction restraining them from interfering with the installation of a natural gas pipeline at Rossport, County Mayo. The plaintiff's solicitor inadvertently included a copy of a solicitor's attendance docket as a part

---

12 *Guinness Peat Properties Ltd v Fitzroy Robinson* [1987] 1 WLR 1027 at 1045–46.

13 *Guinness Peat Properties Ltd v Fitzroy Robinson* [1987] 1 WLR 1027 at 1046 (citing *Goddard v Nationwide Building Soc* [1986] 3 All ER 264, [1986] 3 WLR 734). See also *Derby & Co Ltd v Weldon (No 8)* [1990] 3 All ER 762.

14 *Guinness Peat Properties Ltd v Fitzroy Robinson* [1987] 1 WLR 1027 at 1046.

15 *Lord Ashburton v Pape* [1913] 2 Ch 469. However, in the absence of a colourable claim for injunctive relief, the party who has the privileged material in her hand may use it as secondary evidence in the proceedings. *Goddard v Nationwide Building Society* [1986] 3 All ER 264, [1986] 3 WLR 734; *ISTIL Group Inc v Zahoor* [2003] 2 All ER 252.

16 *IBM Corpn v Phoenix International* [1995] 1 All ER 413.

17 Keane, *Modern Law of Evidence* (7th edn, Oxford University Press, 2008) at p 629.

18 *Shell E & P Ireland Ltd v McGrath (No 2)* [2007] 2 IR 574.

of a book of *inter partes* correspondence in an exhibit to an affidavit grounding the application. The mistake came to light when a representative of the *Irish Times* contacted the plaintiff seeking comments on certain file notes relating to a meeting between the plaintiff and its solicitors that had come into the newspaper's possession. Disjointed excerpts from the attendance docket were published in the newspaper. Some time later, it emerged that the defendants had a copy of the document in their possession. They sought to use the attendance docket in the proceedings to support an allegation of moral turpitude on Shell's part in its conduct in the dispute. It was not disputed that an attendance docket would usually attract privilege. The defendants had argued unsuccessfully that Shell was not entitled to privilege in the instant case because it had been guilty of abuse of process and moral turpitude in its dealings with the defendants. The remaining issue before the court was whether privilege had been lost by the inadvertent disclosure to the defendants.

[6.08] Smyth J distinguished an instance of deliberate disclosure of a privileged communication from a scenario, such as the present, involving inadvertent disclosure. Whereas it was clear that deliberate disclosure would result in the loss of privilege, the question of inadvertent disclosure had not been squarely addressed by the Irish courts. He noted a consistency of view in the relevant English decisions, including *Guinness Peat Properties Ltd*, that in circumstances where it must have been apparent to the solicitors for the other party that the disclosure was as a result of obvious mistake, the court may grant an injunction restraining that party from making use of the document in the proceedings. Smyth J was satisfied that, in the present case, it must have been apparent to the defendants' solicitor that the document was privileged and had been disclosed by reason of mistake.[19]

[6.09] Also before the court was the issue of the efficacy of equitable relief (an injunction restraining a party from making use of a privileged document) where the document has been circulated and confidentiality lost. The defendants challenged Shell's entitlement to the relief sought on the grounds that it was too late to restore the *status quo* and that Shell had failed to move expeditiously to reassert its claim of privilege once the inadvertent disclosure had come to its attention. Smyth J rejected these contentions on the facts. He was satisfied that the document was not circulated to the public but was 'inadvertently given to one or more of the defendants who may have, and probably did, communicate

[19] *Shell E & P Ireland Ltd v McGrath (No 2)* [2007] 2 IR 574 at 585 and 589. In terms of the applicable legal test to govern situations of inadvertent disclosure, Smyth J favoured the more protective approach taken in jurisdictions such as Australia and Canada whereby a court will restrain use of a privileged document that has been disclosed by inadvertence regardless of how obvious the mistake. Because the disclosure by Shell's solicitor was obviously inadvertent, it did not matter which approach was followed in the instant case.

the confidential document to the newspaper'.[20] He took the view that the fact that some disjointed excerpts were printed in the *Irish Times* did not mean that the document was in the public domain.[21] Smyth J was also satisfied that when Shell and its solicitor 'had an apprehension as to who had the document and what use it might be put to' they immediately asserted the privilege.[22]

[6.10] In terms of principle, Smyth J held that the focus of the equitable remedy is not simply the protection of the confidentiality of the communication but also the restraining of its use.[23] This conclusion dovetailed with the learned judge's interpretation of the rationale on which legal professional privilege rests. Earlier in his judgment, Smyth J recalled that the interest of the client in the maintenance of privilege is twofold. Not only has the client an interest in maintaining the confidentiality of the privileged communication but she is also concerned to ensure that the document is not used against her in proceedings, even in a situation where confidentiality is lost or impaired. He quoted with approval from the judgment of Lyndhurst LC in *Holmes v Bradley*:

> 'The principle upon which the rule is established is that communications between a party and his professional advisers, with a view to legal proceedings, should be unfettered: that they should not be restrained by any apprehension of such communications being divulged *and made use of to his prejudice*' [emphasis added].[24]

In conclusion, Smyth J opined that the court should have regard to 'the very important interest that is served by privilege and its important role in the administration of justice'. Thus, in the instant case, it was appropriate to adopt 'a protective approach to privilege' particularly where the documents were revealed inadvertently and the court was satisfied that there was no abuse of process on the privilege holder's behalf.[25]

[6.11] In *Byrne & Another v Shannon Foynes Port Co & Another,* Clarke J analysed the relevant authorities and summarised the test to be applied in cases of inadvertent disclosure as follows:

> 'Firstly the court must consider whether the solicitor seeing the document or documents concerned, realised that a mistake had been made. Secondly, and perhaps more importantly on the basis of the authorities, the court must put itself in the position of a reasonable solicitor and consider whether, on the balance of

20 *Shell E & P Ireland Ltd v McGrath (No 2)* [2007] 2 IR 574 at 586.

21 *Shell E & P Ireland Ltd v McGrath (No 2)* [2007] 2 IR 574 at 585.

22 *Shell E & P Ireland Ltd v McGrath (No 2)* [2007] 2 IR 574 at 586.

23 *Shell E & P Ireland Ltd v McGrath (No 2)* [2007] 2 IR 574 at 587–588 (reviewing English authorities).

24 *Holmes v Bradley* (1844) 1 Ph 476 at 480–481. Smyth J also quoted from the earlier judgment of Brougham LC in *Bolton v Liverpool Corp* (1833) 1 My & K 88 at 94.

25 *Shell E & P Ireland Ltd v McGrath (No 2)* [2007] 2 IR 574 at 589.

probabilities, such solicitor would have taken the disclosure to have been as a result of a mistake.'[26]

Clarke J applied this test in the subsequent case of *Tír na nÓg Projects Ireland Ltd v County Council of County Kerry*.[27] Tír na nÓg sought a declaration of default planning permission on the basis that Kerry County Council had failed to take a decision on a planning application within the statutory time limit. It sought discovery of a document that contained advice by Kerry County Council's solicitor on the course of action to be taken in light of the failure to decide the planning application. The document was openly available on the public planning file for a considerable period of time during which Tír na nÓg had access to it. In these circumstances, Clarke J was not satisfied that the test enunciated above was met.

[6.12] As a preliminary matter, Clarke J dismissed as immaterial to the framing of the test the fact that the disclosure had not occurred in the context of the conventional exchange of court documents:

> 'Where a document which might be the subject of a proper claim of privilege comes to the attention of the other side in litigation, whether as a result of its formal disclosure in the discovery process, by it being inadvertently handed over, as would appear to have happened in *Shell E & P*, or by virtue of it being placed on a public file or otherwise made publicly available, as in the circumstances of this case, does not affect the principle. The underlying test which the court must apply is whether a reasonable person would objectively view any privilege that might have attached to the document as having been waived in the light of the circumstances in which the document had come to the other side's attention. Those circumstances are, therefore, material in that they may affect the proper judgment as to whether, objectively speaking, a party might legitimately take the privilege to have been waived. The circumstances do not, however, affect the test'.

In the present case, the document was available on a public file and Kerry County Council had not given any meaningful explanation as to how the mistake had occurred. Clarke J pointed out that there were many reasons why a local authority might be motivated to place on the public planning record an account of advice received. In the circumstances, Clarke J was not satisfied that it would have been clear to Tír na nÓg that the placing of the document on the record was due to an error on the part of Kerry County Council. He directed discovery of the document on the ground that Kerry County Council must be taken to have waived privilege.

---

26 *Byrne & Another v Shannon Foynes Port Co & Another* [2007] IEHC 315 (7 September 2007), para 5.1.

27 *Tír na nÓg Projects Ireland Ltd v County Council of County Kerry* [2008] IEHC 48 (28 February 2008), para 4.4.

TECHNOLOGICAL DEVELOPMENTS

[6.13] Advances in technology have influenced immeasurably the manner in which we collect, store and exchange information in modern society. The use of electronically stored information, in particular, presents both benefits and challenges to the processes of gathering and exchanging information for the purposes of litigation.

Changes in the Court Rules Relating to Discovery

[6.14] The recent amendments to the rules relating to discovery are enshrined in SI 93/2009, *Rules of the Superior Courts (Discovery)* which entered into force on 16 April 2009.[28] SI 93/2009 introduced important reforms relating to the discovery of electronically stored information. The need for this development was highlighted by *Dome Telecom Ltd v Eircom Ltd*[29] which presented the Supreme Court with the challenge of deciding complex issues relating to the discovery of electronically stored information. The rules now expressly address the subject of electronic discovery[30] and allow for a range of outcomes including the possible appointment of 'an independent expert or person' to undertake the inspection and searching of the documents.[31] While the new provisions adapt the rules to embrace technological developments in the generating, storing and accessing of documents, uncertainties remain. In particular, if discovery of electronically stored information complicates the task of identifying privileged material, the risk of inadvertent disclosure may increase.

US Developments

[6.15] Developments in federal trial practice in the United States illuminate some of the pitfalls and potential solutions. In 2006, the Federal Rules of Civil Procedure governing discovery were amended to require parties to identify and collect electronically stored information (in addition to traditional forms of documentation). Parties must review the information to determine whether any of it should be withheld on grounds of privilege and then produce the non-privileged information for inspection by the other parties. Given the nature and, typically, the extent of the electronic information involved, the review can prove complex and costly. Furthermore, the risks associated with inadvertent disclosure are particularly profound because under federal law waiver may extend beyond the particular item disclosed to all other privileged information relating to the same subject matter.

---

28 SI 93/2009 set out a new version of Ord 31, r 12 which replaces the original. See **Ch 7**.

29 *Dome Telecom Ltd v Eircom Ltd* [2008] 2 IR 727.

30 Order 31, r 12(13) expressly provides that the term 'documents' includes 'all electronically stored information'.

31 Order 31, r 12(3)(a). The independent expert may be agreed by the parties or appointed by the court.

The practical response to this conundrum is the conclusion of non-waiver agreements whereby the parties agree to return inadvertently disclosed documents and, in some instances, to forego privilege review entirely. However, the status of these agreements and, specifically, the willingness of the courts to enforce them *inter partes* and against third parties, remain uncertain.[32]

[6.16] In an attempt to settle law and practice in this area, Congress created a new Federal Rule of Evidence: Rule 502. It limits the effect of inadvertent disclosure in two notable ways. Rule 502(b) provides that inadvertent disclosure will not result in the waiver of privilege if the privilege holder took reasonable steps to prevent disclosure and to rectify the error after the event. In addition, Rule 502(a) clarifies the scope of so-called 'subject matter' waiver. Under its terms, waiver extends to an undisclosed communication only if the waiver is intentional, the disclosed and undisclosed communications relate to the same subject matter, and they ought in fairness to be considered together.

[6.17] Rule 502 also addresses the situation in relation to waiver agreements. Subsection (e) provides: 'An agreement on the effect of disclosure in a Federal proceeding is binding only on the parties to the agreement, unless it is incorporated into a court order'. This provision implicitly recognises that waiver agreements are binding and enforceable between the parties. Furthermore, it creates the possibility that the parties may establish arrangements governing waiver which may bind third parties through the medium of a court order. Finally, Rule 502(d) recognises the overriding power of the court to determine that privilege is not waived by a disclosure connected with the litigation.[33]

Disclosure to a Third Party

[6.18] Because privilege is predicated on confidentiality, waiver may occur outside the trial process through the act of disclosing the privileged information to a third party.[34] There are exceptional circumstances in which privilege survives disclosure. In *Fyffes plc v DCC plc and Others*,[35] the Supreme Court held that limited disclosure in confidence for a particular purpose may be consistent with an assertion of privilege.

The appellant company sued various respondents seeking damages for insider trading in the appellant's shares. The appellant contended that the first and second respondent companies sold shares in the appellant company at a substantial profit at a time when the third respondent was a director of the

---

[32] See, eg, *Hopson v Mayor & City Council of Baltimore* 232 FRD 228 (D Md 2005).

[33] Subsection (d) provides further that where a court determines that privilege has not been waived, the disclosure will not constitute a waiver in any other proceeding.

[34] *Porter v Scott* [1979] NI 6. See generally Heydon, 'Legal Professional Privilege and Third Parties' (1974) 37(6) MLR 601; Auburn, *Legal Professional Privilege: Law and Theory* (Hart Publishing, 2000) ch 11.

[35] *Fyffes plc v DCC plc* [2005] 1 IR 59.

appellant and, in that capacity, in possession of confidential, sensitive information about the appellant's share price. Separate to the civil proceedings, the Stock Exchange investigated dealings in the appellant's shares and referred the matter to the Director of Public Prosecutions (DPP). The respondents sought to persuade the Stock Exchange to reverse its position and encourage the DPP to drop any criminal investigation. In particular, the respondents made available to the Stock Exchange in confidence a number of expert reports prepared for the defence of the appellant's civil claim and designed to show that any information in the possession of the third respondent was not price-sensitive. In the course of the civil proceedings, the appellant sought discovery of these expert reports on the ground that the respondents had forfeited any entitlement to privilege by disclosing the documents to a third party.

[6.19] On appeal, the Supreme Court upheld the decision of Smyth J to refuse discovery. Fennelly J considered the circumstances in which privilege may be lost:

> 'The law, therefore, attaches significant value and accords a high degree of protection to the principle of legal professional privilege. It can, of course, be lost if it is clear that it is being used as a cloak to cover fraud. It may also be overridden by express statutory provision.
>
> Waiver is another matter. Clearly, a party to an action may waive privilege in express terms. A party may also be held to have waived it impliedly, as when a party does not claim privilege, but includes potentially privileged documents in the non-privileged schedule to the affidavit. Equally, a party waives the privilege attaching to documents passing between himself and his solicitor, when he elects to sue the latter ...'[36]

The appellant argued for the general proposition that any disclosure to a third party leads to loss of privilege unless the disclosure is made to a public body and in pursuit of a public duty. Fennelly J noted that no authority had been found to support such a broad and far-reaching principle.[37]

[6.20] The Supreme Court also considered the appellant's argument, based principally on the Australian case of *Goldberg v Ng & Others*,[38] that the question of whether privilege has been waived should be determined by a principle of fairness. The appellant contended that a claim to privilege should be disallowed where a party had made voluntary disclosure of privileged material in circumstances where it would be unfair to deprive the opposing party in the litigation of equal access to it. Fennelly J stated:

---

36 *Fyffes plc v DCC plc* [2005] 1 IR 59 at 67. On disputes arising out of legal advice see para **6.33** *et seq*.

37 *Fyffes plc v DCC plc* [2005] 1 IR 59 at 68.

38 *Goldberg v Ng & Others* [1993] 33 NSWLR 301, 132 ALR 57.

> 'I would conclude, however, that the well-established rule regarding privilege, whether including a notion of fairness or not, goes no further than the proposition that a party who seeks to deploy his privileged documents by partially disclosing them or summarising their effect so as to gain an advantage over his opponent in the action in which they are privileged, runs a serious risk of losing the privilege. I do not deny that the partial disclosure, which has that effect might, in some circumstances, be made to a third party, but it would have to be for the purpose of gaining an advantage in that action. I would add that express stipulations of confidentiality, such as in the present case, will necessarily be a material factor. They will obviously negative any claim of express waiver and most cases of implied waiver.'[39]

Fennelly J concluded that there was 'no relevant nexus' between the disclosures to the Stock Exchange on the one hand and the civil proceedings on the other. Although the criminal investigation concerned the same subject matter as the civil action, criminal and civil proceedings are entirely distinct and there was nothing to suggest that any possible criminal prosecution would have any effect on the civil action.[40] Noting that it was not the court's function to comment on the desirability of the respondents' course of action in seeking to influence the Stock Exchange to persuade the DPP not to proceed with the criminal investigation, Fennelly J recognised that while it was designed to obtain an advantage for the respondents 'it was not an advantage which placed or would have placed the Appellant at any corresponding or related disadvantage in the civil action'.[41]

[6.21] The themes of waiver and loss of privilege were explored in the subsequent High Court case of *Woori Bank & Hanvit LSP Finance Ltd v KDB Ireland Ltd.*[42] The proceedings centred on a series of agreements concluded in October 2000 between the first plaintiff, a Korean bank, the second plaintiff, a company incorporated in Ireland, the defendant, an Irish company and provider of financial services, and others. The agreements permitted the defendant to make investments on behalf of the second plaintiff and, in July 2002, the defendant arranged for the second plaintiff to enter a loan agreement with a Japanese company, AEL Corporation. A dispute arose between the parties

---

39 *Fyffes plc v DCC plc* [2005] 1 IR 59 at 72. McCracken J observed that the concept of fairness, as applied in *Goldberg,* had the undesirable effect of requiring each case to be examined subjectively according to its own particular facts. He continued at p 85: 'While one cannot lay down absolute rules in matters such as this, it is essential that there should be as great a degree of certainty as possible, so that parties can reasonably foresee the result of actions of disclosure taken by them. Were that not so, it is possible that serious injustices could occur because a party might fail to make a disclosure due to the fear that they might lose the benefit of a legal privilege to which they were entitled'.

40 *Fyffes plc v DCC plc* [2005] 1 IR 59 at 72.

41 *Fyffes plc v DCC plc* [2005] 1 IR 59 at 73.

42 *Woori Bank & Hanvit LSP Finance Ltd v KDB Ireland Ltd* [2005] IEHC 451 (21 December 2005) (Finlay Geoghegan J).

regarding the validity of that loan agreement and, more broadly, the extent of the plaintiffs' contractual and other rights. In addition to mounting the present civil proceedings, the first plaintiff laid a criminal complaint under Korean law against an employee of the defendant who it alleged was instrumental in arranging the disputed loan transaction. The defendant in turn laid criminal complaints under Korean law against a representative of the first plaintiff. The transactions at issue were also the subject of investigations by the Board of Inspection and Audit (BAI) and the Financial Supervisory Service (FSS) in Korea.

[6.22] The defendant sought disclosure of various categories of documents over which the plaintiffs asserted legal professional privilege. One category comprised documents that had been disclosed to the Public Prosecutor's Office in Korea. The defendant conceded that by their nature these documents came within the realm of privilege but argued that by disclosing the documents the plaintiff had lost or waived its entitlement to protection.[43] Finlay Geoghegan J found that the documents had been disclosed to the Public Prosecutor for the purposes of supporting its criminal complaint and defending the criminal complaint brought against its representative. She declared herself satisfied further that the plaintiff had taken steps to preserve the confidentiality of the documents notwithstanding the disclosure.[44]

Applying the principles set down by the Supreme Court in *Fyffes plc v DDC plc,* Finlay Geoghegan J held that there had been no waiver or loss of privilege in the documents in question by reason of their disclosure to the Public Prosecutor.[45] However, this conclusion was subject to the reservation that the defendant had adduced only limited facts in support of its application and that the matter might warrant re-opening were other facts to be developed.

[6.23] Factual limitations aside, it is interesting to consider in broad terms the basis on which the defendant sought to distinguish the present case from the facts in *Fyffes*. It invoked the principle of fairness identified in the judgments of McCracken and Fennelly JJ in *Fyffes* and traced to the Australian authority of *Goldberg* noted above. The defendant sought to distinguish *Fyffes* on the ground that the first plaintiff disclosed the documents to the Public Prosecutor in order to gain an advantage over the defendant in the Irish civil proceedings. Thus, it was seeking in effect to establish a tangible link (in this instance between the

43 *Woori Bank & Hanvit LSP Finance Ltd v KDB Ireland Ltd* [2005] IEHC 451 (21 December 2005) (Finlay Geoghegan J) p 12.

44 *Woori Bank & Hanvit LSP Finance Ltd v KDB Ireland Ltd* [2005] IEHC 451 (21 December 2005) (Finlay Geoghegan J) pp 14–15. The plaintiff presented evidence that it had emphasised to the Public Prosecutor the need for utmost confidentiality. In addition, there was evidence before the court that public prosecutors are obliged by Korean law not to disclose information obtained during an investigation.

45 *Woori Bank & Hanvit LSP Finance Ltd v KDB Ireland Ltd* [2005] IEHC 451 (21 December 2005) (Finlay Geoghegan J) p 19.

Korean criminal proceedings and the Irish civil proceedings) which was lacking in *Fyffes*. The specific allegation was that the criminal litigation was commenced in part in order to establish the disputed fact that the first plaintiff had not consented to the AEL loan transaction. In support of this contention, the defendant relied on statements a representative of the plaintiffs had made to the BAI (which had been investigating the disputed transactions). The difficulty for the defendant was that its version of events was directly at odds with the affidavits sworn by the same representative which were before the court. Moreover, the defendant had not sought to cross-examine the plaintiffs' representative on the affidavits. These factual limitations prompted Finlay Geoghegan J to conclude:

> 'I am not satisfied that the defendant on the evidence in this application has established facts which bring the disclosure within the exceptions envisaged by either Fennelly J. or McCracken J. in their judgments in *Fyffes plc v. DCC plc.* In reaching this conclusion however I wish to make clear that this ruling does not preclude the matter being reopened ... '[46]

Legal Aid Board

[6.24] In *Martin & Doorley v Legal Aid Board*,[47] the High Court explored the parameters of privilege in the context of the relationship between a solicitor and a client benefitting from legal aid. The plaintiff solicitors employed by the Legal Aid Board challenged the entitlement of the Board's authorised officers to access and review information contained in individual case files that would attract the protection of privilege in the normal course of the legal professional relationship.

Dismissing the claim, Laffoy J held that the Oireachtas, in establishing the scheme of civil legal aid, had intended to extend the umbrella of privilege to cover the Board, its authorised officers and employees.[48] The learned judge construed s 32(2) of the Civil Legal Aid Act 1995 as conferring a duty on solicitors in question to provide information to an authorised person subject only to the proviso that the information is required by the Board for the purpose of enabling it to discharge its statutory functions.[49] Laffoy J observed that legal professional privilege only becomes operative to shield a client against disclosure in a forum in which the law would otherwise mandate disclosure to a person who is pursuing an agenda adverse to the interest which the client is seeking to protect. She noted: 'That is the *raison d'être* of the privilege and it underscores the client interest which it protects'.[50] Thus, privilege is usually at

[46] *Woori Bank & Hanvit LSP Finance Ltd v KDB Ireland Ltd* [2005] IEHC 451 (21 December 2005) (Finlay Geoghegan J) p 19.

[47] *Martin & Doorley v Legal Aid Board* [2007] 2 IR 759.

[48] *Martin & Doorley v Legal Aid Board* [2007] 2 IR 759 at 777.

[49] *Martin & Doorley v Legal Aid Board* [2007] 2 IR 759 at 771–772.

[50] *Martin & Doorley v Legal Aid Board* [2007] 2 IR 759 at 776.

issue in the context of discovery in *inter partes* litigation but it may arise in other contexts such as the inquisitorial setting of a tribunal of inquiry. The learned judge continued:

> 'The disclosure to an authorised person, which the implementation of the first defendant's decision would involve, is not a disclosure which requires the protection of legal professional privilege and it could not be regarded as a diminution of the protection afforded by that principle. It is a disclosure for the purpose of ensuring that the statutory functions of the first defendant are properly performed.'[51]

[6.25] Given the intra-organisational nature of the disclosure, Laffoy J was satisfied that disclosure would not impact on the client interest that is protected by privilege. She found a further basis for discounting any such danger in the decision of the Supreme Court in *Fyffes*.[52] In his judgment in that case, Fennelly J recognised, *obiter dicta*, that privilege will not be lost where a disclosure to a third party is made in pursuit of some public duty. Laffoy J observed that on the basis of this principle the Oireachtas could have overridden the privilege that would otherwise attach to communications between a client benefitting from legal aid and her solicitor. The learned judge did not consider this to be the effect of the 1995 Act; to the contrary, she adhered to the view that, in this *sui generis* situation, the umbrella of privilege extended beyond the client and solicitor to the Board and its authorised officers and employees. Disclosure to an authorised person constituted a limited disclosure in confidence for a particular purpose. Thus, the Supreme Court's decision in *Fyffes* was 'an absolute assurance' that such a disclosure could not result in the loss of privilege.[53]

JOINT OR COMMON INTEREST

[6.26] Particular issues arise where a solicitor is instructed by two or more clients in relation to a matter in which the clients are jointly interested. The position adopted by the English Court of Appeal is that communications between the solicitor and one of the clients will not be privileged as against the other client but they will be protected from disclosure to any third party.[54] In other words, the clients and the solicitor are located within a circle of confidence from which third parties are excluded. The clients are deemed to have a shared interest and occupy a common position for the purposes of privilege. However, a conflict of interest between the clients may have the effect of breaking the circle of confidence.[55]

---

51 *Martin & Doorley v Legal Aid Board* [2007] 2 IR 759 at 776.

52 *Martin & Doorley v Legal Aid Board* [2007] 2 IR 759 at 778.

53 *Martin & Doorley v Legal Aid Board* [2007] 2 IR 759 at 779.

54 *Buttes Gas and Oil Co v Hammer (No 3)* [1981] QB 223.

55 *TSB Bank plc v Robert Irving & Burns (a firm)* [2000] 2 All ER 826.

The English courts have developed an extensive jurisprudence in relation to common interest privilege.[56] The range of relationships falling within the scope of privilege has been held to include entities within a corporate framework,[57] parties to a conveyancing transaction,[58] and parties to an insurance contract.[59] However, the privilege has been withheld from other relationships such as that between a trade union and its members[60] and company directors and shareholders.[61]

[6.27] In *Moorview Developments Ltd & Others v First Active plc & Others*,[62] Clarke J outlined the approach a trial court should take when faced with an assertion of common interest privilege:

> 'It is clear to me that common interest privilege arises in relation to documentation or materials which would be the subject of either legal professional privilege or litigation privilege in the hands of one person or body, but where the relevant materials are given to a third party who may be said to have a common interest in either the legal advice or the litigation concerned. ... Two questions therefore arise. The first is as to whether the documents would, in the hands of a single party, have the benefit of privilege in the first place. If not, then no question of common interest privilege could arise. If, however, the materials pass that first test but have been released by one party to a second party, then it follows that it is also necessary to ask whether the release was on foot of a common interest in either the relevant litigation or advice. If so, then the documents will remain privileged, notwithstanding their release, by virtue of the doctrine of common interest. If not, then the release may be taken to be a waiver of any privilege which would otherwise have attached to the documents concerned.'[63]

---

56 See *Re Konigsberg (a bankrupt)* [1989] 3 All ER 289; *Guinness Peat Properties Ltd v Fitzroy Robinson Partnership (a firm)* [1987] 2 All ER 716.

57 *Moorview Developments Ltd v First Active plc* [2009] 2 IR 788 at 821 (Clarke J): 'I should note that documents passing to other companies within a group or connected companies where those companies have an interest in the advice or litigation concerned are also covered, as would documents informing such connected entities of such advice or the progress of such litigation'. But see *CAS (Nominees) Ltd v Nottingham Forest plc* [2001] 1 All ER 954 (declining to recognise privilege between company directors and shareholders).

58 *Buttes Gas and Oil Co v Hammer (No 3)* [1981] QB 223; *Re Konigsberg (a bankrupt)* [1989] 3 All ER 289.

59 *Guinness Peat Properties Ltd v Fitzroy Robinson Partnership (a firm)* [1987] 2 All ER 289. See also *Ontario (Attorney General) v Ballard Estate* (1994) 119 DLR (4th) 750 (Ont Gen Div) (beneficiaries and executors have a common interest in relation to estate).

60 *Jones v Great Central Rly Co* [1910] AC 4.

61 *CAS (Nominees) Ltd v Nottingham Forest plc* [2001] 1 All ER 954.

62 *Moorview Developments Ltd & Others v First Active plc & Others* [2009] 2 IR 788.

63 *Moorview Developments Ltd & Others v First Active plc & Others* [2009] 2 IR 788 at 821.

[6.28] These broad principles were endorsed and applied by McGovern J in *Hansfield Developments & Others v Irish Asphalt Ltd & Others.*[64] The proceedings arose out of the construction in North Dublin of three housing estates comprising a total of 681 houses. The plaintiff developers sued the defendant providers of infill or quarry material alleging that their product was defective because it contained a high level of pyrite which caused cracks in the concrete floors of the houses. The plaintiffs were participants in a scheme operated by the National House Building Guarantee Company Ltd (HomeBond) and as a consequence had warranted to the purchasers of the houses they constructed that they would cure any major defects or, with the consent of Homebond, pay the cost of any necessary remedial works. In the event that a participant-builder failed to cure the defects, HomeBond agreed to protect purchasers by providing a remedy and then pursuing the participant-builder.

The defendants sought an order for non-party discovery of certain documents in the possession of HomeBond. The documents comprised communications between the plaintiffs and HomeBond and related to the alleged presence of pyrite and the carrying out of remediation works. The plaintiffs and HomeBond submitted that the documents were protected by litigation privilege; although HomeBond was not a party to the proceedings, it shared a common interest with the plaintiffs which led to the exchange of confidential communications.[65] However, McGovern J held that no such common interest existed between the plaintiffs and HomeBond.[66]

[6.29] In *Redfern Ltd v O'Mahony,*[67] the Supreme Court revisited the issue of waiver by means of disclosure to a third party. Whereas *Fyffes* concerned limited, confidential disclosure to a third party for a particular purpose, the issue in *Redfern* was disclosure to a party having a common interest.

The case had its origins in a complicated set of multi-party arrangements relating to the development of a car park in The Square, Tallaght, County Dublin, a major shopping and commercial enterprise. Square Management Ltd and Alburn, an unlimited company, entered into a joint venture agreement to develop the car park. For the development to take place, it was necessary that all existing licences over the car park be extinguished. To resolve a difficulty in relation to a particular sub-licence, Alburn entered into a separate agreement with the appellants, the beneficial owners of the sub-licence holder. The respondents, Redfern, the parent company of Alburn, sued the appellants for specific performance of that agreement. In their defence, the appellants pleaded

---

64 *Hansfield Developments & Others v Irish Asphalt Ltd & Others* [2009] IEHC 90 (17 February 2009).

65 Relying on *Buttes Gas and Oil v Hammer (No 3)* [1981] QB 223.

66 *Hansfield Developments & Others v Irish Asphalt Ltd & Others* [2009] IEHC 90 (17 February 2009) para 12. The order of discovery was overturned on appeal on separate grounds.

67 *Redfern Ltd v O'Mahony* [2009] IESC 18 (4 March 2009).

that the respondents had been guilty of unreasonable delay and consequently were estopped from seeking to complete the agreement.

[6.30] During discovery, the respondents claimed privilege over an opinion of senior counsel. The appellants sought inspection on the ground that the respondents had waived privilege by disclosing the opinion to the chairman of Square Management Ltd and to a solicitor representing South Dublin County Council. The appellants contended that the disclosures were potentially very wide given that each lessee in The Square development and each member of South Dublin County Council could now request sight of the opinion. The respondents emphasised that the disclosures were made in the context of the joint venture agreement and the proposed disposal of the land by the Council County to Alburn, respectively. As such, they were limited disclosures to parties sharing a common interest and did not evince an intention to publish to the public generally.

[6.31] Finnegan J was satisfied that this case came within the general principles discussed by Fennelly J in *Fyffes*. Applying those principles to the facts in *Redfern,* Finnegan J concluded:

> 'If the document comes into the public domain privilege will be lost. It will not, however, be lost where there is limited disclosure for a particular purpose or to parties with a common interest. The disclosure relied upon by the appellants here is limited and was to parties having a common interest with the respondent in the proposed development of the car park. Such disclosure does not evince an intention to waive privilege. I am satisfied there has been no waiver of privilege in respect of the opinion sought to be inspected.'[68]

The Supreme Court thus upheld the decision of the trial judge refusing to order inspection of the opinion of the senior counsel.

Putting the Privileged Communication in Issue

[6.32] Where a party puts the substance of a privileged communication in issue in legal proceedings, she will be deemed to have impliedly waived privilege.[69] The classic scenario is one in which a party seeks to rely on a document containing legal advice but at the same time refuses to disclose that advice to the other party or parties.[70]

---

68 *Redfern Ltd v O'Mahony* [2009] IESC 18 (4 March 2009).

69 See generally Auburn, *Legal Professional Privilege: Law and Theory* (Hart Publishing, 2000) ch 10. Similarly, privilege does not apply where the adverse party was the very source of the information and consequently is aware of it: *McKay v McKay* [1988] NI 611 (CA).

70 *Brennan and Others v Sunderland City Council and Others* [2009] ICR 479, 483.

Disputes Arising Out of Legal Advice

[6.33] A relatively straightforward example is a dispute between a client and her lawyer arising out of legal advice proffered by the lawyer. A party waives the privilege attaching to oral communications or documents passing between herself and her lawyer when she elects to sue the lawyer.[71] Lynch J stated the rule thus in *McMullen v Carty:*[72]

> 'When a client sues his solicitor for damages for alleged negligence arising out of the conduct of previous litigation against third parties and especially as in this case arising out of the settlement of such previous litigation the client thereby puts in issue all the communications as between the solicitor and the client and the barrister and the client and also as between the barrister and the solicitor relevant to the settlement of the case and thereby impliedly waives the privilege of confidentiality. For example the client may give evidence that he was advised by the solicitor A.B.C. and that he should therefore settle his case but that as matters turned out A.B.C. was wrong and that he should not in fact have settled the case: whereas the solicitor may wish to give evidence that both he and counsel advised the client X.Y.Z. and that in those circumstances the client should settle. It would be manifestly unjust and wrong if the solicitor was precluded by the rule of confidentiality from making his case before the court that both he and counsel advised the client X.Y.Z. and that the settlement was indeed advantageous to the client. These facts are put in issue by the client who thereby impliedly waives his privilege of confidentiality.'[73]

The question before the court was whether the barrister, if called by either party, could be compelled to give evidence as to his advice to the client and the solicitor in circumstances where the solicitor alone is sued. The Supreme Court held that the barrister could be so compelled where his testimony was relevant to the issue of whether the solicitor was negligent.[74]

[6.34] Waiver will not extend to communications and documents passing between the client and another lawyer newly appointed to represent her in the suit against her former legal adviser.[75] In *Paragon Finance plc v Freshfields*,[76] the plaintiff brought a claim in negligence against the defendant firm of solicitors for damages arising out of advice received in relation to the creation of securitised mortgages. Following a fall in the property market, there were numerous defaults on the mortgages in question but insurers refused to indemnify the plaintiff on the ground that the agreed loan to value ratio had not been complied with. The claim against the insurers was settled and the plaintiff sought to recover its outstanding losses from the defendant. In the course of

---

71 *Fyffes plc v DCC plc* [2005] 1 IR 59; *Kershaw v Whelan* [1996] 1 WLR 358.

72 *McMullen v Carty* (27 January 1998, unreported) SC.

73 *McMullen v Carty* (27 January 1998, unreported) SC at pp 9–10.

74 *McMullen v Carty* (27 January 1998, unreported) SC at p 10.

75 *Paragaon Finance plc v Freshfields* [1999] 1 WLR 1183 at 1192.

76 *Paragaon Finance plc v Freshfields* [1999] 1 WLR 1183.

discovery, the defendant sought the disclosure of communications between the plaintiff and a different law firm, Slaughter and May, which had acted for the plaintiff in its claim against the insurers. In the High Court, Buckley J granted inspection on the basis that a plaintiff suing a solicitor for negligence may not claim privilege in relation to similar transactions involving a different solicitor.[77]

[6.35] Allowing the appeal, the Court of Appeal held that whereas the plaintiff had impliedly waived privilege over confidential communications between itself and the defendant, there was no corresponding waiver of privilege in relation to communications between the plaintiff and Slaughter and May since that confidential relationship had not been brought into the public domain by the pleadings. Parting company with Australian authority, the court held that while unfairness to an opponent informed the principle that the mere instigation of proceedings by a client against her solicitor resulted in the loss of privilege, it did not similarly affect transactions with other solicitors.[78]

[6.36] In *Lillicrap & Another v Nalder & Son (A Firm) & Another*,[79] the Court of Appeal espoused a common sense approach to the scope of waiver of privilege in circumstances where a client sues her lawyer. Dillon LJ emphasised that waiver is not unlimited: 'There is no waiver for a roving search into anything else in which the solicitor or any other solicitor may have happened to have acted for the clients'.[80] At the same time, Dillon LJ recognised that waiver must go far enough, not merely to entitle the plaintiff to establish her cause of action, but also to enable the defendant to establish any possible defence.[81]

Deploying Privileged Materials in Proceedings

[6.37] Whereas the principles that apply to proceedings between the client and lawyer are reasonably well settled, the rules that govern the deployment of privileged material in other proceedings are somewhat uncertain.

In *Hannigan v Director of Public Prosecutions*,[82] the applicant appealed against an order of the High Court refusing inspection of a document disclosed by the DPP during the course of judicial review proceedings. The document was a letter sent by the DPP to the gardaí concerning the District Court prosecution of the applicant which was the subject of the judicial review. The Supreme Court held that the DPP had impliedly waived privilege by deploying the document in the proceedings. Hardiman J observed: 'The status of a document, from the point of view of privilege or immunity from disclosure, changes once it has been

[77] Relying on *Hayes & Another v Dowdling & Others* [1996] PNLR 578.

[78] Judgment of Lord Bingham relying on *Nederlandse Reassurantie Groep Holding NV v Bacon & Woodrow & Others* [1995] 1 All ER 976.

[79] *Lillicrap v Nalder & Son* [1993] 1 WLR 94.

[80] *Lillicrap v Nalder & Son* [1993] 1 WLR 94 at 99.

[81] *Lillicrap v Nalder & Son* [1993] 1 WLR 94 at 99.

[82] *Hannigan v Director of Public Prosecutions* [2001] 1 IR 378.

referred to in pleadings or affidavits'.[83] Referring with approval to the relevant discussion in *Matthews and Malek on Discovery*, Hardiman J stated:

> 'The general rule is that where privileged material is deployed in court in an interlocutory application, privilege in that and any associated material is waived.'[84]

[6.38] The English courts have emphasised the principle of fairness as the underlying rationale underpinning the legal rules in this area. Lord Denning placed the principle in context in *Burnell v British Transport Commission*:

> 'It would be most unfair that cross-examining counsel should use part of the document which was to his advantage and not allow anyone, not even the judge or the opposing counsel, a sight of the rest of the document, much of which might have been against him'.[85]

Thus, where a party has deployed a significant part of legal advice received, fairness may require that she disclose the advice in its totality.[86] In essence, a party will not be permitted to 'gain an advantage in litigation' by 'cherry picking', selecting favourable aspects of relevant information for presentation to the court while withholding unfavourable aspects.[87]

[6.39] The courts have grappled with the determination of when privileged material can be said to be deployed in the proceedings. The English authorities distinguish between mere reference to a document by a party and actual reliance on the document in the proceedings.[88]

The circumstances in which a party puts privileged material in issue were considered by the Supreme Court in *Redfern Ltd v O'Mahony*,[89] the basic facts of which are set out above at para **6.29** *et seq*.

In their defence to the action for specific performance of the agreement relating to the sub-licence, the appellants submitted that the respondents had delayed unreasonably thereby obliging the appellants to seek alternative

---

83 *Hannigan v Director of Public Prosecutions* [2001] 1 IR 378 at 383.

84 *Hannigan v Director of Public Prosecutions* [2001] 1 IR 378. The principle in *Hannigan* was applied in *Egan v O'Toole* [2005] IESC 53 (29 July 2005). In a civil context, see also *Desmond v Times Newspapers Ltd* [2009] IEHC 271 (12 June 2009) (Dunne J).

85 *Burnell v British Transport Commission* [1956] 1 QB 187, 190. *See also Great Atlantic Insurance Co v Home Insurance Co* [1981] 1 WLR 529, 538; *Dunlop Slazenger Int'l Ltd v Joe Bloggs Sports Ltd* [2003] EWCA Civ 901.

86 *Nea Kateria Maritime Co Ltd v Atlantic & Great Lakes Steamship Corp (No 2)* [1981] Com LR 138.

87 *Sunderland City Council v Brennan and Others* [2009] ICR 479, 484. The Irish courts adopt an analogous stance to the admission into evidence of parts of statements taken from an accused person during custodial interviews: *People (DPP) v Diver* [2005] 3 IR 270.

88 See, eg, *Dunlop Slazenger Int'l Ltd v Joe Bloggs Sports Ltd* [2003] EWCA Civ 901; *Expandable Ltd and Others v Rubin* [2008] 1 WLR 1999 (CA); *Sunderland City Council v Brennan and Others* [2009] ICR 479.

89 *Redfern Ltd v O'Mahony* [2009] IESC 18 (4 March 2009), (2010) 28 ILT 246.

funding. During discovery, the appellants claimed privilege over legal advice they had obtained in relation to the alternative funding agreement. They conceded that they intended to rely on the fact that this legal advice was obtained in order to demonstrate that the alternative funding agreement was not designed to interfere with their contractual relationship with the respondents. Nevertheless, the appellants stressed that the legal advice sought or given would not be introduced into evidence. The respondents took the position that the appellants had impliedly waived privilege by relying on the legal advice in this manner in the proceedings. Specifically, the appellants had put in issue their state of mind in entering into the alternative funding agreement and this could be determined only on inspection of the legal advice. Thus the respondents were asking the court to accept the broad proposition that in any proceeding (and not merely an action brought by the client against her lawyer) privilege is impliedly waived where the privileged communication is in itself a material fact.

[6.40] Finnegan J reviewed a relevant line of authority in the Australian courts[90] which suggests that privilege may be lost in the following circumstances. First, where a party pleads the privileged document as a relevant fact;[91] second, where the court might be misled if the document is not available;[92] and, third, where a party relies on her state of mind and it would be unfair to permit her to assert privilege over communications passing between her and her legal advisers which might bear upon the existence of that state of mind.[93]

[6.41] Fairness to the party opposing privilege is a central theme in the Australian cases. In contrast, the English courts have rejected any general proposition that unfairness to an opponent is a sufficient basis to establish an implied waiver of privilege. Fairness is a material consideration in certain limited circumstances. Where a client instigates proceedings against her solicitor, it would be unfair to allow the client to open the relationship by asserting the claim and at the same time to seek to enforce the duty of confidence owed by the solicitor.[94] Loss of privilege is triggered in such instances by the mere instigation of proceedings. However, this species of waiver is generally limited to suits by a client against her solicitor and, even then, to communications between the client and that solicitor – communications

---

90 Including *Hong Kong Bank of Australia Ltd v Murphy* [1993] 2 VR 419 (High Court of Australia); *Telstra Corp v BT Australasia Pty Ltd* 85 FCR 152, [1985] 156 ALR 634 (Federal Court of Australia).

91 *Data Access Corp v Powerflex Services Pty Ltd* [1994] AIPC 91.

92 *Hong Kong Bank of Australia Ltd v Murphy* [1993] 2 VR 419 (High Court of Australia).

93 *Wardrope v Dunne* [1996] 1 Qd R 224.

94 *Nederlandse Reassurantie Groep Holding NV v Bacon & Woodrow & Others* [1995] 1 All ER 976; *Paragon Finance plc v Freshfields* [1999] 1 WLR 1183.

between the client and other lawyers, however closely related or relevant, remain privileged.[95]

[6.42] Favouring English over Australian authority, Finnegan J rejected any general proposition that unfairness to an opponent will result in implied waiver of privilege and expressly endorsed Fennelly J's statement in *Fyffes* that there is no judicial balancing exercise to be carried out between the privilege maintained by one party and the possible unfairness caused to the other party. Finnegan J recognised that, in particular, there is no general implied waiver of privileged material merely because a state of mind or certain actions are in issue.[96] The learned judge accepted that 'a party by its pleadings or by deployment in court may waive legal professional privilege: this will arise where the contents and effect of the legal advice are disclosed'. In the instant case, however, the appellants would be relying only on the fact that legal advice had been obtained and not on the contents and effect of that advice. In conclusion, the Supreme Court allowed the appeal and refused inspection of the appellants' documents over which privilege had been asserted.

[6.43] The concept of putting privileged material in issue has also been considered in the context of proceedings before tribunals of inquiry. In *Ahern v Mahon*,[97] a Divisional High Court held that a person whose conduct is under examination by such a tribunal should be regarded as being in the same position as a party to High Court litigation and, as such, entitled to the protection of litigation privilege. It followed that, as a person to whom *Re Haughey*[98] rights applied, former Taoiseach Bertie Ahern could assert privilege over communications between his legal advisers and an expert retained by him in connection with the proceedings of the Tribunal of Inquiry into Certain Planning Matters and Payments. The Mahon Tribunal raised the alternative argument that Ahern had waived any entitlement to claim privilege by deploying the documents in question in a prepared statement which was read into the record of the public hearings before the tribunal.

The court considered the question whether the passages in the prepared statement in which Ahern referred to his expert amounted to deployment such as to waive the privilege to which he would otherwise be entitled. Kelly J answered

---

95 Finnegan J noted a second instance in which fairness is a material consideration, namely, where a party makes partial disclosure of legal advice, it would be unfair to deprive the other party and the court of an opportunity of satisfying themselves that the information disclosed represents the whole of the material relevant to the issue in question (citing *R v Secretary of State for Transport, ex parte Factortame & Others* (1997) The Times, 16 May). The application of the principle in this second instance is discussed above.

96 Following English authority, notably *Farm Assist Ltd (In Liquidation) v Secretary of State for Environment, Food and Rural Affairs* [2008] All ER (d) 124 (Dec) and declining to follow Australian authority.

97 *Ahern v Mahon* [2008] IEHC 119 (8 May 2008) (Divisional High Court).

98 *Re Haughey* [1971] IR 217.

the question in the negative, observing that the reference to the expert was 'in general terms' and 'far removed from what occurred in *Hannigan*'s case'.[99]

[6.44] In a ruling handed down in March 2010, the Tribunal of Inquiry into Payments to Politicians and Related Matters (Moriarty Tribunal) addressed the issue of the implied waiver of legal professional privilege through possible deployment in tribunal proceedings.[100] The ruling centred on an opinion of counsel dated 9 May 1996 that had been provided to the Department of Transport, Energy and Communications in the weeks leading up to the grant of the second GSM mobile telecommunications licence. Departmental witnesses had referred to the opinion during the course of their evidence before the Tribunal and, in addition, counsel for Mr Dennis O'Brien had put passages of the opinion to a witness during cross-examination. The issue before the Tribunal was whether the Department had deployed the opinion in the proceedings and thereby waived privilege by acquiescing in what had occurred. In relation to the references to the opinion during the course of evidence in chief, the Tribunal took the view that departmental witnesses could not be presumed to be authorised to waive privilege on the Department's behalf.[101] The Tribunal's conclusion that the use of the opinion in cross-examination did not result in a waiver of privilege rested on a different line of reasoning. The Tribunal opined that the concept of deployment as envisioned in *Hannigan v DPP*[102] required 'some conscious and deliberate use of selected portions of the privileged document by the party in whom the privilege is vested'.[103] Although counsel for the Department had not objected to the cross-examination conducted by counsel for Mr O'Brien, the Tribunal ruled that the Department's 'mere acquiescence' in what had occurred lacked 'the requisite deliberation or involvement to constitute a 'deployment' by the Department in the terms contemplated by the Supreme Court in the Hannigan case'.[104]

---

99 *Ahern v Mahon* [2008] IEHC 119 (8 May 2008) at p 15. Kelly J accepted that when the expert came to testify before the tribunal, he could be asked to give evidence as to the factual material that he used in order to form his opinion and as to the instructions that were given to him. Nevertheless, 'the liceity that line of questioning' did not justify 'a trawl through the entire of the solicitor's file in advance of his testimony'.

100 Tribunal of Inquiry into Payments to Politicians and Related Matters, Revised Tribunal Ruling Dated 24 March 2010 Re Opinion Dated 9 May 1996.

101 Revised Tribunal Ruling Dated 24 March 2010 Re Opinion Dated 9 May 1996, para 21. In addition, the Tribunal considered that some of the references to the opinion did not rise to the level of substantive disclosure.

102 *Hannigan v DPP* [2001]1 IR 378.

103 Revised Tribunal Ruling Dated 24 March 2010 Re Opinion Dated 9 May 1996, para 25.

104 Revised Tribunal Ruling Dated 24 March 2010 Re Opinion Dated 9 May 1996, para 25.

Chapter 7

Civil Procedure

Introduction

[7.01] The bulk of academic discussion on legal professional privilege centres on the substantive legal aspects of the subject whereas, by contrast, procedural aspects of privilege have attracted less attention. This chapter seeks to locate legal professional privilege in its procedural setting and considers pertinent questions such as the timing of assertions of privilege, the manner in which allegedly privileged information is presented to the court, and the burden of proof resting on the proponent and any opponent of the claim of privilege.

Discovery

[7.02] In modern times, most claims of legal professional privilege relate to evidence in documentary form.[1] The procedure whereby documents relevant to civil proceedings are disclosed prior to trial is known as discovery[2] and its parameters are sketched in the rules of the trial courts.[3] 'Inter party discovery' refers to the disclosure and exchange of documents between the various parties to the proceedings. Discovery may be undertaken voluntarily on the basis of an agreement between the parties or, alternatively, on foot of a court order.

1 The term 'documentary evidence' tends to be broadly defined and extends beyond written documents in the classic sense to embrace information recorded or stored by a myriad of means. Typical examples are graphs, photographs, computer-generated text and images and electronic communications. *McCarthy v O'Flynn* [1979] IR 127. Order 31, r 12(13) states that for purposes of rr 12 and 29, the term 'documents' includes all electronically stored information.

2 See generally, Delany and McGrath, *Civil Procedure in the Superior Courts* (2nd edn, Thomson Round Hall, 2005) ch 10; Abrahamson, Dwyer and Fitzpatrick, *Discovery and Disclosure* (Thomson Round Hall, 2007); Reid (ed), *Civil Litigation* (Oxford University Press, 2009) ch 12; Ó Floinn, *Practice and Procedure in the Superior Courts* (2nd edn, Bloomsbury Professional, 2008) p 283 *et seq*; O'Neill, *Ancillary Discovery* (Bloomsbury Professional, 2009); Barron, *Practice and Procedure in the Master's Court* (2nd edn, Round Hall, 2001) ch 3.

3 RSC 1986 as amended, Ord 31, r 12 (inter party discovery), Ord 31, r 29 (non-party discovery); CCR as amended, Ord 32, r 1 (inter party discovery), Ord 32, r 9 (non-party discovery), DCR as amended, Ord 46A. The present discussion deals exclusively with the relevant Rules of the Superior Courts. These rules have been amended on three occasions: Rules of the Superior Courts (No 2) of 1993 (SI 265/1993); Rules of the Superior Courts (No 2) (Discovery) (1999) (SI 233/1999); and Rules of the Superior Courts (Discovery) (2009) (SI 93/2009).

Occasionally a court may direct 'non-party discovery' of documents in the possession or control of a person who is not a party to the action.

[7.03] Discovery purports to serve several tangible purposes within our system of civil litigation. First, the procedure safeguards the integrity of judicial fact finding and decision making by ensuring that courts have at their disposal the full gamut of evidence that is relevant to the proceedings. In *AIB Bank plc v Ernst & Whinney*, Finlay CJ stated that the basic purpose of discovery is 'to ensure as far as possible that the full facts concerning any matter in dispute before the court are capable of being presented to the court by the parties concerned'.[4] The procedure thus guarantees 'justice on full information, rather than on a limited or partial revelation of the facts arising in a particular action'.[5] Second, discovery has the salutary effect of defining the scope of the dispute and narrowing the issues between the parties. In this respect it further contributes to the administration of justice by facilitating the resolution of the case 'in as speedy and cost efficient a manner as possible' whether by settlement or trial.[6] Indeed, by assisting the parties in their pre-trial preparations,[7] discovery vindicates their evidentiary rights and, more broadly, their entitlement to fair procedures. Specifically, the procedure enables a party to learn about and inspect documents on which another party intends to rely at trial and, subsequently, to prevent that other party from adducing evidence improperly withheld.[8]

[7.04] A valid assertion of legal professional privilege entitles a party or non-party to refuse to produce for inspection a document that would be otherwise susceptible to disclosure within the parameters of discovery. As such, privilege swims against discovery's general current in favour of transparency and disclosure. For this reason, the courts will not permit privilege to be used as a cloak to conceal documents that should be available for use in the proceedings. The rules strive to reach a compromise between supporting legitimate claims of privilege yet at the same time preventing the entitlement from being abused by requiring that the *existence* of a privileged document must be disclosed even if the contents of the document may be legitimately withheld.

---

4 *AIB Bank plc v Ernst & Whinney* [1993] 1 IR 375 at 390.

5 *AIB Bank plc v Ernst & Whinney* [1993] 1 IR 375 at 390.

6 Delany and McGrath, *Civil Procedure in the Superior Courts* (2nd edn, Thomson Round Hall, 2005) at para 10.03 (noting judicial differences of opinion over whether discovery is intended to enable settlement or trial).

7 *Galvin v Graham Twomey* [1994] 2 ILRM 315 at 318 (*per* Henchy J).

8 *McCarthy v O'Flynn* [1979] IR 127 at 129 (*per* Henchy J) .

AMENDMENTS TO THE RULES OF THE SUPERIOR COURTS

[7.05] The Rules of the Superior Courts relating to discovery have been substantially amended on two occasions: in 1999, some 13 years after the entry into force of the rules in their original form, and again, a decade later, in 2009.[9]

The 1999 Amendments

[7.06] The brief discussion above concerning the purposes of discovery reflects the many advantages that the procedure may bring to civil proceedings particularly in terms of defining the issues and expediting the proceedings. The rules relating to discovery as incorporated in the original Rules of the Superior Courts travelled some distance towards achieving these goals. While discovery was undoubtedly viewed as 'an extremely valuable legal procedure',[10] the case law in the decade following the introduction of the rules evinced increasing concern on the part of the courts that the procedure was being over-used and, at times, misused. The difficulty lay in part in the liberal provision in the rules for general orders of discovery which could potentially impose excessive burdens on parties making discovery.[11] However, judges were also alive to the possibility that discovery could be used as a tactic in the adversarial process to conduct fishing expeditions, swamp the other side with oppressive demands for disclosure and needlessly increase the length and cost of the proceedings.[12] Fennelly J summarised the position in *Ryanair plc v Aer Rianta cpt*: '[the change made in 1999] exemplifies ... growing concern about the dangers of unnecessarily costly and protracted litigation and, in particular, the burdens on parties and the courts arising from excessive resort to automatic blanket discovery'. The learned judge extolled the virtues of 'expedition and economy' as elements in the 'just and proper conduct of litigation'.[13]

The 1999 Amendments introduced a new Ord 31, r 12[14] which alleviated some of these concerns by rendering discovery a more narrow and particularised procedure.[15] The new rule dispensed with general orders of discovery and placed on the shoulders of the party seeking discovery the burden of establishing that the procedure is necessary in the individual case.[16]

---

9 A prior amendment, providing for voluntary discovery, was introduced in 1993. Rules of the Superior Courts (No. 2) of 1993 (SI 265/1993).

10 *Irish Nationwide Building Society v Charlton* (5 March 1997, unreported) SC (*per* Murphy J).

11 *Ryanair plc v Aer Rianta cpt* [2003] 4 IR 264, 277 (*per* Fennelly J).

12 See, eg, *Murphy v Minister for Defence* [1991] 2 IR 161; *Hannon v Commissioners of Public Works* [2001] IEHC 59; *Swords v Western Proteins Ltd* [2001] 1 IR 324.

13 *Ryanair plc v Aer Rianta cpt* [2003] 4 IR 264 at 277.

14 The new rule entered into force on 3 August 1999: SI 233/1999.

15 See Delany and McGrath, *Civil Procedure in the Superior Courts* (2nd edn, Thomson Round Hall, 2005) paras 10.22–10.24.

16 *Ryanair plc v Aer Rianta cpt* [2003] 4 IR 264, 275 (*per* Fennelly J).

The 2009 Amendments

[7.07] The recent amendments to the rules relating to discovery are enshrined in SI 93/2009, *Rules of the Superior Courts (Discovery)* which entered into force on 16 April 2009.[17] SI 93/2009 did not alter discovery in its essential characteristics but targeted certain specific aspects of the procedure.

The principal reform was the incorporation within the rules of provisions relating to the discovery of electronically stored information. The need for this development was highlighted by *Dome Telecom Ltd v Eircom Ltd*[18] which presented the Supreme Court with the challenge of deciding complex issues relating to the discovery of electronically stored information. The rules now expressly address the subject of electronic discovery[19] and allow for a range of outcomes including the possible appointment of 'an independent expert or person' to undertake the inspection and searching of the documents.[20] While the new provisions go a considerable way towards adapting the rules to embrace technological developments in the generating, storing and accessing of documents, they house potential difficulties and ambiguities.[21] It remains to be seen how the new provisions will play out in practice.

[7.08] SI 93/2009 extended the powers of the court in relation to discovery in certain interesting respects. The new rule etches in formal terms the broad discretion that the Master and the Court have long exercised in practice to order discovery on the terms sought or on more limited terms. Thus, discovery may be ordered in respect of some or all of the categories of documents sought or limited to certain documents or classes of documents within those categories.[22]

The new rule also vests in the court the authority to vary an order for discovery or an agreement to make voluntary discovery where the court is satisfied that further discovery is necessary or that the discovery originally ordered or agreed is 'unreasonable having regard to the cost or other burden of providing discovery'.[23] This development reflects in part a growing emphasis in the case law on the potential burden of discovery as a factor influencing the fairness of the procedure. Nevertheless, the courts will need to exercise this jurisdiction sparingly if they are to avoid the drawbacks that would accompany the regular re-opening of settled arrangements for discovery.[24]

---

17 SI 93/2009 set out a new version of Ord 31, r 12 which replaces the original.

18 *Dome Telecom Ltd v Eircom Ltd* [2008] 2 IR 727.

19 Order 31, r 12(13) expressly provides that the term 'documents' includes 'all electronically stored information'.

20 Order 31, r 12(3)(b). The independent expert may be agreed by the parties or appointed by the court.

21 Abrahamson (ed), 'Amendments to Court Rules' (2009) 5(1) JCPP 2.

22 For discussion of the pre-existing practice see, eg, *Framus Ltd v CRH plc* [2004] 2 IR 20.

23 Order 31, r 12(11).

24 Abrahamson (ed), 'Amendments to Court Rules' (2009) 5(1) JCPP 2.

[7.09] Another change to the rules introduced by SI 93/2009 has heightened the degree of specificity required in the classification of documents in the affidavit of discovery. The new rule stipulates that 'documents of the same or a similar nature and not in electronic form, when numerous, shall so far as is possible be grouped together and numbered or otherwise sufficiently marked so as to be identifiable'.[25] Delany and Egan McGrath observe that '[t]his provision does not reflect general practice and may prove difficult to implement'.[26] In a related development, the new rule provides that the affidavit shall list documents 'in a manner corresponding with the categories in the agreement or order for discovery' and 'in a sequence corresponding with the manner in which the documents or information have been stored or kept in the usual course of business' by the party making discovery.[27] This requirement will likely increase the procedural burden resting on the party making discovery particularly where there is a lack of symmetry between the categorisation of documents in the order or agreement and the system of classification in the usual course of business.

Interpretation of the Rules of the Superior Courts

[7.10] The relevant Rules of the Superior Courts provide the starting point for the determination of issues relating to discovery. However, in recent years the courts have indicated a willingness to transcend the strict letter of the rules where appropriate and adopt a proactive approach to their interpretation.[28] The willingness of the members of the Supreme Court to adapt the rules to take account of technological developments in *Dome Telecom Ltd v Eircom Ltd*[29] is illustrative of this trend. In the course of his judgment in that case, Geoghegan J stated:

> '... I would reject any idea that the right to discovery of documents should be exclusively based on an interpretation (literal or otherwise) of the relevant rule of court. According to Halsbury's *Laws of England* (4th ed.), vol. 13, para. 1 footnote 3, the discovery of documents "was originally an equitable device employed in the Court of Chancery for obtaining the disclosure and inspection of relevant documents as well as the disclosure and admissions of relevant facts." It had a more limited history in the common law courts but from and after the Judicature Act, the chancery practice applied in all courts though of course ever since the Judicature Act, there has been a rule of court regulating discovery. In modern times, courts are not necessarily hidebound by interpretation of a

---

25 Order 31, r 12(4)(a).

26 Delany and Egan McGrath, 'The Discovery Rules – Judicial Proactivity and S.I. 2009/93' (2010) 3 ILT 42 at 46.

27 Order 31, r 12(4)(b). Similarly, the party making discovery must provide the document for inspection within these parameters.

28 See, eg, Delany and Egan McGrath, 'The Discovery Rules – Judicial Proactivity and S.I. 2009/93' (2010) 3 ILT 42 at 42–44.

29 *Dome Telecom Ltd v Eircom Ltd* [2008] 2 IR 726.

> particular rule of court. More general concepts of ensuring fair procedures and efficient case management are frequently overriding considerations. The rules of court are important and adherence to them is important but if an obvious problem of fair procedures or efficient case management arises in proceedings, the court, if there is no rule in existence precisely covering the situation, has an inherent power to fashion its own procedure and even if there was a rule applicable, the court is not necessarily hidebound by it.'[30]

The circumstances in which the courts will supplement or even depart from the rules remain exceptional however. In practical terms, the Supreme Court has emphasised the importance of parties adhering to the terms of Ord 31, r 12.[31]

Inter Partes Discovery: Procedural Steps

[7.11] Before applying to the court for an order for discovery, the party must first seek voluntary discovery from the other party.[32] The request must be made by letter in writing[33] specifying the categories of documents in respect of which discovery is sought and the reasons why disclosure of each category is required.[34] Before making an order, the court must be satisfied that 'a reasonable period of time' has elapsed[35] and that the party to whom the request was directed has 'failed, refused or neglected' to make voluntary discovery or has 'ignored' the request.[36] The pre-condition of voluntary discovery may be side-stepped only in exceptional cases 'where by reason of the urgency of the matter or the

30 *Dome Telecom Ltd v Eircom Ltd* [2008] 2 IR 726 at 736.

31 *Taylor v Clonmel Healthcare Ltd* [2004] 1 IR 169, 183. See also *Moorview Developments Ltd v First Active plc* [2009] 2 IR 788. Although a technical breach of Ord 31, r 12 may be waived by the Master or the courts, it may have a bearing on the question of costs.

32 Order 31, r 12(6)(a). The need to seek voluntary discovery as a pre-condition to a court order has long been the practice in the High Court but was formally inserted into the rules in 1993: Rules of the Superior Courts (No 2) 1993 (SI 265/1993). Failure to complete this procedural step may result in a party being ordered to pay the costs of the application to the court: Ord 31, r 12(10).

33 Order 31, r 12(6)(a).

34 Order 31, r 12 (6)(a)(i) and (ii). In the case of electronically stored information, the request must indicate 'whether the applicant seeks the production of documents in searchable form and if so, whether for that purpose the applicant seeks the provision of inspection and searching facilities using any information and communications technology system owned or operated by the party requested': Ord 31 r 12(6)(a)(iii). On the requirement to specify categories of documents, see *Ryanair plc v Aer Rianta cpt* [2003] 4 IR 264 at 279, [2004] 1 ILRM 241 at 254 (*per* McCracken J).

35 Order 31, r 12(6)(b).

36 Order 31, r 12 (6)(c). The pre-condition of voluntary discovery may be dispensed with 'by reason of the urgency of the matter or the consent of the parties, the nature of the case or any other circumstances which to the court seem appropriate': Ord 31, r 21(6). In such circumstances, the court may make 'such order as appears proper' without the need for the applicant to undertake the voluntary procedure: Ord 31, r 21(6). Where discovery has been sought and agreed but not made within the time agreed, the party who sought discovery may make an application to the court: Ord 31, r 12(8).

consent of the parties, the nature of the case or any other circumstances which to the court seem appropriate'.[37] If the request for voluntary discovery is acceded to, the discovery sought and agreed must be made 'in like manner and form' as court-ordered discovery.[38] Furthermore, the rules explicitly state that voluntary discovery shall have 'such effect as if directed by order of the court'.[39]

[7.12] Assuming that the voluntary discovery procedure has been exhausted, the party may seek the imprimatur of the court or, in the first instance, the Master.[40] The rules stipulate that any party may apply to the court by way of motion on notice grounded on an affidavit not later than 28 days after the action has been set down or, in matters which are not set down, 28 days after it has been listed for trial.[41] In practice, discovery will generally be granted only after the pleadings have closed and the matters in issue between the parties have crystallised.[42]

SCOPE OF *INTER PARTES* DISCOVERY

[7.13] The discovery of documents involves two sequential steps: 'the disclosure on affidavit of the existence of relevant documents' and 'the inspection of documents disclosed, except those exempt from production'.[43] The obligation resting on a party to 'make discovery on oath' is substantively broad and extends to 'the documents which are or have been in his possession or power, relating to any matter in question therein'.[44]

[7.14] The traditional practice involved the parties seeking general orders for discovery in the form of applications for all relevant documents in the

---

37 Order 31, r 12(6). *Brian Greene & Co Ltd v Instruelec Services Ltd* [2001] 1 IR 653, [2002] 1 ILRM 237.

38 Order 31, r 12(7).

39 Order 31, r 12(7).

40 Order 63, r 1(6) includes 'an order for discovery, limited or general' within the realm of orders that the Master may make.

41 Order 31, r 9. The 28-day time period for the application for discovery may be extended by order of the court or with the consent of the requested party 'in any case in which it appears just and reasonable to do so': Ord 31, r 9. The court has a discretion to make an order for the costs of the application against a party who has failed to meet the prescribed time period or any extension thereto: Ord 31, r 12(10).

42 *AL v MN* (4 March 2002, unreported) SC; *Medtronic Inc and Others v Guidant Corporation and Others* [2007] IEHC 37 (23 February 2007) (Kelly J). For discussion of the exceptional circumstances in which discovery will be granted prior to the close of pleadings see Delany and McGrath, *Civil Procedure in the Superior Courts* (2nd edn, Thomson Round Hall, 2005) at para 10.11 *et seq*.

43 Reid (ed), *Civil Litigation* (Oxford University Press, 2009) at para 12.1.

44 Order 31, r 12(1). On the concept of 'possession and power' see, eg, *Johnson v Church of Scientology* [2001] 1 IR 682; *Bula Ltd v Tara Mines Ltd* [1994] 1 ILRM 111; *Wicklow County Council v O'Reilly* [2010] IEHC 464 (7 December 2010) (O'Keefe J).

possession, power or procurement of the other side.[45] As originally drafted, the rules did not require the party seeking an order for discovery to file an affidavit and the party resisting the order bore the onus of establishing that discovery was not necessary.[46] The discovery process burgeoned under this broad, open-ended regime buttressed by the historically liberal touchstone of 'relevance' in legal proceedings. Blanket demands for discovery placed excessive burdens on parties in terms of the production of documents and increased the length and cost of litigation.[47] As noted above, this undesirable state of affairs prompted substantial reform of the rules in 1999[48] designed to fashion a more narrow, expeditious and, ultimately, just procedure.[49] The changes essentially put an end to general orders for discovery requiring instead that applicants specify with precision the categories of documents which are sought to be disclosed and the reasons why discovery is necessary.[50]

[7.15] Order 31, r 12 sets out the conditions that frame an application for discovery. In particular, r 12(1) stipulates the level of specificity required in relation to the documents sought:

> 'Any party may apply to the court by way of notice of motion for an order directing any other party to any cause or matter to make discovery on oath of the documents which are or have been in his possession, power or procurement relating to any matter in question therein. Every such notice of motion shall specify the precise categories of documents in respect of which discovery is sought and shall be grounded upon the affidavit of the party seeking such an order of discovery which shall:
>
> (a) verify that the discovery of documents sought is necessary for disposing fairly of the cause or matter or for saving costs;
>
> (b) furnish the reasons why each category of documents is required to be discovered, and
>
> (c) where the discovery sought includes electronically stored information, specify whether such party seeks production of any documents in searchable form and if so, whether for that purpose the party seeking discovery seeks the provision of inspection and searching facilities using any information and communications technology system owned or operated by the party requested.'

45 This remains a possibility in the Circuit and District Courts: Reid (ed), *Civil Litigation* (Oxford University Press, 2009) para 12.4.1.

46 *AIB Banks plc v Ernst & Whinney* [1993] 1 IR 375 at 389 (*per* Finlay CJ).

47 For an insightful account of the conditions that led to reform and the nature of the changes introduced see Delany and McGrath, *Civil Procedure in the Superior Courts* (2nd edn, Thomson Round Hall, 2005) para 10.18 *et seq.*

48 Rules of the Superior Courts (No 2) (Discovery) 1999 (SI 233/1999).

49 *Ryanair plc v Aer Rianta cpt* [2003] 4 IR 264 at 277 (*per* Fennelly J); *Brooks Thomas Ltd v Impac Ltd* [1999] 1 ILRM 171 at 177 (*per* Lynch J).

50 *Taylor v Clonmel Healthcare Ltd* [2004] 1 IR 169, [2004] 2 ILRM 133.

The emphasis on specificity is echoed in the principles governing public interest privilege. Exceptionally, evidence may be privileged from production on the ground that its disclosure would be contrary to the public interest. All forms of privilege could be said to be rooted in the public interest to a greater or lesser extent; legal professional privilege itself furthers the public interest in the administration of justice because it facilitates the full and frank exchange between lawyer and client that is essential to effective legal representation. Nevertheless, as its name suggests, 'public interest privilege' evokes the public interest in a more direct and central sense. Unlike legal professional privilege, the application of public interest privilege is not governed by hard and fast rules. In each case, the trial court must engage in a balancing exercise, weighing the public interest in disclosure against the countervailing public interest in confidentiality.

[7.16] Questions relating to public interest privilege generally arise when a litigant seeks disclosure of a particular document or documents. The protection against disclosure may be broader than legal professional privilege in so far as vindicating the public interest may necessitate keeping the very existence of the information confidential.[51] Nevertheless, the foundational case law in this area affirms that the determination whether information should be withheld is a matter for the judiciary rather than the executive in the exercise of their constitutional mandate to administer justice in our courts. In *Ambiorix Ltd v Minister for the Environment (No 1)*,[52] Finlay CJ inferred from this central tenet certain practical consequences that arise when the executive asserts privilege during the course of legal proceedings:

> (a) The executive cannot prevent the judicial power from examining documents which are relevant to an issue in a civil trial for the purpose of deciding whether they must be produced.
>
> (b) There is no obligation on the judicial power to examine any particular document before deciding that it is exempt from production, and it can and will in many instances uphold a claim of privilege in respect of a document merely on the basis of a description of its nature and contents which it (the judicial power) accepts.
>
> (c) There cannot, accordingly, be a generally applicable class or category of documents exempted from production by reason of the rank in the public service of the person creating them, or of the position of the individual or body intended to use them ...[53]

---

[51] Walsh J recognised as much in the landmark case of *Murphy v Dublin Corporation and the Minister for Local Government* [1972] IR 215. Taking the example of the public interest in the safety of the State, he observed at 234: 'I have referred to non-disclosure and non-production as distinct matters because in certain circumstances the very disclosure of the existence of a document, apart altogether from the question of its production, could in itself be a danger to the security of the State'.

[52] *Ambiorix Ltd v Minister for the Environment (No 1)* [1992] 1 IR 277, [1992] ILRM 209.

[53] *Ambiorix Ltd v Minister for the Environment (No 1)* [1992] 1 IR 277 at 283–284.

These propositions reflect the commonsensical truth that claims of privilege cannot be vetted in any meaningful sense unless the courts are furnished with specific, detailed information about the nature and form of the interest for which protection is sought. Just as in relation to legal professional privilege, specificity in applications for discovery lays the foundation for thorough judicial consideration of executive privilege; when responding to assertions of privilege across diverse contexts of governmental activity, the courts have engaged in close scrutiny of the documents in question.[54]

BURDEN OF PROOF

[7.17] The 1999 amendments to the discovery rules included a profound alteration in the allocation of the burden of proof. The original rules permitted a party to apply for an order without filing an affidavit and provided that the court might refuse or adjourn the application if satisfied that it was 'not necessary either for disposing fairly of the cause or matter or for saving costs'.[55] Consistent with the liberal thrust in favour of discovery, the courts discerned from the rules an implicit onus on the party resisting disclosure to establish that it was 'not necessary' in the circumstances.[56] A dramatic change wrought by the 1999 amendments was the re-allocation of the primary burden of proof.[57] Under Ord 31, r 12, the applicant must now satisfy the court that the documents are relevant to the matter in dispute and that discovery is necessary to dispose fairly of the matter or to save costs.

[7.18] Important practical consequences attended the shifting of the burden of proof from the respondent or opponent of the application for discovery to the applicant or proponent. The demise of orders for general discovery in High Court proceedings has relieved the respondent of an obligation to discover all documents relevant to the issues in dispute; technically speaking, the duty to discover is now limited to documents requested by the applicant. This opens up the possibility that an applicant for discovery may be surprised at trial when another party presents documentary evidence that the applicant failed to request during discovery. The likelihood of ambush may be diminished, however, by strategic considerations:

> 'If a document is regarded as one that the client might wish to rely upon at trial or the disclosure of which would enhance the client's credibility rather than diminish it or the non-disclosure would be evident at trial and diminish the client's credibility, the preference may be to make disclosure even though the

---

54 See, eg, *Gormley v Ireland* [1993] 2 IR 75 (national security); *Breathnach v Ireland (No 3)* [1993] 2 IR 458, [1992] ILRM 75 (prevention and detection of crime); *Incorporated Law Society v Osborne* [1987] ILRM 42 (proper functioning of the public service).

55 Order 31, r 12(3). This condition has since been reformulated in the terms of r 12(2)(a).

56 *AIB Banks plc v Ernst & Whinney* [1993] 1 IR 375 at 388–389 (*per* Finlay CJ).

57 *Ryanair plc v Aer Rianta cpt* [2003] 4 IR 264 at 275 (*per* Fennelly J).

> document has not been requested. In case managed proceedings it is common practice to agree a book of key documents, which requires the disclosure of such documents. A client would therefore be well advised to include such documents in any discovery, whether or not they have been requested.'[58]

From the perspective of the applicant, the system of specific discovery necessitates detailed consideration of the full complement of documents that should be included in a discovery request.

JUSTIFICATIONS FOR *INTER PARTES* DISCOVERY

[7.19] As the text of Ord 31, r 12(1) indicates, the applicant for discovery must establish two central conditions: first, that discovery of the documents in the possession, power or procurement of the other party is relevant to a matter in question in the proceedings; and, second, that discovery is necessary for disposing fairly of the cause or matter or for saving costs. The applicable standard of proof in relation to the first of these conditions is relatively high given that discovery is carried out at such an early stage in the proceedings; the applicant must establish that discovery is relevant as a matter of probability rather than as a mere possibility.[59] As regards the second condition, the applicant must cross the *prima facie* threshold in demonstrating that discovery is necessary for disposing fairly of the cause or matter.[60]

[7.20] The significance of the relevance and necessity requirements for purposes of the present discussion lies in their potential to render moot any claim of privilege. A party who believes she is privileged from disclosing information at trial will be spared the imperative of asserting and establishing her claim if discovery is in any event discounted because it is irrelevant or unnecessary.

Relevance

[7.21] In *Sterling-Winthrop v Farbenfabriken Bayer v AG*,[61] Kenny J approved the classic statement of Brett LJ in *Compagnie Financière et Commerciale du Pacifique v Peruvian Guano Company*[62] concerning the scope of the relevance requirement:

---

58 Reid (ed), *Civil Litigation* (Oxford University Press, 2009) at para 12.6.5.3. The authors observe further that liberal discovery may promote the client's interest by encouraging settlement discussions.

59 *Hannon v Commissioners of Public Works* (4 April 2001, unreported) HC (McCracken J).

60 *Ryanair plc v Aer Rianta cpt* [2003] 4 IR 264, [2004] 1 ILRM 241.

61 *Sterling-Winthrop v Farbenfabriken Bayer v AG* [1967] IR 97 at 101.

62 *Compagnie Financière et Commerciale du Pacifique v Peruvian Guano Company* (1882) 11 QBD 55.

> '... [T]he documents to be produced are not confined to those, which would be evidence either to prove or disprove any matter in question in the action...
>
> The doctrine seems to me to go farther than that and to go as far as the principle which I am about to lay down. It seems to me that every document relates to the matters in question in the action, which not only would be evidence upon any issue, but also which, it is reasonable to suppose, contains information which may – not which must – either directly or indirectly enable the party requiring the affidavit either to advance his own case or to damage the case of his adversary. I have put in the words 'directly or indirectly,' because, as it seems to me, a document can properly be said to contain information which may enable the party requiring the affidavit either to advance his own case or to damage the case of his adversary, if it is a document which may fairly lead him to a train of inquiry, which may have either of these two consequences ...'[63]

Brett LJ's conception of relevance has been endorsed on numerous occasions as the embodiment of the requirement[64] and has continued to feature in judicial reasoning following the 1999 amendments to the rules.[65] The touchstone of the *Peruvian Guano* test is the assistance which any document sought to be discovered may lend to the applicant in advancing her case. As Abrahamson, Dwyer and Fitzpatrick observe, the consequential effect is strikingly expansive:

> 'Requiring an applicant to establish that a document might contain information which directly or indirectly advances his own cause or damages that of his opponent is a broad test and leads in most cases to the refusal of discovery of only the most clearly irrelevant of documents.'[66]

[7.22] Perhaps for this reason, the Irish courts have taken steps to circumscribe the application of the test. In *McKenna v Best Travel Ltd,* Morris J opined: 'It is in my view well settled that it is only documents which would support or defeat an issue that arises in the existing action which are required to be discovered or should be made the subject matter of an order for discovery'.[67] In *Hannon v Commissioners of Public Works,* McCracken J added the important qualification that each of the documents in question must be relevant to an issue raised in the pleadings rather than simply by way of 'submissions as to alleged facts put forward in affidavits'.[68] While the authorities make plain that relevance on the pleadings has become the guiding principle, the task of determining the manner

---

63 *Compagnie Financière et Commerciale du Pacifique v Peruvian Guano Company* (1882) 11 QBD 55 at 62–63.

64 See, eg, *Woodfab Ltd v Coillte Teoranta* (11 August 1995, unreported) HC (Flood J).

65 *Ryanair v Aer Rianta* [2003] 4 IR 264.

66 Abrahamson, Dwyer and Fitzpatrick, *Discovery and Disclosure* (Thomson Round Hall, 2007) para 6.06 (noting further that the 'breadth of the test may owe something to the fact that it was devised at a time when documents were far less abundant than they are now').

67 *McKenna v Best Travel Ltd* [1995] 1 IR 577 at 580.

68 *Hannon v Commissioners of Public Works* (4 April 2001, unreported) HC at p 4. See also *Framus Ltd v CRH plc* [2004] 2 IR 20.

in which documents might bear on the issues pleaded can be deceptively complex.[69] Notwithstanding the breadth of Brett LJ's formulation of relevance in *Peruvian Guano*, the courts will not countenance the use of discovery as a springboard for 'purely speculative investigation'[70] or so-called 'fishing expeditions'.[71] Nor will discovery be ordered where the information in question is sought solely for use in the cross-examination of a witness as to her credibility.[72]

Necessity

[7.23] The second requirement demands of the applicant that she establish the need for discovery of the document or documents in question. Specifically, the applicant must: '(a) verify that the discovery of documents sought is necessary for disposing fairly of the cause or matter or for saving costs and (b) furnish the reasons why each category of documents is required to be discovered'.[73] Although incorporated in the rules as originally drafted, the necessity requirement lay dormant until the 1999 amendments.[74] The reforms sought to rein in an expansive, costly discovery practice by requiring applicants to aver on affidavit that the discovery sought was necessary for disposing fairly of the action or saving costs. The effect was to relocate the necessity requirement centre-stage in the discovery process.

[7.24] The relevance and necessity requirements are generally perceived to go hand-in-hand. *Taylor v Clonmel Healthcare Ltd*[75] is cited for the proposition that where a document is adjudged to be relevant, in most instances it will also be necessary.[76] There may be exceptional cases, however, where necessity will not inexorably follow relevance. The potential significance of necessity as a stand-

---

69 Delany and McGrath, *Civil Procedure in the Superior Courts* (2nd edn, Thomson Round Hall, 2005) para 10.31 (citing cases). The courts have grappled in particular with the vexed question of how much deference should be paid to the deponent of the affidavit of discovery in her assessment of what is relevant. See, eg, *Bula Ltd v Crowley* [1991] 1 IR 220 at 223, [1990] ILRM 756 at 758.

70 *O Company v M Company* [1996] 2 Lloyd's Rep 347 at 350 (*per* Colman J).

71 *Carlow Kilkenny Radio Ltd v Broadcasting Commission* [2003] 3 IR 528; Abrahamson, Dwyer and Fitzpatrick, *Discovery and Disclosure* (Thomson Round Hall, 2007) paras 6.18–6.24 (discussing cases).

72 *Stafford v Revenue Commissioners* (27 March 1996, unreported) SC.

73 Order 31, r 12(1).

74 Abrahamson, Dwyer and Fitzpatrick, *Discovery and Disclosure* (Thomson Round Hall, 2007) paras 6.26–6.27. For a relatively early application of the necessity requirement see *Brooks Thomas Ltd v Impac Ltd* [1999] 1 ILRM 171.

75 *Taylor v Clonmel Healthcare Ltd* [2004] 1 IR 169.

76 See also *Framus Ltd v CRH plc* [2004] 2 IR 20 at 38 (*per* Murray CJ); *Ryanair plc v Aer Rianta cpt* [2003] 4 IR 264, [2004] 1 ILRM 241.

alone criterion was emphasised in *PJ Carroll & Co Ltd v Minister for Health.*[77] In the context of a constitutional challenge to legislation aimed at curbing a particular form of tobacco advertising, the Supreme Court held that whereas certain documentation was relevant, discovery of the documentation was not necessary in the circumstances.

[7.25] The Supreme Court has considered the substantive import of the concept of necessity on a number of occasions. In *Ryanair plc v Aer Rianta cpt*, Fennelly J held that an applicant need not prove that particular categories of documents are 'in any sense absolutely necessary'.[78] He referred with approval to *Cooper Flynn v Radio Telefís Éireann*,[79] a case involving inspection of documents, in which Kelly J distilled from the English authorities 'the useful notion of 'litigious advantage''.[80] Discovery will be necessary if it gives to the applicant a litigious advantage in the guise of information not otherwise available[81] or, conversely, if non-disclosure causes her a litigious disadvantage.[82] The extent of the advantage or disadvantage required to meet the necessity criterion was considered by Lord Salmon in *Science Research Council v Nassé:*

> 'What does 'necessary' in this context mean? It, of course, includes the case where the party applying for an order of discovery and inspection of certain documents could not possibly succeed in the proceedings unless he obtained the order; but it is not confined to such cases. Suppose, for example a man had a slim chance of success without inspection of documents but a very strong chance of success with inspection, surely the proceedings could not be regarded as being fairly disposed of, were he to be denied inspection.'[83]

---

77 *PJ Carroll & Co Ltd v Minister for Health* [2006] IESC 36 (1 June 2006). Geoghegan J observed that 'the separation of the element of necessity from the concept of relevance is, nevertheless, important and has real application in some cases ...'

78 *Ryanair plc v Aer Rianta cpt* [2003] 4 IR 264 at 276.

79 *Cooper Flynn v Radio Telefiis Éireann* [2003] 3 IR 344.

80 *Ryanair plc v Aer Rianta cpt* [2003] 4 IR 264 at 276 (*per* Fennelly J, cautioning nonetheless against substituting a term of art for the words of the rule).

81 *Wallace Smith Trust Co v Deloitte* [1997] 1 WLR 257 (*per* Simon Brown LJ). See also *Air Canada v Secretary of State for Trade* [1983] AC 394. When considering whether discovery is necessary, the courts will have regard to the availability to the applicant of alternative means of proof: *PJ Carroll & Co Ltd v Minister for Health* [2006] IESC 36 (1 June 2006). However, Abrahamson, Dwyer and Fitzpatrick divine some confusion among the authorities on point and conclude that alternative means of proof is best viewed not as a discrete test but rather 'as one of several means of determining whether discovery would confer any litigious advantage on the applicant': *Discovery and Disclosure* (Thomson Round Hall, 2007) at para 6.47. See also Delany and McGrath, *Civil Procedure in the Superior Courts* (2nd edn, Thomson Round Hall, 2005) para 10.54.

82 *Taylor v Anderson* [1995] 1 WLR 447 at 462 (*per* Bingham MR).

83 *Science Research Council v Nassé* [1980] AC 1028 at 1071 quoted with approval by Kelly J in *Cooper Flynn v Radio Telefis Éireann* [2000] 3 IR 344.

[7.26] At the same time, the courts are reluctant to apply too much elasticity to the concept of litigious advantage. In *Framus Ltd v CRH plc*,[84] Murray CJ cautioned that overly broad orders for discovery could place such oppressive burdens of production on respondents as to threaten rather than promote the fair disposal of proceedings. The Chief Justice remarked that 'there must be some proportionality between the extent or volume of the documents to be discovered and the degree to which the documents are likely to advance the case of the applicant or damage the case of his or her opponent in addition to ensuring that no party is taken by surprise by the production of documents at a trial'.[85] The need to balance the litigious advantage discovery bestows on the applicant with the burden and cost involved for the respondent was confirmed in *Dome Telecom Ltd v Eircom plc*,[86] where the Supreme Court overturned an order for discovery of voluminous electronically stored information.

Proportionality

[7.27] In recent years, the Supreme Court has placed increased reliance on the concept of proportionality as a component in assessing the propriety of ordering discovery in a particular case. Delany and Egan McGrath chart an increasingly proactive judicial role in interpreting the Rules of the Superior Courts relevant to the discovery process. They observe:

> 'The most obvious example of this judicial proactivity in the context of discovery is the introduction of the concept of proportionality and, while there is no explicit reference in Order 31, rule 12 to this concept, it is being increasingly referred to as a relevant factor in assessing whether the requirement of 'necessity' has been satisfied on the facts of a particular case.'[87]

[7.28] For example, considerations of proportionality imbued the judgments of the members of the Supreme Court in *Dome Telecom Ltd v Eircom Ltd.*[88] An issue before the court was whether the extensive electronic discovery sought in the proceedings was so oppressive that it be would be unreasonable for the court to sanction it. Both Kearns and Fennelly JJ quoted in their respective judgments the following extract from the judgment of Murray CJ in *Framus Ltd v CRH plc:*

> 'It seems to me that in certain circumstances a too wide ranging order for discovery may be an obstacle to the fair disposal of proceedings rather than the converse. ... [T]he crucial question is whether discovery is necessary for 'disposing fairly of the cause or matter'. I think it follows that there must be some

84 *Framus Ltd v CRH plc* [2004] 2 IR 20.

85 *Framus Ltd v CRH plc* [2004] 2 IR 20 at 38. See also *Ryanair plc v Aer Rianta cpt* [2004] 4 IR 264 at 277, [2004] 1 ILRM 241 at 252 (*per* Fennelly J noting that necessity turns on the totality of relevant circumstances including 'the burden, scale and cost' of discovery).

86 *Dome Telecom Ltd v Eircom plc* [2008] 2 IR 727.

87 Delany and Egan McGrath, 'The Discovery Rules – Judicial Proactivity and S.I. 2009/93' (2010) 3 ILT 42 at 42 (internal citations omitted).

88 *Dome Telecom Ltd v Eircom Ltd* [2008] 2 IR 726.

proportionality between the extent or volume of the documents to be discovered and the degree to which the documents are likely to advance the case of the applicant or damage the case of his or her opponent ...'[89]

[7.29] Kearns J observed that 'the more necessary the document is the more proportionate it will be for the requesting party to obtain discovery' and emphasised the significance of the factual context in which the issue arises.[90] In his dissenting judgment, Geoghegan J distinguished between the concepts of necessity and proportionality. He observed that 'discovery may be necessary and yet so disproportionate as to render it unreasonable for a court to benefit the party seeking discovery by making the order'.[91] However, whereas Fennelly and Kearns JJ concluded that 'the very unusual burden and heavy cost'[92] of the defendant discovering the voluminous, detailed electronic data sought in this particular case outweighed 'the litigious benefit'[93] to the plaintiff, Geoghegan J reached the opposite conclusion.[94]

Whereas the concept of proportionality has been invoked primarily as a counterbalance to the spectre of oppression in the discovery process, its influence has also been felt in other contexts including the discovery of confidential documents.[95]

THE ORDER FOR *INTER PARTES* DISCOVERY

[7.30] The rules provide the Master with considerable latitude in determining how to respond to applications for discovery. On the hearing of the application, the Master may refuse it on the ground that discovery is not necessary or adjourn it if satisfied that discovery is not necessary at that stage in the

89 *Framus Ltd v CRH plc* [2004] 2 IR 20 at para 36 (quoted by Fennelly J in *Dome Telecom Ltd v Eircom Ltd* [2008] 2 IR 726 at 747 and by Kearns J at [2008] 2 IR 726, 771).

90 *Dome Telecom Ltd v Eircom Ltd* [2008] 2 IR 726 at 772. Kearns J noted earlier in his judgment, at 771, that the assessment of what is necessary and proportionate 'must take account of any factual admissions or concessions made by either or both the parties, notably where liability is totally in dispute and where the issue can conveniently be first determined as a result of admissions or concessions made'.

91 *Dome Telecom Ltd v Eircom Ltd* [2008] 2 IR 726 at 738.

92 *Dome Telecom Ltd v Eircom Ltd* [2008] 2 IR 726 at 747 (*per* Fennelly J).

93 *Dome Telecom Ltd v Eircom Ltd* [2008] 2 IR 726 at 747 (*per* Fennelly J).

94 Geoghegan J pointed out, in particular, that the cost of the making the discovery sought should be offset against 'the potential saving in time and cost which may well materialise when the discovery is completed': *Dome Telecom Ltd v Eircom Ltd* [2008] 2 IR 726 at 741. He continued at 741–742: 'It would seem to me that at that stage it is likely that each party will be in a strong position to form a view as to who is going to win this case or if there is to be a win to what extent. At best, the case may more easily settle. But short of settlement there would be every probability, in my view, of considerable narrowing of issues either by agreement or as a consequence of case management'.

95 Delany and Egan McGrath, 'The Discovery Rules – Judicial Proactivity and S.I. 2009/93' (2010) 3 ILT 42 at 43–44 (discussing *Independent Newspapers (Ireland) Ltd v Murphy Junior* [2006] IEHC 276 (28 July 2006) (Clarke J)).

proceedings.[96] Similarly, the Master may refuse or adjourn the application where the applicant has not first sought voluntary discovery from the other party or non-party.[97] Where the Master accedes to the application for discovery, the order may be made 'either in terms of some or all of the categories of documents sought or limited to certain documents or classes of documents within any or all of those categories, or otherwise as may be thought fit'.[98] In addition, the order will set a time-frame for completion of discovery, a period of six weeks being the rule of thumb.[99]

[7.31] Having reviewed the Master's judgments in the area, Delany and McGrath observed in 2005 that the nature and extent of discovery remained controversial:

> 'Since the introduction of the amended rules, the practice in the Master's court has been to adopt much more rigid standards in relation to the granting of discovery. It would also be fair to say that a number of written judgments delivered by the Master following the introduction of the amended discovery rules showed a degree of exasperation about the limited effect which the changes appeared to have had in practice.'[100]

Where the Master makes an order for discovery, any party 'aggrieved' by the order may appeal to the High Court within six days of the perfecting of the order.[101] Similarly, an applicant may appeal a refusal within six days of the date of same.[102]

[7.32] The courts will entertain applications for orders varying the terms of a discovery order or agreement.[103] Applications of this kind may be brought at any time and by 'any party concerned by the effect of an order or agreement for discovery'.[104] Before varying the terms of a discovery order or agreement, the court must be satisfied that one of two conditions is met: either that 'further

---

96 Order 31, r 12(2)(a).

97 Pursuant to Ord 31, r 12(6). The court has a discretion to award the costs of the application against a party who has failed to seek voluntary discovery in advance of coming to court: Ord 31, r 12(10).

98 Order 31, r 12 (2)(b). It is also open to the Master to order discovery on terms as to security for the costs involved: Ord 31, r 12 (2)(b). The rules include special provision for orders in respect of discovery of electronically stored information given the particularities and potential expense involved in inspection of same: Ord 31, r 12(2)(c) and r 12(3). On non-compliance with an order for discovery see *Wicklow County Council v O'Reilly* [2010] IEHC 464 (7 December 2010) (O'Keefe J).

99 Delany and McGrath, *Civil Procedure in the Superior Courts* (2nd edn, Thomson Round Hall, 2005) para 10.57.

100 Delany and McGrath, *Civil Procedure in the Superior Courts* (2nd edn, Thomson Round Hall, 2005) para 10.53.

101 Order 63, r 9(1).

102 Order 63, r 9(1).

103 Order 31, r 12(11).

104 Order 31, r 12(11).

discovery is necessary for disposing fairly of the case or for saving costs'[105] or that the discovery originally ordered or agreed is 'unreasonable' having regard to 'the cost or other burden of providing discovery'.[106] Even where one of these eventualities has transpired, the court 'shall not' make an order varying terms where the applicant has not undertaken the initial step of requesting the other party to agree to the variation.[107] Thus, the rules impose upon the applicant for an order varying terms a procedural pre-condition equivalent to the seeking of voluntary discovery required of the applicant for an original discovery order.[108]

[7.33] To ease the mechanics of the process, the rules stipulate that parties making discovery should list and provide for inspection the documents and information in conformity with the categorisation employed in the agreement or order for discovery.[109] Subject to the terms of the agreement or order, the sequencing of the information should correspond with the manner in which the documents or information are maintained in the party's usual course of business.[110] Where the material includes 'numerous' documents of a similar nature, these documents should be 'grouped together' as far as possible and 'numbered or otherwise sufficiently marked so as to be identifiable'.[111]

PROHIBITION ON USE OF INFORMATION FOR OTHER PURPOSES

[7.34] Where discovery has been agreed or ordered and documents have been disclosed, the party obtaining production is bound to limit her use of the documents to purposes connected with the underlying litigation.[112] In *Ambiorix Ltd v Minister for the Environment (No 1)*,[113] Finlay CJ stated the principle in the following terms:

> 'As a matter of general principle, of course, a party obtaining the production of documents by discovery in an action is prohibited by law from making any use of any description of such documents or the information contained in them

[105] Order 31, r 12(11)(i).

[106] Order 31, r 12(11)(ii).

[107] Order 31, r 12(12).

[108] Specifically, prior to seeking the assistance of the court, the applicant for the order varying terms must have requested the variation by letter in writing to the other party and or allowed that party a reasonable time for agreement. It is only when the party or person requested has 'failed, refused or neglected to agree to such variation or has ignored such request' that the order varying terms can be made: Ord 31, r 12(12).

[109] Order 31, r 12(4)(b).

[110] Order 31, r 12(4)(b).

[111] Order 31, r 12(4)(a).

[112] *R (Kelly) v Warley Magistrates Court* [2007] EWHC 1836.

[113] *Ambiorix Ltd v Minister for the Environment (No 1)* [1992] 1 IR 277.

otherwise than for the purpose of the action. To go outside that prohibition is to commit contempt of court'.[114]

Non-Party Discovery

[7.35] A party to civil legal proceedings may seek discovery from a person who is not a party to the proceedings. Order 31, r 29 provides:

> 'Any person not a party to the cause or matter before the court who appears to the court to be likely to have or to have had in his possession custody or power any documents which are relevant to an issue arising or likely to arise out of the cause or matter ... may by leave of the court upon the application of any party to the said cause or matter be directed by order of the court ... to make discovery of such documents or to permit inspection of such documents. ...'

Non-party discovery marked a procedural departure from traditional practice when introduced with the coming into effect of the Rules of the Superior Courts in 1986. Previously, discovery was exclusively *inter partes* in nature and the courts eschewed attempts to join persons as parties purely for the purpose of extending the scope of discovery *ratio personae*.[115] The procedure is designed to facilitate the pre-trial process by extending the range of relevant information available to the parties.[116] The authority of the Superior Courts Rules Committee to include provision for non-party discovery within the rules has been upheld.[117] Nevertheless, in *Holloway v Belenos Publications Ltd (No 2)*, Barron J emphasised the procedure's special, limited characteristics:

> 'The right to discovery against a non-party does not create an independent enforceable right against such a person. It imposes an obligation on such a person, but one imposed by the court in the same way as a *subpoena*. It has no existence independent of the proceedings in which it is sought.'[118]

[7.36] The conditions governing non-party discovery are broadly similarly to those regulating *inter partes* discovery. Indeed, r 29 expressly states that the provisions of Ord 31 shall apply *mutatis mutandis* to a court order of non-party

---

114 *Ambiorix Ltd v Minister for the Environment (No 1)* [1992] 1 IR 277 at 286. See also *Countyglen plc v Carway* [1995] 1 IR 208; *Greencore plc v Murphy* [1995] 3 IR 520. Exceptionally, the courts may relax the strict application of the principle. See, eg, *Roussel v Farchepro Ltd* [1999] 3 IR 567 discussed in Delany and McGrath, *Civil Procedure in the Superior Courts* (2nd edn, Thomson Round Hall, 2005) para 10.65.

115 *International Trading Group Ltd v Dublin Corporation* [1974] IR 373.

116 *Allied Irish Banks plc v Ernst & Whinney* [1993] 1 IR 375.

117 *Holloway v Belenos Publications Ltd (No 2)* [1988] IR 494; *Fitzpatrick v Independent Newspapers Ltd* [1988] IR 132.

118 *Holloway v Belenos Publications Ltd (No 2)* [1988] IR 494 at 498. See also *Fusco v O'Dea* [1994] 2 IR 93, [1994] 2 ILRM 389 (declining to make an order where the non-party was resident outside the jurisdiction on the ground that r 29 should be construed strictly on its express terms).

discovery as if the order had been directed to a party.[119] There are some significant differences, however. The party seeking non-party discovery bears the onus of establishing two basic conditions,[120] namely, that the non-party 'is likely to have or have had the documents in his possession, custody or power'[121] and that the documents are relevant to an issue in the proceedings.[122] Even where these conditions are satisfied, however, the court retains a discretion to refuse the application because, for example, discovery will cause oppression or prejudice to the non-party[123] or the documents are readily available to be discovered by a party to the action.[124] Typically, the party seeking discovery must give an undertaking as to costs to the non-party.

ASSERTING PRIVILEGE

[7.37] A privilege is distinguishable from a right in that it must be asserted if it is to have effect.[125] Because legal professional privilege belongs to the client, the decision whether or not to assert it is hers.[126] Nevertheless, the lawyer has a duty to inform the client as to the existence of the privilege and to assert the privilege on the client's behalf unless otherwise instructed.[127] Typically, the party seeking discovery must give an undertaking as to costs to the non-party.

[7.38] An evidentiary privilege entitles its holder to escape the obligation resting on a party or non-party to produce for inspection a document relevant to an issue in the proceedings. However, privilege is not a licence to sidestep discovery either entirely or in part. To put it another way, 'in general, the fact that a

---

[119] Thus, for example, before applying to the court the party seeking discovery should first look for voluntary discovery from the non-party: Abrahamson, Dwyer and Fitzpatrick, *Discovery and Disclosure* (Thomson Round Hall, 2007) para 10.15; Delany and McGrath, *Civil Procedure in the Superior Courts* (2nd edn, Thomson Round Hall, 2005) para 10.76. Furthermore, both the application and order for discovery should specify the categories of document to be discovered. Rule 29 provides that the party seeking discovery shall indemnify the non-party in respect of all costs reasonably borne by the non-party.

[120] *Allied Irish Banks plc v Ernst & Whinney* [1993] 1 IR 375.

[121] *Holloway v Belenos Publications Ltd (No 2)* [1988] IR 494.

[122] Abrahamson, Dwyer and Fitzpatrick, *Discovery and Disclosure* (Thomson Round Hall, 2007) para 10.08 (noting that despite some difference in the wording of rr 12 and 29, the relevance requirement is broadly similar in the *inter partes* and non-party contexts).

[123] *Allied Irish Banks plc v Ernst & Whinney* [1993] 1 IR 375; *Ulster Bank Ltd v Byrne* (10 July 1997, unreported) HC (O'Donovan J) (discussed in Delany and McGrath, *Civil Procedure in the Superior Courts* (2nd edn, Thomson Round Hall, 2005) para 10.72).

[124] *Chambers v Times Newspapers Ltd* [1999] 2 IR 424; *Re National Irish Bank* [2006] 2 ILRM 263.

[125] *Bula Ltd v Crowley* [1991] 1 IR 220.

[126] *McMullen v Carty* (27 January 1998, unreported) SC; *Shell E & P Ireland Ltd v McGrath (No 2)* [2007] 2 IR 574 at 580.

[127] *McMullen v Carty* (27 January 1998, unreported) SC.

document is or may be privileged from production is not a ground for refusing discovery of that document.[128] The party or non-party from whom discovery is sought or ordered must discover all relevant documents,[129] thereby conceding that they exist and are presumptively available.[130] In the process, however, the party or non-party may assert privilege over some or all of the documents in question by listing them accordingly in the affidavit of discovery. By asserting privilege in this way, the party or non-party affords the party seeking inspection an opportunity to challenge the assertion and, ultimately, the court an opportunity to determine its validity. Should the court confirm that any document is indeed privileged, the party or non-party will be entitled to refuse to produce it for inspection.[131]

THE FORM IN WHICH THE CLAIM IS PRESENTED

[7.39] The locus of privilege within the discovery process was an influential factor in the changes to the rules introduced in 1999. The lack of specificity in requests and applications for discovery was mimicked by broad and general assertions of privilege. Judicial dissatisfaction with this practice was registered in several cases which presaged the changes to the rules. As Walsh J explained In *Bula Ltd v Tara Mines Ltd (No 4)*: 'Unless documents are identified and properly indicated no particular claim of privilege should be made about anything. One must know what the claim of privilege is'.[132]

In *Bula Ltd v Crowley,*[133] Finlay CJ rejected the notion of assertions of privilege in general terms. The level of specificity required of the party seeking discovery is mirrored in the assertion of privilege. Finlay CJ explained the essence of what is required in the following terms:

> '... an individual listing of the documents with the general classification of privilege claimed in respect of each document indicated in such fashion by enumeration as would convey to a reader of the affidavit the general nature of the document concerned in each individual case together with the broad heading of privilege being claimed for it.'[134]

---

[128] Delany and McGrath, *Civil Procedure in the Superior Courts* (2nd edn, Thomson Round Hall, 2005) at para 10.140.

[129] *Bula Ltd v Tara Mines (No 5)* [1994] 1 IR 487; *Spring Grove Services (Ireland) Ltd v O'Callaghan and Others* (31 July 2000, unreported) HC (Herbert J).

[130] Abrahamson, Dwyer and Fitzpatrick, *Discovery and Disclosure* (Thomson Round Hall, 2007) para 34.07.

[131] Where a challenge to a claim of privilege is likely or inevitable, the court may consider it at the outset along with the broader issue of discovery: *Haughey v Moriarty* (20 January 1998, unreported) HC (Geoghegan J).

[132] *Bula Ltd v Tara Mines Ltd (No 4)* [1991] 1 IR 217 at 218.

[133] *Bula Ltd v Crowley* [1991] 1 IR 220.

[134] *Bula Ltd v Crowley* [1991] 1 IR 220 at 222. See also *O'Brien v Minister for Defence* [1998] 2 ILRM 156. For traditional authority in support see *Worthington v DW & W Railway Co* (1888) 22 LR Ir 310; *Flynn v Northern Banking* (1898) 32 ILTR 67 (discussed in Abrahamson, Dwyer and Fitzpatrick, *Discovery and Disclosure* (Thomson Round Hall, 2007) para 34.10).

[7.40] The form in which a claim of legal professional privilege is presented was considered by the High Court in *Irish Haemophilia Society v Judge Lindsay and Blood Transfusion Board.*[135] The applicant, Irish Haemophilia Society, sought leave to apply for judicial review of a ruling made by the respondent Judge Lindsay in her capacity as Sole Member of the Tribunal of Inquiry into Circumstances of Infection of People with Haemophilia with HIV and Hepatitis C. In the ruling in question, the respondent upheld a claim of legal professional privilege asserted by the notice party, the Blood Transfusion Service Board (BTSB), over certain documents.

The claim of privilege in respect of some 611 documents was made in an affidavit sworn by a witness on behalf of the BTSB. However, the respondent directed the swearing of a supplemental affidavit[136] because although the documents had been adequately categorised in the affidavit, they had not been enumerated individually.[137] A supplemental affidavit was duly sworn, re-asserting the claim to legal professional privilege and describing individually each of the 611 documents over which privilege was asserted.[138] The applicant challenged the claim, questioning the sufficiency of the affidavit on the basis that the 'the documents should have been individually described in a more detailed form'.[139] The respondent was satisfied, however, that the BTSB's supplemental affidavit met the controlling requirements.

[7.41] In the High Court, Kelly J refused leave to apply for judicial review of the respondent's ruling. He recalled the relevant dicta of the Supreme Court in *Bula Ltd v Tara Mines Ltd (No 4)*[140] and *Bula Ltd v Crowley.*[141] Having considered the affidavit carefully, Kelly J concluded that it complied with the Supreme Court's directions. Not only was there 'no necessity to describe the documents in greater detail' than had been done,[142] the learned judge opined that '[t]o do so would run the risk of diluting or perhaps even destroying the privilege which is being asserted'.[143] Kelly J also indicated that it was sufficient to refer to 'counsel' or

[135] *Irish Haemophilia Society v Judge Lindsay and Blood Transfusion Board* (16 May 2001, unreported) HC (Kelly J).

[136] *Irish Haemophilia Society v Judge Lindsay and Blood Transfusion Board* (16 May 2001, unreported) HC at pp 4–5.

[137] *Irish Haemophilia Society v Judge Lindsay and Blood Transfusion Board* (16 May 2001, unreported) HC at p 4.

[138] *Irish Haemophilia Society v Judge Lindsay and Blood Transfusion Board* (16 May 2001, unreported) HC at p 5.

[139] *Irish Haemophilia Society v Judge Lindsay and Blood Transfusion Board* (16 May 2001, unreported) HC at p 10.

[140] *Bula Ltd v Tara Mines Ltd (No 4)* [1991] 1 IR 217.

[141] *Bula Ltd v Crowley* [1991] 1 IR 220.

[142] *Irish Haemophilia Society v Judge Lindsay and Blood Transfusion Board* (16 May 2001, unreported) HC (Kelly J) at p 12.

[143] *Irish Haemophilia Society v Judge Lindsay and Blood Transfusion Board* (16 May 2001, unreported) HC (Kelly J) at p 12.

'expert' in the affidavit of discovery without naming the individuals in question where to do so might lead to the inadvertent disclosure of privileged information.[144]

AFFIDAVIT OF DISCOVERY

[7.42] When making discovery, the party or non-party must swear an affidavit of discovery in the form set out in Form 10 of Appendix C to the Rules of the Superior Courts. The affidavit comprises two schedules, the first of which contains two parts. The First Part of the First Schedule lists all of the documents which the deponent is discovering and the Second Part sets out the items on that list of documents over which the deponent is asserting privilege.[145] In accordance with the guidance offered by the Supreme Court in *Bula Ltd v Tara Mines Ltd (No 4)*[146] and *Bula Ltd v Crowley*,[147] in this Second Part the deponent must list individually each document over which privilege is asserted and describe in general terms the nature of the document and the species of privilege invoked. If the claim of privilege extends to only part of a document, depending on the nature and extent of the privileged material, the party or non-party making discovery may produce the document with the privileged material redacted. If this option is exercised, the description of the document as it appears in the First Part of the First Schedule should make reference to the redaction.[148] In the absence of formal requirements as to the order in which documents should be listed, it is common practice to list them in chronological order and/or within specified categories.[149]

[7.43] The upshot of the changes to the rules is that the courts will not permit parties to make generalised claims of privilege over bundles of documents.[150] At the same time, the courts tend to adopt a purposive approach: sufficient information must be provided so that the other party can assess and respond to the claim and, ultimately, that the court can make any necessary adjudication. Beyond this, however, the courts will not require unnecessarily slavish adherence to detail. For example, a party asserting litigation privilege must include in the affidavit enough information to enable the other side to identify

144 *Irish Haemophilia Society v Judge Lindsay and Blood Transfusion Board* (16 May 2001, unreported) HC (Kelly J) at p 12.

145 The Second Schedule contains a list of relevant documents which the deponent at one time had in his power or possession but which she no longer has in her power or possession.

146 *Bula Ltd v Tara Mines Ltd (No 4)* [1991] 1 IR 217.

147 *Bula Ltd v Crowley* [1991] 1 IR 220.

148 Reid (ed), *Civil Litigation* (Oxford University Press, 2009) para 12.12.2.3.

149 Reid (ed), *Civil Litigation* (Oxford University Press, 2009) para 12.12.2.4. In relation to descriptions of privileged documents, the authors note at para 12.8.1: 'If all documents are in the same category of privilege, this can be set out in one of the general recitals to the affidavit'.

150 *Bula Ltd v Tara Mines Ltd* [1991] 1 IR 217; *O'Brien v Minister for Defence* [1998] 2 ILRM 156.

the type of privilege at issue, such as the statement that the document in question was prepared in contemplation of litigation.[151] Nevertheless, as a general rule the party need not go further and aver that litigation was the dominant purpose for which the document was created.[152]

Challenging a Claim of Privilege

[7.44] If a party fails to make a claim of privilege in the proper way, the other party may seek and the court may order further and better discovery.[153] A substantive challenge to a claim of privilege may be made in several ways. The proper procedure, it seems, is for the party contesting the claim to bring an application to the court by means of a motion for inspection of the document or documents in question.[154]

Burden of Proof

[7.45] Just as a party seeking discovery bears the burden of satisfying the Master or Court that the information is relevant and discovery necessary, so the party resisting discovery on grounds of privilege bears a corresponding onus to justify the withholding of the document or documents in question.[155] The putative privilege holder bears the onus of substantiating her claim.[156]

[7.46] In *Irish Haemophilia Society v Judge Lindsay and Blood Transfusion Board*,[157] the High Court held that once the party asserting privilege has discharged this basic burden, the onus then shifts to the other side to present an evidentiary basis for her challenge. One of the submissions advanced in that case was that Judge Lindsay had improperly reversed the onus of proof by holding that the applicant, as challenger, was required to adduce evidence that

[151] *Worthington v Dublin, Wicklow and Wexford Railway Co* (1888) 22 LR Ir 310.

[152] *Bula Ltd v Crowley* (8 March 1991, unreported) HC (Murphy J) (discussed in Delany and McGrath, *Civil Procedure in the Superior Courts* (2nd edn, Thomson Round Hall, 2005) para 10.142).

[153] *Bula Ltd v Crowley* [1991] 1 IR 220; *Flynn v Northern Banking Co* (1898) 32 ILTR 67.

[154] Delany and McGrath, *Civil Procedure in the Superior Courts* (2nd edn, Thomson Round Hall, 2005) para 10.143 (noting that although the issue is frequently raised by way of a motion for further and better discovery, a motion for inspection is the proper route). See also Abrahamson, Dwyer and Fitzpatrick, *Discovery and Disclosure* (Thomson Round Hall, 2007) para 34.13 (advising that, in the case of privilege claimed in an affidavit of discovery, the motion for inspection should be preceded by a notice to produce); Reid (ed), *Civil Litigation* (Oxford University Press, 2009) para 12.8.3 (listing various procedural options).

[155] *Miley v Flood* [2001] 1 ILRM 489.

[156] *Smurfit Paribas Bank Ltd v AAB Export Finance Ltd* [1990] 1 IR 469; *Buckley v Bough* (2 July 2001, unreported) HC (Morris J) p 4.

[157] *Irish Haemophilia Society v Judge Lindsay and Blood Transfusion Board* (16 May 2001, unreported) HC (Kelly J).

would question the validity of the claim of privilege.[158] Kelly J rejected this argument as contrary to the principles set out in *Smurfit Paribas Bank Ltd v AAB Export Finance Ltd*[159] and *Miley v Flood.*[160] He explained that once a party asserting legal professional privilege discharges the onus of justifying her claim, the burden then shifts to the challenger.[161] In the present case, the BTSB had met its burden through its affidavit of discovery but the applicant had adduced no evidence in support of its challenge.[162]

Inspection by the Court

[7.47] Applications for discovery orders are adjudged on the affidavit evidence and, where the Master deems it appropriate, on the pleadings. The Master's determination turns on whether the applicant has met the central criteria of relevance and necessity and satisfied the procedural requirements set down in the rules. It follows that the documents that form the basis of the application are not necessarily produced for the court's inspection; the decision to grant or refuse the application is generally based on a description of the documents rather than the documents themselves.

[7.48] Where privilege is asserted, the practice of reviewing a description of the document or documents in question may not constitute an adequate means for the adjudication of the claim. The case law firmly supports the authority of the court to inspect the document or documents in question in these circumstances. In *Smurfit Paribas Ltd v AAB Export Finance Ltd*, Finlay CJ stated that 'the question as to whether or not a party to litigation will be privileged to refuse to produce particular evidence is a matter within the sole competence of the courts'.[163] McCarthy J agreed and elaborated further:

> 'It follows that the courts have whatever power is necessary to examine any relevant documents, irrespective of the wishes of the parties and to determine whether any communication, written or otherwise, between a party to litigation and any other person or body is privileged from disclosure.'[164]

---

158 *Irish Haemophilia Society v Judge Lindsay and Blood Transfusion Board* (16 May 2001, unreported) HC (Kelly J) pp 7–9 and 13.

159 *Smurfit Paribas Bank Ltd v AAB Export Finance Ltd* [1990] 1 IR 469, [1990] ILRM 588.

160 *Miley v Flood* [2001] 1 ILRM 489.

161 *Irish Haemophilia Society v Judge Lindsay and Blood Transfusion Board* (16 May 2001, unreported) HC (Kelly J) p 13.

162 Thus, Lindsay J had 'identified and applied the correct principles': *Irish Haemophilia Society v Judge Lindsay and Blood Transfusion Board* (16 May 2001, unreported) HC (Kelly J) p 13.

163 *Smurfit Paribas Ltd v AAB Export Finance Ltd* [1990] 1 IR 469 at 475 (quoting from the judgment of Walsh J in *Murphy v Dublin Corporation* [1972] IR 215, 235).

164 *Smurfit Paribas Ltd v AAB Export Finance Ltd* [1990] 1 IR 469 at 480.

The judicial power to inspect also finds expression in Ord 31, r 20(2) of the Rules of the Superior Courts which applies where the issue is raised by way of an application for order of inspection.

[7.49] It should be recalled that in most cases the court may be satisfied that a description of the documents provides a sufficient basis on which to adjudicate a claim of privilege. Inspection by the court thus remains an exceptional procedure reserved for cases in which a judge considers that she must have sight of the document or documents in question in order to reach a full and proper determination.

EDITING DOCUMENTS

[7.50] In *Duncan v Governor of Portlaoise Prison*, Kelly J provided an example of an extreme instance in which court inspection would be justified:

> 'There may well be a case (although I hope a rare one) where cogent evidence might be adduced to suggest that a claim to legal professional privilege is being wrongfully asserted. In such a case I do not exclude an ability on the part of the court to direct production of the documents in question. Such an exercise would be with a view to ascertaining whether or not the documents were truly privileged.'[165]

These comments were entered by way of a caveat to the forthright rejection of a proposal that the court should go beyond inspection and edit documents with a view to extracting the factual material that should be disclosed to the other side. Kelly J opined that this would represent a serious and unwarranted intrusion into legal professional privilege.[166] He concluded: 'The conduct of such an exercise would, in my view, be much more likely to work against the administration of justice than in its favour'.[167]

CROSS-EXAMINATION

[7.51] Court inspection of documents is just one means whereby an affidavit of discovery may be tested. In *Duncan v Governor of Portlaoise Prison*, Kelly J was also asked to consider the possibility that the deponent of an affidavit of discovery be cross-examined in relation to her claim of privilege. Kelly J recognised that cross-examination of the deponent of an affidavit of discovery might be conducted but only in 'extremely rare circumstances'.[168] He emphasised that ruling out the possibility of cross-examining the deponent

---

165 *Duncan v Governor of Portlaoise Prison* [1997] 1 IR 558 at 576.

166 *Duncan v Governor of Portlaoise Prison* [1997] 1 IR 558 at 576.

167 *Duncan v Governor of Portlaoise Prison* [1997] 1 IR 558 at 576. This position was affirmed by the Supreme Court on appeal. *Quinlivan v Governor of Portlaoise Prison* (5 March 1997, unreported) SC. But see para **7.55** below.

168 *Duncan v Governor of Portlaoise Prison* [1997] 1 IR 558 at 573.

might fetter the courts in their ability 'to adjudicate fully upon the adequacy and accuracy of an affidavit of discovery' as required by the administration of justice.[169] In practice, however, other remedies such as an order for further and better discovery or the delivery of interrogatories constituted more expedient means of testing an affidavit of discovery.[170]

INSPECTION BY LAWYERS

[7.52] A variant on these themes has been raised in other exceptional cases where the dangers posed by disclosure arguably transcend the immediate confines of the litigation so as to prompt calls for the setting of limits on the means whereby discovery is facilitated. Specifically, the courts have considered the possibility of ordering discovery on the condition that the examination of the documents be conducted exclusively by the lawyers representing the applicant; in effect, the applicant would be precluded from learning the contents of the documents either directly through inspection or indirectly from her lawyers. An arrangement of this kind is susceptible to the fundamental objection that it represents an unwarranted intrusion into the relationship between lawyer and client. The Supreme Court has debated this issue on a number of occasions and, surprisingly, its stance has been somewhat inconsistent. A partial explanation may lie in the diversity of contexts in which the issue has surfaced.

[7.53] *Burke v Central Independent Television plc*[171] was a civil action for damages arising out of an alleged libel contained in a television programme concerning the activities of the IRA. During the course of discovery, the defendants objected to the production of documents likely to put at risk the lives or safety of persons identified therein. The Supreme Court held that 'the constitutional right of individual citizens to the protection of their life and their bodily integrity must of necessity take significant precedence over even so important a right' as the right of citizens to the vindication of their good name.[172] The court rejected in forthright terms the suggestion that the risk to lives or safety of persons identified in the documents in question could be alleviated by the expedient of discovery to the lawyers alone. While the proposed arrangement had 'an attractiveness' as a possible bridge between the respective rights, Finlay CJ was satisfied that it was not a procedure that 'could or should properly be adopted by the Court'.[173] He continued:

> 'If these documents are not only to be protected from communication to the plaintiffs in the interests of a possible risk to citizens from that communication, but also from admission in evidence in a public court, the following situation

---

[169] *Duncan v Governor of Portlaoise Prison* [1997] 1 IR 558 at 573.

[170] *Duncan v Governor of Portlaoise Prison* [1997] 1 IR 558 at 573.

[171] *Burke v Central Independent Television plc* [1994] 2 IR 61, [1994] 2 ILRM 161.

[172] *Burke v Central Independent Television plc* [1994] 2 IR 61 at 79 (*per* Finlay CJ).

[173] *Burke v Central Independent Television plc* [1994] 2 IR 61 at 79 (*per* Finlay CJ).

would arise. Lawyers acting on behalf of the plaintiffs would have access to a number of documents some of which might well be significant and weighty tools to be used in cross examination of witnesses adduced on behalf of the defendant and be unable to use such documents or to explain their failure to their own client to use them. This would constitute an unprecedented and wholly undesirable breach in the duty which counsel would owe to their client and in the proper trust which should exist between a client and his/her lawyers.'[174]

[7.54] Two years previously, the Supreme Court expressed an alternative view when considering possible procedural accommodations in connection with assertions of executive or public interest privilege. In *Ambiorix Ltd v Minister for Environment (No 1)*,[175] the plaintiff property developers instituted proceedings challenging the decision of the Minister for the Environment to declare a certain site a 'designated area' under the Urban Renewal Act 1986. The trial judge made an order for discovery of documents relevant to the Minister's decision, rejecting assertions of executive privilege advanced by the various government defendants. The central thrust of the Supreme Court judgments was the affirmation that '[p]ower to compel the production of evidence (which, of course, includes power to compel the production of documents) is an inherent part of the judicial power'[176] with the consequence that '[t]he executive cannot prevent the judicial power from examining documents which are relevant to an issue in a civil trial for the purpose of deciding whether they must be produced'.[177] The documents in question included representations made to government departments by third parties which contained confidential information pertaining to the commercial and financial interests of those third parties. Thus, as a secondary matter, the court considered the possible procedural accommodation within the discovery process of these third party concerns. Although the commercial and financial information was not protected by any privilege, Finlay CJ recalled that there are safeguards within the system against improper disclosure:

'As a matter of general principle, of course, a party obtaining the production of documents by discovery in an action is prohibited by law from making any use of any description of such documents or the information contained in them otherwise than for the purpose of the action. To go outside that prohibition is to commit contempt of court.

Furthermore, the Court has an inherent jurisdiction, I am satisfied, to take such steps as are necessary to regulate the production of documents so as to prohibit any infringement of this restriction.'[178]

[174] *Burke v Central Independent Television plc* [1994] 2 IR 61 at 80.

[175] *Ambiorix Ltd v Minister for Environment (No 1)* [1992] 1 IR 277, [1992] ILRM 209.

[176] *Ambiorix Ltd v Minister for Environment (No 1)* [1992] 1 IR 277 at 283.

[177] *Ambiorix Ltd v Minister for Environment (No 1)* [1992] 1 IR 277 at 283–284 (*per* Finlay CJ).

[178] *Ambiorix Ltd v Minister for Environment (No 1)* [1992] 1 IR 277 at 286. See also *Cooper Flynn v Radio Telefís Éireann* [2000] 3 IR 344, 357 (*per* Kelly J).

[7.55] The learned Chief Justice canvassed two possible procedural accommodations. First, 'a method of editing' the documents in question could be employed and, second, inspection of the documents could be restricted to the lawyers representing the parties obtaining discovery 'who would give to the Court an undertaking that they would not reveal their contents to their clients, except with the special leave of the Court'.[179] However, Finlay CJ's concluding comment implied a preference for maintaining the latter exceptional procedure as a measure of last resort:

> 'I would hear counsel for the plaintiffs and the defendants further on this particular issue in the hope that a simple formula could be devised between them which would give to the plaintiffs adequate information concerning the material matters contained in this particular collection of documents, and would give to the persons who wrote to the Department adequate protection of their commercial and financial interests.'[180]

[7.56] How then can the position in *Ambiorix Ltd v Minister for the Environment (No 1)* be reconciled with the stance in *Burke v Central Independent Television plc*? In the later case of *Ward v Special Criminal Court*[181] the Supreme Court favoured the approach in *Burke v Central Independent Television plc* but stopped short of engaging in any principled analysis of the distinction. At issue in the judicial review proceedings was the proper procedure that should govern assertions of informer privilege in criminal trials and, in particular, defence objections grounded in the well recognised innocence-at-stake exception to the privilege. Invoking the accused's constitutional right to a fair trial, the defence contended that the prosecution was obliged to disclose any information in its possession which would assist the accused in mounting his defence.

[7.57] The Special Criminal Court had fashioned a compromise whereby the defence lawyers could inspect the documents on condition that the contents were not revealed to their client. However, the Supreme Court rejected the proposition that allegedly privileged documents could be disclosed to the lawyers but not to the accused himself as 'not a feasible compromise'.[182] O'Flaherty J emphasised the 'critical role played by counsel for the prosecution in disclosing any possible source of evidence that may help the defence' and ensuring a 'concord' between disclosure and privilege.[183] The authority to dispel any doubt on the issue lay

[179] *Ambiorix Ltd v Minister for Environment (No 1)* [1992] 1 IR 277 at 286.

[180] *Ambiorix Ltd v Minister for Environment (No 1)* [1992] 1 IR 277 at 286.

[181] *Ward v Special Criminal Court* [1999] 1 IR 60, [1998] 2 ILRM 493.

[182] *Ward v Special Criminal Court* [1999] 1 IR 60 at 88. This was the view Carney J had taken in the High Court below. He had stated: 'it does not seem to me that there would be a trial in accordance with constitutional justice if any subsequent legal representatives did not enjoy the full lawyer-client relationship with their client but were under an obligation to keep secrets from him'. [1999] 1 IR 60 at 76.

[183] *Ward v Special Criminal Court* [1999] IR 60 at 87. O'Flaherty J noted that the task of prosecuting counsel was 'not just to *secure* a conviction; rather they must always be ministers of justice'.

ultimately with the trial judge. Whereas trial judges might routinely allow claims of privilege without examining the documents in question, in complicated cases examination may be necessary to determine whether the information contained therein might provide material assistance to the defence.[184] The court adopted a variation of the solution Carney J had proposed in the High Court below, namely, that the trial court should examine the documents at its discretion with a view to determining whether the information contained therein might assist the defence in any material way.[185]

[7.58] O'Flaherty J acknowledged that in *Ambiorix Ltd v Minister for the Environment (No 1)* the Supreme Court had accepted the solution of lawyers alone examining the relevant documents but the learned judge distinguished the precedent on the ground that '*Ambiorix* was a very special case'.[186] He then summarised *Ambiorix* and whereas he refrained from pinpointing with precision the aspects of the case that rendered it special, certain distinguishing features may be inferred.

[7.59] First, *Ambiorix* involved a claim of executive or public interest privilege and, indeed, the central import of the Supreme Court judgments was to underscore the primacy of the judicial function in deciding whether documents in the possession of the government should be disclosed in legal proceedings.[187] It is customary to distinguish claims of public interest privilege from assertions of private privileges, including legal professional privilege, on the basis that whereas private privileges involve the application of pre-determined legal rules, assertions of public interest privilege are resolved case-by-case through judicial balancing of the competing interests in favour of and against disclosure. The distinction arguably supports the implication that courts have greater flexibility when fashioning procedures to bridge the gap between discovery and claims of public interest as opposed to private privilege. This is not an ironclad explanation for this particular conflict in precedent, however, because *Ward* concerned informer privilege which has been classified by some as a species of public interest privilege[188] and by others as a private privilege that requires a judicial balancing exercise when met by the invocation of the innocence-at-stake exception.[189]

[7.60] A more compelling point of distinction lies in the nature of the interests allegedly threatened by the disclosure of the documents. The stakes were high in

---

[184] *Ward v Special Criminal Court* [1999] 1 IR 60 at 87–88.

[185] *Ward v Special Criminal Court* [1999] 1 IR 60 at 76.

[186] *Ward v Special Criminal Court* [1999] 1 IR 60 at 86.

[187] Thus reaffirming the stance adopted in *Murphy v Dublin Corporation* [1972] IR 215.

[188] See, eg, Fennell, *The Law of Evidence in Ireland* (3rd edn, Bloomsbury Professional, 2009) para 8.094. See **Ch 10**.

[189] See, eg, McGrath, *Evidence* (Dublin: Thomson Round Hall, 2005) para 10.181.

both *Burke* and *Ward* in so far as the documents contained revelations which if published could put lives and bodily integrity at risk. This stark reality militated against any disclosure of the documents in question including limited disclosure to the lawyers retained in the respective proceedings. In contrast, the need to protect the commercial and financial interests of third parties, though undoubtedly important, may have influenced the more flexible approach in *Ambiorix*. In a similar vein, the sanctity of the lawyer-client relationship went to the very heart of the constitutional rights of the defence invoked in *Ward* and, moreover, was a more pressing concern in *Burke* than *Ambiorix*.

[7.61] Finally, *Ambiorix* may be distinguished from *Burke* and *Ward* in terms of the relationship between the information sought to be protected and the matters at issue in the legal proceedings. Whereas discovery in *Burke* and disclosure in *Ward* were sought on the premise that the documents in question contained information essential to the proper conduct of the proceedings, 'it was accepted on all sides' in *Ambiorix* that the commercial and financial details of third parties contained in the representations made to government departments 'would be of no possible relevance'.[190] This may well explain a crucial distinguishing factor, namely, the agreement of all parties to the proceedings to the solution of allowing only the lawyers to have sight of the documents. It may be recalled that Finlay CJ couched the procedural accommodation in the swathe of further safeguards: the prohibition on parties using information obtained during discovery for purposes beyond the immediate litigation; the inherent jurisdiction of the court to regulate discovery and prevent any flouting of this prohibition; and, ultimately, the possibility that 'a simple formula' could be devised that would provide the plaintiffs with sufficient information while at the same time lending adequate protection to the interests of the third parties.[191]

INTERROGATORIES

[7.62] Aside from the process of discovery, a party may obtain relevant information from other parties[192] and non-parties[193] by posing interrogatories or questions.[194] The procedure, set down in the Rules of the Superior Courts,[195] allows a party to obtain factual material and concessions from the party being

[190] *Ward v Special Criminal Court* [1999] 1 IR 60 at 86 (*per* O'Flaherty J).

[191] *Ambiorix Ltd v Minister for Environment (No 1)* [1992] 1 IR 277 at 286.

[192] Order 31, r 1.

[193] Order 31, r 29.

[194] *See generally* Abrahamson, Dwyer and Fitzpatrick, *Discovery and Disclosure* (Thomson Round Hall, 2007) ch 14; Barron, *Practice and Procedure in the Master's Court* (2nd edn, Round Hall, 2001) pp 38–42.

[195] Order 31, rr 1–11.

interrogated.[196] It also tends to 'narrow the issues' and 'reduce the area of proof' thereby reducing the length and cost of the proceedings.[197]

[7.63] Interrogatories are typically used as a means of supplementing discovery and are generally delivered after the inspection of documents on foot of discovery. Both procedures are optional, however, with the consequence that a party may opt to forego discovery and simply seek to deliver interrogatories.

[7.64] A party must obtain the leave of the court before delivering interrogatories[198] and courts have occasionally taken the view that the procedure is the exception rather than the norm.[199] The determination whether to order the delivery of interrogatories is similar to the adjudication of applications for discovery and turns principally on considerations of relevance and necessity.[200] However, leave may be declined on particular grounds, for example, where the interrogatories are oppressive or unnecessarily prejudicial[201] or where they rise to the level of cross-examination.[202]

[7.65] Where the court grants leave to deliver interrogatories, the party to be interrogated is obliged to answer.[203] The interrogatories must adhere to a form prescribed in an appendix to the Rules of the Superior Courts.[204] The replies to the interrogatories are given on affidavit and may be admitted as evidence at trial.[205]

[7.66] A party replying to interrogatories may assert privilege by objecting to one or more particular interrogatory. The party should specify the nature of the objection in the affidavit setting out her replies.[206]

---

196 *Mercantile Credit Co of Ireland Ltd v Heelan* [1994] 2 IR 105.

197 *J & LS Goodbody Ltd v Clyde Shipping Co Ltd* (9 May 1967, unreported) SC (*per* Walsh J) quoted in Abrahamson, Dwyer and Fitzpatrick, *Discovery and Disclosure* (Thomson Round Hall, 2007) at para 14.05.

198 Order 31, r 1. Except in cases involving fraud or breach of trust where the leave of the court is not required.

199 *Woodfab Ltd v Coillte Teo* [2000] 1 IR 20.

200 Order 31, r 1 and r 2.

201 *Mercantile Credit Co of Ireland Ltd v Heelan* [1994] 2 IR 105.

202 *McCole v Blood Transfusion Service Board* (11 June 1996, unreported) HC (Laffoy J) (applying the test set down in *Det Danske v KDM* [1994] 2 Lloyd's Rep 534).

203 A party that refrains from answering or answers insufficiently may be subject to a court order to answer or to answer further: Ord 31, r 11.

204 Order 31, r 4, Appendix C, Form No 8. The form set out in the appendix requires the interrogatories to be phrased in the negative and seek 'yes' or 'no' answers.

205 Order 31, rr 8 and 24.

206 Order 31, r 6. Abrahamson, Dwyer and Fitzpatrick, *Discovery and Disclosure* (Thomson Round Hall, 2007) para 34.12 observe that whereas *Smith v Berg* (1877) 36 LT 471 stands for the proposition that a party objecting to answering an interrogatory on a legal point may simply decline to answer, 'it is probably better practice to specify the objection in the replies'.

Chapter 8

Expert Evidence in Personal Injuries Litigation

INTRODUCTION

[8.01] Traditionally, personal injuries actions dominated the dockets of the civil courts and, the establishment of the Personal Injuries Assessment Board[1] notwithstanding, such proceedings continue to occupy a special place in the administration of civil justice. Personal injuries litigation is framed by distinct procedural rules and practices the most notable of which is the provision of far reaching disclosure obligations in relation to expert evidence.[2] Historically, litigation privilege played an important role in protecting from disclosure consultations between lawyers and experts in the preparation and conduct of legal proceedings together with reports and other documents compiled by those experts. The contemporary rules have substantially undercut that protection by requiring parties to reveal and exchange in advance of trial the essence of the expert evidence they propose to adduce. This chapter outlines the procedural requirements in relation to expert trial practice in personal injuries actions with particular emphasis on proceedings for medical negligence. Similar procedures also apply in commercial proceedings[3] and competition proceedings.[4]

EXPERT EVIDENCE IN PERSONAL INJURIES ACTIONS

[8.02] In doctrinal terms, expert evidence assumes the guise of a broad exception to the rule against opinion evidence. As a general rule, witnesses must limit their testimony to facts within their personal knowledge or perception. They are permitted neither to express opinions nor to drawn inferences from the facts that form the basis of their testimony. The underlying premise is that the functions of drawing inferences from stated facts and reaching conclusions on material issues are the exclusive preserve of the finder of fact, whether judge or jury.[5] The exception provides the courts with licence to admit as means of proof the opinions of persons who are acknowledged experts in scientific, technical or

---

1 Personal Injuries Assessment Board Act 2003.

2 Rules of the Superior Courts (Disclosure of Reports and Statements) 1988 (SI 391/1998). On the obligation not to impede access to relevant medical information in personal injuries actions see *McGrory v ESB* [2003] 1 IESC 45 (24 July 2003).

3 Rules of the Superior Courts (Commercial Proceedings) 2004 (SI 2/2004).

4 Rules of the Superior Courts (Competition Proceedings) 2005 (SI 130/2005).

5 *AG (Ruddy) v Kenny* (1960) 94 ILTR 185, 190. Opinion evidence has also been rejected as a species of hearsay: *Wright v Doe d'Tatham* (1838) 5 C & F 670. (contd.../)

other fields.[6] The justification for the admission of such opinion evidence is twofold: first, the disputed facts touch upon a matter beyond ordinary human experience; and, second, the witness possesses specialised knowledge that will assist the finder of fact to resolve the dispute.[7] Such experts are drawn from all walks of life and in the context of personal injuries actions include doctors, psychiatrists and actuaries.[8]

[8.03] In recent years, the use of expert evidence has flourished to the point where, paradoxically, the exception stands shoulder to shoulder with the rule against opinion evidence.[9] Nowhere is this phenomenon more prevalent than in personal injuries litigation where the ubiquity of the expert witness is matched by the influence she exerts over the resolution of the proceedings and the very culture of the courtroom. Specialist fields, such as the complex and contestable terrain of medical negligence actions, have become the paradigm for expert witness practice and the evidentiary testing ground for doctrinal and procedural challenges that impact on all manner of civil litigation. Whereas in former times, the expert witness was a black swan, a rare bird treated with a degree of deference by judges and lawyers alike, experts are now routine participants in litigation and their function has been woven into the adversarial fabric of the courtroom.[10] The procedures governing the presentation of expert opinion are designed to facilitate its admission and, at the same time, limit and control its

5 (\...contd) It is admissible in a miscellany of situations in which the line between fact and opinion is sufficiently blurred that it is difficult to discern whether the witness is testifying as to the former or the latter. A ragbag of statutory provisions also permits the admission of opinion evidence in certain specific circumstances. See generally McGrath, *Evidence* (Thomson Round Hall, 2005) paras 6.45–6.52; Howard, 'Opinion and Expert Evidence' in Howard (ed), *Phipson on Evidence* (15th edn, Sweet & Maxwell, 2000) at paras 37.01–37.09.

6 On the law of expert evidence see generally Heffernan, *Expert Evidence: Fingerprints and DNA* (First Law, 2006) chs 1 and 2; Heffernan, 'Expert Evidence in Medical Negligence Litigation' in Craven and Binchy (eds), *Medical Negligence Litigation: Emerging Issues* (First Law, 2008) 110; Heffernan, 'Gauging the Reliability of Scientific Evidence in Tort' (2006) 6(1) JSIJ 140; McGrath, *Evidence* (Thomson Round Hall, 2005) ch 6; Fennell, *Law of Evidence in Ireland* (2nd edn, Lexis Nexis, 2003) ch 6; Healy, *Irish Laws of Evidence* (Thomson Round Hall, 2004) ch 12; Kelleher, 'Expert Evidence in Ireland' (1996) 14 ILTR 42; O'Flaherty, 'The Expert Witness and the Courts' (1997) 3 MLJI 3.

7 *Folks v Chadd* (1782) 3 Doug KB 157; *AG (Ruddy) v Kenny* (1960) 94 ILTR 185.

8 These are some of the 'experts' that appear on the non-exhaustive list contained in RSC, Ord 39, r 45(1).

9 As early as 1960, Lavery J observed: 'This is the age of experts qualified to give opinions in every field of human knowledge – whether science, medical or other, in accountancy, finance, handwriting and technical matters in every aspect of manufacturing process and so on. I would certainly not wish to minimise the value of such evidence, but a sense of proportion should not be lost. There are innumerable incidents of everyday life upon which an ordinary person can express a useful opinion and one which ought to be admitted': *AG (Ruddy) v Kenny* (1960) 94 ILTR 185 at 189.

10 See generally Ormrod, 'Scientific Evidence in Court' [1968] Crim LR 241; Kenny, 'The Expert in Court' (1983) 99 LQR 197.

role in legal proceedings. The basic principles of fairness and reciprocity that underpin the disclosure of evidence apply with particular force in relation to experts. Where one side presents expert evidence, the other side is entitled to respond by testing that evidence and by presenting independent expert opinion.

EXPERT SUPPORT TO PURSUE A CLAIM

[8.04] From the outset of personal injuries proceedings, legal practitioners must give due consideration to the nature and extent of expert opinion that will be required in the prosecution or defence of the action. Experts tend to be enlisted at the very outset of the process, even before the point at which legal proceedings have been formally initiated. Given the need to initiate proceedings within the two-year limitation period imposed by s 7 of the Civil Liability and Courts Act 2004, lawyers must act promptly to determine the issues requiring expert opinion, the number and kind of experts required, and the identity of potential experts whether located in Ireland or, more usually, abroad.[11]

In proceedings for medical negligence, in particular, the immediate engagement of experts has become a necessity. As Barr J explained in *Reidy v National Maternity Hospital*, a plaintiff must have reasonable medical grounds to justify the commencement of a lawsuit:

> '[I]t is irresponsible and an abuse of the process of the Court to lodge a professional medical negligence action against institutions such as hospitals and professional personnel without first ascertaining that there are reasonable grounds for so doing. Initiation and prosecution of an action in negligence on behalf of the plaintiff against the hospital necessarily requires appropriate expert evidence to support it.'[12]

[8.05] The need for 'some credible evidence to support the plaintiff's case' was subsequently recognised by the Supreme Court in *Cooke v Cronin*.[13] Denham J stated:

> 'To issue proceedings alleging professional negligence puts an individual in a situation where for professional or practice reasons to have the case proceed in open Court may be perceived and feared to that professional as being detrimental to his professional reputation and practice. This fear should not be utilized by unprofessional conduct.'[14]

---

[11] For a comprehensive discussion of the commencement of personal injuries proceedings see Delany and McGrath, *Civil Procedure in the Superior Courts* (2nd edn, Thomson Round Hall, 2005) ch 25.

[12] *Reidy v National Maternity Hospital* (31 July 1997, unreported) HC. See also *Cooke v Cronin* (14 July 1999, unreported) SC; *Quinn v Mid Western Health Board* [2005] 2 ILRM 180.

[13] *Cooke v Cronin* (14 July 1999, unreported).

[14] *Cooke v Cronin* (14 July 1999, unreported), para 10.

[8.06] This sentiment was echoed by Geoghegan J in *Sugg v O'Keefe* in relation to the dismissal of a medical negligence action:

> 'This action would have been regarded by all courts as in fact an abuse of the process of the courts and at the very least as unsustainable once there was not some backup evidence in the form of a report obtained in advance of the action or certainly, obtained in advance of [a motion to strike] from a medical expert that supported the plaintiff's claim.'[15]

This reality turns virtually on its head the traditional premise in relation to the admissibility of expert evidence, namely, that an onus rests on the party tendering an expert witness to demonstrate the need for his or her testimony in the given case. Now the law not only concedes that need in proceedings for medical negligence but, in addition, requires the plaintiff to secure a medical report supporting his or her case before proceedings are instituted.

[8.07] Conducting a preliminary investigation involving communicating with experts to ascertain whether there are reasonable grounds for initiating proceedings can be a complicated and time consuming process. The recent case of *Creevy v Kinsella and Others*[16] suggests that courts will be mindful of the practical constraints involved while at the same time not condoning delay for its own sake. The issue before the court was whether the need to carry out such a preliminary investigation constituted a 'good reason' (other than a reason relating to service) to justify the renewal of a plenary summons under Ord 8, r 1. The plaintiff sought to pursue a claim for negligence arising out of the birth of her twins in October 2001. The plenary summons was issued in August 2004, renewed in April 2006 and ultimately served on the various defendants in September 2006. The plaintiff had obtained expert medical reports which advised that a further report from an anaesthetist should be obtained but had encountered difficulty in this regard. Dunne J refused the defendants' application to set aside the renewal of the summons concluding that the delay was inordinate but not inexcusable in the circumstances. She concluded: 'I accept the principle that the need to investigate the basis of the claim is not a licence to delay but on the facts of this case, I am satisfied that the plaintiff and her advisors have not overstepped the boundaries of what is permissible'.[17] Dunne J went on to hold that prejudice to the plaintiff in not renewing the summons would far outweigh any prejudice to the defendants.[18]

---

15 *Sugg v O'Keefe* (14 October 2005, unreported) SC.

16 *Creevy v Kinsella and Others* [2008] IEHC 100 (17 April 2008).

17 But see *Faughnan v Maguire* [2006] IEHC 282 (23 June 2006) (delay of 12 years in joining a defendant was inordinate and inexcusable and significant prejudice would result). See also *Keane v Western Health Board* [2006] IEHC 283 (2 October 2006).

18 On defendant prejudice in this regard, see *O'Grady v Southern Health Board* [2007] IEHC 38 (2 February 2007).

EXPERT REPORTS IN PERSONAL INJURIES ACTIONS

[8.08] The formal presentation of expert evidence unfolds in two stages. Having been enlisted by a party to prospective legal proceedings, the expert will compile a written report in advance of trial. Although orality remains the guiding principle for ordinary witnesses, expert evidence is initially furnished in documentary form and, at least in civil proceedings, there is an emerging trend in the common law world in favour of admitting it in that guise at trial.[19] Expert reports are exchanged during discovery[20] and typically have an important bearing on settlement negotiations.[21] The law governing expert evidence in personal injuries actions has undergone considerable change in recent years with the introduction of a series of measures designed to minimise personal injuries litigation, expedite proceedings and reduce costs.[22] The principal evidentiary import has been the rolling back of legal professional privilege and the traditional protection parties enjoyed from disclosing their preparations for trial.

[8.09] SI 391/1998 governs the disclosure of expert reports in personal injuries actions.[23] Its provisions were inserted into Ord 39 of the Rules of the Superior Courts as rr 45 to 51.

Rule 46(1) provides:

> 'The plaintiff in an action shall furnish to the other party or parties or their respective solicitors (as the case may be) a schedule listing all reports from expert witnesses intended to be called within one month of the service of the notice of trial in respect of the action or within such further time as may be agreed by the parties or permitted by the Court.
>
> Within seven days of receipt of the plaintiff's schedule, the defendant or any other party or parties shall furnish to the plaintiff or any other party or parties a schedule listing all reports from expert witnesses intended to be called. Within seven days of the receipt of the schedule of the defendant or other party or parties, the parties shall exchange copies of the reports listed in the relevant schedule.'

---

19 See, eg, English Civil Procedure Rules, Part 35, and accompanying practice direction.

20 See Rules of the Superior Courts (No 6) (Disclosure of Reports and Statements) 1998, SI 391/1998 (adding a new Part VI to Ord 39). See generally Delany and McGrath, *Civil Procedure in the Superior Courts* (2nd edn, Thomson Round Hall, 2005) paras 25.44–25.79; Abrahamson, Dwyer and Fitzpatrick, *Discovery and Disclosure* (Thomson Round Hall, 2007) ch 29; Healy, *Irish Laws of Evidence* (Thomson Round Hall, 2004), p 386 *et seq*.

21 Abrahamson, Dwyer and Fitzpatrick, *Discovery and Disclosure* (Thomson Round Hall, 2007) paras 25.36–43.

22 Rules of the Superior Courts (No 6) (Disclosure of Reports and Statements) 1998, SI 391/1998; Civil Liability and Courts Act 2004.

23 Rules of the Superior Courts (No 6) (Disclosure of Reports and Statements) 1998, SI 391/1998, which replaced Rules of the Superior Courts (Disclosure of Reports and Statements) 1997, SI 348/1997.

The concept of an 'expert report' is broadly defined for the purposes of disclosure and extends to any report or statement from an intended expert containing 'the substance of the evidence to be adduced'.[24] Rule 45(1)(e) states:

> '"report"' means a report or reports or statement from accountants, actuaries, architects, dentists, doctors, occupational therapists, psychologists, psychiatrists, scientists, or any other expert whatsoever intended to be called to give evidence in relation to an issue in an action and containing the substance of the evidence to be adduced and shall also include any maps, drawings, photographs, graphs, charts, calculations or other like matter referred to in any such report'.[25]

Experts

[8.10] The net is case wide over the potential range of witnesses to whom the rules apply. In addition to the species of expert listed in r 45(1)(e) to whom the rules might be said to routinely govern, it extends to 'any other expert whatsoever'. Section 2 of the Civil Liability and Courts Act 2004 defines expert evidence as 'evidence of fact or opinion given by a person who would not be competent to give such evidence unless he or she had a special skill or expertise'. The wording of r 45(1)(e) hints at a liberal construction of expertise embracing not only skills and experience traditionally recognised but also scientific or medical knowledge of a novel or unconventional kind.[26]

[8.11] On a literal reading, r 45(1)(e) is also broad in so far as it applies to any intended witness who is an expert regardless of the nature of her intended testimony. For example, so read it covers a treating doctor who may be called primarily for her factual account of relevant events (and who may even be a named party to the proceedings). This reading is consistent with s 2 of the Civil Liability and Courts Act 2004 which refers to 'evidence of fact or opinion'.

Nevertheless, the courts will not allow disclosure to take privilege hostage and thereby excessively inhibit the parties in their preparation for trial. For example, in *Sullivan v Kieran*,[27] O'Neill J refused to order disclosure from the defendant doctor of a letter he had written to his indemnifiers on the basis that disclosure would undermine the important confidence that existed in communications between the defendant and his lawyers and indemnifiers.

---

24 RSC, Ord 39, r 45(1).

25 It continues: 'Any copy report (including a copy report in the form of a letter), copy statement or copy letter however made, recorded or retained from any such expert mentioned above intended to be called to give evidence in relation to an issue or action and containing the substance of the evidence to be adduced, the original of which has been concealed, destroyed, lost mislaid or is not otherwise readily available, shall also be deemed to be a report for the purposes of this rule'.

26 For a discussion on the definition of an expert see Law Reform Commission *Consultation Paper on Expert Evidence* (LRC CP 52–2008, December 2008) ch 3.

27 *Sullivan v Kieran* (11 February 2004, unreported) HC.

[8.12] The obligation to disclose is limited in the sense that it applies to any expert witness 'intended to be called to give evidence in relation to an issue in the action'. Where a party enlists the services of an expert in an exclusively advisory capacity and does not intend to call the expert to give evidence, her report is privileged from disclosure.[28]

[8.13] Care must be taken in relation to witnesses who provide expert advice to a party in the capacity of employees. In *Galvin v Murray*, the Supreme Court held that the defendant County Council could not resist disclosing the reports of their expert employee engineers on the basis that the reports contained observations that an independent expert might not have provided and that the defendant did not wish to disclose. As Murphy J explained:

> '[I]t seems to me that the two engineers are beyond doubt experts and, accordingly, if the second defendant is determined to call them as witnesses to give evidence of a technical nature included in the reports, that those documents would fall squarely within the disclosure rules. … The fact that an engineer is employed by one or other of the parties may affect his independence with a consequent reduction in the weight to be attached to his evidence but it could not deprive him of his status as an expert.'[29]

Thus, the decision of the party to call the expert to give evidence triggers the application of the rules; assuming the expert is so called, her relationship with the party does not alter the obligation to disclose. Finally, it should be noted that the decision to call an expert to give evidence is not written in stone. In *Kincaid v Aer Lingus Teoranta*, the Supreme Court held that, prior to exchanging reports, a party may change its mind with respect to calling a particular expert witness and withdraw her name from its schedule of witness reports.[30]

The Content of the Expert Report

[8.14] A second issue concerns the material that must be disclosed. Rule 45(1)(e) refers to a report or statement from the witness in relation to an issue in the action and containing 'the substance of the evidence to be adduced'. The intention, presumably, is to require the parties to disclose not just the expert's description of the relevant facts or circumstances but also the substance of the opinion that constitutes the very justification for calling the expert to testify.[31] The depth and breadth of the obligation to disclose is underscored by the reference in r 45(1)(e) to the need to include 'any maps, drawings, photographs, graphs, charts, calculations or other like matter' to which the expert refers. It is

[28] *Galvin v Murray* [2001] 1 IR 331 (expert employee); *Fyffes plc v DCC plc* [2005] 1 IR 59 (disclosure of advisory expert report to a third party).

[29] *Galvin v Murray* [2001] 1 IR 331.

[30] *Kincaid v Aer Lingus Teoranta* [2003] 2 IR 314.

[31] *Ollett v Bristol Aerojet Ltd* [1979] 1 WLR 1197 at 1197 (*per* Ackner J).

further reinforced by s 45(3) of the Courts and Court Officers Act 1995 which lends the term 'expert report' a broad construction.[32]

[8.15] The meaning of the phrase 'maps, drawings, photographs, graphs, charts, calculations or other like matters referred to in any such report' was considered in *Doherty v North Western Health Board.*[33] Following the exchange of expert reports, the defendant sought an order compelling the first third party to furnish certain documents that two expert medical witnesses had referred to in their respective reports. The documents included solicitor-client correspondence and the first third party resisted disclosure on the ground that the documents were privileged. Finnegan P rejected the defendant's submission that the documents came within the phrase 'other like matter referred to in any such report':

> 'The phrase 'other like matter referred to in any such report' must be construed *ejusdem generis* with the words preceding it. I am satisfied that the documents referred to by [the two expert witnesses] cannot be considered as a like matter to a map, drawing, photograph, graph, chart or calculation. There is accordingly no obligation to disclose the same or to exchange the same arising under Order 39 rule 46(1) the documents in question not coming within the definition of report.'[34]

Again, this case serves as a reminder that the courts will give effect to the legislative intention to favour disclosure over privilege but only in so far as that intention is reflected in the rules.

[8.16] *Payne v Shovlin*[35] has shed some additional light on the meaning of 'expert report' for the purposes of the obligation to disclose. The Supreme Court held that where an expert compiles two reports, a preliminary report and subsequently a final report, the first report is not necessarily exempt from disclosure. The party contended that it was not obliged to disclose the preliminary report because it did not contain the expert's final views or intended evidence in chief. Kearns J stated:

> 'The relevant test, it seems to me, is whether or not the 'substance' of the evidence to be given, or part of it, is contained in the first report even if the views in that first report are later altered or modified or even given subject to qualification in such first report.'[36]

---

32 Delany and McGrath, *Civil Procedure in the Superior Courts* (2nd edn, Thomson Round Hall, 2005) para 25.57.

33 *Doherty v North Western Health Board* [2005] IEHC 404 (1 December 2005).

34 *Doherty v North Western Health Board* [2005] IEHC 404 (1 December 2005).

35 *Payne v Shovlin* [2006] 2 ILRM 1, [2007] 1 IR 114.

36 *Payne v Shovlin* [2006] 2 ILRM 1 at 11, [2007] 1 IR 114 at 130. See also *Carlson v Townsend* [2001] 1 WLR 2415.

Unfavourable Information

[8.17] There are divergent views as to whether the rules are designed solely to remove the element of surprise and therefore do not require a party to disclose information unfavourable to her case or whether they support disclosure *per se* and consequently extend to the bad as well as the good aspects of the expert's opinion. In *Galvin v Murray*, Murphy J took the former view: 'Clearly, the disclosure rules are designed to forewarn other parties of expert evidence with which they may be confronted. The rules have no role to play in investigating strengths or weaknesses of an opponent's case'.[37] This position was endorsed by Geoghegan J in *Kincaid v Aer Lingus Teoranta.*[38] Arguably it finds support in a literal, common sense reading of the rules: what is required to be disclosed is the substance of the evidence the expert *intends* to give in examination-in-chief and not any conceivable concession she might be forced to make on cross-examination.

[8.18] The view that the rules are designed to support disclosure *per se* starts with the premise that a party decides to call an expert because she believes that, on balance, the expert's evidence will be more favourable than not; having made that decision, the party must live with it, and call the expert on the basis of all the evidence that she can give. Delany and McGrath find support for the latter interpretation elsewhere in the rules[39] and go on to observe:

> 'Interpreted in this way, the disclosure rules serve to reinforce the duties and responsibilities owed by an expert to the court and can be viewed as, at least in part, an attempt to restore in some small measure the impartiality and independence of experts which was originally the hallmark and, indeed, to some extent, the justification for their evidence but which has become very much eroded in recent years. The knowledge that any report or statement by him has been disclosed should discourage attempts by an expert to tailor his evidence in court for the benefit of the party calling him, as he could well find himself being cross-examined on an inconsistent statement made by him in a previous report. ...The practical effect is more likely to be that experts will simply become more careful in drafting their reports to omit anything that could be construed as damaging to the case of the party retaining them, reserving such comments for oral communication. ...'[40]

[8.19] In *Payne v Shovlin*, Kearns J quoted from the judgment Murphy J in *Galvin v Murray* and went on to observe:

---

[37] *Galvin v Murray* [2001] 1 IR 331 at 336.

[38] *Kincaid v Aer Lingus Teoranta* [2003] 2 IR 314.

[39] Specifically, r 50 which permits a party to apply for an order of exemption from disclosure in the interests of justice and which the authors argue would not be necessary if a party was obliged merely to disclose a 'sanitised expert report': Delany and McGrath, *Civil Procedure in the Superior Courts* (2nd edn, Thomson Round Hall, 2005) at para 25.63.

[40] Delany and McGrath, *Civil Procedure in the Superior Courts* (2nd edn, Thomson Round Hall, 2005) para 25.64 (internal citations omitted).

> 'No one could cavil at or disagree with this proposition and it is common case between the parties before this court that the mischief of ambush and/or surprise is something to be avoided. However, the failure to produce an earlier report which contains a view different from that contained in the final report may produce exactly the kind of surprises about which Murphy J. and Geoghegan J. warned.'[41]

Kearns J rejected the suggestion that the objective of preventing surprises necessarily leads to a 'will say' form of disclosure. Rather, the rules require 'such production or disclosure of reports that will ensure that surprises do not occur, either in the course of examination-in-chief or in cross-examination of an expert witness'. While this judgment may not set down a bright-line in relation to what must be disclosed for the purposes of the rules, it goes further than previous cases in elucidating the amorphous phrase 'the substance of the evidence to be adduced'. More generally, it suggests a judicial leaning towards a more robust interpretation of a party's disclosure obligations.

Disclosure

[8.20] Rule 46 set down a timetable for the exchange of expert reports and the names and addresses of all witnesses intended to be called.[42] It provides that within seven days of the receipt by the plaintiff of the schedule of the defendant or other party or parties, 'the parties shall exchange copies of the reports in the relevant schedule'.[43] In *Kincaid v Aer Lingus Teoranta*, Geoghegan J suggested that exchange should be contemporaneous so as to guard against the mischief of abuse of the procedure.[44]

[8.21] The obligation to disclose is a continuing one and applies to any additional expert reports or statements received by a party after the initial exchange.[45] Conversely, a party may withdraw any previously disclosed report by confirming that she no longer intends to call the expert as a witness.[46] The act of withdrawal is deemed to reactivate any privilege that originally existed in relation to the report.[47]

---

41 *Payne v Shovlin* [2006] 2 ILRM 1 at 12, [2007] 1 IR 114 at 131.

42 Order 39, r 46. Service of expert reports may be effected by letter in writing enclosing the report and sent by ordinary pre-paid post.

43 Order 39, r 46(1).

44 *Kincaid v Aer Lingus Teoranta* [2003] 2 IR 314 at 320. Order 39, r 46(3) states 'where a party or his or her solicitor certifies in writing that no report exists which requires to be exchanged pursuant to subrule 1, any other party shall, on the expiry of the time fixed, agreed or permitted (as the case may be) deliver any report within the meaning of the section to all other parties to the proceedings'.

45 Order 39, r 46(4).

46 Order 39, r 46(6).

47 Order 39, r 46(6).

[8.22] The rules provide that directions of the court may be sought in relation to any alleged default in compliance with the obligation to disclose.[48] The court may deal with an instance of non-compliance in a number of ways, such as adjourning the action to permit compliance or prohibiting the errant party from adducing the evidence in question.[49] A party may also apply to the court for an order that in the interests of justice a particular report or statement should not be disclosed.[50]

EXPERT TESTIMONY

[8.23] Where the case goes to trial, the expert may be called to testify by the party that enlisted her services and, whether or not so called, may be subject to cross-examination by any other party. In personal injuries actions, the court may direct that evidence be given by affidavit although in such instances the witness nevertheless remains subject to possible cross-examination.[51] The desirability of admitting medical evidence in documentary form, thereby obviating the need for *viva voce* evidence, was reflected in a practice direction dated 8 September 1993. It urges counsel to consider whether the attendance of experts at trial is necessary and, where appropriate, to request that the court admit expert reports in evidence without recourse to oral testimony.[52] The practice direction also provides that where experts take the stand, their reports should be made available to the court, admitted in evidence, and form the basis for the examination of the witness.[53] As regards oral testimony, given the adversarial nature of the trial process, the testifying expert can anticipate a tough grilling from cross-examining counsel in relation to her qualifications, expertise and substantive conclusions, together with critical rebuttal evidence from the experts retained by the other parties.

[8.24] The expert witness enjoys a somewhat exalted status in the trial process by virtue of her role in assisting the jury on a matter outside ordinary human experience. Although the expert must take the oath and deliver her testimony in a manner not unlike the ordinary or lay witness, the substance of her evidence and the manner in which it is delivered are otherwise governed by special rules and practices. Lay witnesses must generally limit their testimony to facts within their personal knowledge or perception thereby allowing the jury to carry out their essential function of drawing the necessary inferences from the stated

48 Order 39, r 47.

49 Order 39, r 48.

50 Order 39, r 50.

51 Section19 of the Civil Liability and Courts Act 2004.

52 On the dangers of judicial reliance on documentary expert evidence without the benefit of expert oral testimony, see *Curran v Finn* (20 May 1999, unreported) SC.

53 Delany and McGrath, *Civil Procedure in the Superior Courts* (2nd edn, Thomson Round Hall, 2005) para 25.86.

facts. The expert witness, in contrast, assists the jury in drawing those very inferences and, by virtue of this dependency, enjoys wide latitude in relation to the scope of her testimony.

[8.25] Expert opinion embodies the application of the expert's training and experience to the facts of the case. In compiling her report and delivering her evidence, the expert may base her opinion on facts both within and outside her personal knowledge. She may testify as to matters of opinion and may incorporate secondary material, such as documents, videotapes or the views of other experts, that would otherwise fall foul of the rule against hearsay.[54] Indeed, much of the relevant factual information on which the expert relies may have been gleaned second-hand. Of course, the facts on which her opinion is based must be proved by admissible evidence either by the expert herself or independently. In other words, facts outside the expert's personal knowledge may form the basis of her opinion but because they are technically hearsay, they must be proved at some point in the proceedings by other, independent evidence.[55] This technical obstacle is side-stepped in examination-in-chief through the expedient of counsel asking the witness to couch her expert opinion in hypothetical terms. The opinion is elicited in the form of responses to a series of hypothetical questions that assume facts that have yet to be proved by the party presenting the expert testimony. The expert's opinion is thus intrinsically linked to the promised proof of the facts on which the hypothesis is based.[56]

[8.26] The expert is permitted to draw inferences from facts; indeed, the value of expert opinion may lie in the inferential light it may shine on matters that have left the court in the dark. However, the insight offered by the expert frequently eschews any firm distinction between fact and inference. By virtue of her skill and training, the expert may be equipped not only to draw inferences from observed fact but also to perceive facts that would escape the lay person.[57] Attempts to identify the precise point at which the expert departs from the realm of fact into that of opinion are consequently somewhat futile and it may be more helpful simply to observe that courts generally adopt a flexible attitude to the testimony of experts on matters within their field of expertise. In particular, experts may marshal a wide range of material in support of their opinions, including the views of their peers.[58]

[8.27] The basis for the expert opinion has been a source of controversy in the Irish courts. During examination-in-chief, the expert is typically asked to

[54] On the rule against hearsay, see McGrath, *Evidence* (Thomson Round Hall, 2005) ch 5; Healy, *Irish Laws of Evidence* (Thomson Round Hall, 2004) ch 9; Fennell, *Law of Evidence in Ireland* (2nd edn, Lexis Nexis, 2003) ch 9.

[55] *RT v VP* [1990] 1 IR 545 at 551; *R v Somers* [1963] 1 WLR 1306.

[56] *Conley v Strain* [1988] IR 628.

[57] Howard, 'Opinion and Expert Evidence' in Howard (ed), *Phipson on Evidence* (15th edn, Sweet & Maxwell, 2000) at para 37.10.

[58] *Foyle and Bann Fisheries Ltd v AG* (1949) 83 ILTR 29.

explain both the facts and the criteria or standards on which her opinion is based. The premise behind this line of questioning is that the court should be appraised not only of the expert's conclusions but also of the *method* by which those conclusions were reached. Armed with this information, the court is then in a position to test the accuracy of the expert's conclusions and to exercise independent judgment on the ultimate issue in dispute.[59] In criminal trials involving juries and in quasi-inquisitorial proceedings, such as those relating to the welfare of children, judges may need to ensure that expert witnesses adequately explain the methodologies that underpin their conclusions.[60] A less interventionist judicial stance is generally adopted in the strictly adversarial context of proceedings in tort. However, the complexity of medical evidence provides a compelling practical rationale for raising the bar on expert testimony. The key to judicial comprehension of expert opinion may lie in the clear, logical and adequate explication of the predicate scientific methodology. Just as the expert must explain the basis for her conclusions, so counsel bears a corresponding responsibility to ask questions of the witness that will facilitate the proper presentation of the evidence.

Law Reform Commission's Provisional Recommendation

[8.28] In its *Consultation Paper on Expert Evidence*,[61] the Law Reform Commission noted that although pre-trial disclosure of expert reports has been the subject of significant statutory amendment, 'there is comparably little guidance relating to the requisite content of such reports'.[62] This struck the Commission as surprising given that the report forms 'the fundamental basis of all expert evidence'.[63] The Commission sought to fill this lacuna with a provisional recommendation that expert reports should assume a set form and structure that might include the following elements:

(1) The report must be addressed to the court and not to the party or parties from whom instructions have been received.

(2) The expert's qualifications and experience should be outlined in detail and relevant certificates of proof attached.

(3) The terms and conditions of the appointment of the expert witness including the payment arrangements should be explained.

(4) All material instructions, oral and written, which were given to the expert, and on the basis of which the report was written must be outlined.

(5) If a potential conflict of interest arises, the facts relating to this should be stated.

---

59 *Davie v Edinburgh Magistrates* [1953] SC 34.

60 *State (D & D) v Groarke* [1990] 1 IR 305, [1990] ILRM 130; *Southern Health Board v CH* [1996] 2 ILRM 142; *Re N* (14 March 1996, unreported) CA.

61 LRC CP 52-2008 (December 2008).

62 LRC CP 52-2008 (December 2008) para 5.141.

63 LRC CP 52-2008 (December 2008) para 5.141.

(6) All relevant information relating to the issue, including that which is capable of detracting from the expert's opinion, should be outlined.

(7) All materials used by the expert in coming to the opinion, clearly distinguishing between matters of fact and matters of opinion.

(8) Where tests or experiments have been conducted in the course of creating the report all related information must be included such as methodologies, results and details about the individuals and qualification of those involved in the carrying out of these tests.

(9) The expert should indicate if the opinion is provisional or conditional on certain factors, or if they believe they cannot give a formal opinion on the issue without further information, or where they believe they cannot make an opinion without qualification.

(10) A signed declaration that the contents of the report are true and that the expert understands the overriding duty owed to the court and that the report has been created in compliance with this.

(11) If, subsequent to the completion of the report, an expert changes his opinion on any material issue in the report, the expert witness must state this in a supplementary report.[64]

[8.29] The Commission's proposal draws on experience in England and Wales[65] and Australia.[66] Experts, lawyers and courts alike would undoubtedly benefit from guidelines relating to the role of the expert in general and to the content and form of expert evidence in particular. It is the Commission's premise that establishing a list of compulsory elements for expert reports will raise the standard of report writing and, by ensuring greater consistency, assist the court in comparing expert opinions presented by the various parties in the adversarial contest.[67] In all likelihood, this issue will form the basis of a final recommendation in the Commission's report on expert evidence. It is hoped that the Commission will avail of the opportunity to consider the broader question of the use of expert reports in the trial process and the possible extension of the current practice in relation to personal injuries and commercial litigation to the full gamut of civil proceedings.

---

[64] LRC CP 52-2008 (December 2008) para 5.202.

[65] Civil Procedure Rules, Part 35, r 35.10; Practice Direction Part 35; Civil Justice Council Protocol for the Instruction of Experts in Civil Claims, Part 13 (2005) discussed in LRC CP 52-2008 (December 2008) paras 5.179–5.187.

[66] Notably the Federal Court of Australia Practice Direction: *Guidelines for Expert Witnesses in Proceedings in the Federal Court* (Version 5, 2007) discussed in the LRC CP 52-2008 (December 2008) paras 5.189–5.192.

[67] LRC CP 52-2008 (December 2008) para 5.199. The Commission indicated that it was holding over consideration of a separate, significant suggestion that expert reports might be admitted without the need for accompanying expert testimony to its deliberations on hearsay: LRC CP 52-2008 (December 2008) para 5.216. However, while its *Consultation Paper on Hearsay in Civil and Criminal Cases* (LRC CP 60–2010, March 2010) makes several general recommendations for reform of hearsay in civil cases, it does not appear to contain any specific recommendation in this regard.

Chapter 9

Criminal Procedure

INTRODUCTION

[9.01] Criminal trials differ from civil proceedings in certain fundamental respects that are reflected in important distinctions in relation to procedure and evidence. The object of civil proceedings is to determine the rights and obligations of parties and, where appropriate, the allocation of remedies, notably compensation. The court is essentially adjudicating on the merits of a private dispute and, under the Irish system of civil justice, does so on the basis of the adversarial paradigm.

[9.02] Criminal conduct, in contrast, is presumptively the concern of society at large and prosecutions are almost invariably brought by the State, through the office of the Director of Public Prosecutions (DPP) or the Garda Síochána. The criminal justice system is characterised by an inherent tension between the interests of the community in general and victims of crime in particular in the prevention and detection of crime and the multiplicity of rights vested in a criminal defendant,[1] both as an individual and as a person charged with a criminal offence, under the Constitution[2] and international human rights standards.[3] Consequently, the system incorporates important safeguards designed to protect the rights of the accused and counterbalance prosecutorial advantage.[4] The accused is the beneficiary of a basket of special evidentiary rules designed to protect her from prejudice in the gathering of evidence by the gardaí and its presentation at trial by the prosecution.[5] Other practical

---

1 Conway, Daly and Schweppe, *Irish Criminal Justice: Theory, Process and Procedure* (Clarus Press, 2010) para 1.10.

2 Such as the right to liberty under Art 40.4.1°, unenumerated personal rights under Art 40.3, and the right to a trial in due course of law under Art 38.1.

3 Notably under the European Convention for the Protection of Human Rights and Fundamental Freedoms 1953 (ECHR) as incorporated into Irish law by the European Convention on Human Rights Act 2002.

4 Such as the right to a jury trial for non-minor offences pursuant to Art 38.5 of the Constitution and the presumption of innocence implicit in the right to a trial in due course of law under Art 38.1.

5 Leading examples include the law governing the admissibility of confessions and the rules excluding evidence of an accused's bad character or prior misconduct.

protections include the provision by the State of legal aid to any person formally charged with a criminal offence and generally at risk of a custodial sentence.[6]

[9.03] This chapter and the following two chapters explore the broad issues of privilege and access to legal advice in three particular contexts of the criminal trial process. This chapter opens with an overview of the law relating to disclosure in criminal proceedings. Procedures relating to claims of privilege, as they have been developed by the courts in the context of informer privilege, are then discussed in Ch 10. Chapter 11 analyses pre-trial access to legal advice and the implications for privilege of procedures governing the drawing of inferences from a suspect's silence in response to custodial questioning.

DISCLOSURE

[9.04] The law and practice governing disclosure[7] is markedly different in the setting of the criminal as opposed to the civil trial. Whereas civil proceedings are adversarial in the strict sense, certain aspects of the criminal trial are 'inconsistent with a pure adversarial contest'.[8] Disclosure is an area of trial practice where the adversarial model has been adapted in important respects to accommodate the unique character of the criminal process.

[9.05] The prosecution is under a general duty to disclose any information that could assist the defence. This duty is a necessary correlation of the accused's right to fair trial[9] and specifically, her rights to equality of arms[10] and an adequate opportunity to present her case.[11] Consequently, the prosecution is

---

6 Criminal Justice (Legal Aid) Act 1962; *State (Healy) v Donoghue* [1967] IR 325; *Costigan v Judge Brady* (6 February 2004, unreported) HC; *Neeson v Judge Brady* [2008] IEHC 182 (11 June 2008). Criminal suspects (ie, persons who have been arrested and detained on suspicion of having committed a criminal offence but not formally charged) enjoy no such right to State-provided legal assistance. This omission has a significant bearing on the meaningful exercise of the right of access to a solicitor in custodial detention. See **Ch 11**.

7 See generally O'Malley, *The Criminal Process* (Thomson Round Hall, 2009) ch 18; Abrahamson, Dwyer and Fitzpatrick, *Discovery and Disclosure* (Thomson Round Hall, 2007) chs 20–28; Walsh, *Criminal Procedure* (Thomson Round Hall, 2002) paras 14.45–52; Dwyer, 'The Duty of Disclosure in Criminal Proceedings' (1993) 3(1) ICLJ 66; Charleton, McDermott and Bolger, *Criminal Law* (Butterworths, 1999) para 2.80 *et seq*; Charleton and Reidy, 'Disclosure in Criminal Cases: Tripping Up the Prosecution in a Legal Vacuum' (2010) 20(2) ICLJ 44 & (2010) 20(3) ICLJ 70.

8 Walsh, *Criminal Procedure* (Thomson Round Hall, 2002) para 14.45. See generally *Code of Conduct for the Bar of Ireland* (July 2010) Ch 10, 'Duty of a Barrister in the Conduct of a Criminal Case'.

9 As protected by Art 38.1 of the Constitution and Art 6 of the ECHR.

10 *State (Healy) v Donoghue* [1976] IR 325. The jurisprudence of the European Court of Human Rights is replete with references to equality of arms as an incident of the right to fair trial. See, eg, *Rowe and Davis v United Kingdom* (2000) 30 EHRR 1.

11 See, eg, *Re Haughey* [1971] IR 217; *People (DPP) v Tuite* (1983) 2 Frewen 175; *Edwards v United Kingdom* (1992) 15 EHRR 417. (contd.../)

obliged to furnish the defence with details of the case that it intends to make at trial and the evidence it will adduce. By comparison, the disclosure obligations of the defence are far less onerous. The defence is under no reciprocal duty of general disclosure; its burden is limited to disclosure of certain information in particular instances prescribed by statute.[12] The operation of disparate burdens of disclosure is consistent with the allocation of the burden of proof in a criminal trial: whereas the prosecution bears the legal burden of proving each element of the offence beyond a reasonable doubt, the defence is under no corresponding duty to establish a defence save in the case of certain recognised exceptions.[13] The disparity in the duties imposed on the parties constitutes one of the ways in which the system strives to redress the inherent imbalance in power between the prosecution and defence. It is thus reflective of the broader prosecutorial duty to assist the court in ensuring that justice is administered fairly and effectively.[14]

[9.06] The practice of discovery in civil proceedings is prescribed by an intricate code of court rules and a substantial body of case law. In contrast, the paucity of legal regulation governing the practice of criminal disclosure is striking. The prosecutorial duty of disclosure is rooted in the common law and governed in part by statute; as noted, the limited obligations resting on the defence are based on a series of legislative provisions. There is no general, overarching statutory procedure governing disclosure, nor any applicable rules of court. Moreover, the common law rules and principles in the area remain surprisingly underdeveloped.

Absence of Discovery

[9.07] In *DPP v Sweeney*,[15] the Supreme Court held that the discovery procedure does not apply in criminal proceedings. Having analysed in detail the history of discovery, Geoghegan J concluded that the procedure is inappropriate in a criminal context:

> 'Only the prosecution must show its hand. Subject to some modern statutory exceptions in relation to alibi evidence, the defence is entitled to spring surprises

---

11 (\...contd) See generally Heffernan and Imwinkelried, 'The Accused's Constitutional Right to Introduce Critical, Demonstrably Reliable, Exculpatory Evidence' (2005) 40 Irish Jurist (ns) 111.

12 See, eg, s 20 of the Criminal Justice Act 1984 (alibi evidence); s 19 of the Criminal Law (Insanity) Act 2006 (evidence of the accused's mental condition).

13 Notably, where the accused raises the defence of insanity, where a fact is within the peculiar knowledge of the accused and where a statute reverses the allocation of the legal burden of proof. In each of these instances, the standard of proof required of the accused is proof on the balance of probabilities. See, eg, *O'Leary v Attorney General* [1993] 1 IR 102 (HC); *Hardy v Ireland* [1994] 2 IR 550; *Rock v Ireland* [1997] 3 IR 484.

14 O'Malley, *The Criminal Process* (Thomson Round Hall, 2009) para 18.01.

15 *DPP v Sweeney* [2001] 4 IR 102, [2001] 1 ILRM 532.

> and, above all, is perfectly entitled, pending trial, to give no indication as to what issues might be raised. In that state of affairs, discovery of documents under the Rules of Court is wholly inappropriate and it is another reason why those rules never have been intended to apply to criminal proceedings'.[16]

However, as Keane CJ noted in *DH v Groarke*, '[t]he fact that discovery in the form provided for in the rules for civil litigation is not available in criminal proceedings does not have as a necessary consequence an erosion of the fair procedures to which defendants are entitled'.[17]

[9.08] A difference of judicial opinion has emerged as to whether, and if so to what extent, the absence of an elaborate procedure may warrant greater flexibility on the part of the courts when faced with issues of criminal disclosure. In *PG v DPP*,[18] Hardiman J, commenting *obiter dicta*, lamented the absence of 'a satisfactory provision for disclosure or discovery in criminal cases'.[19] In that case, the Supreme Court dismissed an appeal against the refusal of an application to injunct the applicant's trial for sexual offences on the grounds of delay and prosecutorial failure to disclose certain evidence. Hardiman J took issue with the respondent's contention 'that disclosure is always or primarily a matter for the trial judge'.[20] The learned judge opined that until such time as an adequate procedure for criminal disclosure is put in place, 'an applicant is, in a suitable case, entitled to raise the question of disclosure on judicial review'.[21] In contrast Fennelly J, writing for a majority of the Supreme Court, took the view that matters of disclosure fall primarily within the province of the trial judge and are not matters for judicial review 'except to the extent that an accused person can show that, having taken all reasonable steps to obtain disclosure, necessary material is being withheld from him to such an extent as to give rise to a real risk of an unfair trial'.[22]

Disclosure by the Prosecution

[9.09] The prosecution must disclose any document that could be of assistance to the accused in establishing a defence, in damaging the prosecution case or in

16 *DPP v Sweeney* [2001] 4 IR 102 at 109–110.

17 *DH v Groarke* [2002] 3 IR 522 at 531.

18 *PG v DPP* [2007] 3 IR 39.

19 *PG v DPP* [2007] 3 IR 39 at 42–43.

20 *PG v DPP* [2007] 3 IR 39 at 42.

21 *PG v DPP* [2007] 3 IR 39 at 42–43. The judgment continues at 43: 'In particular, it appears to me that an applicant in an old sex abuse case may be entitled to sight of all statements in the nature of complaints or disclosures of alleged abuse. In many instances these will be the only 'islands of fact' available to an applicant. It will clearly be of the greatest importance to establish if there is consistency over time in the complaints made, or if they evolved over time, and if so why'.

22 *PG v DPP* [2007] 3 IR 39 at 55–56.

providing a lead on evidence that goes to either of these two matters.[23] The corresponding right of the defence 'to see relevant documentation in the hands of the prosecution' derives from 'the constitutional obligation on the court to ensure fair procedures'.[24]

Charleton and Reidy have captured the essence of the prosecutorial duty in the following terms:

> 'The whole process of disclosure is, by the way, a fishing exercise: a process of finding out prior to the trial where the relative strength of each side lies, or in a criminal case as the law now stands, the strengths and weaknesses of the prosecution side. The prosecution are obliged not only to make their case, that the accused can be proved guilty beyond a reasonable doubt, but to make available to the defence any material which might reasonably tend to show that the accused is innocent, or to lead to the disclosure of other material or facts that, considered reasonably, might make a case of innocence as a result from such disclosure. Any infirmities in relation to their own witnesses should, therefore, be disclosed.'[25]

[9.10] In proceedings on indictment, the prosecution's duty of disclosure is discharged primarily by serving on the defence the so-called 'book of evidence' which sets out the evidence on which the prosecution intends to rely at trial. Nevertheless, the prosecution's duty to disclose material to the defence extends further than this. The prosecution is obliged to furnish the defence with all relevant evidence[26] in its possession[27] so that the defence has the option of relying on such evidence, even where the prosecution does not wish to do so.[28] Thus, for example, the prosecution must disclose the statement of a material witness whom it does not intend to call to testify at trial.[29] Other documents ordinarily disclosed include copies of all statements made by the accused,[30] the

---

23 *DPP v Ward* [1999] 1 IR 60 at 71. See generally Director of Public Prosecutions, *Guidelines for Prosecutors* (revised November 2010), ch 9.

24 *People (DPP) v Sweeney* [2001] 4 IR 102 at 108 (*per* Geoghegan J).

25 Charleton and Reidy, 'Disclosure in Criminal Cases: Tripping Up the Prosecution in a Legal Vacuum' (2010) 20(2) ICLJ 44 at 47.

26 For analysis of comparative common law tests of relevance in this context see O'Malley, *The Criminal Process* (Thomson Round Hall, 2009) paras 18.03–18.05.

27 On the possible disclosure of information outside the prosecution's possession see *PG v DPP* [2007] 3 IR 39.

28 *People (DPP) v Tuite* (1983) 2 Frewen 175 at 180 (*per* McCarthy J).

29 *Ward v Special Criminal Court* [1999] 1 IR 60. In *DPP v Lacy* [2005] IECCA 70 (12 May 2005), the Court of Criminal Appeal held that the exercise by the prosecution of their discretion in relation to the calling of witnesses could affect the interests of justice and the fairness of proceedings. Good reasons must be adduced where a witness included in the book of evidence is not called or tendered. On the duty to disclose in a retrial transcripts of testimony given at the first trial see *Traynor v Judge Delahunt* [2008] IEHC 272 (31 July 2008) (McMahon J).

30 Including a video recorded interview if available, pursuant to Criminal Justice Act 2007, s 56.

accused's custody record,[31] and the previous convictions of any prosecution witness.[32]

With regard to the timeframe for disclosure, the courts have recognised that the duty to disclose is ongoing and continuing. It follows that while the prosecution should disclose all relevant evidence at the outset, it must also provide the defence with any additional material that emerges during the course of the trial process.[33]

Book of Evidence

[9.11] In proceedings on indictment, ss 4B and 4C of the Criminal Procedure Act 1967[34] require the prosecution to provide the accused with an array of documents, commonly known as the book of evidence, comprising the evidence on which the prosecution intends to rely at trial.[35] Section 4B provides for service by the prosecutor on the accused or her solicitor of the following documents:

(a) a statement of the charges against the accused;

(b) a copy of any sworn information in writing upon which the proceedings were initiated;

(c) a list of the witnesses the prosecutor proposes to call at the trial;

(d) a statement of the evidence that is expected to be given by each of them;

(e) a copy of any document containing information which it is proposed to give in evidence by virtue of Part II of the Criminal Evidence Act;[36]

(f) where appropriate, a copy of a certificate under s 6(1) of that Act;[37]

(g) a list of exhibits (if any).[38]

---

31 The gardaí are required to maintain a custody record in accordance with the Criminal Justice Act 1984 (Treatment of Persons in Custody in Garda Síochána Stations) Regulations 1987 (SI 119/1987).

32 *People (DPP) v Kelly* [1987] IR 596.

33 Indeed, the duty subsists even after the close of the trial in respect of newly discovered information. O'Malley, *The Criminal Process* (Thomson Round Hall, 2009) para. 18.07 (discussing *People (DPP) v Nevin* (13 December 2001, unreported) CCA).

34 As inserted by s 9 of the Criminal Justice Act 1999.

35 See generally Abrahamson, Dwyer and Fitzpatrick, *Discovery and Disclosure* (Thomson Round Hall, 2007) ch 21; Hogan and Whyte, *JM Kelly: The Irish Constitution* (4th edn, Bloomsbury Professional, 2004) para 6.5.75.

36 These documents comprise records compiled in the ordinary course of business and records compiled on behalf of public bodies which are admissible under an exception to the rule against hearsay set out in Part II of the 1992 Act.

37 Namely, a certificate relating to business records.

38 In addition to these materials, in relation to sexual or violent offences and trafficking, pornography and inchoate offences, the prosecutor must give the accused an opportunity to view a video-recording of any pre-recorded interview of a complainant who is under the age of 14 years: ss 15 and 16(1)(b) of the Criminal Evidence Act 1992 as amended.

[9.12] The book of evidence must be served within 42 days after the accused first appears in the District Court charged with an indictable offence[39] although the period may be extended where the District Judge is satisfied that there is good reason and that it would be in the interests of justice to do so.[40]

[9.13] In deference to the continuing nature of the prosecutorial duty to disclose, s 4C provides that the prosecutor shall furnish the defence with any additional documents that come to light after the book of evidence has been served. The material in question includes a list of any further witnesses the prosecutor intends to call to testify together with the statements of the anticipated evidence of any such proposed witnesses,[41] any further evidence that is expected from sources already listed in the Book of Evidence[42] and a copy of any deposition taken.[43]

SUMMARY PROCEEDINGS

[9.14] The statutory obligation resting on the prosecution to prepare and serve a book of evidence applies only in proceedings on indictment.[44] In *DPP v Gary Doyle*,[45] the Supreme Court confirmed that no corresponding duty arises in

---

39 Section 4B(1). Section 37(b)(1)(a)(i) of the Criminal Procedure Act 2010 substitutes a new s 4B(1). It provides that the prosecutor shall cause the documents to be served 'on the accused or his or her solicitor (if any) not later than 42 days from the date on which—

> the accused, on being informed by the District Court of his or her right to be tried by a jury, objects to being tried summarily or the prosecutor informs the court that he or she does not consent to the person being tried summarily for the offence concerned or,
>
> in the case of an offence in respect of which the prosecutor may elect either summarily or on indictment, the prosecutor elects to try the offence on indictment, or
>
> the District Court determines that the facts alleged do not constitute a minor offence and are not fit to be tried summarily'.

This section was entered into force by the Criminal Procedure Act 2010 (Commencement) Order 2010 (SI 41/2010).

40 Section 4B(3). The legislation allows for the possibility of further extensions: s 4B(4). Where the District Judge refuses to grant an extension, the proceedings shall be struck out without prejudice to the institution of further proceedings: s 4B(5) and (6).

41 Section 4C(1)(a) and (b).

42 Such as a statement of further evidence expected to be given by a witness whose name appears on the list already served: s 4C(c). The prosecutor must also disclose a list of any further exhibits: s 4C(g). The accused is entitled to inspect all exhibits listed in the Book of Evidence or contained in any list subsequently served: s 4D.

43 Section 4C(f). Provision for the taking of depositions is contained in s 4F and for the admissibility of same in s 4G.

44 See generally, Hogan and Whyte, *JM Kelly: The Irish Constitution* (4th edn, Bloomsbury Professional, 2004) para 6.5.76–6.5.79; Abrahamson, Dwyer and Fitzpatrick, *Discovery and Disclosure* (Thomson Round Hall, 2007) ch 27; Dwyer, 'The Duty of Disclosure in Criminal Proceedings' (1993) 3(1) ICLJ 66.

45 *DPP v Gary Doyle* [1994] 2 IR 286.

summary proceedings. The accused was charged with various indictable offences under the Larceny Act 1916 and consented to the summary jurisdiction of the District Court. At trial, counsel for the defence challenged the failure of the prosecution to furnish the accused in advance of the trial with the statements of key witnesses who were to testify for the prosecution. On a consultative case stated to the High Court, Geoghegan J held that there was no general obligation on the prosecution to disclose the statements of proposed witnesses where an indictable charge was being disposed of by way of summary trial.[46] However, the learned judge did not rule out the possibility that disclosure might be required in exceptional circumstances:

> '[I]f in any given case fair procedures dictate that an accused in a summary trial should be given advance notice of the material evidence against him, then the judge should not embark on the trial unless this is done.'[47]

[9.15] These conclusions were affirmed by the Supreme Court. Holding that there is no general obligation on the prosecution to disclose proposed witness statements where an indictable charge is being disposed of by way of summary trial, Denham J stated: 'The trial is summary, it is not a halfway house between an indictable and summary trial'.[48] Denham J further endorsed the qualification on the general obligation recognised by the High Court:

> '[T]he applicant retains at all times his constitutional rights to fair procedures and if he requires, and it is in the interests of justice, that he be furnished with statements, or indeed other documents held by the prosecution, which will be evidence in his trial, then he is so entitled. It is a matter for the trial judge to determine in each case.'[49]

Failure to Disclose

[9.16] As Fennelly J made plain in his judgment in *PG v DPP*,[50] an accused person who seeks to enjoin her trial on the basis that the prosecution has failed to disclose material evidence faces a heavy burden: the accused must satisfy the court that 'having taken all reasonable steps to obtain disclosure, necessary material is being withheld from him to such an extent as to give rise to a real risk of an unfair trial'.[51]

[9.17] The task of assessing the impact of a failure to disclose evidence on the fairness of a trial is more straightforward where the challenge is mounted post trial in the form of an appeal against conviction in so far as the court has the

---

46 *DPP v Gary Doyle* [1994] 2 IR 286 at 292.
47 *DPP v Gary Doyle* [1994] 2 IR 286 at 292.
48 *DPP v Gary Doyle* [1994] 2 IR 286 at 302.
49 *DPP v Gary Doyle* [1994] 2 IR 286 at 302.
50 *PG v DPP* [2007] 3 IR 39.
51 *PG v DPP* [2007] 3 IR 39 at 42–43.

benefit of analysing the trial retrospectively. In *DPP v Dundon*,[52] Kearns J, delivering judgment for the Court of Criminal Appeal, stated that a failure on the part of the prosecution to make full pre-trial disclosure 'must be shown to have been important, as distinct from technical or trivial if a conviction is to be regarded as unsafe'. The learned judge went on to explain that the Court of Criminal Appeal must engage with the facts in order to ascertain whether an impugned omission disadvantaged the defence in such a way as to render the trial unfair or the jury verdict unsafe in the particular circumstances of the individual case. The enquiry was analogous to the test for the duty to seek out and preserve evidence, discussed below, and conditioned by 'the commonsense parameters' governing the scope of that duty.[53]

The Duty to Seek Out and Preserve Evidence

[9.18] The disclosure obligations resting on the State rest not only on the prosecution but also on the gardaí in carrying out their functions of investigating crime and gathering evidence. The effective enjoyment by the defence of a right to disclosure assumes a duty on the part of the gardaí to obtain relevant evidence and to preserve it for possible use at trial.[54] The extent of this duty to seek out and preserve evidence has been the subject of a vibrant discourse in the Superior Courts over the past several years.[55] The general principle, recognised for well over a century,[56] was set out by Hardiman J in *Braddish v DPP*:

> 'It is the duty of the Gardaí, arising from their unique investigative role, to seek out and preserve all evidence having a bearing or potential bearing on the issue of guilt or innocence. This is so whether the prosecution propose to rely on the evidence or not, and regardless of whether it assists the case the prosecution is advancing or not.'[57]

Questions surrounding the nature and extent of this duty have tended to surface in judicial review proceedings in which the High Court is asked to enjoin a criminal trial on the ground that a failure to preserve evidence has resulted in a breach of fair procedures.[58]

---

52 *DPP v Dundon* [2007] IECCA 64 (25 July 2007).

53 *DPP v Dundon* [2007] IECCA 64 (25 July 2007).

54 O'Malley, *The Criminal Process* (Thomson Round Hall, 2009) para 18.36.

55 For a more detailed discussion see Heffernan, 'The Duty to Preserve' in Bacik and Heffernan (eds), *Criminal Law and Procedure: Current Issues and Emerging Trends* (First Law, 2009) 53.

56 *Dillon v O'Brien and Davis* (1887) 20 LR IR 300.

57 *Braddish v DPP* [2001] 3 IR 127; [2002] 1 ILRM 151 at 157.

58 An early and fairly typical case is *Murphy v DPP* [1989] ILRM 81. Lynch J held that 'evidence relevant to guilt or innocence must so far as is necessary and practicable be kept until the conclusion of the trial'. This duty extended to 'articles which may give rise to the reasonable possibility of securing relevant evidence'.

[9.19] In *Braddish v DPP*,[59] the Supreme Court held that evidence relevant to guilt or innocence, including material that may give rise to a reasonable possibility of securing relevant evidence, must be retained, so far as is necessary and practicable, until the conclusion of the trial. The obligation that rested on the gardaí by virtue of their unique investigative role extended not only to material with a direct and established evidential significance but also to material that might reasonably lead to other relevant evidence.

[9.20] The principles set down in *Braddish* have been revisited in several subsequent cases.[60] The salient characteristics of the duty to preserve may be summarised as follows.[61]

(1) The courts have emphasised repeatedly that the duty does not lend itself to a precise, exhaustive definition and that it must be interpreted realistically on the facts of each individual case.[62]

(2) The prosecution is obliged to disclose to the defence all relevant evidence within its possession. It follows that evidence relevant to guilt or innocence must be kept until the conclusion of the trial in so far as this is necessary and practicable. Relevant evidence for this purpose includes evidence that may indirectly assist the accused by providing a lead to other information that might undermine the prosecution case or support the defence case.[63]

(3) Exceptionally the obligation resting on the gardaí may go beyond simply retaining and preserving evidence and extend to seeking out evidence that may assist the defence.[64] However, the courts have not imposed any general obligation on the gardaí to seek out and take possession of evidence.[65]

(4) Expectations as to what is reasonably required of the gardaí are tempered by considerations of necessity and practicality in contemporary policing.[66] Thus, the duty must be interpreted in a 'fair and reasonable manner' and cannot be construed as requiring the gardaí to engage in a 'disproportionate

---

59 *Braddish v DPP* [2001] 3 IR 127, [2002] 1 ILRM 151.

60 Such as *Dunne v DPP* [2002] 3 IR 305; *Bowes v DPP; McGrath v DPP* [2003] 2 IR 25; *Scully v DPP* [2005] 1 IR 242; *McFarlane v DPP* [2008] IESC 7 (5 March 2008).

61 For a judicial summary of the principal factors relevant to whether a court will make an order prohibiting a trial, see the judgment of Fennelly J in *Savage v DPP* [2009] 1 IR 185.

62 *Braddish v DPP* [2001] 3 IR 127 at 135.

63 *People (DPP) v Meleady* [1995] 2 IR 517; *Dunne v DPP* [2002] 2 IR 25. Compare *McGrath v DPP* [2003] 2 IR 25 with *Bowes v DPP* [2003] 2 IR 25.

64 *Dunne v DPP* [2002] 3 IR 305.

65 *Whelton v DJ O'Leary* [2010] IESC 63 (21 December 2010) *per* Fennelly J para 51. (The proceedings in this case took the form of an appeal from an order of the High Court refusing the appellant's application for judicial review by way of *certiorari* of his conviction in the District Court on a charge of theft.)

66 *People (DPP) v Murphy* [1989] ILRM 71. See *Byrne v DPP* [2010] IESC 54 (17 November 2010) *per* O'Donnell J at p 9: 'The duty to seek out and preserve evidence, is one which must, on all the authorities, be interpreted realistically. In that context, the fact the gardaí have never had the particular evidence in their possession, but made efforts to obtain it, is relevant in the assessment of the case made'.

commitment of manpower and resources in an exhaustive search for every conceivable kind of evidence'.[67] Where the evidence comprises property belonging to third parties, some consideration should be given to the need to return the property to its rightful owner at the earliest opportunity.[68]

(5) There is an onus on the defence to act promptly in requesting material considered to be relevant.[69] At the same time, the gardaí and the prosecution must act reasonably in ensuring that information and material is disclosed to the defence in a timely fashion.[70]

(6) The onus of proof on an accused who seeks an order prohibiting her trial is to establish a real risk that she could not obtain a fair trial.[71] This means an unfairness that cannot be avoided by appropriate rulings and directions on the part of the trial judge.[72] The prohibition of a trial must be based on more than a remote, theoretical or fanciful possibility. The exercise of the court's jurisdiction must be careful and realistic.[73]

(7) The focus of the court's inquiry must be on the fairness of the eventual trial in the absence of the missing evidence.[74] Neither the shortcomings in the investigative process nor the question of fault should concern the court (except in so far as they impact on the prospects of a fair trial).[75]

(8) The impact of the lost evidence must be considered in the context of all the evidence likely to be put forward at trial.[76] It will depend in part on the prosecution's case and proposed evidence[77] and on the extent to which the evidence might have assisted the defence in presenting an alternative theory to that presented by the prosecution.[78] The availability to the defence of

---

67 *Braddish v DPP* [2001] 3 IR 127 at 135; *Mitchell v DPP* [2000] 2 ILRM 396; *Scully v DPP* [2005] 1 IR 242; *Connolly v DPP* [2003] 4 IR 121.

68 *Rogers v DPP* [1992] 2 ILRM 695; *Connolly v DPP* [2003] 4 IR 121.

69 *Rogers v DPP* [1992] 2 ILRM 695; *Mitchell v DPP* [2000] 2 ILRM 396; *Scully v DPP* [2005] 1 IR 242; *Savage v DPP* [2009] 1 IR 185.

70 *Ludlow v DPP* [2009] 1 IR 640.

71 *Toohey v DPP* [2008] IESC 64 (3 December 2008).

72 *Z v DPP* [1994] 2 IR 476 at 506–507 (*per* Finlay CJ); *Bowes v DPP* [2003] 2 IR 25.

73 *Dunne v DPP* [2002] 2 IR 305 at 323–324; *McFarlane v DPP* [2006] IESC 11 (7 March 2006); *Perry v Judges of the Circuit Court and the DPP* [2008] IESC 58 (28 October 2008).

74 *McFarlane v DPP* [2006] IESC 11 (7 March 2006).

75 *Bowes v DPP* [2003] 2 IR 25 at 35.

76 *CD v DPP* [2009] IESC 70 (23 October 2009).

77 *Ludlow v DPP* [2009] 1 IR 640; *Perry v Judges of the Circuit Court and the DPP* [2008] IESC 58 (28 October 2008); *McHugh v DPP* [2009] IESC 15 (24 February 2009). The Supreme Court has recognised that exceptionally it may be necessary to take account of extraneous factors when assessing the likely impact of lost evidence on the fairness of the trial: *O'Brien v DPP* [2008] IESC 67 (16 December 2008) (lost evidence *in tandem* with a history of animosity between the applicant and the witnesses).

78 *Savage v DPP* [2009] 1 IR 185; *Perry v Judges of the Circuit Court and the DPP* [2008] IESC 58 (28 October 2008).

alternative evidence that can provide a viable substitute for the lost evidence will undermine an application for relief.[79]

[9.21] *Ludlow v DPP*[80] is one of the rare cases relating to the duty to preserve which resulted in an injunction restraining the DPP from continuing a prosecution, in this instance for the offence of dangerous driving causing death. The applicant, a truck driver, was involved in a road traffic accident on a public road in County Carlow, early on an Autumn afternoon. At a bend in the road, his truck allegedly slid onto the other side and collided with a car travelling in the opposite direction. The driver of the car, who had been accompanied by his wife and child, died three days later as a result of injuries sustained in the collision. Although neither vehicle had been travelling excessively fast, it was raining, as it had been for most of the day, and the surface of the road was greasy. The applicant's truck was examined at the scene by a Public Service Vehicle Inspector who noted in his report that some of the tyres were excessively worn and would have contributed to loss of control in wet conditions. The truck was returned to its owner, the applicant's employer, that same day. Not having been requested to preserve the tyres, he disposed of them shortly afterwards.

[9.22] *Ludlow* bucks the trend of missing evidence cases by virtue of the relative ease with which the Supreme Court identified a real risk of an unfair trial. The court was satisfied that the condition of the tyres was the ultimate issue on which the prosecution's case would turn. Against this backdrop, the evidentiary implications for the defence of the absence of tyres were stark. Hardiman J put the matter thus:

> 'This is a case where the defendant is charged with a criminal offence carrying a maximum sentence of ten years imprisonment. The case against him is based wholly on a forensic examination of the tyres. Without, in my view, any fault on his part, the prosecution's forensic evidence will be given by a qualified and skilled expert whose evidence will be virtually impossible to rebut because the defendant does not have available to him the tyres on an examination on which it is based. I do not see that the defendant can be compelled to admit, or to assume, the accuracy of the prosecution's expert evidence, measurements or photographs and neither has it been suggested in evidence that the photographs permit one to gauge the precise depth of the thread of the tyres. This is a case where a faction of a millimetre may be the difference between guilt and innocence.'[81]

[9.23] Denham J echoed these sentiments, observing that neither the photographs nor the garda statements were adequate in the circumstances to vindicate the applicant's right to a fair trial. The prosecution's case, it seems,

---

[79] *Savage v DPP* [2009] 1 IR 185; *Ludlow v DPP* [2009] 1 IR 640. In her judgments in these cases, Denham J delivered constructive best practice directions to the gardaí regarding the duty to preserve in cases arising out of road traffic accidents.

[80] *Ludlow v DPP* [2009] 1 IR 640.

[81] *Ludlow v DPP* [2009] 1 IR 640 at 661.

plays an influential part in the potential nexus between missing evidence and unfairness at trial. In particular, the viability of alternative evidence (as a substitute for evidence lost through a breach of the duty to preserve) turns in no small measure on the nature of the allegations levelled against the applicant.[82] However, the courts must also consider the positive evidentiary value of lost evidence for an accused, for example, in providing a tangible explanation of the facts favourable to the defence.[83]

[9.24] The trickle of cases that preceded the Supreme Court's decision in *Braddish* has since evolved into a steady stream. The ubiquity of requests for injunctive relief and appeals from refusals to grant same has encouraged the courts to emphasise the limits of the duty to preserve. In the recent case of *Byrne v DPP*,[84] the Supreme Court made plain that applications to enjoin criminal trials on the basis of missing evidence will be granted only in exceptional circumstances. O'Donnell J stated:

> 'In my view, having considered the decided cases, the position has now been reached where it can be said that other than perhaps the very straight forward type of Braddish case, it would now require something exceptional to persuade a court to prohibit a trial. This is in my view in accordance with principle ...
>
> The manner in which the Constitution contemplates that a fair trial is normally guaranteed, is through the trial and if necessary appeal processes of the Courts established under the Constitution. The primary onus of ensuring that that right is vindicated lies on the court of trial which will itself be a court established under the Constitution and obliged to administer justice pursuant to Article 34. It is in my view therefore, entirely consistent with the constitutional order, to observe that it will only be in exceptional cases, that Superior Courts should intervene and prohibit a trial, particularly on the basis that evidence is sought to be adduced ... or is not available ... .'[85]

Statutory Provision for the Return of Property Used as Evidence

[9.25] The Criminal Procedure Act 2010 incorporates a legislative initiative aimed at tackling some of the practical difficulties that have led to the plethora of missing evidence cases outlined above. Section 35 applies where property that is to be entered in evidence in a criminal trial is either returned to its owner

---

[82] See also *Savage v DPP* [2009] 1 IR 185; *Toohey v DPP* [2008] IESC 64 (3 December 2008).

[83] See, eg, *Perry v Judges of the Circuit Court and the DPP* [2008] IESC 58 (28 October 2008) in which the appellant sought unsuccessfully to counter the prosecution's charge of dangerous driving with the alternative explanation that the steering of the car he was driving had locked immediately prior to the collision and that the failure of the gardaí to preserve the vehicle for inspection necessarily impaired his ability to press that theory home. See also *Kelly v DPP* [2007] IESC 69 (21 December 2007).

[84] *Byrne v DPP* [2010] IESC 54 (17 November 2010).

[85] *Byrne v DPP* [2010] IESC 54 (17 November 2010) at p 6.

or disposed of prior to the commencement of the trial.[86] Where the prosecution intends to return or dispose of such property, it must serve notice on the accused at least 23 days in advance.[87] The notice must contain a description of the property,[88] a statement of its relevance to the proceedings, one or more photographs of the property and any report arising out of the analysis of the property that the prosecution intends to present in evidence.[89]

[9.26] Not later than seven days after service of the prosecution notice, the defence must in turn serve a notice of its own indicating one of three courses of action: (a) that the defence agrees to the return or disposal of the property; (b) that the defence wishes to provide the prosecution with a report of its own; or (c) that the defence requires the property to be available as an exhibit at trial.[90] Where the defence chooses the second option, ie, to serve notice of a defence report, service of the report itself must follow within a further seven days;[91] the prosecution must then indicate not later than three days before the start of the trial whether it intends to accept or reject the report.[92]

[9.27] Section 35 goes on to prescribe the steps the gardaí must take in the event that the accused agrees to the return or disposal of the property or the prosecution accepts the defence report on the property. Responsibility for causing the property to be returned or disposed of rests with a member of the gardaí not below the rank of inspector; she must keep a written record of the return or disposal and in the case of return procure a written receipt from the owner.[93]

[9.28] Section 35(8) formalises an important new exception to the rule against hearsay. Where the accused agrees to return or disposal of the property and accepts a prosecution report on the property, 'the prosecution report is proof of the facts stated therein, unless the contrary is shown'.[94] In the alternative event that the defence serves a report which is accepted by the prosecution, 'the defence report of evidence is proof of the facts stated therein, unless the contrary is shown'.[95] Furthermore, where the defence requires the property to be

---

86 Criminal Procedure Act 2010, s 35(1). Entered into force by the Criminal Procedure Act 2010 (Commencement) Order 2010 (SI 414/2010).

87 Section 35(2).

88 Section 35(3). The description must be sufficiently detailed for the property to be identified.

89 Section 35(3). This extends to analysis of any material found in or on the property.

90 Section 35(4).

91 Section 35(5). This provision applies notwithstanding s 34 of the 2010 Act which imposes a new obligation on the defence to disclose details of any expert evidence they intend to adduce at trial.

92 Section 35(6).

93 Section 35(7).

94 Section 35(8)(a).

95 Section 35(8)(b).

available as an exhibit at trial, 'the property may be admitted as evidence in any trial in which the property is otherwise admissible'.[96] Finally, in any other scenario, a prosecution report or a defence report 'may be admitted as evidence in any trial in which the property is otherwise admissible'.[97] Section 35(9) closes the section with a principle that might otherwise be assumed to apply, namely, that any person who prepares information contained in a prosecution or defence report may be called to give evidence 'in relation to all or any part of the report' and may be cross-examined on such evidence.

DISCLOSURE BY NON-PARTIES

[9.29] The extent of a putative right on the part of an accused to production of documents in the possession of non-parties presents interesting questions, considered but not resolved in all respects, by the Irish courts.[98] There is no bar to the defence seeking voluntary disclosure by a non-party; if the non-party does not accede to the request, however, can the defence obtain a court order directing the non-party to disclose the information in question? As noted above, in *People (DPP) v Sweeney*,[99] the Supreme Court held that the rules relating to discovery of documents, including third party discovery, do not apply in criminal trials.[100] In *Sweeney*, Geoghegan J quoted with approval the reasoning of then Circuit Judge Moriarty in *People (DPP) v Flynn*,[101] as expressed in the headnote:

> (1) While O.31, r.29 of the Rules of the Superior Courts 1986 leaves open the possibility of ordering discovery in criminal cases, there was no authority which would support the making of such an order.
>
> (2) The principle that each party should be entitled to know from the other in advance any information that would enhance his own case or destroy his adversary's case was less applicable in criminal proceedings where the entire burden of proof rested on the prosecution.
>
> (3) Discovery was intended to be mutual between the parties and it could not be mutual in a criminal case because it would not be ordered against the accused. It followed that a non-party should not be subject to a greater obligation that could be imposed on the accused.
>
> (4) ....

96 Section 35(8)(c).

97 Section 35(8)(d).

98 See generally Abrahamson, Dwyer and Fitzpatrick, *Discovery and Disclosure* (Thomson Round Hall, 2007) ch 24.

99 *People (DPP) v Sweeney* [2001] 4 IR 102.

100 See also *DH v Judge Groarke* [2002] 3 IR 522.

101 *People (DPP) v Flynn* [1996] 1 ILRM 317.

(5) ... If the prosecution cannot obtain evidence disclosure of which is necessary for the purposes of the defence, the accused may be entitled to a direction on the relevant counts.[102]

[9.30] In *DH v Groarke*,[103] the Supreme Court declined an invitation to resile from its stance in *Sweeney*. At issue in the case was the disclosure, prior to the applicant's trial on charges of indecent and sexual assault, of notes compiled by social workers based on conversations they had held with the complainant. The Supreme Court found no basis on which to exercise its exceptional jurisdiction to depart from one of its previous decisions. Keane CJ was satisfied, in any event, that the decision in *Sweeney* was 'correct in point of law'.[104] He identified a fundamental distinction between civil and criminal proceedings: whereas in civil proceedings the court is in a position to ascertain from the pleadings the issues and likely relevance of documentation, in a trial on indictment the issues remain undefined until the accused has been arraigned and pleaded, at the very earliest. Consequently, discovery in a trial on indictment would be 'a wholly one-sided process', which was clearly not the envisioned objective of the *inter partes* and non-party procedures fashioned in the rules of court.

[9.31] Keane CJ remained confident, however, that the absence of discovery in criminal proceedings did not have as a necessary consequence 'an erosion of the fair procedures to which defendants are entitled'.[105] In *obiter dicta*, he suggested that in the instant case the deposition stage had provided an opportunity for production of the notes in the possession of the social workers. In addition, the social workers could be required by the defence to attend at trial and produce any relevant documents pursuant to a subpoena *duces tecum*.[106]

[9.32] The *obiter dicta* of Keane CJ were distinguished in the later case of *JF v DPP*[107] in which the Supreme Court rejected as a general rule the use of depositions and subpoenas as a means of obtaining non-party disclosure. The case originated in attempts by the legal advisers of the appellant, who had been charged with sexual offences, to obtain confidential reports in the hands of the Midland Health Board. The latter claimed that the reports were privileged because they referred to interviews of a therapeutic nature. The defence sought to take depositions and/or serve subpoenas *duces tecum* on a number of health board employees and social workers. On a consultative case stated, Macken J

102 Quoted by Geoghegan J in *People (DPP) v Sweeney* [2001] 4 IR 102 at 110–111. Geoghegan J at 111 described Judge Moriarty's reasons as 'impeccable' save that they did not advert to 'the contextual limitation on the definitions' contained in the rules.

103 *DH v Groarke* [2002] 3 IR 522.

104 *DH v Groarke* [2002] 3 IR 522 at 531.

105 *DH v Groarke* [2002] 3 IR 522 at 531.

106 *DH v Groarke* [2002] 3 IR 522 at 531–532.

107 *JF v DPP* [2008] 1 IR 753.

rejected this use of depositions and subpoenas[108] and the Supreme Court, in turn, upheld her reasoning and this result. Geoghegan J endorsed Macken J's characterisation of the deposition procedure as 'a means of ascertaining whether there is sufficient evidence or material upon which a judge of the District Court may determine to send forward a defendant for trial'.[109] He concluded that '[t]he device of using or, more accurately, misusing the deposition procedure is an even less appropriate method of getting around the difficulty of obtaining documents from a third party than the condemned use of the civil discovery procedure'.[110] As against this position, the applicant had sought to rely on the *obiter dicta* of Keane CJ in *DH v Groarke*, quoted above, but Geoghegan J distinguished those comments:

> 'I agree with the view of the High Court judge that that statement must be read in context and did not have the wide meaning contended for. The crucial difference was that in that case the social workers had actually made a statement and appeared in the book of evidence and accordingly, it was appropriate to have that person examined in the course of a deposition hearing. The later part of the passage related to the trial itself.'[111]

In *JF*, Geoghegan J expressly left over to another day the possible resolution of 'undecided issues as to a right to procurement of documentation from a third party which is at least a State or a State funded body'.[112]

[9.33] If the defence is precluded from obtaining an order directing a non-party to disclose relevant material, the issue remains whether the prosecution can be compelled to procure the information in question. In other words, does the prosecution's duty to disclose extend to material outside its immediate possession and, if so, how broad is the prosecutorial obligation to procure information that might assist the defence?

[9.34] In *PG v DPP*,[113] the applicant sought an injunction by way of judicial review restraining his prosecution for sexual offences allegedly committed more than 20 years previously. One of the grounds on which the applicant sought relief was that the failure of the DPP to disclose certain information had deprived the applicant of his right to a fair trial. That information included the clinical notes of psychological experts who had attended one of the complainants. In response to a request from the solicitors acting for the applicant for disclosure of information relating to the therapy, the Chief State

---

108 *JF v DPP* [2005] IEHC 198 (10 June 2003).

109 *JF v DPP* [2008] 1 IR 753 at 759.

110 *JF v DPP* [2008] 1 IR 753 at 760–761.

111 *JF v DPP* [2008] 1 IR 753 at 760.

112 *JF v DPP* [2008] 1 IR 753 at 760. It was the opinion of Geoghegan J that an issue of this kind would have to be decided in a suitable case by the court of trial and on notice to the DPP, the body in question and the Attorney General.

113 *PG v DPP* [2007] 3 IR 39.

Solicitor provided details of the expert therapist and a copy of a letter from the therapist stating that he was not prepared to disclose the material as it would be unethical and a breach of client confidentiality.[114] Fennelly J stated:

> 'I accept, nonetheless, that, in the ordinary way, the applicant would normally, as a matter of fairness, be entitled to disclosure of [the] clinical notes for the purpose of cross-examination, if they were in the possession of the prosecution. However, the respondent is not in possession of these notes and has made reasonable efforts to obtain them.'[115]

[9.35] In *DPP v JF*,[116] Geoghegan J reflected, *obiter dicta*, on the propriety of limiting the scope of the prosecutorial obligation to disclose to matters strictly within the DPP's possession:

> '[The] obligation of the prosecution has been traditionally viewed by the Director of Public Prosecutions as logically confined to documents within his possession or lawful procurement. It may be arguable as to whether this is too narrow a view of the obligations of the Director of Public Prosecutions. Certainly, the guidelines of the Attorney General of England and Wales relating to disclosure seem to suggest a rather wider obligation in that jurisdiction. This whole problem has been coped with in different ways in the jurisdictions of England and Wales, Canada, New South Wales, the United States of America and no doubt elsewhere also. These are areas still to be explored ...'[117]

[9.36] The issue of disclosure by a non-party was addressed in a lengthy, detailed judgment of Edwards J in *The Health Service Executive v Judge Michael White*.[118] The case originated in the death of Evelyn Joel, the mother of the third notice party, in Wexford General Hospital in January 2006.[119] Evelyn Joel had been diagnosed with multiple sclerosis in October 2000 and had resided in the home of the third notice party and the latter's partner, the second notice party, since November 2004. It was alleged that at the time of her admission to hospital, Evelyn Joel was in an extremely malnourished condition and was suffering from neglect. Her death was the subject of two enquiries, a review by the HSE and a criminal investigation by the gardaí. The second and third notice parties were ultimately charged with unlawful killing and reckless endangerment.[120] The solicitor acting for the third notice party sought disclosure of the report of the committee that had conducted the HSE review and the

---

114 These facts are detailed in the judgment of Fennelly J, *PG v DPP* [2007] 3 IR 39 at 52.

115 *PG v DPP* [2007] 3 IR 39 at 55. Fennelly J remarked further that the court could not direct the DPP 'as to how to perform his functions'.

116 *JF v DPP* [2008] 1 IR 753.

117 *JF v DPP* [2008] 1 IR 753 at 755–756.

118 *The Health Service Executive v Judge Michael White* [2009] IEHC 242 (22 May 2009).

119 These facts are taken from the judgment of Edwards J, *The Health Service Executive v Judge Michael White* [2009] IEHC 242.

120 Contrary to the common law and s 13 of the Non-Fatal Offences Against the Person Act 1997, respectively.

material that had been before the committee. The Chief State Solicitor sought voluntary disclosure from the HSE and whereas the latter was willing to disclose material that had been available prior to the investigation, it refused to release the report or any material generated during the course of the investigation on the ground that persons who might be adversely affected by the findings had not had an opportunity to present their views. In response to an application brought by the third notice party in the Circuit Court, Judge White ordered the HSE to make disclosure of certain documents relevant to the prosecution but not the draft report of the investigating committee. The HSE, in turn, sought relief in the High Court by way of judicial review, including an order of *certiorari* quashing Judge White's order.

[9.37] The issue that Judge White had faced in the Circuit Court was whether there was a real and substantial risk that the notice parties might not receive a fair trial unless the material in the possession of the HSE was made available. Judge White ordered disclosure on the premise that it was necessary to safeguard the right to a fair trial and, moreover, that it was inherently within the power of the Circuit Court to issue the order in circumstances such as these.[121] In the High Court, Edwards J conducted a careful analysis of the law relating to judicial jurisdiction. He surmised that Judge White's direction could not be characterised as a 'disclosure order' in the strict sense because it was non-binding in so far as it would not be open to the trial judge to sanction the prosecutor for non-compliance; nor could it be described as an 'order for discovery' because discovery is not available in criminal proceedings. Judge White had thus made 'a novel order' which was 'in certain respects, but not in other respects, analogous or akin to an order for third party discovery on the civil side'.[122] Edwards J held that, although Judge White had acted with the worthy motive of accommodating the competing interests at issue, he was not justified in fashioning this novel remedy.[123] Whereas Edwards J lamented the unsatisfactory lacuna in the law as it currently stands, he contended that crafting a legal mechanism whereby a non-party can be compelled to disclose material in its possession that is potentially relevant to a criminal proceeding is primarily a matter for the legislature. In his opinion, the *obiter dicta* of Geoghegan J in *JF v DPP* merely identified scope for arguing that State or State-funded bodies might be situated differently to other non-parties and that this was an issue that would have to be decided in a suitable case.

121 *The Health Service Executive v Judge Michael White* [2009] IEHC 242 p 60. Judge White alluded to indications from the Supreme Court that the trial judge had the power to make such an order; Edwards J took this as a reference to the *obiter dicta* of Geoghegan J in *JF v DPP* [2008] 1 IR 753.

122 *The Health Service Executive v Judge Michael White* [2009] IEHC 242 at pp 70–71.

123 *The Health Service Executive v Judge Michael White* [2009] IEHC 242 p 71.

DEFENCE DISCLOSURE

[9.38] An accused is under no general duty to disclose his defence to the prosecution in advance of trial.[124] This principle, and the imbalance it strikes as against the prosecutorial duty to disclose, derives from the constitutionally and internationally protected rights of the defence including the presumption of innocence and the privilege against self incrimination.[125]

[9.39] The Oireachtas has carved out some notable exceptions to the principle of non-disclosure, however. One of the instances in which statute requires the defence to disclose information to the prosecution in advance of trial is where the accused intends to present alibi evidence in a trial on indictment. Section 20 of the Criminal Justice Act 1984[126] provides that the accused must give notice of the particulars of the alibi, including the name and address of the witness, if known, or any information in her possession which might be of material assistance in finding the witness.[127] The notice must be given in writing within 14 days of service of the Book of Evidence.[128]

Other examples of limited statutory dutics to disclosc include notice of an intention to call a witness on a charge of membership of an unlawful organisation,[129] and notice of an intention to present evidence of the accused's mental condition.[130]

[9.40] The Balance in the Criminal Law Review Group[131] criticised the disparity between the advance disclosure required of the prosecution and the defence in criminal cases. Characterising the current disclosure arrangements as 'imbalanced and unsatisfactory', the Group considered various options for reform. They noted, in particular, some of the practical difficulties that might attend more liberal provision for defence disclosure. The Group's overall conclusion was as follows:

> 'On balance, and having regard to the difficulties of moving to a defence statement regime, we consider that, in the first instance, the obligation of additional disclosure should be limited to the expert or technical reports or witness statement of experts on which the defendant seeks to rely. Provision

---

124 On defence disclosure see generally Abrahamson, Dwyer and Fitzpatrick, *Discovery and Disclosure* (Thomson Round Hall, 2007) ch 28.

125 Walsh, *Criminal Procedure* (Thomson Round Hall, 2002) para 19.31.

126 As amended.

127 Section 20(1) states specifically that 'the accused shall not without the leave of the court adduce evidence in support of an alibi unless, before the end of the prescribed period, he gives notice of particulars of the alibi'.

128 Section 20(8).

129 Offences Against the State (Amendment) Act 1998, s 3(1) (as amended by s 24 of the Criminal Justice Act 1999).

130 Section 19(1) of the Criminal Law (Insanity) Act 2006.

131 Final Report of the Balance in the Criminal Law Review Group (Dublin, 2007) ch 4.

> should be made that, following such disclosure, the prosecution would not be entitled to call any witness making such a report without the consent of the defendant.
>
> We likewise consider that it should not be open to the prosecution to require the defence to tender a witness where a report or witness statement has been furnished, but the defence does not, in the event, wish to call the witness at the trial.
>
> We recognise that, in many circumstances, the obtaining of expert evidence may take a longer period of time and, in such instances, the defence should be permitted to give details of the efforts being made to obtain a statement if the statement itself is not to hand at the time for disclosure. But, in any event, such reports should be disclosed well in advance of trial.'[132]

The Group also recommended that the defence should generally be required to provide advance notice of an intention to cast an imputation on the character of the deceased in a homicide case or an incapacitated witness in an assault case.[133]

Expert Witnesses Called by the Defence

[9.41] The recently enacted Criminal Procedure Act 2010[134] introduces a new statutory disclosure obligation for the defence drawing on the recommendations of the balance in the Criminal Law Review Group. Section 34(1) requires the defence to seek and obtain the leave of the court before calling an expert witness[135] or presenting expert evidence.[136] In addition, the defence is required by s 34(2) to give notice in writing to the prosecution of its intention to call an expert or present expert evidence at least 10 days in advance of the scheduled date for the trial.[137] This requirement applies regardless of whether the evidence in question is to be adduced in response to expert evidence presented by the prosecution.

---

132 Final Report of the Balance in the Criminal Law Review Group (Dublin, 2007) at pp 173–174.

133 Final Report of the Balance in the Criminal Law Review Group (Dublin, 2007) pp 144–145. These recommendations have also influenced the amendment to the character evidence provision in the Criminal Justice (Evidence) Act 1924 contained in s 33 of the Criminal Procedure Act 2010.

134 Entered into force by the Criminal Procedure Act 2010 (Commencement) Order 2010 (SI 414/2010).

135 An 'expert witness' is defined in s 34(9) as 'a person who appears to the court to possess the appropriate qualifications or experience about the matter to which the expert's evidence relates'.

136 The term 'expert evidence' is defined in s 34(9) as 'evidence of fact or opinion given by an expert witness'.

137 Section 34(7) states that notice may be given by delivering it to the prosecutor, or by leaving it at his or her office or by sending it by registered post to his or her office'.

[9.42] In addition to the name and address of the expert witness,[138] the notice must include:

> 'any report prepared by the expert witness concerning a matter relevant to the case, including details of any analysis carried out by or on behalf of, or relied upon by, the expert witness, or a summary of the findings of the expert witness.'[139]

However, a failure on the part of the defence to include such a report or summary will not be a bar to the granting of leave provided the court is satisfied that the defence took 'all reasonable steps' to procure it before giving notice.[140]

[9.43] Section 34 sets out certain additional conditions which must be fulfilled before leave may be granted. Specifically, the court must be satisfied

(1) that 'the expert evidence to be adduced satisfies the requirements of any enactment or rule of law relating to evidence';[141]

(2) that if notice was not given in a timely fashion, 'it would not, in all the circumstances of the case, have been reasonably possible for the defence to have done so'[142] or that a matter has arisen from the prosecution's expert evidence which 'it was not reasonably possible for the defence to have anticipated' and 'it would be in the interests of justice for that matter to be further examined in order to establish its relevance to the case'.[143]

The court must afford the prosecution an opportunity to be heard where the defence has failed to meet the basic conditions of s 34, ie, where the defence seeks leave, but no report or summary has been disclosed or notice was not given in a timely fashion.[144]

Where the court grants leave, s 34(8) provides that the prosecution shall be given 'a reasonable opportunity to consider the report or summary' before the expert witness testifies or the expert evidence is 'otherwise adduced'.

[9.44] In *Markey v Minister for Justice and Law Reform*,[145] the High Court recently rejected a challenge to s 34 grounded in the Constitution and the European Convention on Human Rights. The applicant for judicial review, who had been sent forward for trial for offences under the Road Traffic Acts, contended that s 34 interfered with his rights in multiple respects: the new provision placed an accused at a material disadvantage by inhibiting the ability of the defence to test the prosecution evidence; the disclosure requirements

[138] Section 34(3)(a).

[139] Section 34(3)(b).

[140] Section 34(4).

[141] Section 34(5).

[142] Section 34(5)(b).

[143] Section 34(5)(c).

[144] In the words of s 35(6), 'the prosecution shall be heard in an application under subsection (4) or (5)'.

[145] *Markey v Minister for Justice and Law Reform* [2011] IEHC 39 (4 February 2011) (Kearns J).

encroached on an accused's right to silence; and the absence of corresponding obligations for the prosecution was unequal and unfair. Kearns J was inclined to accept the respondents' view that the instant application was premature and hypothetical. However, given the importance of the substantive issue, he proceeded to decide the application on the merits. Having recalled the views of the Balance of the Criminal Law Review Group, which had influenced the legislation, and considered certain case law cited by the applicant, Kearns J rejected the contention that section 34 placed the defence at a unique procedural disadvantage. Noting that "[q]uite different obligations devolve on the two sides to a criminal trial", he observed:

> 'To characterise the obligations imposed on the different sides to a criminal trial as an evenly balanced see-saw which becomes totally unbalanced by the imposition of a requirement to notify the prosecution and seek leave in respect of expert evidence upon which the defence proposes to rely strikes me as astonishing and unreal. As the report of the expert group makes clear, it was the disadvantage and inequality being suffered by the prosecution (and, by extension, the public interest in the successful prosecution of crime) which required to be addressed in new legislation. ...'[146]

Later in his judgment, Kearns J noted that 'there is no rule of law or requirement in the Constitution that the procedures available to an accused person must be identical to those available to the prosecution'.[147] Moreover, any potential unfairness to an accused could be avoided through the exercise by the trial judge of her discretionary powers.[148] Overall, Kearns J was satisfied that any interference with protected rights occasioned by section 34 was limited and proportionate 'when placed in balance with the public interest in an effective and balanced prosecution system'.[149]

APPLICATION FOR DISMISSAL OF CHARGES

[9.45] In advance of a trial on indictment, an accused may apply for a dismissal of the charges under s 4E of the Criminal Procedure Act 1967.[150] The substantive foundation for such an application is the contention that the prosecution lacks a sufficient case to justify proceeding to trial. Whether the defence is required to provide the prosecution with advance notice of the

146 *Markey v Minister for Justice and Law Reform* [2011] IEHC 39 (4 February 2011) (Kearns J) at p 8.

147 *Markey v Minister for Justice and Law Reform* [2011] IEHC 39 (4 February 2011) (Kearns J) at p 9.

148 *Markey v Minister for Justice and Law Reform* [2011] IEHC 39 (4 February 2011) (Kearns J) at p 10.

149 *Markey v Minister for Justice and Law Reform* [2011] IEHC 39 (4 February 2011) (Kearns J) at p 11. Kearns J, at p 11, also rejected an argument that section 34 may adversely affect legal professional privilege.

150 As inserted by Criminal Justice Act 1999, s 9.

grounds upon which the application will be based was considered in *Phipps v Judge Desmond Hogan*.[151] The Supreme Court upheld the decision of Quirke J that to infer such a requirement from s 4E would be inconsistent with the presumption of innocence and the burden of proof in criminal proceedings.

[9.46] Before the Supreme Court, the DPP argued that, even in the absence of an express statutory power to oblige a defendant to give notice of the grounds for an application, such a power is implicit in the inherent authority of the trial judge to manage proceedings in her court. Hardiman J rejected this contention, opining that the right to a trial in due course of law precludes the implied interpretation of a power to require disclosure where the statute does not expressly say as much. Given that the prosecution has full access to the facts as the gardaí see them as well as its Book of Evidence and proofs advised by senior counsel, he considered it 'unlikely in the extreme' that the prosecution would be 'embarrassed' by the need to demonstrate the sufficiency of the case against the defendant. If necessary, the prosecution could apply to the trial judge for an adjournment; in addition, the prosecution may appeal the determination of an application under s 4E.

151 *Phipps v Judge Desmond Hogan* [2007] IESC 68 (20 December 2007).

Chapter 10

Procedural Accommodations: Informer Privilege

[10.01] As we have seen, the procedural dimension of legal professional privilege in criminal proceedings remains relatively undeveloped in this jurisdiction. In contrast, the application of informer privilege has generated a more substantial case law. This chapter explores some of the procedural accommodations that the courts have fashioned in response to the challenges presented by this strand of privilege. It begins, however, with an analysis of the substantive aspect of informer privilege.

INFORMER PRIVILEGE

[10.02] Law enforcement authorities have long enjoyed a privilege from disclosing the identity of their informers.[1] O'Flaherty J captured the general judicial attitude in *Ward v Special Criminal Court* when he stated: 'I hold that the informer's privilege is of ancient origin and that it is essential for the prevention and detection of crime and, therefore, the preservation of law and order....'[2]

The justification for the privilege is said to be grounded in two public policies: the need to preserve the valued contribution of informers to the prevention and detection of crime[3] and the imperative of protecting the informers' lives and safety.[4] The existence of these distinct but related rationales

1 *AG v Briant* (1846) 15 M & W 169 at 185 (*per* Pollock CB: 'The rule clearly established and acted on is this, that in a public prosecution a witness cannot be asked such questions as will disclose the informer, if he be a third person ... and we think the principle of the rule applies to the case where a witness is asked if he himself is the informer' quoted by Lord Esher MR in *Marks v Beyfus* (1890) 25 QBD 494 at 498). *R v Smith O'Brien* (1848) 7 St Tr NS 123; *R v Hardy* 24 St Tr 199

2 *Ward v Special Criminal Court* [1999] 1 IR 60 at 88.

3 *D v NSPCC* [1978] AC 171 at 218 (*per* Lord Diplock). The privilege is thought to encourage individuals to report past or likely future unlawful activities to the police and other law enforcement authorities. Without the safeguard of anonymity, informers might be discouraged from providing information vital to the fight against crime: *Alfred Crompton Amusement Machines Ltd v Customs and Excise Commissioners (No 2)* [1974] AC 405, 434; *R v Hennessey* (1978) 68 Cr App R 410, 426.

4 *R v Hennessy* (1978) 68 Cr App R 419 at 426 (*per* Lawton LJ). O'Connor reasons that the privilege safeguards the position of the informer by protecting her, first, from the risk of physical harm should her identity become known and, second, from the possibility of social ostracism arising from any perception that the informer betrayed an individual for financial gain: O'Connor, 'The Privilege of Non-Disclosure and Informers' (1980) Irish Jurist 111 at 112.

may account for some uncertainty about the classification of the privilege: informer privilege has been recognised as a strand of public interest privilege and also as a common law privilege in its own right.[5]

[10.03] Notwithstanding unambivalent judicial recognition of the existence of the privilege, there is considerable uncertainty about its scope. In the first place, the privilege clearly protects the *identity* of an informer but it is not clear how far it sweeps, if at all, in protecting other information from disclosure, such as the substance of communications between the informer and law enforcement authorities. Common sense suggests that the anonymity of an informer may be lost in a number of ways beyond divulging the individual's name and address. In order to protect the informer's life and safety, it may be necessary to withhold aspects of her evidence that would reveal her identity. However, lending informer privilege too broad a construction could substantially undercut the general principle of disclosure. The judgment of the Supreme Court in *Ward* hints at some judicial flexibility in this regard. Although the Supreme Court was not asked to decide the point directly, the court seemed willing to countenance the withholding of *information* provided by informers in a particular case.[6]

[10.04] The rigidity of the rule is a further matter for consideration. Whereas the courts have generally referred to informer privilege in robust terms, they have been equally firm in recognising an exception where it can be shown that divulging the identity of an informer will establish the innocence of the accused. Even beyond this, there are occasional judicial dicta to the effect that disclosure may be warranted to ensure justice in particular circumstances.[7] What remains unclear is the method whereby the courts should import this element of

---

5 *Howlin v Morris* [2004] 2 ILRM 53. McGrath takes the view that 'it is better regarded as a distinct category of privilege because, except where the 'innocence-at-stake' exception is at issue, its application does not involve any case by case balancing exercise': McGrath, *Evidence* (Thomson Round Hall, 2005) para 10.181. In contrast, Fennell concludes that 'adjudications on the balancing of public interests will inevitably arise in such areas' with the consequence that 'it is much better to categorise these as cases of public interest immunity, amenable in such manner to judicial discretion or control'. Fennell, *The Law of Evidence in Ireland* (3rd edn, Bloomsbury Professional, 2009) para 8.94. Having analysed *People (DPP) v Kelly* [2006] 3 IR 115, Fennell concludes at para 8.98: 'Informer privilege then, although referred to as though it is a separate heading of private privilege, is in fact part of public or state privilege. It is not one of those very limited and jealously guarded headings of private privilege, such as lawyer/client privilege, which has existed for many years'.

6 In *Director of Consumer Affairs v Sugar Distributors* [1991] 1 IR 225, Costello J painted the privilege with a similarly broad brush. He held that all documents forwarded by a complainant to the Director of Consumer Affairs concerning alleged anti-competitive practices should be protected from disclosure. Costello J reasoned, at pp 228–229, that the assurance of confidence in relation to information given to the Director and in some instances the names of complainants was necessary to the proper functioning by the Director of his statutory powers. Of course, in many instances the information will be used as evidence in the proceedings with the consequence that its disclosure will no longer be contested.

7 *AG v Simpson* [1959] IR 105 at 133.

flexibility. It seems that the traditional conception of informer privilege as a rule subject to exception has been gradually eclipsed by a more discretionary, case specific balancing exercise.[8]

EVOLVING CONTEXT

[10.05] In terms of scope, establishing the contexts in which the privilege operates has been the principal preoccupation of the Irish courts and consequently warrants detailed consideration. O'Connor defines an informer as 'a person who voluntarily supplies information to law enforcement officials concerning violations of the law'.[9] This captures the broad, common sense approach which has characterised the development of the case law. Although traditionally limited to police and prison informers, the privilege has evolved to embrace the giving of information to statutory bodies and officeholders engaged in the enforcement of the law in a wider sense. The Irish courts have tended to follow the lead of their English counterparts in this regard, a development which is perhaps not surprising given the similarities in law enforcement structures and protocols. The test applied by the courts appears somewhat counterintuitive in so far as the issue of whether an assertion of informer privilege should be upheld depends not on the character of the informer but on the status and function of the entity to which the information is given in confidence.

Given the significant role that informers play in the prevention and detection of crime, preserving the anonymity of police informers has always been the core objective of the privilege. The principal concern is that if the identity of police informers were revealed 'these sources of information would dry up and the police would be hindered in their duty of preventing and detecting crime'.[10]

[10.06] The case law suggests that the courts afford garda witnesses considerable leeway when asserting informer privilege and tend to take at face value claims that maintaining confidentiality is necessary. In *People (DPP) v Eccles, McPhillips and McShane*,[11] one of the grounds on which the second

---

8 The incorporation of the ECHR in England and Wales has influenced a noteworthy shift in emphasis in favour of a fact-intensive approach to informer privilege whereby the courts balance the public interests in favour of and against disclosure in particular cases. See *Chief Constable of Greater Manchester Police v McNally* [2002] EWCA Civ 14, [2002] CrimLR 832.

9 O'Connor, 'The Privilege of Non-Disclosure and Informers' (1980) Irish Jurist 111 at 111. O'Connor observes further that financial inducements may be provided by the authorities in return for information: 'The Privilege of Non-Disclosure and Informers' (1980) Irish Jurist 111 at note 4 (citing the exceptional example of the Irish Government's offer of a reward for information leading to the arrest and conviction of Earl Mountbatten's assassins).

10 *D v NSPCC* [1978] AC 171 at 218 (*per* Lord Diplock). *Breathnach v Ireland (No 3)* [1993] 2 IR 458 at 469 (information supplied in confidence to the gardaí should not in general be disclosed).

11 *People (DPP) v Eccles, McPhillips and McShane* (1986) 3 Frewen 36.

applicant sought leave to appeal against his conviction for capital murder concerned the validity of an order extending the period for which he was detained under s 30 of the Offences Against the State Act 1939. At trial, the garda chief superintendent asserted privilege against disclosing the source of information on which he based his decision to order the extension. Indeed, during cross-examination, he refused to indicate whether his source was a garda officer or a civilian. The Court of Criminal Appeal recognised that a member of the Garda Síochána is not entitled to claim privilege in respect of information received from another member of the force. Nevertheless, the Court affirmed the decision of the Special Criminal Court to uphold the claim of privilege, citing the exceptional circumstances of the case and the witness's opinion that it would be dangerous to indicate whether the source was police or civilian.[12] *Eccles* was followed in the later case of *People (DPP) v Reddan.*[13] The second applicant was arrested at the home of her uncle during a search for firearms carried out on foot of a warrant. The Court of Criminal Appeal upheld the entitlement of the superintendent who granted the warrant to preserve the anonymity of a fellow garda who had provided him with the information on which he based his decision. The court accepted the superintendent's explanation that revealing the identity of the garda who gave him the information would endanger the original source in turn.[14]

[10.07] The considerations that underpin the protection afforded to police informers also apply to prison informers. In *State (Comerford) v Governor of Mountjoy Prison*,[15] the High Court refused to make an absolute order of *habeas corpus* in respect of a remand prisoner who had been transferred to the wing of Mountjoy Prison housing convicted prisoners because the prison authorities feared that he might be party to an escape conspiracy. In his evidence, the Governor claimed privilege in respect of a confidential source for this information. Barrington J had 'no hesitation' in accepting the Governor's explanation and was 'quite satisfied' that the Governor 'could not responsibly disclose the source of this information' to the prisoner.[16]

---

12 *People (DPP) v Eccles, McPhillips and McShane* (1986) 3 Frewen 36 at 63. The chief superintendent also stated in his testimony that he believed he could claim privilege in respect of confidential information obtained from a fellow officer (at 61–62). On claims of public interest privilege in respect of communications between members of the gardaí see *AG v Simpson* [1959] IR 105; *DPP (Hanley) v Holly* [1984] ILRM 149.

13 *People (DPP) v Reddan* [1995] 3 IR 560.

14 *People (DPP) v Reddan* [1995] 3 IR 560 at 572.

15 *State (Comerford) v Governor of Mountjoy Prison* [1981] ILRM 86.

16 *State (Comerford) v Governor of Mountjoy Prison* [1981] ILRM 86 at 88. Although satisfied that the Governor's decisions were motivated by administrative and security reasons, Barrington J held that the circumstances of the prisoner's detention were irregular and in breach of the provision in the Prison Rules for the separation of remand prisoners and convicted prisoners. Nevertheless, he concluded that the irregularity was not such as to render the prisoner's detention unlawful or to entitle him to an absolute order of *habeas corpus*.

[10.08] Although responsibility for the enforcement of the law lies primarily in the hands of the Garda Síochána, there are several other bodies that are entrusted with the power to perform at least some law enforcement functions in specific contexts. In England, the privilege was first applied by analogy in *R v Lewes Justices, ex parte Secretary of State for the Home Department*,[17] where protection from disclosure was sought in relation to the identity of persons providing information to the Gaming Board. The House of Lords held that the Gaming Board was entitled to maintain the anonymity of its informers because, like the police, it was operating under statutory authority as an organ of law enforcement.

[10.09] The case of *D v NSPCC*[18] marked a watershed in the extension of informer privilege. The House of Lords held that the privilege extends to the identity of persons who provide the National Society of Prevention of Cruelty to Children (NSPCC) with information that a child is being abused or neglected. The NSPCC is a voluntary society incorporated by royal charter. At the time of the proceedings, the NSPCC was empowered to bring care proceedings under s 1 of the Children and Young Persons Act 1969 but was not under any statutory duty to do so. The case originated in a complaint to the NSPCC that the 14-month-old daughter of Mrs D had been ill-treated over a period of weeks. An inspector of the NSPCC called to Mrs D's home to ascertain the condition of the child and discovered that the complaint was unfounded. Mrs D sought the name of the informer but the NSPCC refused. Mrs D then sued the NSPCC seeking damages for personal injuries alleged to have resulted from the NSPCC's failure to properly investigate the complaint and the manner of the inspector's call which had caused her severe and continuing shock. She also sought an order that the NSPCC disclose all documents relating to the complaint and the identity of the complainant.

[10.10] Lord Diplock observed that the fact that information has been communicated by one person to another in confidence is not of itself sufficient to protect the information or the identity of the informer from disclosure in a court of law. In his words,

> '[t]he private promise of confidentiality must yield to the general public interest that in the administration of justice truth will out unless by reason of the character of the information or the relationship of the recipient of the information to the informant a more important public interest in confidentiality is served by protecting the information or the identity of the informant from disclosure in a court of law.'[19]

---

17 *R v Lewes Justices, ex parte Secretary of State for the Home Department* [1973] AC 388.

18 *D v NSPCC* [1978] AC 171, [1977] 1 All ER 589.

19 *D v NSPCC* [1978] AC 171 at 218 (citing *Alfred Crompton Amusement Machines Ltd v Customs and Excise Commissioners (No2)* [1974] AC 405 at 433–434). Lord Hailsham approached the issue in a similar frame of mind, observing that any attempt to withhold relevant evidence had to be justified and 'jealously scrutinised': [1978] AC 171 at 223.

Lord Diplock considered the public interest in protecting the identity of NSPCC informers to be analogous to that of police informers. Noting that the Lords had not hesitated in extending privilege to persons who provide information to the Gaming Board, he stated:

> 'Your Lordships' sense of values might well be open to reproach if this House were to treat the confidentiality of information given to those who are authorised by statute to institute proceedings for the protection of neglected or ill-treated children as entitled to less favourable treatment in a court of law than information given to the Gaming Board so that gaming may be kept clean.'[20]

Of the three categories of persons authorised to bring care proceedings – local authorities, the police and the NSPCC – the rationale for protecting the anonymity of informers was arguably strongest in the case of the NSPCC. Lord Diplock referred to the evidence as showing that the public were more ready to bring information to the NSPCC 'presumably because it is not associated in the public mind with officialdom'.[21]

[10.11] In Ireland, the High Court adopted the reasoning of *D v NSPCC* in *Director of Consumer Affairs v Sugar Distributors Ltd.*[22] The High Court upheld a claim of privilege over the identity of persons informing to the Director of Consumer Affairs in relation to allegations of suspected anti-competitive behaviour contrary to the Restrictive Practices Act 1972. Costello J recognised a long established general rule to the effect that 'the identity of police informers need not be disclosed as otherwise the information to enable the police to deter and detect crime might not be forthcoming'.[23] Having quoted from the judgment

---

20 *D v NSPCC* [1978] AC 171 at 218. Later in his judgment, at 219, Lord Diplock opined that the public interest in preserving the anonymity of NSPCC informers was of no less weight than police informers and of greater weight than informers of the Gaming Board. Lord Hailsham concluded, at 230, that as bodies empowered to institute care proceedings, 'the police, the local authority and the society stand on the same footing'. For a similar view see the judgment of Lord Simon, at 241 ('There can be no material distinction between police and/or local authorities on the one hand and the appellants on the other as regards the protection of children. It follows that, on the strictest analogical approach and as a matter of legal rule, the appellants are bound to refuse to disclose their sources of information'). Lord Edmund-Davies, at 245, reached the same destination by way of a different route; he opined that where a confidential relationship exists and disclosure would be in breach of 'some ethical or social value involving the public interest', the court has a discretion to uphold a refusal to disclose if on balance the public interest is best so served.

21 *D v NSPCC* [1978] AC 171 at 219. Lord Hailsham, at 229, relied on the undisputed evidence of the NSPCC that an entity which solicits information on condition of confidentiality would suffer a 'drastic reduction' in the flow of information available to it. It is noteworthy that some of the Lords cautioned against a broad reading of the extension of privilege: see, eg, Lord Diplock at 219 and Lord Simon at 235–237.

22 *Director of Consumer Affairs v Sugar Distributors Ltd* [1991] 1 IR 225, [1991] ILRM 395.

23 *Director of Consumer Affairs v Sugar Distributors Ltd* [1991] 1 IR 225 at 227.

of Lord Diplock in *D v NSPCC*, he reviewed the statutory law enforcement functions of the Director of Consumer Affairs. The learned judge continued:

> 'I am satisfied that it is in the public interest that the court should protect the effective functioning by the Director of his statutory powers. I am further satisfied that to enable him to exercise his powers effectively he must be able to assure complainants that information given to him (and, indeed, in certain circumstances the names of complainants) will be treated in confidence and not disclosed as otherwise complaints may not be forthcoming and breaches of ministerial orders are likely to go undetected.[24]

[10.12] It appears from the report of the case that the identities of the complainant and of other firms mentioned in the documents that comprised the complaint were known at the time of the proceedings. The submission advanced by the Director was broad in its potential reach: it was his contention that he was not required to permit inspection of documents that had come into his possession as part of a complaint made to him by a member of the public.[25] The protection sought and received related not to the identity of the Director's informers but to the full gamut of information conveyed. Costello J concluded: 'The requisite protection should embrace all documents forwarded by a complainant with a complaint'.[26] However, it is clear from the language of the judgment that Costello J was not laying down a broad rule to bind future trial courts. The discussion clearly locates the claim within the contours of public interest privilege which, given the inherent judicial balancing of competing public interests, implicitly limits the ruling to the particularities of the case. Indeed, Costello J expressly recognised that the protection is necessarily qualified:

> 'When a claim is made, as it has been in this case, that it is not in the public interest that relevant documents in the Director's possession should not be inspected, the court should examine the documents. If satisfied that they form part of a complaint made to the Director by a member of the public that a breach of the restrictive practices legislation or orders made thereunder has occurred inspection should not be allowed unless the court concludes that the documents might tend to show that the defendant had not committed the wrongful acts alleged against him.'[27]

[10.13] The reasoning in *Director of Consumer Affairs v Sugar Distributors* arguably supports the application of privilege to complainants and complaints made to any statutory body vested with law enforcement powers such as Customs and Excise, the Revenue Commissioners and the Competition

---

24 *Director of Consumer Affairs v Sugar Distributors Ltd* [1991] 1 IR 225 at 228–229.

25 *Director of Consumer Affairs v Sugar Distributors Ltd* [1991] 1 IR 225 at 227.

26 *Director of Consumer Affairs v Sugar Distributors Ltd* [1991] 1 IR 225 at 229.

27 *Director of Consumer Affairs v Sugar Distributors Ltd* [1991] 1 IR 225 at 229.

Authority.[28] However, the limits of informer privilege were drawn in another judgment on point by Costello J in *Buckley v Incorporated Law Society of Ireland.*[29] Distinguishing *Director of Consumer Affairs v Sugar Distributors*, Costello J rejected the Incorporated Law Society's claim that it was privileged from disclosing the identity of persons who made complaints over alleged professional misconduct on the part of a solicitor. The case had its origins in an accident suffered by the plaintiff at work. The plaintiff instructed a solicitor who so delayed instituting proceedings in respect of the accident that the plaintiff's claim became statute barred. The solicitor had been the subject of complaints to the Incorporated Law Society and the plaintiff ultimately sued the Law Society for damages arising out of the Society's decision to renew the solicitor's practising certificate in the face of those complaints. One of the grounds on which the Law Society sought to resist disclosure of documents relating to the complaints was the public interest in the prevention and detection of crime.

[10.14] The determinative difference between the two cases lay in the respective duties of the defendant Law Society and the Director of Consumer Affairs. Costello J explained:

> 'There is, it seems to me, a crucial distinction between the duties of the defendant and those of the Director of Consumer Affairs. The Director is concerned to investigate possible breaches of the criminal law whilst the defendant is concerned with investigating allegations of professional misconduct. The fact that in some cases misconduct might involve breaches of the criminal law does not alter the fundamental nature of the defendant's statutory duties.'[30]

The issue before the court was whether informer privilege should extend to complaints made to a professional disciplinary body relating to professional misconduct. In an interesting twist, Costello J invoked *Smurfit Paribas Bank Ltd*

---

28 In *Alfred Crompton Amusement Machines Ltd v Customs and Excise Commissioners (No 2)* [1974] AC 405, the House of Lords rejected the notion that information handed over to the authorities in confidence should be privileged by reason of confidentiality alone. Nevertheless, balancing the public interests on the facts of the case presented, it held that the Customs and Excise Commissioners should not be forced to disclose information of this kind since public knowledge that the Commissioners could not keep such information secret might be harmful to the conduct of their statutory functions. In *Wallace Smith Trust Co Ltd v Deloitte Haskins and Sells* [1996] 4 All ER 403, the liquidators of the plaintiff company brought proceedings against the defendants for breach of duty in contract and tort in failing to detect that the company's business was being fraudulently conducted. The defendants asserted privilege over tapes and transcripts of interviews between officers of the Serious Fraud Office and a partner and employee of the company. The documents in question contained information disclosed to a public body under compulsion of law but neither the trial judge not the Court of Appeal was persuaded that this was sufficient to support a claim of public interest immunity.

29 *Buckley v Incorporated Law Society of Ireland* [1994] 2 IR 44.

30 *Buckley v Incorporated Law Society of Ireland* [1994] 2 IR 44 at 50.

v AAB Expert Finance Ltd[31] in which Finlay CJ discussed the possible extension of the scope of legal professional privilege (as opposed to public interest privilege). As against the restriction on full disclosure inherent in privilege the court had to consider the suggested disadvantage if disclosure were allowed, namely, that 'persons with legitimate complaints may be discouraged by fear of public disclosure of their private affairs from coming forward, thus reducing the effectiveness of the defendant's supervisory role'.[32] Costello J concluded that on balance the public interest did not favour disclosure:

> 'It seems to me that it is a demonstrable probability ... that if inspection is refused this will result in the frustration of the court's duty to ascertain the truth and do justice between the parties. On the other hand, in my estimation, if inspection is allowed the risk that complainants will be deterred from approaching the defendant is not a very great one'.[33]

[10.15] The concluding remark by the learned judge to the effect that 'consideration of the public interest' did not 'require' the extension of informer privilege is worthy of note. The choice of words echoes the sentiment of Finlay CJ in *Smurfit Paribas Bank Ltd* that privilege constitutes an exception to the general rule in favour of disclosure and as such must be construed narrowly. Notwithstanding the court's consideration of the disadvantages that would accompany the granting and refusal of discovery respectively, it seems that this was not an even balancing exercise. Both public interest privilege and private privilege characteristics are discernible in the court's discussion in *Director of Consumer Affairs v Sugar Distributors Ltd* and *Buckley v Incorporated Law Society.*

OTHER POTENTIAL CONTEXTS

[10.16] The question remains how far the courts may be willing to go in extending informer privilege. In *D v NSPCC*, Lord Hailsham speculated about the possibility of further extensions: 'The categories of public interest are not

[31] *Smurfit Paribas Bank Ltd v AAB Expert Finance Ltd* [1990] 1 IR 469, [1990] ILRM 588.

[32] *Buckley v Incorporated Law Society of Ireland* [1994] 2 IR 44 at 51.

[33] *Buckley v Incorporated Law Society of Ireland* [1994] 2 IR 44 at 51. The English High Court has taken a different view in the context of the duties of the Law Society of England and Wales. In *Buckley v The Law Society (No 2)* [1984] 1 WLR 1101, Megarry VC held that the principles laid down in *D v NSPCC* [1978] AC 171 applied to persons providing confidential information to the Law Society about dishonest conduct on the part of solicitors. The public interest to be protected was 'the effective functioning of the Law Society in exercising its statutory functions in protecting moneys held by solicitors on behalf of members of the public, as well as the probity and good repute of the solicitors' profession' which Megarry VC considered 'at least as important' as the efficient functioning of the Gaming Board, which supported informer privilege in *R v Lewes Justices, ex parte Secretary of State for the Home Department* [1973] AC 388.

closed, and must alter from time to time whether by restriction or extension as social conditions and social legislation develop'.[34] Reviewing the English case law, Phipson has pointed to a possible distinction between investigating authorities which have statutory or quasi-statutory powers to obtain information and those which rely on voluntary information.[35]

[10.17] The position under Irish law seems less amenable to precise demarcation. As the case law outlined above suggests, the courts approach the question from the premise that any further extension of informer privilege would have to be justified as an exceptional restriction on the general rule of full disclosure. In order to justify the extension of privilege, the privilege-holder would have to draw a credible analogy between the case presented and the paradigm of the police informer. The key would lie in the function of the entity to which the information is given, its law enforcement powers and its contribution to the prevention and detection of crime.

Informers of Child Abuse

[10.18] The landmark case of *D v NSPCC*[36] placed in sharp relief the role that privilege can play in ensuring that allegations of child abuse or neglect are brought to the attention of the relevant authorities.[37]

In its 1990 *Report on Child Sexual Abuse*,[38] the Law Reform Commission recommended that greater protected be afforded to informers. The Oireachtas responded with the Protections for Persons Reporting Child Abuse Act 1998 which shields an informer from civil liability arising out of allegations of child abuse[39] communicated to the gardaí and certain other designated persons.[40] The protection afforded by the Act is dependent upon the informer having acted reasonably and in good faith when forming and communicating the opinion of the existence of abuse.[41]

[10.19] The current state of the law has been criticised by Geoffrey Shannon in his capacity as Special Rapporteur on Child Protection. In his 2007 Report, he called for a more comprehensive, coherent statutory regime. The Report states:

---

34 *D v NSPCC* [1978] AC 171 at 230.

35 Malek (ed), *Phipson on Evidence* (16th edn, Sweet & Maxwell, 2005) para 25.32 discerns another, seemingly unrelated trend, that '[s]ince the Human Rights Act 1998, the courts are increasingly adopting a case-specific approach to the disclosure of the identity of informants in civil cases,' (citing *Chief Constable for Greater Manchester v McNally* (2002) 2 Cr App R 27).

36 *D v NSPCC* [1978] AC 171, [1977] 1 All ER 589.

37 See generally Fennell, *The Law of Evidence in Ireland* (3rd edn, Bloomsbury Professional, 2009) para 8.102 *et seq.*

38 Law Reform Commission, *Report on Child Sexual Abuse* (LRC 32-1990) p 11.

39 Section 3. Section 4 protects employees from penalisation by employers for having reported child abuse.

40 Section 2.

41 Section 5 imposes criminal penalties for false reporting.

> 'There is a need to extend the category of persons/bodies that enjoy immunity from suit in respect of communications concerning child abuse. In addition to those already protected by the 1998 Act others involved in the care of children should be included eg employees of certain child agencies, school counsellors and others in similar positions. In addition, the legislation should be amended so as to deem the actual communication to be privileged.'[42]

The Report observes that the extension of categories of privilege in Ireland is relatively rare due to what it characterises as 'the prevailing philosophy of the balance lying in favour of the court having all available information before it so as to make an informed decision'. Shannon goes on to recommend that privilege should be decided on a case-by-case basis.[43]

Parliamentary Informers

[10.20] Informer privilege has also arisen outside the setting of the executive branch of government in the guise of the protection afforded to individuals who provide information in confidence to members of the Oireachtas. Understandably, the courts have chosen to address the issue principally under the rubric of parliamentary privilege.[44] Nevertheless, the case law indicates that informer privilege may play a supporting role.

[10.21] In *Goodman International v Hamilton (No 3)*,[45] the High Court held that certain members of the Oireachtas who testified before the Tribunal of Inquiry into the Beef Processing Industry were not obliged to disclose the identity of their sources. Geoghegan J took the view that the privilege claimed had 'a direct public interest dimension far beyond the mere private interest in confidentiality'.[46] He gleaned from the line of Irish authorities relating to public interest privilege a judicial rejection of any kind of class or category of privilege that would automatically override the general rule in favour of disclosure of relevant evidence.[47] He stated:

> 'I think that most Irish people would regard it as important that matters of actual or potential public concern may be confidentially brought to the attention of elected national public representatives without fear of the confidence being broken. But I do not believe that most people would expect an absolute rule of non-disclosure that could brook no exceptions. If disclosure of the source was

42 Shannon, *Report of the Special Rapporteur on Child Protection* (November, 2007) para 5.3.4.

43 Shannon, *Report of the Special Rapporteur on Child Protection* (November, 2007) para 5.3.4.

44 On parliamentary privilege see *Ahern v Mahon* [2008] IEHC 119 (8 May 2008, Divisional Court); Hogan & Whyte, *JM Kelly: The Irish Constitution* (4th edn, Bloomsbury Professional, 2004) para 4.2.140 *et seq.*

45 *Goodman International v Hamilton (No 3)* [1993] 3 IR 320. See McHugh, 'Members of Oireachtas Entitled to Claim Common Law Privilege on their Informants – Chairman of Beef Tribunal' (June 1993) ILT 119.

46 *Goodman International v Hamilton (No 3)* [1993] 3 IR 320 at 325.

47 *Goodman International v Hamilton (No 3)* [1993] 3 IR 320 at 326.

> relevant to the guilt or innocence of an accused in a trial for a serious criminal offence then justice and the public interest might require disclosure.'[48]

Drawing from the judgment of Lord Edmund Davies in *D v NSPCC*,[49] Geoghegan J concluded that whether the members of the Oireachtas should be required to disclose the identity of their sources was a matter for the discretion of Mr Justice Liam Hamilton, the sole member of the Tribunal. In the circumstances of the case, Geoghegan J opined that the discretion should be exercised in favour of non-disclosure.[50]

[10.22] The Supreme Court considered the question over a decade later in *Howlin v Morris*.[51] The applicant member of Dáil Éireann challenged by way of judicial review an order of the respondent, Mr Justice Frederick Morris, the sole member of the Tribunal of Inquiry into Complaints Concerning Some Gardaí of the Donegal Division, requiring the applicant to disclose his source of confidential information. The allegations of garda misfeasance that had emanated from that source had led to the establishment of the Tribunal. The High Court quashed the order, holding that the information was protected by the parliamentary privilege enshrined in Article 15 of the Constitution.[52] However, the Supreme Court allowed the respondent's appeal. The court held that the conditions of parliamentary privilege had not been met with the consequence that the only kind of privilege that could conceivably avail the applicant was the common law privilege which the High Court had not found it necessary to consider. Geoghegan J observed that the phrase 'common law privilege' was a misnomer because it was not privilege 'in the strict sense' but rather 'a question of public interest immunity'.[53] Hardiman J echoed this sentiment in so far as he observed that '[s]uch a privilege would clearly not be an absolute one'.[54] Assuming that it were open to the court to consider submissions on the issue, Hardiman J could find no fault with the respondent's decision rejecting the claim of privilege in the circumstances of the case.[55]

Garda Complaints

[10.23] A possible further extension of informer privilege was considered by the Supreme Court in *Skeffington v Rooney*.[56] The plaintiff brought proceedings

---

48 *Goodman International v Hamilton (No 3)* [1993] 3 IR 320 at 327.

49 *D v NSPCC* [1978] 1 AC 171 at 245; [1977] 1 All ER 589 at 618.

50 These circumstances included 'the fact that the unknown informants could not reasonably have expected that, through an accidental and erroneous understanding of constitutional privilege, the members of the Oireachtas laid themselves open to being forced to disclose': *Goodman International v Hamilton (No 3)* [1993] 3 IR 320 at 329–330.

51 *Howlin v Morris* [2006] 1 ILRM 440, [2006] 2 IR 321.

52 *Howlin v Morris* [2004] 2 ILRM 53, [2006] 2 IR 321 (Kearns J).

53 *Howlin v Morris* [2006] 1 ILRM 440 at 480, [2006] 2 IR 321 at 387.

54 *Howlin v Morris* [2006] 1 ILRM 440 at 462, [2006] 2 IR 321 at 371.

55 *Howlin v Morris* [2006] 1 ILRM 440 at 462, [2006] 2 IR 321 at 372.

56 *Skeffington v Rooney* [1997] 1 IR 22.

against two garda officers claiming damages for personal injuries arising out of an alleged incident of assault and negligent driving. The incident had been the subject of a complaint by the plaintiff to the Garda Síochána Complaints Board and the plaintiff sought discovery of all documents in the possession of the Board relating to the complaint. The Board relied on s 12 of the Garda Síochána (Complaints) Act 1986 which prohibited the disclosure of confidential information by members or staff of the Board. Counsel for the Board contended further that subjecting the Board to orders of discovery might have the negative effect of discouraging persons alleging misconduct against the gardaí from making complaints and render garda officers more reluctant to co-operate with the Board's inquiries.[57] In the High Court, Barr J concluded that the plaintiff was entitled to discovery and, on appeal by the Board, the Supreme Court affirmed this ruling.

[10.24] The Supreme Court resolved the case under the rubric of public interest privilege, divining the applicable principles of law from the judgment of Finlay CJ in *Ambiorix Ltd v Minister for the Environment (No 1)*.[58] Keane J traced from the category of public interest in the detection and prevention of crime the principle that courts should allow the anonymity of informers to be preserved.[59] In the context of the present case, Keane J recognised the importance of the 1986 Act in protecting the rights of citizens who complain of misconduct and maintaining public confidence in the Garda Síochána.[60] He took note of the concern voiced in the evidence of the Board that the efficacy of its continuing work would be affected if members of the public and the gardaí could not be assured of the confidentiality of statements made by them to the Board.[61] Keane J acknowledged that where documents relating to a complaint to a board are sought by a party to litigation other than the complainant, a court might be justified in refusing discovery; indeed, the court might follow the approach proposed by Costello J in *Director of Consumer Affairs v Sugar Distributors Ltd* of examining the documents with a view to ascertaining whether the interests of justice required disclosure in the circumstances of the particular case. However, those considerations did not arise in the present case where the documentation about the complaint was being sought by the complainant himself.[62]

---

57 *Skeffington v Rooney* [1997] 1 IR 22 at 27.

58 *Ambiorix Ltd v Minister for the Environment (No 1)* [1992] 1 IR 277 at 283.

59 *Skeffington v Rooney* [1997] 1 IR 22 at 32.

60 *Skeffington v Rooney* [1997] 1 IR 22 at 30.

61 This argument had found a receptive audience in the English Court of Appeal in *Neilson v Lougharne* [1981] QB 736 where it held that statements taken by the police in pursuance of a statutory police inquiry were privileged.

62 *Skeffington v Rooney* [1997] 1 IR 22 at 36. Nor was the Supreme Court convinced that the Garda Síochána (Complaints) Act 1986, s 12 had any direct bearing on the case; in the view of Keane J, at 37, the provision was not 'in any sense a prohibition on the production to a court in the interests of justice of documents in the Board's possession which are relevant to proceedings before that court'.

Skeffington v Rooney seems typical on its facts of cases of this kind, namely instances where an individual aggrieved with the conduct of the gardaí first lodges a complaint with the Board and later institutes a civil action. Nevertheless, the result in this case clearly leaves open the possibility of informer privilege in proceedings instituted by a person other than the individual who lodged the initial complaint.[63]

Innocence at Stake

[10.25] The vast majority of cases relating to informer privilege centre on persons providing information to the gardaí during the course of investigations that leads to criminal proceedings. This classic scenario is subject to an important exception which is a gloss as ancient as the privilege itself. Under this 'innocence-at-stake' exception, the identity of the informer must be disclosed if the trial judge is satisfied that disclosure will lead to the exoneration of the accused. As Lord Esher explained in *Marks v Beyfus:*

> '[I]f upon a trial of a prisoner the judge should be of the opinion that the disclosure of the name of the informant is necessary or right in order to shew the prisoner's innocence, then one public policy is in conflict with another public policy, and that which says that an innocent man is not to be condemned when his innocence can be proved is the policy that must prevail'.[64]

[10.26] The Criminal Division of the English Court of Appeal applied this principle in *R v Agar*[65] which involved an appeal against a conviction for possession of drugs with intent to supply. The appellant's case at trial had been that he had been entrapped by the police acting in concert with an informer. Nevertheless, the trial judge ruled that the appellant's counsel should not put in cross-examination of police witnesses any questions that might elicit the informer's role in the investigation. The Court of Appeal quashed the conviction on the ground that the appellant had been unduly hindered in the presentation of his defence. Lord Mustill stated:

---

63 A new system for the investigation and review of complaints by a Garda Ombusdman Commission was established by the Garda Síochána Act 2005, as amended.

64 *Marks v Beyfus* (1890) 25 QBD 494 at 498 (CA). This view was echoed by Bowen LJ, at 500, who opined that the only exception to the rule of non-disclosure would be 'upon a criminal trial, when the judge if he saw the strict enforcement of the rule would be likely to cause a miscarriage of justice, might relax it in favorem innocentiae; if he did not do so, there would be a risk of innocent people being convicted'. Later in his judgment, Lord Esher MR said of the exception: '[T]his rule of public policy is not a matter of discretion; it is a rule of law, and as such should be applied by the judge at the trial ...'. The underlying proceedings took the form of an action against several defendants for maliciously and without reasonable and probable cause conspiring to institute and instituting a prosecution for fraud against the plaintiff. Lord Esher MR, at 499, was of the opinion that the rule of non-disclosure of informers applied not only to a criminal trial but also to any subsequent civil action for malicious prosecution. See also *R v Hennessey* (1978) 68 Cr App R 419, 426; *R v Hallett* [1986] Crim LR 462.

65 *R v Agar* [1990] 2 All ER 442.

'The question as we see it is whether in the particular circumstances of the trial it would have been possible, with a reasonable degree of ingenuity, to have put the appellant's case to the officers without, as an integral part of the exercise, inquiring of the officers whether it was true that they had got their information from X. As already indicated, we do not see how this could have been done. By adhering to the ruling counsel was in effect forced to emasculate his client's attack on the police. Now it is certainly not the case that a defendant can circumvent the rule of public police so as to find out the name of the person who had informed on him, for his own future reference and possible reprisal, simply by pretending that something is part of his case, when in truth it adds nothing to it. And it may be, and we emphasise 'may', that if the defence is manifestly frivolous and doomed to failure the trial judge may conclude that it must be sacrificed to the general public interest in the protection of informers. We do not see the present case in this light. There was a strong, and absent any contrary indication, overwhelming public interest in keeping secret the source of information; but, as the authorities show, there was an even stronger public interest in allowing a defendant to put forward a tenable case in its best light.'[66]

[10.27] The notion that the identity of an informer should be disclosed where 'the needs of justice so require' was accepted by Davitt P in *AG v Simpson.*[67] Costello J recognised as much in *Director of Consumer Affairs v Sugar Distributors Ltd* when he observed that inspection of documents conveyed to the Director as part of a complaint of alleged wrongdoing should not be allowed 'unless the court concludes that the documents might tend to show that the defendant had not committed the wrongful acts alleged against him'.[68] The accused bears the burden of demonstrating that 'for good reason the need to protect the liberty of the subject should prevail over the need to protect informers'.[69]

[10.28] The High Court judgment of Carney J in *Ward v Special Criminal Court*[70] shed some light on the difficult question of how probative of innocence the evidence must be in order to qualify for the exception. The common law authorities fashioned a relatively narrow exception; as the quotation from the judgment of Lord Esher in *Marks v Beyfus* suggests, the courts spoke in terms of evidence that would exonerate the accused. In contrast, the fair trial rights of an accused might be thought to support a more broadly defined exception that would mandate disclosure of any information necessary to the presentation of a proper defence. Although Carney J chose not to characterise the exception in constitutional terms, he seemed to prefer the broad interpretation: he directed

66 *R v Agar* [1990] 2 All ER 442 at 448.

67 *AG v Simpson* [1959] IR 105 at 133.

68 *Director of Consumer Affairs v Sugar Distributors Ltd* [1991] 1 IR 225 at 229. See also *Breathnach v Ireland (No 3)* [1993] 2 IR 458 at 469; *Skeffington v Rooney* [1997] 1 IR 22.

69 *R v Hennessey* (1978) 68 Cr App R 419 at 426 (*per* Lawton LJ).

70 *Ward v Special Criminal Court* [1999] 1 IR 60.

the Special Criminal Court to examine the documents in question to determine 'whether any of them might help the defence case, help to disparage the prosecution case or give a lead to other evidence'.[71]

[10.29] In *Howlin v Morris*,[72] the Supreme Court held that the innocence-at-stake exception was not limited to the setting of a criminal trial but applied to proceedings before the Tribunal of Inquiry into Complaints Concerning Some Gardaí in the Donegal Division. Hardiman J stated:

> 'The Oireachtas has thought it necessary that a tribunal should investigate allegations that 'a large number of convictions were achieved by planting evidence', and that two assistant commissioners of An Garda Síochána were aware of this. This is an allegation of the corruption of the criminal trial process itself by gardaí. To hold that an 'innocence at stake' exception to privilege could have applied during the trial process (which was allegedly corrupted and during which the allegations were in any event unknown) but not during the investigation into the alleged corruption would be an absurdity. It would ensure the frustration of the inquiry which the Oireachtas itself has set in motion. These allegations raise in terms the prospect that people have been framed and thereby convicted of criminal offences. In my view this presents an 'innocence at stake' situation in an acute form.'[73]

CONSTITUTIONAL IMPLICATIONS

[10.30] The traditional cast of informer privilege and the innocence-at-stake exception thereto has taken on an individual rights / human rights complexion in recent years. In a criminal proceeding, any attempt by the prosecution to invoke an evidentiary privilege is open to the fundamental objection that non-disclosure may infringe the right of the accused to a trial in due course of law pursuant to Article 38.1 of the Constitution and the corresponding right to a fair trial under art 6 the European Convention on Human Rights (ECHR).[74] In the landmark case of *People (DPP) v Kelly*,[75] the traditional assertion of the innocent-at-stake exception was essentially recast in constitutional terms. At issue before the Supreme Court was whether restrictions on the right of the defence to cross-

71 *Ward v Special Criminal Court* [1999] 1 IR 60 at 76.

72 *Howlin v Morris* [2006] 1 ILRM 440, [2006] 2 IR 321.

73 *Howlin v Morris* [2006] 1 ILRM 440 at 462, [2006] 2 IR 321 at 372.

74 The following discussion draws substantially on Heffernan, 'Evidentiary Rights under Article 38.1: The Right to Fair Trial and Informer Privilege' in Carolan and Doyle (eds), *The Irish Constitution* (Thomson Round Hall, 2009) pp 278–292 and reproduces in part Heffernan, 'Evidence and National Security: "Belief Evidence" in the Irish Special Criminal Court' (2009) 15 Eur Pub L 65.

75 *People (DPP) v Kelly* [2006] 3 IR 115. See Fennell, *The Law of Evidence in Ireland* (3rd edn, Bloomsbury Professional, 2009) paras.8.97–8.98; King, 'The Right to Fair Trial v The Claim of Privilege' (2007) 17 ICLJ 17.

examine a prosecution witness deemed necessary to protect the identity of police informers violated the accused's right to a fair trial.

[10.31] The applicant, Martin Kelly, was convicted by the Special Criminal Court of membership of the IRA contrary to s 21 of the Offences Against the State Act 1939, as amended, and sentenced to a term of imprisonment of four years. At trial, Garda Chief Superintendent Philip Kelly[76] took the stand and testified that he believed that the applicant had been a member of the IRA at the material time. During cross-examination, Chief Superintendent Kelly refused to reveal the basis for his belief on the ground that disclosing the identity of his informers would endanger their lives and threaten ongoing garda operations against the IRA. The Special Criminal Court upheld the claim of informer privilege and reasoned that the public interest in the prevention and detection of crime and the preservation of the safety of the informers took precedence over the right of the accused to a fair trial. The applicant challenged his subsequent conviction contending that the failure of the trial court to investigate the reasonableness of the claim of privilege constituted a breach of Article 38.1. The Court of Criminal Appeal held that the trial had not been tainted by unfairness, a conclusion that was affirmed by a unanimous Supreme Court.

[10.32] The bulk of the respective judgments of Geoghegan and Fennelly JJ was devoted to analysis of the constitutionality of belief evidence. Section 3(2) of the Offences Against the State (Amendment) Act 1972 bestows upon the prosecution an evidentiary prop in establishing the offence of membership of an unlawful organisation contrary to s 21 of the Offences Against the State Act 1939. It provides:

> 'Where an officer of the Garda Síochána, not below the rank of Chief Superintendent, in giving evidence in proceedings relating to an offence under the said section 21, states that he believes that the accused was at the material time a member of an unlawful organisation, the statement shall be evidence that he was then such a member.'

The subsection creates a controversial exception to the common law rule against the admission of opinion evidence by legislating in bald terms for the admissibility of testimony directed at the ultimate issue in the proceedings. It effectively takes the matter of admissibility out of judicial hands by providing that the prosecution need only tender the witness in the customary way and the witness's statement of belief 'shall be evidence'. Equally significant is a reality not reflected in the face of s 3(2), namely, the legal and practical constraints on the ability of the defence to challenge belief evidence. The defence is prohibited from tendering witnesses to offer evidence in the form of beliefs or opinions that would contradict the testimony of the chief superintendent. The legislation does not condition the belief, for example with a requirement that it be 'reasonable'

76 Seemingly, the garda chief superintendent was not related to the applicant.

or based on objective criteria. The defence can proceed on the premise that such conditions are implicit and seek to shake the belief through the course of cross-examination. But herein lies the paradox: the chief superintendent can escape any rigorous testing of the basis for her belief through the expedient of informer privilege.[77]

[10.33] In *People (DPP) v Kelly*, the Supreme Court unanimously concluded that the restrictions on the cross-examination necessary to protect the identity of informers had not tainted the fairness of Kelly's trial. The court's task in deciding the appeal was expedited by a body of case law concerning the application of s 3(2). In particular, the constitutionality of belief evidence had previously been upheld in *O'Leary v Attorney General* when the High Court rejected the contention that s 3(2) offended the presumption of innocence by shifting the burden of proof from the prosecution to the defence, in essence requiring an accused to establish that she was not a member of an unlawful organisation at the material time.[78]

[10.34] Geoghegan J, writing for a majority of the Supreme Court in *Kelly*,[79] recognised the importance of the presumption of constitutionality, to which s 3(2) was entitled, given the limitation on the right to cross-examination inherent in its terms. He observed that s 3(2) had been enacted in response to the legitimate concern that it is frequently not possible to adduce direct evidence of membership of an illegal organisation from lay witnesses who fear reprisal.[80] Counsel for the DPP had submitted two possible constructions of s 3(2): first, that it permits evidence of the chief superintendent's belief but not evidence about the basis for the belief; and, second, that it permits evidence about the basis for the belief but not to the extent that it interferes with a legitimate plea of privilege. Geoghegan J favoured the latter construction on the premise that the

[77] Robinson notes that the elevation of possibly dubious police intelligence to the status of evidence, immune from challenge, was one of the principal criticisms levelled against s 3(2) in the debates within the Oireachtas leading to the passage of the 1972 Act. Robinson, *The Special Criminal Court* (1974) p 31.

[78] *O'Leary v Attorney General* [1993] 1 IR 102 (HC). Costello J took the view, at 109, that s 3(2) imposed no more than an evidential burden on the accused without disturbing the underlying legal burden on the prosecution to establish the offence. No constitutional infringement occurred because the accused could elect not to call any evidence and still be entitled to an acquittal if the prosecution's evidence did not establish guilt beyond a reasonable doubt.

[79] Murray CJ, Denham and Kearns JJ.

[80] Geoghegan J stated: 'It is a reasonable inference to draw that the subsection was enacted out of bitter experience. It is carefully crafted ensuring that the belief evidence must come from an officer of the Garda Síochána not below the rank of Chief Superintendent. This is with a view to ensuring trust and credibility as far as possible ... I have no doubt that in so far as [counsel for the defence] was limited in his cross-examination of Chief Superintendent Kelly, permission for this limitation was inherent in the subsection itself ...' *People (DPP) v Kelly* [2006] 3 IR 115 at 121.

former (the preferred reading of the DPP) would involve a disproportionately broad interference with an accused's rights.[81]

[10.35] Concurring with the result but writing separately, Fennelly J characterised the issue raised by the appeal as 'both important and difficult' because '[i]t sets the policy of the legislation in suppressing dangerous and threatening unlawful organisations against the presumption of innocence and the imperative of a fair trial'.[82] Quoting extensively from the Supreme Court's jurisprudence on fair procedures and from decisions of the United States Supreme Court and the European Court of Human Rights, Fennelly J emphasised the central place that the right to cross-examination occupies on the landscape of the guarantee of a fair trial. While restrictions may be imposed on the right to cross-examination for overriding reasons of public interest, they must not stray beyond what is strictly necessary and must not imperil the overall fairness of the particular trial.[83] The exceptional, limited recourse to belief evidence under the extraordinary legislative regime governing offences against the State was justified in Fennelly's view by a combination of factors including the decision of the Oireachtas to limit belief evidence to members of the Garda Síochána of particularly high rank; the fact that belief evidence is restricted to the confines of the regime for offences against the State; the presumption of constitutionality; and the requirement that the restriction on the right to cross-examine is limited to the extent that is strictly necessary to achieve the subsection's clear objectives.[84]

[10.36] The weight that the courts afford to belief evidence influenced the reasoning of the Supreme Court. The majority commended the DPP's practice of not initiating prosecutions solely on belief evidence and that of the Special Criminal Court of not convicting on belief evidence alone. However, Geoghegan J considered that these 'self-imposed restrictions' were not required by law.[85] Fennelly J, in contrast, opined that an accused would have 'a powerful argument' based on the denial of his or her rights where such evidence constituted 'the sole plank in the prosecution's case'.[86] Both judges based their ultimate conclusion that Kelly had received a fair trial in part on the existence of prosecution evidence other than the belief evidence of the chief superintendent.

[10.37] *Kelly* is indicative of a fundamental shift in the framing of issues of privilege and disclosure. Whereas in civil proceedings the law responds to

---

81 *People (DPP) v Kelly* [2006] 3 IR 115 at 121 (noting that there might be cases in which the chief superintendent's belief is not based on information from informers and that the restriction on the right to cross-examine had to be kept to a minimum).

82 *People (DPP) v Kelly* [2006] 3 IR 115 at 129.

83 *People (DPP) v Kelly* [2006] 3 IR 115 at 146.

84 *People (DPP) v Kelly* [2006] 3 IR 115 at 146–147.

85 *People (DPP) v Kelly* [2006] 3 IR 115 at 122.

86 *People (DPP) v Kelly* [2006] 3 IR 115 at 147.

assertions of privilege through the balancing of competing public policies whether in the form of pre-determined rules or as a matter of judicial discretion, in criminal proceedings the issue is now presented in its constitutional and human rights frame: does prosecutorial reliance on privilege affect the right of an accused to a fair trial? From the standpoint of the defence, *Kelly* underscores the limited scope for appellate review of evidentiary rulings of this kind.[87] This relates in part to the conception of evidentiary rights under Article 38.1;[88] in cases such as *Kelly* the resolution of a specific difficult issue of principle is partially obscured by fact intensive analysis conjured by the benchmark of the 'overall fairness' of the trial. Whereas this approach allows the courts to tailor their response to the particularities of individual cases, it inhibits the divining of general principles that would guide future practice with certainty and precision.

[10.38] It is important to recall that belief evidence constitutes a special case; it is rare that informer privilege operates *in tandem* with evidence that has a statutory mandate much less the backing of the legislative regime governing scheduled offences. It does not follow that the Supreme Court would be willing to countenance a comparable interference with the rights of the defence in the prosecution of ordinary as opposed to extraordinary offences. If revealing the identity of an informer would substantially assist an accused in presenting a defence to a serious charge such as murder or armed robbery, the restriction on the right to cross-examine upheld in *Kelly* might not pass constitutional muster. The trial judge would have to weigh the competing public interests in the factual setting of the particular case. Clearly, the stronger the prosecution argument that the life or safety of an informer would be endangered by disclosing her identity, the greater the challenge facing the defence in persuading the court to recognise the innocence-at-stake exception.

[10.39] One area of criminal justice where belief evidence and informer privilege may guide future developments is the investigation and prosecution of offences relating to organised crime. The Criminal Justice (Amendment) Act 2009 provides for additional measures with respect to combating organised crime[89] including the creation of the offences of directing a criminal organisation[90] and participating in the activities of a criminal organisation.[91] In relation to proceedings for these offences, s 7 legislates for a mechanism corresponding to belief evidence in the form of a new s 71B of the Criminal

---

87 Subsequent cases on all fours include *People (DPP) v Matthews* [2007] IECCA 23 (29 March 2007); *People (DPP) v Vincent Kelly* [2007] IECCA 110 (6 December 2007); *People (DPP) v Birney & Others* [2007] 1 IR 337; *People (DPP) v Binead and Donohue* [2007] 1 IR 374.

88 See generally Heffernan and Imwinkelried, 'The Accused's Constitutional Right to Introduce Critical, Demonstrably Reliable, Exculpatory Evidence' (2005) 40 Irish Jurist (ns) 111.

89 Long title.

90 Section 5 (inserting Criminal Justice act 2006, s 71A).

91 Section 6 (replacing Criminal Justice Act 2006, s 72).

Justice Act 2006. It renders admissible in evidence, as to the existence of a particular criminal organisation, the opinion of any present or former member of the gardaí who appears to the trial court to be 'an appropriate expert'.[92]

PROCEDURE

[10.40] In criminal proceedings, it is incumbent on the trial court to ensure not only that the accused's substantive rights are adequately protected but also that fair procedures are observed in the determination of those rights. Particularly challenging procedural questions arise where the defence raises the innocence-at-stake exception in an attempt to defeat an assertion of informer privilege. The evidence that is the subject of the claim must necessarily be disclosed to the trial judge if she is to reach a meaningful determination as to whether the assertion of privilege should be upheld. The issue is whether the material should also be disclosed to the defence and, if so, by what procedure. Disclosure is arguably necessary in our adversarial system in order to vindicate the accused's right to a fair trial; on the other hand, disclosure to the defence may defeat the purpose of the privilege by endangering the safety and security of the informer. How then should the court resolve the dilemma?

[10.41] The issue was considered by the Supreme Court in *Ward v Special Criminal Court.*[93] Prior to the trial of Paul Ward before the Special Criminal Court for the murder of journalist Veronica Guerin, the defence sought the disclosure of documents containing some 40 statements made to the gardaí by various informers. The prosecution asserted privilege on the basis that the statements had been given in confidence and that revealing the identity of the informers would put their lives at risk. The defence took the position that the prosecution was obliged to disclose any information which could assist Ward in establishing a defence and that this obligation necessarily took precedence over any claim of privilege.

[10.42] The Special Criminal Court reached a compromise: if Ward was prepared to waive his right to inspect the documents personally or be informed of their contents, the court would direct the prosecution to turn them over to Ward's lawyers on the condition of strict confidence. In the event that the lawyers formed the view that any particular document contained information that might be relevant to the defence and consequently required further

---

92 Section 7 (inserting Criminal Justice Act 2006, s 71B(1)). Section 71B(2) defines 'expertise' as 'experience, specialised knowledge or qualifications'. The Explanatory Memorandum describes the new provision in the following somewhat confusing terms: '*Section 7* inserts a new section after section 71 of the Criminal Justice Act 2006 to provide for proof of the evidence of the existence of a criminal organisation. This will enhance the ability to bring prosecutions for offences of directing or participating in organised crime'.

93 *Ward v Special Criminal Court* [1999] 1 IR 60, [1998] 2 ILRM 493. See generally Charleton, McDermott and Bolger, *Criminal Law* (Lexis Nexis, 1999) para 2.86 *et seq.*

instruction from their client, the court would consider an application for the document to be disclosed to Ward himself. However, if Ward was not prepared to waive his rights in this manner, the documents would be examined solely by the court which would then determine whether any of the documents should be disclosed.

[10.43] The DPP instituted proceedings in the High Court by way of judicial review and obtained an order of *certiorari* quashing the Special Criminal Court's ruling. Carney J noted that there was not a great deal of difference between the parties as regards the applicable law and that the issue presented was 'more in the area of mechanics than principle'.[94] In his view, the Special Criminal Court had created an unworkable solution and had exceeded its jurisdiction in 'fundamentally altering the established relationship between defence lawyers and their client'.[95] Carney J continued:

> 'It does not seem to be any answer that the notice party has consented to his legal team having sight of the statements on the terms that they are not disclosed to him without leave of the court. His present legal team could be discharged at any time and it does not seem to me that there would be a trial in accordance with constitutional justice if any subsequent legal representatives did not enjoy the full lawyer-client relationship with their client but were under an obligation to keep secrets from him'.[96]

Carney J directed that the Special Criminal Court should examine the documents in question and determine 'whether any of them might help the defence case, help to disparage the prosecution case or give a lead to other evidence'.[97]

[10.44] Ward appealed this decision and sought, in effect, the restoration of the Special Criminal Court's compromise formula as a means of ensuring a trial in due course of law under Article 38.1.[98] A unanimous Supreme Court dismissed the appeal and affirmed Carney J's conclusion that permitting Ward's lawyers to see the document, but not Ward himself, was not a realistic procedure. O'Flaherty J, writing for the court, stated that he would vary Carney J's judgment only to the extent of removing the *direction* to the Special Criminal Court to examine the documents. The decision whether to examine the documents, O'Flaherty J concluded, was a matter for the discretion of the trial judge. The court emphasised the particular responsibilities of prosecution

94 *Ward v Special Criminal Court* [1999] 1 IR 60 at 71.

95 *Ward v Special Criminal Court* [1999] 1 IR 60 at 75.

96 *Ward v Special Criminal Court* [1999] 1 IR 60 at 76.

97 *Ward v Special Criminal Court* [1999] 1 IR 60 at 76.

98 Judgment of O'Flaherty J summarising counsel's submissions: *Ward v Special Criminal Court* [1999] 1 IR 60 at 84.

counsel in ensuring the fairness of the trial which include a duty to disclose any source of evidence that might assist the defence.[99]

[10.45] This procedural issue has arisen in even starker terms in a series of cases concerning so-called 'belief evidence' proffered by the prosecution in trials for membership of an unlawful organisation contrary to s 21 of the Offences Against the State Act 1939. As discussed above, s 3(2) of the Offences Against the State (Amendment) Act 1972 creates a controversial exception to the common law rule against the admission of opinion evidence by legislating for the admissibility of testimony directed at the ultimate issue in the proceedings. The procedural challenge presented by such a proffer of belief evidence is that the confidential information which forms the basis of the assertion of privilege is not reduced to written form as it was in *Ward v Special Criminal Court*. If the information is revealed at trial it will take the form of oral testimony and, specifically, answers given by the witness to questions put in cross-examination. Consequently, the possibility of the prosecution handing over documents to be inspected by the court does not arise. How then should the trial court respond to an assertion of privilege in circumstances such as these? As noted, the question of appropriate procedures has assumed increased importance with the enactment of provision for opinion evidence, along the lines of belief evidence, in relation to organised crime under the Criminal Justice (Amendment) Act 2009.

[10.46] The Supreme Court did not address this procedural dimension in *People (DPP) v Kelly*,[100] presumably because the court was in a position to answer the question referred to it on the substantive constitutional law. The troubling question remains, however, as to the appropriate procedural steps that a trial court should take in order to review the evidence in question. An assessment of this kind may be required in any proceeding in which a court must respond to an assertion of privilege; unless the outcome is unquestionably clear, the trial court may need to review the information in order to dispose of the claim of privilege in a meaningful way.

[10.47] The Special Criminal Court considered the issue in *People (DPP) v Binead and Donoghue*,[101] another case involving a challenge to belief evidence.

---

[99] In *R v Agar* [1990] 2 All ER 442, the English Court of Appeal cast doubt on the propriety of a proceeding conducted in the judge's private room the content of which counsel was forbidden to disclose to the defendant. Although it was not necessary for the Court of Appeal to decide the issue, in *obiter dicta* Lord Mustill stated at 448: 'As this court has repeatedly emphasised, discussions in the judge's room, with the defendant absent, are an expedient of last resort. This appeal demonstrates once again how things can go wrong, and how a real sense of injustice may be engendered in the absent client. This is not to say that a solution was easy to find, but we are sure that with some resource it would have been possible to deal with the matter in open court ...'

[100] *People (DPP) v Kelly* [2006] 3 IR 115.

[101] *People (DPP) v Binéad and Donoghue* (28 November 2004, unreported) SCC, discussed at para **10.57**.

The claim of privilege arose during the course of cross-examination of a chief superintendent who refused to answer questions relating to his confidential sources. The Special Criminal Court took the view that the fairness of the trial would be placed in jeopardy if 'no enquiry whatsoever' were made into the basis of the chief superintendent's belief.[102] The court considered whether an appropriate mechanism could be devised which would 'build a bridge' between the accused's constitutional rights and the claim of privilege.[103] The court was not persuaded that it had jurisdiction to take the 'radical step' of appointing a special counsel or advocate.[104] Nevertheless, the court decided that it could and should examine some of the documentation that the witness asserted had influenced his belief and rejected the suggestion that the defence should be informed about the detail of the material made available to the court.[105] On a perusal of those files, the court declared itself satisfied that the witness had adequate and reliable information upon which he could legitimately form the stated opinion and, moreover, that there was nothing in the information that would assist the accused in establishing their innocence.[106]

THE ECHR

[10.48] Prosecutorial claims of privilege may impact upon the substantive and procedural rights of accused persons under art 6 of the ECHR. The Convention's fair trial guarantee includes in art 6(3) certain minimum rights to which a criminal defendant is entitled including the right 'to examine or have examined witnesses on his behalf under the same conditions as witnesses against him'.[107] In a series of cases across a diverse range of contexts the European Court of Human Rights has stipulated that art 6 protects core evidentiary rights such as equality of arms, the laying of evidence with a view to adversarial argument, and the right to challenge and question witnesses.[108]

[10.49] The Strasbourg case law also supports the need to withhold evidence from the defence in order to preserve the fundamental rights of others or to safeguard important public interests.[109] Where a State party restricts the

[102] *People (DPP) v Binéad and Donoghue* (28 November 2004, unreported) SCC at p 21.
[103] *People (DPP) v Binéad and Donoghue* (28 November 2004, unreported) SCC at p 8.
[104] *People (DPP) v Binéad and Donoghue* (28 November 2004, unreported) SCC at p 21.
[105] *People (DPP) v Binéad and Donoghue* (28 November 2004, unreported) SCC at pp 21–22.
[106] *People (DPP) v Binéad and Donoghue* (28 November 2004, unreported) SCC at p 22.
[107] Article 6(3)(d).
[108] See, eg, *Ludi v Switzerland* (1993) 15 EHRR 173 para 49; *Saidi v France* (1994) 17 EHRR 251 para 43; *Rowe v United Kingdom* (2000) 30 EHRR 1 para 60; *Dowsett v United Kingdom* (2004) 38 EHRR 41 para 41; *Taal v Estonia* (App No 13249/02, judgment of 22 November 2005) para 31.
[109] *V v Finland* (App No 40412/98, judgment of 24 April 2007) para 75.

disclosure of evidence to the defence, it bears the burden of demonstrating that the rule or practice is compatible with art 6.[110] The bar on the permissibility of such measures is set high: the State must persuade the court that the restriction is strictly necessary to serve countervailing public interest (such as the protection of the anonymity of police sources)[111] and that convictions are not secured solely or substantially on evidence procured through the restricted measure.[112] Of crucial importance to the present discussion is the additional requirement that the national trial courts make any necessary procedural accommodations to counterbalance the difficulties created for the defence.[113]

[10.50] In *Kostovski v Netherlands*,[114] the court held that the use as evidence of statements given to the police by anonymous witnesses rendered the applicant's trial for armed robbery unfair. The court observed that in principle all evidence must be produced in the presence of the accused at a public hearing with a view to adversarial argument but that this did not preclude entirely the use of pre-trial witness statements provided that the rights of the defence are respected.[115] These rights generally require that an accused be afforded an adequate and proper opportunity to question and challenge a witness giving evidence against her either at the time the witness makes her statement or at some later stage in the proceedings.[116]

[10.51] In a similar vein, the court found in *Van Mechelen v Netherlands* that the applicants' rights had been violated where their convictions for attempted manslaughter and robbery with the threat of violence were based to a decisive extent on pre-trial statements made by anonymous police officers whom the defence had no opportunity to question.[117] The witnesses had been interrogated by an investigating judge in a hearing from which the accused and their counsel were excluded but to which they had access via sound link. The court did not consider this a proper substitute for the direct questioning of a witness by the defence which provides opportunities to observe the demeanour of the witness and test his or her credibility and the reliability of the witness's account.[118]

---

[110] *Van Mechelen & Others v Netherlands* (1997) 25 EHRR 647 at 674 (para 60).

[111] *Van Mechelen & Others v Netherlands* (1997) 25 EHRR 647 at 674 (para 60); *W v Finland* (App No 14151/02, judgment of 24 April 2007).

[112] *Doorson v Netherlands* (1996) 22 EHRR 330 (para 78); *Mild and Virtanen v Finland* (App Nos 39481 and 40227/98, judgment of 26 July 2005).

[113] *Doorson v Netherlands* (1996) 22 EHRR 330; *Van Mechelen and Others v Netherlands* (1997) 25 EHRR 647. See also *SN v Sweden* (2004) 39 EHRR 13; *PS v Germany* [2003] 36 EHRR 61.

[114] *Kostovski v Netherlands* (1990) 12 EHRR 343 at paras 42 and 45.

[115] *Kostovski v Netherlands* (1990) 12 EHRR 343 at 447 (para 41).

[116] *Kostovski v Netherlands* (1990) 12 EHRR 343 at 448–449 (paras 42 and 45). See also *Luca v Italy* (2003) 36 EHRR 46; *Birutis and Others v Lithuania* (App Nos 47698/99 and 48115/99, judgment of 28 March 2002).

[117] *Van Mechelen v Netherlands* (1997) 25 EHRR 647.

[118] *Van Mechelen v Netherlands* (1997) 25 EHRR 647 at 674–675 (paras 59 and 62).

[10.52] The implication it seems is that anonymous sources may play a limited role in the investigative and trial processes. The European Court has stressed that its function in such cases is not to second-guess the national courts' assessment of the necessity of non-disclosure but rather to ensure that the national decision-making procedure complied with the requirements of adversarial proceedings and adequately protected the interests of the accused.[119] States may conceal the identity of certain witnesses provided that anonymity is justified (for example, by virtue of a genuine fear of witness intimidation) and the defence is given adequate opportunity to challenge their evidence. It follows that the focus of the court's analysis is the procedures the national authorities have in place to counterbalance the detriment to the defence.

[10.53] In *Doorson v Netherlands*,[120] for example, the applicant was convicted of drug-related offences and the European Court concluded that the authorities were justified in preserving the anonymity of the witnesses in question in the face of threats of violence from drug dealers.[121] Doorson's case was distinguishable from that of Kostovski because although the use of anonymous witnesses presented difficulties for the defence, they were counterbalanced by a procedure at the appeals stage conducted by an investigating judge. Counsel for the defence was not only present at this hearing but entitled to ask any question of the witness other than a question that might lead to the disclosure of the witness's identity.[122] Procedural variations have met with the court's approval in a number of cases against the United Kingdom arising out of assertions of public interest immunity. For example, in *PH and JH v United Kingdom*,[123] the rights of the applicant were found not to have been infringed where the withholding of information took the form of a refusal on the part of a police officer to answer certain questions during cross-examination. Following the refusal, the trial judge had put the questions to the witness in the confidential confines of chambers. On the basis of that *ex parte* exchange, the judge had concluded that some of the answers should not be disclosed in open court.

---

[119] *Dowsett v United Kingdom* (2004) 38 EHRR 41 at 858. See also *Rowe and Davis v United Kingdom* (2000) 30 EHRR 1 (violation where prosecution had withheld relevant evidence without notifying the judge); *Jasper v United Kingdom* (2000) 30 EHRR 441 at 458 (para 55) and *Fitt v United Kingdom* (2000) 30 EHRR 480 at 511–12 (para 48) (no violation where the material withheld on grounds of public interest immunity formed no part of the prosecution's case and was not put to the jury).

[120] *Doorson v Netherlands* (1996) 22 EHRR 330.

[121] But see *Krasniki v Czech Republic* (App No 51277/99, judgment of 28 February 2006), para 83 where the court was not satisfied that preserving the anonymity of the witness was a justifiable encroachment of the rights of the defence.

[122] *Krasniki v Czech Republic* (App No 51277/99, judgment of 28 February 2006) at 359 (para 73).

[123] *PH and JH v United Kingdom* (2008) 46 EHRR 51.

[10.54] Even assuming that counterbalancing procedures are sufficient to compensate for the detriment anonymous witnesses impose on the defence, the Strasbourg jurisprudence contains the additional safeguard that a conviction should never be based either solely or 'to a decisive extent' on anonymous statements.[124] In *Taal v Estonia*,[125] for example, the court held that the applicant's trial had been unfair because his conviction on a charge of extortion had been based to a decisive extent on statements of witnesses he had been unable to question at trial.[126] Similarly, the United Kingdom was found to have violated the Convention in *Edwards and Lewis v United Kingdom*,[127] where the undisclosed material related to an issue of fact at trial, namely, whether the applicants had been entrapped by undercover police officers and informers into committing the offences for which they were charged. Without access to this material, the defence was impaired in its ability to argue an issue which had the potential to determine the outcome of the trial.[128]

[10.55] Indeed, it is striking that in several cases in which the court has determined that the requirements of art 6 had been met, it has rested its determination on a combination of these factors: the sufficiency of the procedural accommodation and the limited use the national authorities made of the confidential information. In *Jasper v United Kingdom*[129] and *Fitt v United Kingdom*,[130] decided on the same day, a bare majority of the court found no violation of the Convention where the withholding of information had been accompanied by procedural safeguards and the material in question formed no part of the evidence put to the jury.[131]

---

124 *Doorson v Netherlands* (1996) 22 EHRR 330, para 76. On the facts of the case itself, the court was satisfied that the national court of appeal had rested its determination on additional albeit limited evidence: 340–341 and 360–361 (paras 34 and 78).

125 *Taal v Estonia* (App No 13249/02, judgment of 22 November 2005).

126 *Taal v Estonia* (App No 13249/02, judgment of 22 November 2005), para 33. The prosecution alleged that the applicant had made telephone calls threatening to explode a bomb in a supermarket if his demands for a sum of money were not met. The case file presented to the court included the statements of witnesses, one of whom was anonymous, purporting to identify the applicant, together with tape recordings of various phone calls. When the witnesses failed to appear, the court proceeded to convict the applicant on the basis of the information contained in the case file. See also *Luca v Italy* (2003) 36 EHRR 46, para 43 (finding a violation); *Birutis and Others v Lithuania* (App Nos 47698/99 and 48115/99, judgment of 28 March 2002) (finding a violation); *Mild and Virtanen v Finland* (App Nos 39481/98 and 40227/98, judgment of 26 July 2005) (finding no violation); *Krasniki v Czech Republic* (App No 51277/99, judgment of 28 February 2006), para 84 (finding a violation).

127 *Edwards and Lewis v United Kingdom* (2005) 40 EHRR 24.

128 *Edwards and Lewis v United Kingdom* (2005) 40 EHRR 24 at 59 (para 46).

129 *Jasper v United Kingdom* (2000) 30 EHRR 441.

130 *Fitt v United Kingdom* (2000) 30 EHRR 480.

131 With respect to the procedural safeguards, the court noted that the issue of disclosure was kept under assessment by the trial judge at all times, (contd.../)

The ECHR in the Irish Courts

[10.56] In *People (DPP) v Kelly*,[132] the Supreme Court was asked to analyse belief evidence through the prism of the Constitution but not that of the ECHR. Other than acknowledging that the parties had cited Strasbourg case law, the majority judgment of Geoghegan J makes no mention of the Convention. The reasoning and result reached by Fennelly J is similarly grounded in an analysis of Article 38.1 of the Constitution. Nevertheless, his judgment includes an examination of art 6(3) of the Convention and cases such as *Kostovski* and *Doorson*. Fennelly J concluded that 'all of the authorities cited from all the relevant jurisdictions demonstrate that there is an inescapable obligation on the courts to guarantee the overall fairness of a trial'.[133] The claim of privilege had the potential for unfairness in this case because it infringed the normal right of the accused to have access to the material that underlay the belief expressed. Even so, Fennelly J accepted that the 'compelling circumstances' identified by the respondent DPP in support of belief evidence constituted 'sufficient justification for its introduction, while, at the same time, demonstrating a concern to respect such necessary limitations'.[134] Thus, the implication is that the use of belief evidence in *Kelly* was consistent with the Convention standard of a trial that is fair overall.

[10.57] The compatibility of belief evidence with the Convention's fair trial guarantee has been considered by the Irish courts on a number of occasions. Perhaps the most in-depth examination was conducted by the Special Criminal Court in *People (DPP) v Binead and Donoghue*,[135] discussed at para **10.47**. One of the strands of evidence presented by the prosecution at trial was the testimony of a chief superintendent that he believed that the two accused were members of the IRA at the material time. Under cross-examination, the chief superintendent indicated that this belief was based on oral and written communications from

---

131 (contd.../) the trial judge was fully versed in the evidence and was in a position to monitor its relevance to the defence both before and during the trial, and the defence was kept informed and permitted to make submissions to the court and participate in the decision-making process as far as possible without revealing the material which the prosecution sought to keep secret: *Jasper v United Kingdom* (2000) 30 EHRR 441 at 485 (paras 54 and 56), *Fitt v United Kingdom* (2000) 30 EHRR 480 at 511–512 (paras 47–49). In *Fitt*, the defence was afforded the additional safeguard of a summary of the material in question. The dissenting judges were not satisfied that the procedures in question afforded the applicants an adequate opportunity to make informed submissions on the issue of non-disclosure. An alternative procedure canvassed by the dissenters was the possibility of *ex parte* applications made to a judge other than the trial judge. A procedure of this kind would avoid the trial judge seeing the material and possibly having to discount it at a later stage in the proceedings. See dissenting opinions of Judges Palm, Fischbach, Vajic, Thonassen, Tsatsa-Nikolovska and Traja.

132 *People (DPP) v Kelly* [2006] 3 IR 115.

133 *People (DPP) v Kelly* [2006] 3 IR 115 at 146.

134 *People (DPP) v Kelly* [2006] 3 IR 115 at 146–147.

135 *People (DPP) v Binead and Donoghue* (18 November 2004, unreported) SCC.

sources both within and outside the gardaí. He claimed privilege in respect of those matters on the ground that disclosure of his sources would endanger lives and hamper ongoing activities relating to State security. The accused argued that they would be deprived of a fair trial if they were not permitted to know the source of the witness's belief. In particular, denying the defence an opportunity to investigate whether or not there was any reasonable basis for the belief infringed the presumption of innocence and the principle of equality of arms. The court stated:

> '[I]f no enquiry whatsoever is made into the basis of Chief Superintendent Kelly's belief, there is substance to the defence argument that there is an imbalance in the trial in favour of the prosecution and an absence of equality of arms which could be interpreted as a lack of fairness insofar as the accused are concerned. The court is also of the view that art 6 of the European Convention on Human Rights, which is now part of the domestic law in this country, does augment the traditional rights of an accused person in the course of his/her trial, in that, it is now the law that one of their minimum rights is the right to examine and *have examined* [the emphasis is that of the court] witnesses against them. In the context of this case, this right would appear to the court to include the right to have Chief Superintendent Kelly examined with regard to the basis for this belief.'[136]

However, the court accepted that informer privilege 'is still very much a part of the law of this country'[137] and that the chief superintendent could not be compelled to disclose the identity of persons who are sources of information or, indeed, matters that would endanger State security.[138] The prosecution made available to the court documentation containing some of the information that had influenced the chief superintendent in forming his opinion. The court was satisfied that the information constituted an adequate and reliable basis for the chief superintendent's opinion and, furthermore, that it would not assist the accused in establishing their innocence.[139]

[10.58] The Court of Criminal Appeal has upheld the use of belief evidence against the yardstick of the Convention in a number of cases[140] and declined invitations to refer the matter back to the Supreme Court.[141] The intriguing

[136] *People (DPP) v Binead and Donoghue* (18 November 2004, unreported) SCC at p 21.

[137] *People (DPP) v Binead and Donoghue* (18 November 2004, unreported) SCC at p 21.

[138] *People (DPP) v Binead and Donoghue* (18 November 2004, unreported) SCC at p 21.

[139] *People (DPP) v Binead and Donohue* (18 November 2004, unreported) SCC at p 22. This decision was affirmed by the Court of Criminal Appeal: *People (DPP) v Donoghue* [2007] IECCA 97 citing the CCA's earlier opinion reported as *People (DPP) v Binead* [2007] 1 IR 374 (refusing an application for leave to appeal).

[140] *People (DPP) v Matthews* [2007] 2 IR 169; *People (DPP) v Donoghue* [2007] IECCA 97; *People (DPP) v Binead* [2007] 1 IR 374; *DPP v Vincent Kelly* [2007] IECCA 110, 6 December 2007) p 9.

[141] *People (DPP) v Donohue* [2007] IECCA 97 (26 October 2007) p 3; *DPP v Matthews* [2007] IECCA 23 (29 March 2007) p 6; *DPP v Vincent Kelly* [2007] IECCA 110 (6 December 2007) p 9.

question of the compatibility of belief evidence with the Convention may be less straightforward than the outcome of these cases implies. There are broad similarities between the European Court's review under art 6 of the Convention and the Supreme Court's analysis under Article 38.1 of the Constitution. Nevertheless, one is not a mirror-image of the other. There is no Strasbourg precedent on all-fours with belief evidence in general much less belief evidence coupled with informer privilege in particular. The case law makes plain that the use of hearsay statements is permissible provided that the defence has an opportunity to test the evidence at some stage in the proceedings. Of course, in cases such as *Kelly*, the prosecution is not seeking to admit third party out-of-court statements as evidence but rather to incorporate them indirectly into the witness's in-court opinion. The scenario may be factually distinct from cases like *Van Mechelen* and *Doorson* but it raises the same fundamental problem of denying the defence an adequate opportunity to test the evidence. Irish law recognises that expert witnesses may proffer opinions and that they may draw on hearsay when so doing. But belief evidence under s 3(2) is not expert evidence in the classic sense but rather evidence in the form of non-scientific opinion that cannot be empirically validated and that incorporates hearsay in an *ad hoc*, unpredictable fashion. In any event, expert evidence is subject to the self-same safeguard that it be open to challenge by the other side. Moreover, whereas a party can respond to expert evidence by tendering its own expert witness, s 3(2) obviously does not bestow on the defence the right to tender an expert witness to rebut the belief of the chief superintendent.

[10.59] It is reasonably clear that Irish law and practice under s 3(2) conforms to the expectations of the European Court up to a point. The European Court and the Irish Supreme Court are in accord that an evidentiary shortcut such as the use of belief evidence in tandem with informer privilege constitutes a restriction on the rights to which an accused is normally entitled but equally that such a restriction is in principle permissible provided that it is strictly necessary. But can it be said that the restrictions on the right to cross-examination that were upheld in *Kelly* represent the least restrictive means of achieving the legitimate State objectives of protecting lives and preserving security? The outcome in *Kelly* was influenced in large measure by the Supreme Court's perception that preserving informer privilege was necessary in the exceptional context of the offences against the State regime.[142] But the notion of strict necessity is also manifest in the case law requirement of a procedure whereby the trial judge can enquire into the basis for the witness's belief and, specifically, the justification for maintaining the anonymity of sources in a particular instance.

[142] That said, the judgments eloquently explain the justification for the introduction of s 3(2) in 1972 without engaging the question whether the provision remains strictly necessary some three decades following its enactment and several years after the formal cessation of hostilities in Northern Ireland. For further discussion see Heffernan, 'Evidence and National Security: 'Belief Evidence' in the Irish Special Criminal Court' (2009) Eur Pub L 65 at 84.

[10.60] The Irish procedure for asserting claims of informer privilege incorporates certain safeguards of which the European Court has approved, namely, it assigns to the trial court a supervisory role and enables the defence to make submissions and participate up to the point of revealing the protected information. Indeed, one might go further and predict that the European Court would look favourably on the approach endorsed by the Supreme Court in *Ward v Special Criminal Court* and the procedure applied by the Special Criminal Court in *People (DPP) v Binead and Donoghue* whereby privileged information in documentary form was submitted to the court so that it could peruse and independently assess the cogency of the claim for confidentiality.

[10.61] The conundrum is embodied in a case such as *Kelly* where the confidential information is not reduced to writing and the Irish courts respond to the assertion of privilege by restricting the defence's right to cross-examine the witness. Irish practice stops short of the kind of counterbalancing procedures utilised in English practice such as special advocates[143] and the questioning of witnesses by the judge in chambers.[144] In the absence of an equivalent procedure, it is doubtful whether Irish law conforms to the requirements of art 6(3). Although in *Kelly* the Supreme Court held that the existing procedure comports with the constitutional fair trial guarantee and the Court of Criminal Appeal has subsequently interpreted that holding as supporting the same conclusion with respect to the Convention. Nevertheless, the question whether Irish law and practice provides an adequate counterbalance to the restriction on the rights of the defence may be more complicated than the recent case law would suggest and certainly warrants close scrutiny.

[10.62] Even if the procedure were deemed sufficient, an accused may be denied a fair trial if the evidentiary restriction has a direct bearing on the outcome of the proceedings. In several of the Strasbourg cases discussed above, restrictions were held not to violate the Convention because the material that was withheld from the defence was not used as evidence at trial. The same cannot be said of any case involving a statement of belief under s 3(2) which, by its very design, is offered as direct proof of the offence charged. It seems clear that a trial in which belief evidence based on privileged information constituted the sole basis on which an accused was convicted of membership of an unlawful organisation would not be a fair trial within the meaning of art 6. Although the Irish courts have recognised that s 3(2) does not bar a conviction in such circumstances, it is unlikely that the issue will reach the European Court given the Special Criminal Court's current preference for corroboration. A more likely

---

143 See *R v H and Others* [2004] 2 WLR 335.

144 *PG and JH v United Kingdom* (2008) 46 EHRR 51. The absence of juries in the Special Criminal Court may pose an additional obstacle to the extent that the court may view protected information for the purpose of assessing the claim of privilege and then be required to discount it when weighing the evidence as finder of fact.

prospect would be a case in which the corroborative evidence mustered by the prosecution lends such negligible support that the conviction rests 'to a decisive extent' on the untested belief evidence.[145] Finally, whereas the Irish law governing informer privilege has been dominated by the context of belief evidence, it is important to consider the ramifications of the case law for proceedings involving ordinary as opposed to extraordinary offences.

[145] For example, how might the European Court respond to a scenario in which an applicant was convicted of membership of an unlawful organisation and the prosecution's evidence comprised belief evidence corroborated by inferences drawn from the applicant's silence during custodial questioning? See, eg, *People (DPP) v Binead* [2007] 1 IR 374.

Chapter 11

Pre-trial Legal Advice

Introduction

[11.01] This chapter considers various issues surrounding access to legal advice and questions of privilege in the specific context of pre-trial criminal procedure.[1] The right of a suspect to consult with a lawyer while detained in custody has been recognised as implicit in the Constitution and the European Convention on Human Rights (ECHR) and is firmly established in statute and case law. It is a right of 'reasonable' access to legal advice and the discussion addresses the nature and scope of the right and the import of this qualification. The chapter then explores the application of the right to the procedures for the drawing of inferences at trial from an accused's silence in response to custodial questioning introduced by the Criminal Justice Act 2007. Particular emphasis is placed on the implications of inference-drawing procedures for legal professional privilege.

The Right of Access to Pre-Trial Legal Advice

[11.02] Of the various constitutional rights that may trigger the application of the exclusionary rule in relation to evidence gathered during the course of custodial detention, the right of reasonable access to a lawyer is particularly significant in practice.[2] Even assuming that a suspect has been made aware of the panoply of rights to which she is entitled, the provision of independent, professional legal advice may have a crucial bearing on her understanding of the nature and extent of those rights and her strategy in respect of custodial questioning.[3] Legal advice may assist the suspect in navigating the complex terrain of the law relating to the making of statements and the drawing of inferences from silence and the rules governing the gathering of forensic scientific evidence. More broadly, the safeguard of legal advice goes some way

1 The chapter reproduces in part Heffernan, 'The Right to Legal Advice, Reasonable Access and the Remedy of Excluding Evidence' (2011) 1 Crim L & Proc Rev (forthcoming).

2 See generally O'Malley, *The Criminal Process* (Thomson Round Hall, 2009) ch 8; Conway, Daly and Schweppe, *Irish Criminal Justice: Theory, Process and Procedure* (Clarus Press, 2010) paras 3.46–3.75; Walsh, *Criminal Procedure* (Thomson Round Hall, 2002) ch 5D and ch 11; Hogan and Whyte, *JM Kelly: The Irish Constitution* (4th edn, Bloomsbury Professional, 2004) para 6.5.152 *et seq*; Wycherley, 'Custodial Legal Advice in Ireland – Lessons from England and Wales' Pt 1 (2010) 28 ILT 170 and Pt II (2010) 28 ILT 190.

3 *People (DPP) v Healy* [1990] 2 IR 73, 81, [1990] ILRM 313 (*per* Finlay CJ).

towards redressing the inherent imbalance of power in the relationship between the suspect and the gardaí.[4]

[11.03] The right of a suspect in custodial detention to consult a solicitor is a relatively modern ingredient in our system of criminal justice. Historically, the gardaí were prohibited from detaining persons purely for the purposes of interrogation or obtaining evidence in relation to the commission of ordinary offences. Whereas the courts recognised a right of access to legal advice in the limited context of offences against the State,[5] it was only with the introduction of the broader legislative foundation for custodial questioning in the Criminal Justice Act 1984 that the right took centre-stage. The Oireachtas placed the right of access to a lawyer on a statutory footing in s 5[6] but, more dramatically, the Supreme Court recognised the right's implicit constitutional credentials some six years later in the seminal case of *People (DPP) v Healy.*[7] Finlay CJ stated:

> '... I am driven to the conclusion that such an important and fundamental standard of fairness in the administration of justice as the right of access to a lawyer must be deemed to be constitutional in its origin, and that to classify it as merely legal would be to undermine its importance and the completeness of the protection of it which the courts are obliged to give.'[8]

[11.04] A point of enormous practical significance inherent in the 'completeness' of the constitutional protection is the fact that a deliberate and conscious breach of the right of access to legal advice will trigger the remedy of the exclusion of evidence obtained as a result, in the absence of any extraordinary excluding circumstances.[9]

---

4 *Magee v United Kingdom* (2001) 31 EHRR 822, 835.

5 Detention for questioning prior to charge was permissible only under s 30 of the Offences Against the State Act 1939. See, eg, *Re Emergency Powers Bill 1976* [1977] IR 159, 173; *People (DPP) v Madden* [1977] IR 336; Keane, 'Detention Without Charge and the Criminal Justice (Drug Trafficking) Act 1996' (1997) 7(1) ICLJ 1.

6 See also regs 8 and 9 of the Criminal Justice Act 1984 (Treatment of Persons in Custody in Garda Síochána Stations) Regulations 1987 (SI 119/1987).

7 *People (DPP) v Healy* [1990] 2 IR 73, [1990] ILRM 313.

8 *People (DPP) v Healy* [1990] 2 IR 73 at 81. The judgment does not cite any particular provision of the Constitution from which the right might be implied. It might potentially derive from the guarantee of a criminal trial in due course of law in Art 38.1 and the corresponding provision in Art 40.3 for fair procedures and protection against self incrimination in quasi-criminal proceedings. Another reason for sourcing the right in Art 40.3 is the possibility that access to a lawyer may avert the risk that a suspect will be subjected to physical or psychological coercion. Arguably, the right may be a necessary incident of other constitutional rights such as the right to liberty which is expressly recognised in Art 40.4.1°.

9 *People (AG) v O'Brien* [1965] IR 142; *People (DPP) v Kenny* [1990] 1 IR 110. For recent consideration of the application of the exclusionary rule in this context see *DPP v AD* [2008] IECCA 101 (25 July 2008); *DPP v McCrea* [2009] IEHC 39 (28 January 2009) (Edwards J), [2010] IESC 60 (9 December 2010); *DPP v Creed* [2009] IECCA 95 (31 July 2009). For analysis see Heffernan, 'The Right to Legal Advice, Reasonable Access and the Remedy of Excluding Evidence' (2011) 1 Crim L & Proc Rev (forthcoming).

[11.05] The constitutional protection afforded to the right of access to a lawyer is mirrored by the fair trial guarantee of the ECHR. As the European Court of Human Rights observed in *Murray v United Kingdom*, a right of access to pre-trial legal assistance is implicit in art 6:

> 'National laws may attach consequences to the attitude of an accused at the initial stages of police interrogation which are decisive for the prospects of the defence in any subsequent criminal proceedings. In such circumstances Article 6 will normally require that the accused be allowed to benefit from the assistance of a lawyer already at the initial stages of police interrogation.'[10]

REASONABLE ACCESS

[11.06] Despite the symbolism associated with access to legal advice, the contours of the right are not drawn with precision. Over the years, a lack of coherence in the Irish case law has led to uncertainty over its scope and application.

The right of access to legal advice is one of reasonable access only and the courts have expended considerable energy teasing out the implications of this limitation. In *People (DPP) v Madden*, the Court of Criminal Appeal advocated a flexible, contextual approach to the concept of reasonable access:

> '... the word 'reasonable' must be construed having regard to all the circumstances of each individual case and, in particular, as to the time at which access is requested and the availability of the legal adviser or advisers sought.'[11]

The court went on to endorse the traditional view that the gardaí were not obliged to proffer the assistance of a lawyer where the suspect had not expressly requested it. This interpretation of the right of access to legal advice was extremely restrictive; because at that time the gardaí were not required by law to inform a suspect of his right of access to legal advice, there could be no meaningful enjoyment of the right unless the suspect was independently aware of his entitlement and expressly invoked it.[12]

[11.07] The position post-*Healy* is considerably more protective in the sense that the right of a suspect to be informed of his right of access to legal advice is no longer in doubt.[13] However, considerable uncertainty lingers over the additional

---

10 *Murray v United Kingdom* (1996) 22 EHRR 29 at 66, para 63.

11 *People (DPP) v Madden* [1977] IR 336 at 355.

12 *People (DPP) v Madden* [1977] IR 336 at 356. See also *People (DPP) v Farrell* [1978] IR 13; *People (DPP) v Pringle* (1981) 2 Frewen 57.

35 Section 5(1) of the Criminal Justice Act 1984 provides that where a person not below 17 years of age is detained in a garda station pursuant to the Act, the member in charge 'shall inform him or cause him to be informed without delay that he is entitled to consult a solicitor'. The self same duty applies by virtue of s 5(2) where the detained person is less than 17 years of age but is copper fastened by an obligation to inform or cause to be informed 'as soon as practicable' a parent or guardian of the fact and place of detention as well as the entitlement to consult a solicitor. (contd.../)

steps, if any, the gardaí must take to facilitate access.[14] This uncertainty in our domestic law is echoed to an extent by the jurisprudence of the European Court of Human Rights which recognises that the right may be restricted 'for good cause'.[15] The Convention analysis involves not the application of precisely defined rules but rather case-by-case assessment of whether a cited restriction on the right of access has had the effect of depriving a particular accused of a fair hearing.[16]

[11.08] Section 5 of the 1984 Act provides that if, having been informed of his right, the suspect asks to consult with a solicitor, the member in charge of the garda station 'shall cause the solicitor ... to be notified as soon as practicable'.[17] It seems that the obligation resting on the gardaí arises only where, having been informed of the right, the suspect chooses to exercise it. Even then, the gardaí will have fulfilled their obligation where they have made reasonable efforts to facilitate access. The standard set out in s 5 is replicated in the Custody Regulations[18] which specify further that the right is one of reasonable access 'to a solicitor of [the suspect's] choice'.[19] Whether access to a named solicitor can be secured will depend upon the practical constraint of the solicitor's availability.[20] Nevertheless, the regulations emphasise that difficulties in facilitating a consultation with a solicitor of choice will not obviate the need for the gardaí to take other steps to vindicate the right:

> 'if the solicitor ... cannot be contacted within a reasonable time or if the solicitor is unable or unwilling to attend at the station, the person shall be given an opportunity to ask for another solicitor ... and, if the person asks for another solicitor ... the member in charge shall notify or cause to be notified that other solicitor .. accordingly as soon as practicable.'[21]

[11.09] A breach of this or any other relevant provision of the Custody Regulations will not necessarily lead to the exclusion of any evidence obtained on foot of the breach. Section 7(3) of the Criminal Justice Act 1984 expressly

---

13 (\...contd) Regulation 8(1) of the Custody Regulations 1987 requires the member in charge to explain or cause to be explained to the arrested person that, if she does not wish to exercise the right immediately, she will not be precluded from doing so at a later time. These protections have since been extended to detention pursuant to other statutory powers.

14 The principal focus in this chapter is the concept of reasonable access in the context of inference-drawing procedures. For a discussion of other aspects of the subject see Heffernan, 'The Right to Legal Advice, Reasonable Access and the Remedy of Excluding Evidence' (2011) 1 Crim L & Proc Rev (forthcoming).

15 *Murray v United Kingdom* (1996) 22 EHRR 29 at 66, para 63.

16 *Murray v United Kingdom* (1996) 22 EHRR 29 at 66, para 63.

17 Section 5(1) and, in the case of detainees under 17 years of age, s 5(2).

18 Regulation 9(2)(a)(i).

19 Regulation 11(1).

20 *DPP v McCrea* [2010] IESC 60 (9 December 2010) pp 7–8 (*per* Hardiman J).

21 Regulation 9(2)(a)(ii).

states that a failure on the part of any member of the gardaí to observe any provision of the regulations shall not 'of itself affect ... the admissibility in evidence of any statement made by him'. In *DPP v Spratt*, O'Hanlon J construed the subsection to mean that non-compliance with the regulations would not result in the automatic exclusion from evidence of 'all that was done and said while the accused person was in custody'.[22] Subsequent courts have confirmed the view that in every case it is a matter for the trial judge to adjudicate on the impact of non-compliance on the prosecution's evidence.[23] One might analyse the issue through an alternative lens and say that evidence procured as a result of a breach of the regulations may be classified as unlawfully obtained (as opposed to unconstitutionally obtained) with the consequence that its admissibility is a matter for the discretion of the trial judge guided by the principles set down by Kingsmill Moore J in *People (AG) v O'Brien.*[24] Of course, where a suspect has made one or more statements in response to custodial questioning, non-compliance with the regulations may be a factor in the trial court's general assessment of whether the statements were voluntary and the product of fair procedures in the totality of the circumstances of the case.[25]

[11.10] While s 5 of the 1984 Act and the Custody Regulations provide some guidance on the right of access to legal advice, neither legislative text resolves authoritatively the myriad issues surrounding the application of the right of reasonable access to legal advice. In a series of cases, the Superior Courts have sought to fill this lacuna by mapping the specific contours of the right.

IMMEDIATE ACCESS FOLLOWING THE SOLICITOR'S ARRIVAL

[11.11] In *Healy*,[26] the respondent was arrested under s 30 of the Offences Against the State Act 1939 on suspicion of unlawful possession of firearms and interviewed at a garda station for several hours. While the respondent was in the course of giving a formal statement to the gardaí, a solicitor retained by his family arrived at the station and requested access to the respondent. The solicitor was informed by the gardaí that the respondent was making a statement and, over his objections, the solicitor was denied access to the respondent until the statement had been completed. The significance of the statement was ultimately profound in that it constituted the only evidence tendered against the respondent at his trial before the Central Criminal Court. The detective superintendent in charge of the investigation testified that he had been aware

22 *DPP v Spratt* [1995] 1 IR 585, 591 [1995] 2 ILRM 117. The judgment continued: 'It appears to be left to the court of trial to adjudicate in every case as to the impact the non compliance with the regulations should have on the case for the prosecution'.

23 See, eg, *People (DPP) v Darcy* (29 July 1997, unreported) CCA.

24 *People (AG) v O'Brien* [1965] IR 142.

25 *People (DPP) v Shaw* [1982] IR 1.

26 *People (DPP) v Healy* [1990] 2 IR 73, [1990] ILRM 313.

that the respondent was in the process of making a statement but that he had not permitted him immediate access to the solicitor because it would have been bad manners to interrupt the interview. The garda officers who had been taking the respondent's statement had not been aware of the solicitor's arrival at the station. The trial judge excluded the statement on the basis that it had been unlawfully obtained. The respondent had been denied his right of instant access to his solicitor and the court could not be satisfied that any incriminating admissions had been made prior to that denial.

[11.12] An appeal by the DPP against the trial judge's decision to direct the jury to acquit was dismissed by a unanimous Supreme Court. While the decision in *Healy* is renowned principally for its landmark elevation of the right of access to legal advice to the constitutional plain, the decision shed instructive light on the concept of reasonable access to legal advice. Finlay CJ explained:

> 'A right of reasonable access to a solicitor in a detained person, I am satisfied, means, in the event of the arrival of a solicitor at a Garda station in which a person is detained, immediate right of that person to be told of the arrival and, if he requests it, immediate access. The only thing that could justify the postponement of informing the detained person of the arrival of the solicitor or of immediately complying with a request made by the detained person when so informed, for access to him, would be reasons which objectively viewed from the point of view of the interest or welfare of the detained person, would be viewed by the court as being valid.'[27]

The Chief Justice expressly rejected the DPP's suggestion that the fact that a detained person was in the course of making a statement could possibly be an objectively valid reason for postponing at least informing him of the solicitor's arrival and asking him whether he wished to suspend the making of the statement in order to consult with the solicitor.[28] This was precisely the course of action which should have been followed in *Healy*.

[11.13] The judgment in *Healy* was delivered during a period in which the Supreme Court was developing the exclusionary rule in relation to unconstitutionally obtained evidence set down in *People (AG) v O'Brien*.[29] The acknowledgement in *Healy* that the right of access to legal advice is constitutional in status was significant in this context because of the implication that a breach of the right would lead to the exclusion of evidence obtained proximate to that breach. However, the Supreme Court also availed of the opportunity to clarify another disputed aspect of the rule, namely, the requirement that the breach of the suspect's rights be 'conscious and deliberate'. Finlay CJ made plain his view that the requirement must be objectively defined:

---

27 *People (DPP) v Healy* [1990] 2 IR 73 at 81.

28 *People (DPP) v Healy* [1990] 2 IR 73 at 81.

29 *People (AG) v O'Brien* [1965] IR 142.

> 'I reject completely the submission made on behalf of the Director of Public Prosecutions that the test to be applied to the question of reasonable access is a subjective test in the mind of the jailer of the detained person. The test is whether the superintendent's refusal of access was a conscious and deliberate act, as it clearly was. The fact that he may not have appreciated that his refusal was a breach of the respondent's constitutional right is immaterial.'[30]

Finlay CJ characterised the failure to inform the respondent of the presence of the solicitor and the postponement of access until after the statement was completed as both a deliberate and conscious violation of the respondent's constitutional right of access to legal advice and 'a complete failure to observe reasonable standards of fairness in the procedure of his interrogation'.[31]

Questioning Prior to Access

[11.14] The judgment in *Healy* clarified an important aspect of the right of reasonable access: as soon as a solicitor arrives at the garda station, the suspect has the right to be informed and to consult with the solicitor immediately should she wish to do so. However, the duty resting on the gardaí prior to the arrival of the solicitor at the station remained unresolved. A decade later, in *People (DPP) v Buck*,[32] the Supreme Court was asked to elucidate the steps the gardaí must take when a suspect requests access to a solicitor and, furthermore, the licence, if any, the gardaí enjoy to question the suspect prior to the solicitor's arrival at the station.

[11.15] The appellant was arrested on the afternoon of Sunday 14 July 1996 and detained in Cahir garda station, County Tipperary, in connection with the murder of a man. During the course of garda questioning, the appellant admitted that he had engaged in drug transactions with the deceased but denied any involvement in his death. He requested access to a solicitor and indicated that he did not wish to answer any questions. The member in charge tried unsuccessfully to contact two solicitors nominated by the appellant in turn and thereafter to contact other solicitors and the gardaí continued to question the appellant while these attempts were ongoing. A solicitor who was contacted that evening arrived at the garda station at 8.33pm but after a consultation he informed the gardaí that he would not be representing the appellant.

[11.16] Later that evening and again the following morning the appellant made inculpatory statements to the gardaí. At the appellant's trial for murder before the Central Criminal Court, the judge admitted these statements into evidence over the objections of the defence. The trial judge also accepted the evidence of the member in charge that it had been difficult to contact a solicitor, it having

30 *People (DPP) v Healy* [1990] 2 IR 73 at 81.

31 *People (DPP) v Healy* [1990] 2 IR 73 at 82.

32 *People (DPP) v Buck* [2002] 2 IR 268.

been a Sunday afternoon in Summer and there having been a large sporting event on in the area, and the evidence of the solicitor that he had advised the appellant that he was not required to make a statement. An appeal against the appellant's conviction was dismissed by the Court of Criminal Appeal which certified the following point of law of exceptional importance for the consideration of the Supreme Court: where the gardaí arrest a person at a time and in circumstances where it is likely that there will be difficulty in contacting a solicitor, does the questioning of the arrested person, before he has had access to a solicitor but after he had sought such access, constitute a conscious and deliberate violation of his constitutional rights rendering inadmissible any inculpatory statement made?

[11.17] It was the view of Keane CJ that the right of access to a solicitor could not be said to have necessarily been denied in circumstances such as these. He recalled the ruling of Finlay CJ in *Healy* which implied that an incriminating statement made *prior* to the arrival of the solicitor would have been admissible since, at that point, there would have been neither a deliberate and conscious violation of the accused's right nor a breach of fair procedures requiring the exclusion of the statement.[33] Keane CJ further distilled from *Healy* the important caveat that a breach of the right of access to a solicitor would render a statement inadmissible only where the two events (the beach of the right and the obtaining of the statement) were causatively linked.[34]

[11.18] Keane CJ eschewed the application of 'a rigid exclusionary rule that would treat such statements as inadmissible without any regard to the circumstances prevailing in the particular case'.[35] The Chief Justice preferred to place the evidentiary determination firmly in the hands of the trial judge:

> 'It would also seem to me that, where a person being detained under a statutory provision asks for a solicitor to be present and the gardaí make *bona fide* attempts to comply with that request, the admissibility of any incriminating statement made by the person concerned before the arrival of the solicitor should be decided by the trial judge as a matter of discretion ... based on considerations of fairness to the accused and public policy.'[36]

As a vehicle for the elucidation of the concept of reasonable access to legal advice, the judgment is noteworthy in two respects. First, where a suspect requests access, the gardaí are obliged to make *bona fide*, reasonable attempts to secure the presence of a solicitor. The use by Keane CJ of both terms ('*bona fide*' and 'reasonable') at different points in the judgment suggests that the standard should be measured by an objective and not merely a subjective

[33] *People (DPP) v Buck* [2002] 2 IR 268, 279–280.

[34] *People (DPP) v Buck* [2002] 2 IR 268 at 280.

[35] *People (DPP) v Buck* [2002] 2 IR 268 at 280.

[36] *People (DPP) v Buck* [2002] 2 IR 268 at 281.

yardstick.[37] Whether the standard has been met or not is a matter for the trial judge to determine first and foremost on an examination of the facts of the particular case. Thus, in *Buck*, the Supreme Court accepted the trial judge's finding that the gardaí had met their obligations by making reasonable attempts to contact the solicitor nominated by the appellant and, when he proved unavailable to act, seeking to obtain the services of other solicitors.

[11.19] The second significant gloss on the right of reasonable access relates to the propriety of questioning a suspect after access has been requested but before the arrival of the solicitor at the station. The Custody Regulations presaged this issue with the inclusion of a provision restraining the taking of a formal statement during this time period. Regulation 12(6) states:

> 'Where an arrested person asks for a solicitor, he shall not be asked to make a written statement in relation to an offence until a reasonable time for the attendance of the solicitor has elapsed.'

Nevertheless, the regulations place no restraint on the posing of questions or the recording of oral answers.[38]

[11.20] *Buck* suggests that there is nothing to prevent the gardaí from proceeding with an interview provided that they are engaging in *bona fide* efforts to contact a solicitor and thereby to facilitate consultation.[39] Keane CJ couched the question in terms of whether at the time of questioning there has been a deliberate and conscious violation of the suspect's constitutional rights that would require the exclusion at trial of any statement made.[40] It follows that provided the gardaí are making *bona fide* attempts to secure the presence of a solicitor, no question of a deliberate and conscious breach of the right of reasonable access to legal advice arises.

[11.21] The *bona fide* standard set in *Buck* was applied by the Central Criminal Court in *People (DPP) v O'Brien.*[41] Following his arrest and detention in Pearse Street garda station in Dublin City Centre, the appellant requested access to legal advice. He did not request the presence of any particular solicitor and the gardaí contacted a busy solo practitioner whose offices were in the far suburb of

---

37 This is consistent with the prevailing judicial understanding of the phrase 'deliberate and conscious breach' for the purposes of the exclusionary rule. See, eg, *People (DPP) v Healy* [1990] 2 IR 73, 81.

38 Note the view of Walsh J in his dissenting judgment in *People (DPP) v Conroy* [1986] IR 460, 479 that the practice of the gardaí pressing ahead with questioning prior to the arrival of a solicitor was constitutionally forbidden.

39 See Hogan and Whyte, *JM Kelly: The Irish Constitution* (4th edn, Bloomsbury Professional, 2004) para 6.5.159.

40 *People (DPP) v Buck* [2002] 2 IR 268, 281.

41 *People (DPP) v O'Brien* [2005] 2 IR 206 (SC). See Daly, 'Does the Buck Stop Here? An Examination of the Pre-Trial Right to Legal Advice in Light of O'Brien v DPP' (2006) 28 DULJ 345.

Tallaght and who practised primarily in the Tallaght area. Due to his commitments, the solicitor did not attend the garda station until some four and a half hours after the accused's request to gardaí. During the period between the request and the arrival, the appellant was interviewed by the gardaí on at least two occasions. The trial judge held that by questioning the appellant in advance of the solicitor's arrival, the gardaí had deliberately and consciously breached his constitutional right of access. Given the circumstances of the solicitor's practice, the gardaí must have known that a considerable delay was inevitable.[42]

[11.22] The decision of the Court of Criminal Appeal in *DPP v Gormley*[43] lends grist to the mill of *Buck*. The applicant was arrested at his apartment and brought to the garda station at 2pm on a Sunday afternoon. At 2.15pm, he requested a consultation with either of two named solicitors. The gardaí made various attempts to contact one of these solicitors. The solicitor in question telephoned the garda station at 3.05pm, indicating that he would arrive at the station shortly after 4pm. The first interview commenced at 3.10pm and terminated at 4.46pm, just two minutes before the solicitor's arrival. In seeking leave to appeal, the applicant challenged the admission into evidence of inculpatory statements he had allegedly made during this first interview. Delivering judgment for the Court of Criminal Appeal, Finnegan J stated:

> 'Where the detained person requests access to a solicitor the Gardaí are under a duty to make *bona fide* attempts to give effect to the request and a failure to do so will constitute a breach of the suspect's constitutional right of access and render his detention unlawful. However, so long as reasonable efforts are being made to contact the solicitor there is no prohibition on the Gardaí proceeding to question him.'[44]

[11.23] The court accepted the trial judge's determination that the attempts by the gardaí to make contact with the solicitor nominated by the applicant were *bona fide* and reasonable in the circumstances. Finnegan J recognised that '[d]ifficulties can, of course, arise where arrest is effected over a weekend when access to a solicitor may be difficult to arrange'.[45] However, given the timeframe of the relevant events, there was no suggestion that there had been any deliberate attempt to frustrate the applicant's access to a solicitor.

---

42 This particular ruling by the trial judge was not at issue in the accused's subsequent appeal which was referred ultimately to the Supreme Court. *People (DPP) v O'Brien* [2005] 2 IR 206, 209.

43 *DPP v Gormley* [2009] IECCA 86 (27 July 2009).

44 *DPP v Gormley* [2009] IECCA 86 (27 July 2009) at p 5 (citing *People (DPP) v Buck* [2002] 2 IR 268).

45 *DPP v Gormley* [2009] IECCA 86 at p 5.

QUESTIONING PRIOR TO ACCESS: THE ECHR

[11.24] Whether the practice of questioning a suspect pending the arrival of a requested solicitor is compatible with the ECHR is another matter. Developments before the European Court of Human Rights and the UK Supreme Court suggest that Irish law and practice falls short of evolving European standards.

[11.25] Article 6(1) of the ECHR provides that '[i]n the determination ... of any criminal charge against him, everyone is entitled to a fair and public hearing ... by an independent and impartial tribunal established by law ...' art 6(3)(c) states that the minimum rights enjoyed by a person charged with a criminal offence include 'the right to defend himself in person or through legal assistance' of his own choosing or provided by the State. Although art 6 does not on its face prescribe a right to pre-trial legal advice, the European Court of Human Rights has construed such a right as implicit in its terms.[46] In a series of cases dating back to the 1990s, the court has questioned the propriety of interrogating a suspect prior to affording him access to legal advice where inferences may be drawn at any subsequent trial from the suspect's silence. The concept of fair procedures in art 6 is considered by the court to be undermined where the suspect is confronted with the fundamental dilemma of choosing to remain silent and run the risk that negative inferences will be drawn or opting to break his silence and face the possibility of prejudicing his defence.[47]

[11.26] In the 2008 case of *Salduz v Turkey*,[48] the Grand Chamber took the bold step of recognising the right of access to a lawyer as an essential pre-condition to any form of custodial questioning, including but not limited to the context of inference-drawing procedures. Enveloping the right firmly within the folds of the privilege against self incrimination,[49] a unanimous Grand Chamber declared:

> '... the Court finds that in order for the right to a fair trial to remain sufficiently 'practical and effective' article 6(1) requires that, as a rule, access to a lawyer should be provided as from the first interrogation of a suspect by the police, unless it is demonstrated in the light of the particular circumstances of each case that there are compelling reasons to restrict this right. Even where compelling reasons may exceptionally justify denial of access to a lawyer, such restriction – whatever its justification – must not unduly prejudice the rights of the accused under article 6. The rights of the defence will in principle be irretrievably

[46] *Murray v United Kingdom* (1996) 22 EHRR 29. However, the court has recognised that the right is not absolute and comprises one element, among others, in the concept of a fair trial: *Imbrioscia v Switzerland* (1993) 17 EHRR 441; *Brennan v United Kingdom* (2001) 34 EHRR 18.

[47] *Imbrioscia v Switzerland* (1993) 17 EHRR 441; *Brennan v United Kingdom* (2001) 34 EHRR 18; *Averill v United Kingdom* (2001) 31 EHRR 839.

[48] *Salduz v Turkey* (2008) 49 EHRR 421.

[49] *Saunders v United Kingdom* (1996) 23 EHRR 313.

prejudiced when incriminating statements made during police interrogation without access to a lawyer are used for a conviction'.[50]

Applying *Salduz v Turkey*, the UK Supreme Court recently held that Scottish law is incompatible with the ECHR in so far as it fails to vindicate the right of a detained person to have access to a lawyer prior to being interviewed. In *Cadder v Her Majesty's Advocate*,[51] the court rejected the conventional wisdom that the guarantees otherwise available under the Scottish system were sufficient to secure a fair trial.[52] Unlike its Scottish counterpart, Irish practice on questioning prior to access is grounded in case law rather than statute.[53] Nevertheless, the substantive similarities between the respective laws outweigh the differences. The decision in *Cadder* underscores the isolated position that Ireland occupies among the membership of the Council of Europe and suggests that steps should be taken to guarantee access to legal advice prior to questioning in line with the Strasbourg jurisprudence.[54]

CONSULTATION

[11.27] The right of access of legal advice presumes an entitlement to consult a lawyer in private. This is confirmed by reg 11(1) of the Custody Regulations, which states: 'An arrested person shall have reasonable access to a solicitor of his choice and be enabled to communicate with him privately'. The right to consult in private suggests that the conditions in which the consultation takes place must be such as to permit unfettered confidential communication between the suspect and her lawyer. Regulation 11(3) states in this regard that the consultation 'may take place in the sight but out of the hearing of a member' of the gardaí.[55]

---

50 *Salduz v Turkey* (2008) 49 EHRR 421, para 55. The court has maintained this stance in a number of subsequent cases. See, eg, *Amutgan v Turkey* (App No 5138/04, 3 February 2009); *Plonka v Poland* (App No 20310/02, 31 March 2009); *Brusco v France* (App No 1466/07, 14 October 2010). It is interesting to note that in *Salduz*, Judge Bratza (the President of the Grand Chamber) and three other judges would have gone further and held that 'as a rule, a suspect should be granted access to legal advice from the moment he is taken into police custody or pre-trial detention': para O-12.

51 *Cadder v Her Majesty's Advocate* [2010] UKSC 43 (26 October 2010).

52 *Cadder v Her Majesty's Advocate* [2010] UKSC 43 (26 October 2010) para 50 (overturning *Her Majesty's Advocate v McLean* [2010] SLT 73). Those safeguards included the requirement that, in order to convict, any admissions made by the detainee must be supported by corroborating evidence.

53 Criminal Procedure (Scotland) Act 1995, ss 14 and 15.

54 *Cadder v Her Majesty's Advocate* [2010] UKSC 43, para 49.

55 Criminal Justice Act (Treatment of Persons in Custody in Garda Síochána Stations) Regulations 1987 (SI 119/1987), reg 11.

[11.28] In *People (DPP) v Finnegan*, the Court of Criminal Appeal held that where a detainee consults with a solicitor by telephone, he or she has 'a constitutional right to make that call in private'.[56] During the course of questioning and sometime after the accused had met with his solicitor in person, the accused requested a telephone conversation with the solicitor. The gardaí acceded to this request but the conversation took place within the hearing of one or more members of the gardaí. The Court of Criminal Appeal held that evidence of an interview that took place subsequent to the conversation was inadmissible.

[11.29] The European Court of Human Rights has recognised that the right of a suspect to communicate with her lawyer out of the hearing of a third person is a basic requirement of a fair trial. In *Brennan v United Kingdom*,[57] the court observed:

> 'If a lawyer were unable to confer with his client and receive confidential instructions from him without surveillance, his assistance would lose most of its usefulness, whereas the Convention is intended to guarantee rights that are practical and effective.'[58]

The court held that the presence of a police officer within hearing during the applicant's first consultation with his solicitor infringed the effective exercise of the rights of the defence and constituted a violation of art 6(3) read in conjunction with art 6(1).[59] The applicant had been arrested in connection with the investigation of terrorist offences and detained at the special holding centre at Castlereagh in Belfast. He had been tried before a single judge for a total of 18 serious offences and found guilty on all counts. The trial judge had found that the presence of the police officer during the applicant's consultation with his solicitor served the purpose identified by the governing legislation of preventing information being passed on to suspects still at large. However, the court was not persuaded that this justification had traction in the present case:

> 'There was however no allegation that the solicitor was in fact likely to collaborate in such an attempt, and it was unclear to what extent a police officer would be able to spot a coded message if one was in fact passed. At most, it appears that the presence of the police officer would have had some effect in inhibiting any improper communication of information, assuming there was any risk that such might take place. While the Court finds that there is no reason to doubt the good faith of the police in imposing and implementing this measure – there is no suggestion, as was pointed out by the Government, that the police sought to use the opportunity to obtain evidence for their own purposes – it

56 *People (DPP) v Finnegan* (15 July 1997, unreported) CCA (*per* Barrington J).

57 *Brennan v United Kingdom* (2002) 34 EHRR 18.

58 *Brennan v United Kingdom* (2002) 34 EHRR 18, para 58 (internal citation omitted).

59 *Brennan v United Kingdom* (2002) 34 EHRR 18, para 63.

nonetheless finds no compelling reason arising in this case for the imposition of the restriction.'[60]

[11.30] The case law proceeds in the main on the premise that access to legal advice generally necessitates consultation with a solicitor in person as opposed to other means. Consultation by the telephone may also be utilised in practice although it seems doubtful that the right of access would be effectively protected if telephone were the only medium through which a suspect was enabled to consult with her solicitor during the entire course of her detention.

[11.31] Consultation by telephone may also affect the obligations of the gardaí during the crucial time period between a suspect's request to consult with a solicitor and the solicitor's arrival at the garda station. Any bar to immediate questioning would be removed if, by affording the suspect an opportunity to speak to a solicitor by telephone pending the solicitor's arrival, the gardaí can be said to be adequately respecting the right of access to legal advice. The point does not appear to have been authoritatively resolved by the Irish courts. Nevertheless, the general tenor of the case law strongly suggests that effective protection of the right necessitates a face-to-face consultation.

[11.32] Assuming then that consultation by telephone is best classified as a secondary and additional means of accessing legal advice, whether the gardaí are obliged to comply with a request for a telephone consultation is an open question. Delivering the judgment of the Court of Criminal Appeal in *Finnegan*, Barrington J noted that 'the right to make a telephone call to a solicitor may not be, *per se*, a constitutional right' (before going on to hold that, nevertheless, once the telephone call is allowed, the right to make that call *in private* is constitutionally protected).[61]

Presence of a Lawyer and Access to Record of Interview

[11.33] The right of access to legal advice has been more liberally construed in other jurisdictions. The prevailing view in common law countries such as the United Kingdom and the United States is that that rights of a suspect are adequately protected only through provision for the presence of the lawyer during custodial interrogation. The threshold of the right of reasonable access set by the Irish courts is considerably lower in that it appears to be satisfied in practice by periodic consultation outside the immediate setting of the custodial interview. Writing in 2000, White estimated the practical entitlement as a consultation between lawyer and suspect for approximately 10 minutes out of every hour of detention or one hour out of every six hours of detention. He argued that *Healy* provides a cogent basis for recognising a right on the part of a suspect to the presence of her lawyer, and with it the provision of on-the-spot

[60] *Brennan v United Kingdom* (2002) 34 EHRR 18, para 59.

[61] *People (DPP) v Finnegan* (15 July 1997, unreported) CCA.

advice, during the interview itself.[62] However, the courts have eschewed any such entitlement.[63]

[11.34] In *Lavery v Member in Charge, Carrickmacross Garda Síochána Station*,[64] the Supreme Court upheld various provisions of the Offences Against the State Act (Amendment) Act 1998 against challenges grounded in the constitutional rights of silence and of access to legal advice. The Act, which was passed in response to the Omagh bomb atrocity, attaches negative consequences to the decision on the part of a suspect detained under the Offences Against the State Act 1939, as amended, to remain silent in the face of custodial questioning. Specifically, the Act permits the drawing of inferences at trial from the failure of a suspect to mention facts later relied on in her defence.[65] It also makes it an offence for a person to remain silent without reasonable excuse, when she has information which she knows or believes might materially assist the gardaí.[66]

[11.35] The applicant was arrested on suspicion of membership of an unlawful organisation and detained at Carrickmacross garda station for 60 hours. During that time, the applicant met his solicitor in person on two occasions and consulted with him on the telephone once. The gardaí refused the solicitor's request that the interviews be electronically recorded or, alternatively, that a full and complete written record be taken by hand. The solicitor was also refused access to the garda notes of interview that were actually taken.

In the High Court, McGuinness J accepted the applicant's submission that the new legislation necessitated access on the part of the solicitor to the documentation he required and that, once the solicitor was refused, the applicant's detention became unlawful. She granted the application for *habeas corpus* and ordered the applicant's release. On appeal by the State, the Supreme Court overturned the judgment and reversed the order.

[11.36] The net issue before the Supreme Court was whether, in light of the encroachments on the right to silence prescribed by the 1998 Act, a person detained under the Offences Against the State regime is entitled (a) to the

---

[62] See, eg, White, 'The Confessional State: Police Interrogation in the Irish Republic: Part II' (2000) 102 ICLJ 2 at 2–3.

[63] Reporting in 1978, the O'Briain Committee recommended that a solicitor should be able to attend a custodial interview as an observer: *Report of the Committee to Recommend Certain Safeguards for Persons in Custody and for Members of An Garda Síochána* (Dublin, 1978) Prl 7158. The Martin Committee did not support this approach but opted instead to recommend the safeguard of the mandatory electronic recording of custodial interviews: *Report of the Committee to Enquire Into Certain Aspects of Criminal Procedure* (Dublin, 1990) p 46.

[64] *Lavery v Member in Charge, Carrickmacross Garda Síochána Station* [1999] 2 IR 390. See also *People v Binéad* [2007] 1 IR 374.

[65] Sections 2 and 5.

[66] Section 9.

presence of her solicitor during questioning and (b) to the solicitor having access to the garda notes of interview. In a relatively short judgment, O'Flaherty J discounted each of these suggested entitlements. He acknowledged that the detention of a person in custody would be rendered unlawful by a blanket denial of access to legal advice. Nevertheless, 'the gardaí must be allowed to exercise their powers of interrogation as they think right, provided they act reasonably'.[67] O'Flaherty J rejected the suggestion that the gardai were required to give a solicitor 'regular updates and running accounts' of the progress of their investigations. He continued:

> 'The solicitor is not entitled to be present at the interviews. Neither was it open to the applicant, or his solicitor, to prescribe the manner by which the interviews might be conducted, or where.'[68]

O'Flaherty J recognised an apparent inconsistency in the State's position that whereas a detained person is entitled to see the notes of interview, her solicitor is not. Nevertheless, the learned judge held that this 'somewhat incongruous course of conduct' did not render the detention unlawful.[69] He noted further that this legal position governs only until the detained person is charged; from that point moving forward, both the accused and her legal adviser are entitled to all relevant documentation.[70]

[11.37] The Supreme Court judgment in *Lavery* is disappointing in several respects. The failure of the court to address directly the interaction between the right to silence and the right of access to legal advice in the specific context of the 1998 Act is regrettable.[71] The general terms in which O'Flaherty J couched the right of reasonable access to legal advice failed to take account of the need for heightened access posed by the negative consequences that could potentially flow from a decision on the part of the applicant to remain silent in response to certain questions.

[11.38] Arguably, the presence of the applicant's solicitor during questioning or the provision to the solicitor of access to the garda notes of interview was necessary in order for the applicant to be properly advised regarding the likelihood that her silence would permit the court to draw negative inferences at trial or leave her open to prosecution for failure to disclose material information. The point has been eloquently put by Hogan and Whyte thus:

> '... if the right of access to a lawyer is to be a meaningful one in cases where the suspect has been detained under s 30 of the Offences Against the State Act 1939,

67 *Lavery v Member in Charge, Carrickmacross Garda Síochána Station* [1999] 2 IR 390 at 395.
68 *Lavery v Member in Charge, Carrickmacross Garda Síochána Station* [1999] 2 IR 390 at 396.
69 *Lavery v Member in Charge, Carrickmacross Garda Síochána Station* [1999] 2 IR 390 at 396.
70 *Lavery v Member in Charge, Carrickmacross Garda Síochána Station* [1999] 2 IR 390 at 396.
71 The same considerations applied to the inference-drawing mechanism contained in Criminal Justice (Drug Trafficking) Act 1996, s 7, since amended by the Criminal Justice Act 2007.

> then the lawyer must be at least entitled to know the gist of the case put to the client during the course of the interview. How otherwise could a suspect discover whether he ran the risk of adverse inferences being drawn by virtue of his silence or his failure to disclose material facts on which he later proposes to rely in his defence?'[72]

Indeed, the uncertainty surrounding the decision whether to respond to questions or remain silent in these circumstances is reminiscent of the flawed conditions surrounding the operation of s 52 of the Offences Against the State Act 1939, criticised by the European Court of Human Rights in *Heaney v Ireland.*[73]

PRACTICAL CONSIDERATIONS

[11.39] Notwithstanding a relative bounty of case law on the subject, the concept of reasonable access to legal advice remains regrettably amorphous. In practice, the sufficiency of garda efforts to facilitate access for a particular suspect tends to turn on the trial judge's determination of what is fair and reasonable in the circumstances. The case law makes plain that suspects in Ireland lack certain of the entitlements enjoyed by suspects in other common law jurisdictions such as the United Kingdom and the United States such as access to a lawyer prior to the commencement of interrogation, the presence of a lawyer during questioning, and access by the lawyer to notes or recordings of custodial interviews.

[11.40] Considerations of doctrine aside, certain practical factors inhibit the exercise of the right of access to a lawyer. The cost of legal advice and representation is an important consideration. An accused is entitled to the services of a lawyer at the expense of the State for the purposes of legal representation at trial.[74] However, this entitlement does not extend to the pre-trial custodial process.[75] The Criminal Justice (Legal Aid) Act 1962 did not include provision for the payment of solicitors to consult with suspects detained in garda stations who would be eligible due to their lack of financial means. Some 15 years later, the Tormey Committee recommended that the law be changed to allow for remuneration for services rendered to eligible clients prior to the preferment of a charge.[76] Writing in 1997, Keane observed:

> '... a solicitor who attends at a garda station for the purpose of advising an indigent detainee does so at some personal or financial sacrifice. Admittedly, payment may follow for work done subsequently, if the detention culminates in

---

72 Hogan and Whyte, *JM Kelly: The Irish Constitution* (4th edn, Bloomsbury Professional, 2004) at para.6.5.161.

73 *Heaney v Ireland* (2000) 33 EHRR 12.

74 *State (Healy) v Donoghue* [1976] IR 325.

75 *State (O) v Daly* [1977] IR 312.

76 Criminal Aid Review Committee Report (Dublin, 1977) Prl 9986.

> the preferring of a charge and legal aid is then granted by a court. Yet there is no small irony in the observation that a solicitor receives no remuneration at all if his advice to such a client should result in, or contribute to, a decision not to charge. And perhaps the real question is whether solicitors can continue to advise effectively at garda stations on a *pro bono publico* basis where their client's detention without charge can be extended up to a seven-day period.'[77]

No such change in the law has been forthcoming. Difficulties in the provision of legal services to suspects are attributable in part to the absence in Ireland of a State-funded duty solicitor scheme.[78] There has been a modest change in practice through the introduction by the Department of Justice in 2002 of a non-statutory Garda Station Legal Advice Scheme.[79]

[11.41] Recent years have seen a welcome improvement in the availability of the electronic recording of interviews. The importance of maintaining a complete and accurate contemporaneous record of the questioning of a suspect is acknowledged in reg 12 of the Custody Regulations[80] and r 9 of the Judges' Rules. Ireland has lagged behind other countries in reaping the recognised benefits of this technology; the Electronic Recording Regulations,[81] passed as late as 1997, set up a permissive rather than mandatory regime which provides considerable latitude to the gardaí.[82] This lacklustre approach has attracted the criticism of the European Committee for the Prevention of Torture.[83] Moreover, the courts have grown increasingly impatient with tardiness in the practical implementation of electronic recording and in a series of cases have made plain that they will not tolerate failures to electronically record interviews other than for very good reasons.[84]

---

77 Keane, 'Detention Without Charge and the Criminal Justice (Drug Trafficking) Act 1996' (1997) 7(1) ICLJ 1 at 9.

78 See Criminal Legal Aid Review Committee Final Report (Dublin, 2002) ch 3.

79 Walsh, *Criminal Procedure* (Thomson Round Hall, 2002) para 11.18. Conway, Daly and Schweppe, *Irish Criminal Justice: Theory, Process and Procedure* (Clarus Press, 2010) para 3.65, have highlighted the limits of the scheme: 'Only persons in receipt of Social Welfare payments or earning less than €20,316 *per annum* are entitled to free legal advice. As an administrative scheme it, as such, creates no right to free legal advice for a detained suspect and places no specific obligation on gardaí to inform the detained suspect of the existence of the scheme or the possibility that he may be able to obtain legal advice free of charge if eligible under its terms' (internal citation omitted).

80 Criminal Justice Act 1984 (Treatment of Persons in Custody in Garda Síochána Stations) Regulations 1987 (SI 119/1987).

81 Criminal Justice Act 1984 (Electronic Recording of Interviews) Regulations 1997, SI 74/1997.

82 See, eg, *People (DPP) v Holland* (15 June 1998, unreported) CCA.

83 See, eg, Report to the Government of Ireland on the Visit to Ireland carried out by the European Committee for the Prevention of Torture and Inhuman and Degrading Treatment or Punishment from 2–13 October 2006, CPI/Inf (2007) 40, paras 19–20.

84 See, eg, *People (DPP) v Connolly* [2003] 2 IR 1; *People (DPP) v Michael Murphy* [2005] 4 IR 504; *People (DPP) v Diver* [2005] 3 IR 270; *People (DPP) v O'Neill* [2007] IECCA 6 (16 March 2007).

[11.42] Nevertheless, the relatively recent case law continues to evince scenarios in which trial courts are willing to exercise their discretion to admit evidence of interviews that have not been video-recorded and the appellate courts to uphold such rulings. For example, in *People (DPP) v Cunningham*,[85] the applicant sought leave to appeal his conviction for murder on several grounds including alleged error on the part of the trial judge in refusing to exclude evidence of garda interviews that were not electronically recorded. The applicant had been brought for questioning to Dundalk garda station which lacked electronic recording facilities. The appropriate facilities were in place in Carrickmacross, which was located some 13 miles away in a different garda division, and also at Drogheda and Kells, but the trial judge accepted that moving the interviews to these locations would have disrupted the investigation. The judge also had regard to the fact that the events unfolded on Christmas Eve, 'a busy family and social occasion'.

[11.43] The Court of Criminal Appeal upheld the decision to admit the interviews recorded by conventional as opposed to electronic means. Noting that the trial judge had carefully considered all the circumstances and heard detailed submissions, Finnegan J recalled that s 27(4) of the Criminal Justice Act 1984 expressly provides that a failure to comply with the Electronic Recording Regulations shall not by itself render evidence inadmissible and that the subsection is 'without prejudice to any power of the court to exclude evidence at its discretion'. The Court of Criminal Appeal was satisfied that the trial judge's discretion had been exercised properly in this case.[86]

[11.44] The expectation that the electronic recording of custodial interviews has become the norm is reflected in the Criminal Justice Act 2007. The general inference-drawing provision inserted into the new s 19A of the Criminal Justice Act 1984[87] includes the safeguard that the interview must have been electronically recorded or the suspect must have consented to it not being so recorded.[88]

---

85 *People (DPP) v Cunningham* [2007] IECCA 49 (24 May 2007).

86 Practical considerations were also to the fore in *People (DPP) v PA* [2008] IECCA 21 (21 February 2008) in which the Court of Criminal Appeal refused leave to appeal against a conviction for the offence of making a false statement of sexual abuse. The applicant challenged the voluntariness of statements made during the third of four custodial interviews, the only one of such interviews that was not electronically recorded. In relation to the failure to electronically record the interview in question, the court accepted the gardaí's explanation that the electronic recording equipment (and the room in the garda station in which the equipment was situated) was in use at the relevant time. Citing s 27(4) of the Criminal Justice Act 1984 (which provides that any failure to comply with the Electronic Recording Regulations shall not by itself render inadmissible in evidence anything said during questioning), the court had regard to the other circumstances in the case and determined that they were cumulatively insufficient to render inadmissible the statements made during the third interview.

87 By Criminal Justice Act 2007, s 30.

88 Section 19A(6).

Section 57(1) of the 2007 Act provides for the admissibility in evidence of an electronic recording and/or the transcript of such a recording. The subsection is limited by its terms to a recording of the questioning of an accused in connection with the investigation of an offence for which she is on trial. The effect is to facilitate the use of electronic recording as proof at trial without displacing the evidentiary value of statements recorded by traditional means.

[11.45] Section 57(3) expressly preserves the admissibility of a statement recorded in writing whether or not the statement was signed by the accused and irrespective of whether it was electronically recorded. This is a somewhat curious inclusion given the legislative premise that electronic recording is now routine.[89] Exceptional circumstances may arise in which electronic recording is not feasible and a statement is taken by conventional means. But the section goes further and permits the possibility, however remote, of the admission at a trial of both electronic and written recordings, for example where a discrepancy between the two versions is alleged. Where the statement is electronically recorded, s 57(2) dispenses with the obligation on the gardaí to make a contemporaneous written record of an interview with a suspect; the electronically recorded statement may be admissible notwithstanding that it is not in writing and signed by the accused.

[11.46] Where the questioning of a suspect has been audio or video recorded, s 56 states that a copy of the recording shall be given to the person (or her legal representative) only where the person is before a court charged with an offence and then only if the court so directs, and subject to such conditions as the court may specify. This measure revoked reg 16 of the Electronic Recording Regulations which had obliged the gardaí to provide a copy in response to a written request unless the superintendent believed 'on reasonable grounds' that to do so would prejudice an ongoing investigation or endanger the safety, security and well being of another person.

INFERENCE DRAWING UNDER THE CRIMINAL JUSTICE ACT 2007

[11.47] The conclusion that the appeal in *Lavery* was an opportunity lost is underscored by recent statutory developments: the extension of inference-drawing procedures to the full gamut of ordinary offences under the Criminal Justice Act 2007[90] renders all the more acute the need to define with precision the right to legal advice in the contemporary custodial setting.

---

89 Explanatory memorandum p 12.

90 See generally McGillicuddy, 'Restrictions on the Right to Silence under the Criminal Justice Act 2007 – Part 1' (2008) 18(3) ICLJ 77 and 'Part 2' (2008) 18(4) ICLJ 112; Daly, 'Silence and Solicitors: Lessons Learned from England and Wales?' (2007) 17(2) ICLJ 2.

[11.48] The Oireachtas included limited provision for the drawing of inferences in the Criminal Justice Act 1984 as originally drafted.[91] Section 18 permits a court to draw inferences from the failure of an accused to account for the presence of an object, substance or mark on her person or in her possession. Section 19 allows for the drawing of inferences from the failure or refusal of an accused to account for her presence at a particular location. In *Rock v Ireland*,[92] the Supreme Court upheld the constitutionality of these provisions relying in part on the existence of statutory safeguards: the suspect must be cautioned about the consequences of failing or refusing to answer; an inference adverse to the accused may only be drawn where the court deems it proper; an inference may corroborate other items of evidence but cannot support a conviction standing alone.

[11.49] Limited provision for the drawing of inferences from an accused's silence in response to custodial questioning was included in s 7 of the Criminal Justice (Drug Trafficking) Act 1996[93] and s 2 of the Offences Against the State (Amendment) Act 1998 (the legislation at issue in *Lavery*). In *People (DPP) v Finnerty*,[94] the Supreme Court asserted the broad proposition that, in the absence of these kinds of express statutory inference-drawing mechanisms, a suspect is entitled to remain silent during questioning without running the risk that any negative evidentiary consequences will ensue at trial. It followed that it was permissible neither for the prosecution to cross-examine an accused about her refusal to answer questions nor for the trial judge to comment on the refusal in her charge to the jury.[95]

[11.50] The possibility that the Oireachtas might curtail the right to silence by the enactment of more liberal provision for the drawing of inferences from a failure or refusal to answer questions was canvassed in the Leahy Report in 1998[96] and the Balance in the Criminal Law Review Group Report in 2007.[97]

---

91 See generally, Hogan and Whyte, *JM Kelly: The Irish Constitution* (4th edn, Bloomsbury Professional, 2004) para 6.5.99 *et seq*.

92 *Rock v Ireland* [1997] 3 IR 484.

93 See *People (DPP) v Bowes* [2004] 4 IR 223.

94 *People (DPP) v Finnerty* [1999] 4 IR 364.

95 *People (DPP) v Finnerty* [1999] 4 IR 364; *People (DPP) v Coddington* (31 May 2001, unreported) CCA; *People (DPP) v MA* [2005] IECCA 93. See also Criminal Justice (Evidence) Act 1924, s 1(b), which prohibits the prosecution from passing any comment on the accused's silence.

96 *Report of the Expert Group Appointed to Consider Changes in the Criminal Law which were Recommended in the Garda SMI Report* (1998), Recommendation 6, pp 31–36.

97 *Final Report of the Balance in the Criminal Law Review Group* (March 2007), pp 80–98.

Having considered arguments both in favour of and against change,[98] and having explored various models for reform of the right to silence,[99] the Review Group issued a recommendation, broadly in line with that of the Leahy Committee,[100] for a statutory provision to allow an inference to be drawn from an accused's failure to mention a defence on which she subsequently relies:[101]

> 'The Review Group sees a certain logic in permitting a defendant to be challenged on a defence which emerges very late in the day. To permit such a challenge would, of necessity, involve an exploration of whether the defence was mentioned in the Garda interview.'[102]

[11.51] Nevertheless, the proposal differed from the pre-existing inference-drawing provisions in significant respects. For example, the proposed inference-drawing provision was limited to the question of recent invention of a defence; it did not invite the trier of fact to hold that a false defence amounted to corroboration and nor did it permit a more general inference as to guilt to be drawn. Moreover, the Review Group did not intend its provision to extend to a situation in which a defence was legitimately withheld in the garda interview but volunteered shortly afterwards, 'where the detained person was in shock, for example, or embarrassed, or incapable of applying his or her mind to the position'.[103]

Among the safeguards that the Review Group recommended should accompany provision for the drawing of inferences were an amended form of caution and the recording of interviews (or the consent of the detained person to the non-recording of the interview). However, the Review Group rejected the possible safeguard that an accused person be entitled to have a lawyer present

---

98 *Final Report of the Balance in the Criminal Law Review Group* (March 2007), pp 67–73. The Review Group also identified some of the practical policing concerns that supported reform. Having noted that the principal reason for extended periods of custodial detention in the Criminal Justice Act 2006 was hope on the part of the gardaí that suspects would feel compelled to speak about their involvement in crimes and to make full confessions, the Review Group observed at p 27:

> Some of the submissions to the Review Group made the point that experienced criminals exploit the present system by 'running down the clock' by having frequent consultations with solicitors or visits from family members. In an increasing number of cases involving the detention of non-nationals, it is also necessary for the Gardaí to secure the services of an interpreter. All of this serves to reduce the time available to the Gardaí for effective interrogation. In other cases experienced suspects can simply resort to standard anti-interrogation techniques by simply staring at a spot on the wall and refuse to say anything [internal citations omitted].

99 *Final Report of the Balance in the Criminal Law Review Group* (March 2007), pp 80–92.

100 *Report of the Expert Group Appointed to Consider Changes in the Criminal Law which were Recommended in the Garda SMI Report* (1998), Recommendation 6.

101 *Final Report of the Balance in the Criminal Law Review Group* (March 2007), pp 84–90.

102 *Final Report of the Balance in the Criminal Law Review Group* (March 2007), p 86.

103 *Final Report of the Balance in the Criminal Law Review Group* (March 2007), p 87.

during the interview on the ground that it would be unduly restrictive on the prosecution and the police.[104]

[11.52] Part 4 of the Criminal Justice Act 2007 developed the law in this area in two salient respects. First, it amended the specific inference-drawing provisions contained in the Criminal Justice Act 1984, the Criminal Justice (Drug Trafficking Act) 1996 and the Offences Against the State (Amendment) Act 1998. The 2007 Act extended the scope of ss 18 and 19 of the 1984 Act and refined and strengthened the statutory safeguards that conditioned the drawing of inferences. In particular, the amended sections state that the accused must have been afforded a reasonable opportunity to consult a solicitor before the failure or refusal occurred.[105] The 2007 Act made corresponding amendments to the inference-drawing procedure contained in s 2 of the 1998 Act and repealed s 7 of the 1996 Act.[106]

[11.53] Second, the central plank of Part 4 of the 2007 Act is a general inference-drawing mechanism, similar in substance to s 2 of the 1998 Act and the former s 7 of the 1996, but applicable in relation to the full gamut of ordinary arrestable offences. The enactment took the guise of a new s 19A inserted into the 1984 Act.[107] It permits a court to draw such inferences 'as may appear proper' from the failure of an accused to mention particular facts where that failure is tendered in evidence in proceedings for an arrestable offence.[108] The predicate questioning may take place at various stages during the pre-trial process: at any time before the accused is charged with the offence; at the time when the accused is so charged; and at the time when the accused is informed by a garda officer of the possibility of prosecution for the offence.[109]

[11.54] Section 19A is broader in scope that the statutory provision recommended by the Review Group. The basis for the drawing of inferences is that the accused 'failed to mention any fact relied on in his or her defence in [the] proceedings, being a fact which clearly called for an explanation from him or her when so questioned, charged or informed, as the case may be'. The court (whether judge, judges or jury subject to the judge's directions) may draw such inferences when determining whether the accused is guilty of the offence charged or of any other offence of which she could lawfully be convicted on that charge.[110] However, the power to draw inference may also be invoked at an

[104] *Final Report of the Balance in the Criminal Law Review Group* (March 2007), p 90.

[105] Sections 18(3)(b) and 19(3)(b).

[106] Criminal Justice Act 2007, s 3. Presumably on the premise that the questioning of persons detained under that Act is covered by the broader provision for inference-drawing contained in the Part 4 of the 2007 Act.

[107] By Criminal Justice Act 2007, s 30.

[108] Section 19A(1).

[109] Section 19A(1)(a) and (b).

[110] Section 19A(1).

earlier juncture in the proceedings when the court determines whether a charge should be dismissed or whether there is no case to answer. In relation to the conditions under which inferences may be drawn, the wording of s 19A mirrors that of amended ss 18 and 19 of the 1984 Act. Thus, an inference may corroborate other evidence[111] but an accused may not be convicted solely or mainly on an inference. The accused must have been cautioned in ordinary language[112] and the questioning must have been electronically recorded unless the accused consented to it not being so recorded.[113] Particularly pertinent to the present discussion is the stipulation that the accused must have been afforded a reasonable opportunity to consult a solicitor before the failure to mention a material fact occurred.[114]

[11.55] Taken collectively, the inference-drawing provisions of the 2007 Act represent a substantial encroachment on the right to silence under Irish law. The general inference-drawing provision contained in the new s 19A inserted into the 1984 Act effectively rolls back the benchmark set in *Finnerty.* A weakness in the measure is the failure to counterbalance the diminution in the right to silence with a strengthened right of access to legal advice. As we shall see, the European Court of Human Rights has underscored the complementary protection that these respective rights provide against the backdrop of inference-drawing procedures.[115] Although s 19A(3)(b) incorporates the requirement that a suspect be afforded a reasonable opportunity to consult a solicitor, arguably the Oireachtas should have gone further and legislated for the presence of the solicitor during questioning or, at a minimum, for the solicitor's access to the record of interview.

Inference Drawing under the ECHR

[11.56] In *Murray v United Kingdom*, the European Court of Human Rights upheld the drawing of incriminating inferences under Northern Irish legislation against a challenge grounded in art 6, the fair trial guarantee of the ECHR. The applicant had been convicted of aiding and abetting unlawful imprisonment and sentenced to eight years in prison after a trial in which adverse inferences had been drawn from the applicant's silence during police questioning.

[11.57] Although emphasising that its role was confined to assessing the fairness of the applicant's trial, the court couched its judgment in terms which shed light on the broader issue of the compatibility of inference-drawing mechanisms with the Convention. It observed that inference-drawing fell somewhere between two extremes: on the one hand, it was 'self-evident' that a

[111] Section 19A(1).
[112] Section 19A(1)(a).
[113] Section 19A(6).
[114] Section 19A(3)(b).
[115] *Murray v United Kingdom* (1996) 22 EHRR 29.

conviction could not be based 'solely or mainly' on such inferences but, on the other, it could not be said that an accused's decision to remain silent should necessarily have no bearing on the court's evaluation of the evidence against him.[116] The court stated:

> 'Whether the drawing of adverse inferences from an accused's silence infringes Article 6 is a matter to be determined in the light of all the circumstances of the case, having particular regard to the situations where inferences may be drawn, the weight attached to them by the national courts in their assessment of the evidence and the degree of compulsion inherent in the situation.'[117]

In the applicant's case, the court was satisfied that the legislation contained sufficient safeguards[118] and that the drawing of inferences in the circumstances was 'a matter of common sense' on the facts[119] and could not be regarded as 'unfair or unreasonable'.[120]

[11.58] In *Murray*, the applicant had been denied access to a lawyer for the first 48 hours of his detention. The European Court examined this issue separately and concluded that the denial of access to a lawyer constituted a breach of art 6.[121] Ironically, the finding of a violation of the Convention's standards in relation to the provision of legal advice did not disturb the court's conclusion that the drawing of inferences had been neither unfair nor unreasonable.[122] The applicant had argued that the question of access to a solicitor was inextricably entwined with the drawing of inferences; he argued that the legislation set a trap because if an accused remained silent under police questioning, inferences of one kind or another could be drawn regardless of whether the accused subsequently gave evidence at trial or maintained his silence throughout the proceedings.[123] However, the court was not willing to speculate either about the

---

116 *Murray v United Kingdom* (1996) 22 EHRR 29 at 61, para 47.

117 *Murray v United Kingdom* (1996) 22 EHRR 29 at 61, para 47.

118 Notably that silence was not in itself considered an indication of guilt; there was no compulsion to speak in that silence was not a criminal offence and did not render an accused susceptible to contempt of court; an accused was given appropriate warnings; and the trial judge had a common sense discretion whether to draw an inference in any particular case: *Murray v United Kingdom* (1996) 22 EHRR 29, paras 48–51.

119 The prosecution evidence was that when the police entered a house where a person had been held captive by the IRA, they had come upon the applicant coming down the stairs. The person held captive had also given evidence which placed the applicant in the house. The inferences drawn by the trial judge related specifically to the applicant's failure to account to the police for his presence in the house and his failure to give evidence in his own defence when so requested by the court under the relevant legislation: *Murray v United Kingdom* (1996) 22 EHRR 29, paras 52–54.

120 *Murray v United Kingdom* (1996) 22 EHRR 29, para 54. The finding that there had been no breach of Article 6(1) and (2) was reached by 14 votes to 5.

121 Article 6(1) in conjunction with 6(3). On this issue the court divided 12 to 7.

122 *Murray v United Kingdom* (1996) 22 EHRR 29, para 56.

123 *Murray v United Kingdom* (1996) 22 EHRR 29, para 55.

inferences that could possibly have been drawn under the legislation or about the reasons behind the legal advice the applicant was ultimately given.[124]

[11.59] It is difficult to reconcile the court's finding that the drawing of inferences was fair and reasonable with its determination that the denial of access to legal advice was incompatible with the rights of the accused under art 6. The court was forthright in its condemnation of the denial of access to legal advice where an accused may be subject to inference-drawing procedures:

> 'The Court is of the opinion that the scheme contained in the Order is such that it is of paramount importance for the rights of the defence that an accused has access to a lawyer at the initial stages of police interrogation. It observes in this context that, under the Order, at the beginning of police interrogation, the accused is confronted with a fundamental dilemma relating to his defence. If he chooses to remain silent, adverse inferences may be drawn against him in accordance with the provisions of the Order. On the other hand, if the accused opts to break his silence during the course of interrogation, he runs the risk of prejudicing his defence without necessarily removing the possibility of inferences being drawn against him.[125]

The court concluded that 'under such conditions' the concept of fairness enshrined in art 6 requires that that accused has the benefit of the assistance of a lawyer even at the initial stages of police questioning. The denial of access for the first 48 hours of questioning, 'in a situation where the rights of the defence may well be irretrievably prejudiced' was incompatible with art 6.[126] The judicial rhetoric on the importance of the right in the context of inference-drawing procedures and the court's recognition of the heightened need for legal advice are striking. It is all the more curious then that the court should uphold as reasonable and fair the drawing of inferences from the applicant's silence at a time when he was being unlawfully deprived of his right of access to a lawyer.

[11.60] Some four years later, the European Court tackled head-on the relationship between the right of access to a lawyer and the propriety of the drawing of inferences from silence in *Condron v United Kingdom.*[127] The applicants claimed that their right to a fair trial was violated by the decision of the trial judge to leave the jury with the option of drawing an adverse inference from their silence during police interviews. The applicants were intoxicated at the time of their arrest. They were afforded access to a solicitor who was present during the totality of the interviews. At trial, the applicants took the stand and

---

124 *Murray v United Kingdom* (1996) 22 EHRR 29, para 56. The applicant had been interviewed on 12 occasions prior to being granted access to his solicitor. At that point, the solicitor advised the applicant to remain silent partly because he had maintained silence already during the interview and partly because the solicitor would not be permitted to remain present during questioning (para 59).

125 *Murray v United Kingdom* (1996) 22 EHRR 29, para 66.

126 *Murray v United Kingdom* (1996) 22 EHRR 29, para 66.

127 *Condron v United Kingdom* (2001) 31 EHRR 1.

explained that they had held their silence on the strength of their solicitor's advice that they were unfit to answer questions.[128] As the European Court observed, *Condron* was factually distinguishable from *Murray* in certain respects. In particular, the function of drawing inferences under the relevant legislation rested with the jury, properly directed.[129] The trial judge drew the jury's attention to the applicants' explanation for their silence but in terms that left the jurors at liberty to draw an adverse inference notwithstanding that they may have been satisfied that the explanation was plausible. The European Court was not satisfied with the sufficiency of this direction:

> 'In the Court's opinion, as a matter of fairness, the jury should have been directed that it could only draw an adverse inference if satisfied that the applicants' silence at the police interview could only sensibly be attributed to their having no answer or none that would stand up to cross-examination.'[130]

[11.61] A unanimous court concluded that the jury had not been properly directed and that the imperfection in the direction could not be remedied on appeal. The formula employed by the trial judge could not be said to reflect the balance that the court sought to strike in *Murray* between the right to silence and the circumstances in which an adverse inference may be drawn from silence.[131] Consequently, the applicants had not received a fair hearing within the meaning of art 6(1) of the Convention.[132]

[11.62] In *Condron*, the European Court reinforced its determination in *Murray* that the compatibility of inference-drawing with art 6 of necessitates a case specific assessment of the totality of the circumstances including 'the situations where inferences may be drawn, the weight to be attached to them by the national courts in their assessment of the evidence and the degree of compulsion inherent in the situation'.[133] This approach was again endorsed in *Averill v United Kingdom*,[134] in which the court found no violation of art 6 where inferences had been drawn from the applicant's silence during multiple interviews conducted over several days.[135]

---

[128] This was confirmed by the solicitor in the *voir dire* proceedings: *Condron v United Kingdom* (2001) 31 EHRR 1, para 61.

[129] *Condron v United Kingdom* (2001) 31 EHRR 1, para 57. In addition, unlike Murray, the applicants gave evidence at their trial and offered an explanation for their silence during police interviews.

[130] *Condron v United Kingdom* (2001) 31 EHRR 1, para 61.

[131] *Condron v United Kingdom* (2001) 31 EHRR 1, para 61.

[132] *Condron v United Kingdom* (2001) 31 EHRR 1, para 66.

[133] *Condron v United Kingdom* (2001) 31 EHRR 1, para 56.

[134] *Averill v United Kingdom* (2001) 31 EHRR 83.

[135] By 6 votes to 1. Like Murray, the applicant had been denied access to a lawyer, in his case for the first 24 hours of his detention. Notwithstanding the result, the court took the occasion of *Averill* to emphasise that the absence of a lawyer is a relevant factor to be weighed in the balance between respecting the right to silence and permitting the reasonable drawing of inferences.

[11.63] An issue raised but not examined by the court in *Murray* was whether an accused is entitled to have his solicitor present during police interviews.[136] The wording of the judgment seems to reflect a judicial assumption that the right of access is a right to consult a lawyer with a view to receiving legal advice rather than an entitlement to the lawyer's presence at interview.[137] This is reinforced by the court's subsequent judgment in *Brennan v United Kingdom*[138] which also arose out of an arrest and detention in Northern Ireland in connection with terrorist offences. Although the applicant had been denied access to his solicitor for a 24-hour period, his evidentiary challenge concerned the admissibility of statements he had made after he had consulted with his solicitor. It was the applicant's contention that the absence of his lawyer during interviews, coupled with the failure of the police to electronically record the interviews, contributed to the oppressiveness of the interrogation process.[139]

[11.64] The European Court began its assessment by recalling that the admissibility of evidence is principally a matter for the national courts to determine. The court will intervene only where the national court's assessment of the evidence was arbitrary or capricious or, in the case of confessions, the guarantees to safeguard the reliability of the evidence were manifestly inadequate.[140] In the present case, the circumstances in which the statements were obtained 'were subjected to strict scrutiny' on a *voir dire* at which the applicant was represented and were extensively reviewed on appeal.[141] While acknowledging that the presence of a lawyer during questioning enhances the protection of Convention rights, the court stopped short of prescribing it as an essential condition of a fair trial:

> 'The applicant has argued that in the absence of independent evidence of video or taped records of police interview, and the absence of the accused's solicitor, there are considerable difficulties for an accused to convince a court, against the testimony of the police officers, that any oppression took place. The Court agrees that the recording of interviews provides a safeguard against police misconduct, as does the attendance of the suspect's lawyer. However, it is not persuaded that these are an indispensable precondition of fairness within the meaning of Article 6 § 1 of the Convention. The essential issue in each application brought before this Court remains whether in the circumstances of the individual case the applicant received a fair trial.'[142]

The court was satisfied that in the present case the adversarial procedure conducted before the trial court (at which evidence was heard from the

[136] *Murray v United Kingdom* (1996) 22 EHRR 29 at 67, para 69.

[137] *Murray v United Kingdom* (1996) 22 EHRR 29 at 67, para 69.

[138] *Brennan v United Kingdom* (2002) 34 EHRR 18.

[139] *Brennan v United Kingdom* (2002) 34 EHRR 18, para 49.

[140] *Brennan v United Kingdom* (2002) 34 EHRR 18, para 51.

[141] *Brennan v United Kingdom* (2002) 34 EHRR 18, para 52.

[142] *Brennan v United Kingdom* (2002) 34 EHRR 18, para 53.

applicant, psychological experts, the various police officers involved in the interrogations and the police doctors who examined the applicant during his detention) was capable of bringing to light any oppressive conduct by the police.[143]

The protections afforded to suspects in *Murray* and *Brennan* have been strengthened by the 2008 decision of the Court of Human Rights in *Salduz v Turkey*[144] discussed at para **11.26** above. The Grand Chamber recognised the right of access to a lawyer as an essential pre-condition to custodial questioning.

Legal Advice to Remain Silent

[11.65] Section 19A of the Criminal Justice Act 2007 is modelled on legislation in England and Wales, s 34 of the Criminal Justice and Public Order Act 1994, which has itself been the subject of controversial discourse. The scenario presented by *Condron v United Kingdom* has given rise to particular difficulty. Where the accused remains silent during police questioning and then gives evidence at trial that her silence was based on legal advice received from her solicitor, how should the jury assess the veracity of the proffered justification? Placing the issue in the frame of the Irish legislation, McGillicuddy contends that a delicate balancing act will be required:

> 'On the one hand, the courts may not want to allow defendants to avoid s.19A altogether by merely stating that they were relying on legal advice to stay silent during an interview so that no inference can be drawn. To permit otherwise will allow legal advice to circumvent the entire workings of the section by becoming a shield against inferences being drawn in all circumstances.
>
> On the other hand, once it is accepted that a person has a right to legal advice then it is important that legal privilege attaches to those conversations between the solicitor and the client so that the solicitor can provide appropriate advice to her client. If legal professional privilege is weakened by the operation of s.19A then that will create other issues in relation to the constitutional right of access to legal advice and how intrusive the inquiries into the discussions between the solicitor and the accused could be.'[145]

If a suspect genuinely relies on the advice of her solicitor to remain silent and, moreover, this legal advice constitutes the sole reason for her failure to mention a fact later relied on in her defence, would the drawing of an adverse inference

143 *Brennan v United Kingdom* (2002) 34 EHRR 18, para 53.

144 *Salduz v Turkey* (2008) 49 EHRR 421.

145 McGillicuddy, 'Restrictions on the Right to Silence under the Criminal Justice Act 2007 – Part 1' (2008) 18(3) ICLJ 77 at 84. Daly has suggested that anecdotally it seems that the gardaí had been slow to invoke the terms of the pre-existing inference-drawing provisions, such as s 7 of the 1996 Act, 'due to their knowledge of the definitional disarray caused by the similarly phrased s.34 in the English courts': Daly, 'Silence and Solicitors: Lessons Learned from England and Wales?' (2007) 17(2) ICLJ 2 at 6.

compromise the fairness of her trial?[146] The English courts have developed a convoluted and contradictory jurisprudence on point.

[11.66] In *R v Betts and Hall*,[147] the Court of Appeal focused on the sincerity of an accused's reliance on legal advice to remain silent. The issue for the jury was whether the accused's claim that his or her silence was attributable to legal advice was in fact genuine. In quashing the appellants' convictions on the ground that the jury had not been properly directed, Kaye LJ noted that that jurymay have failed to appreciate that they could only draw inferences if they were sure that the appellants' failure to mention facts was based on something other than mere legal advice.[148] In a subsequent reversal of reasoning, the Court of Appeal declared in *R v Howell*[149] that genuine reliance on legal advice is not the exclusive benchmark for the drawing of inferences:

> 'We do not consider, *pace* the reasoning in *Betts & Hall*, that once it is shown that the advice (of whatever quality) has genuinely been relied on as the reason for the suspect's remaining silent, adverse comment is thereby disallowed. The premise of such a position is that in such circumstances it is in principle not reasonable to expect the suspect to mention the facts in question. We do not believe that it is so. What is reasonable depends on all the circumstances.'[150]

Thus, the court upheld the trial judge's direction to the jury that reasonableness rather than genuineness should be the touchstone for assessing the accused's reliance on legal advice. The essence of the holding in *Howell* is that the genuine reliance on legal advice to remain silent is not in itself sufficient to bar the drawing of adverse inferences.[151] Academic commentators are divided on whether *Howell* sanctioned an objective test over the seemingly subjective approach in *Betts & Hall* and, more generally, whether the decisions can be reconciled.[152]

---

146 See Daly 'Silence and Solicitors: Lessons Learned from England and Wales?' (2007) 17(2) ICLJ 2.

147 *R v Betts and Hall* [2001] EWCA Crim 224, [2001] 2 Cr App R 257. For a review of earlier English and Northern Irish case law see Easton, 'Legal Advice, Common Sense and the Right to Silence' (1998) 2 E & P 109. For an empirically-based assessment of the effect of the relevant legislation in the 1990s, see Jackson, 'Silence and Proof: Extending the Boundaries of Criminal Proceedings in the United Kingdom' (2001) 5 E & P 145.

148 *R v Betts and Hall* [2001] EWCA Crim 224, [2001] 2 Cr App R 257, para 55.

149 *R v Howell* [2003] EWCA Crim 1. See Choo and Jennings, 'Silence on Legal Advice Revisited: *R v Howell*' (2003) 7 E & P 185.

150 *R v Howell* [2003] EWCA Crim 1, para 24.

151 This approach was approved in the subsequent case of *R v Knight* [2003] EWCA Crim 1977.

152 See, eg, Choo and Jennings, 'Silence and Legal Advice Revisited: *R v Howell*' (2003) 7 E & P 185; Malik, 'Silence on Legal Advice: Clarity But Not Justice?: *R v Beckles*' (2005) 9 E & P 211; Cooper, 'Legal Advice and Pre-Trial Silence – Unreasonable Developments' (2006) 10 E & P 60; Daly, 'Silence and Solicitors: Lessons Learned from England and Wales?' (2007) 17(2) 2.

[11.67] Whatever the merits of this debate, the Court of Appeal has continued to emphasise the prevailing importance of reasonableness in the assessment of an accused's decision to remain silent. In *R v Hoare & Pierce*,[153] the court recalled that s 34 requires the jury to determine whether it was 'reasonable' for the accused to remain silent in the circumstances. Auld J declared:

> 'The question in the end, which is for the jury, is whether regardless of advice, genuinely given and genuinely accepted, an accused has remained silent not because of that advice but because he had no or no satisfactory explanation to give.'[154]

This approach apparently draws strength from the common-sense assumption underpinning the legislation that when confronted with an accusation an innocent person would normally give an explanation. The assumption is problematic, however, in so far as common sense may be 'unreliable, impressionistic and unsystematic' and, moreover, it may 'wrongly equate silence with guilt and fail to take account of other possible factors which underlie the silence, including fear, anxiety, confusion, the desire to protect someone else, embarrassment, outrage and anger'.[155]

[11.68] The jury's assessment of the reasonableness of an accused's decision to act on legal advice honestly given and genuinely accepted may place both the accused and her solicitor in an awkward position. Indeed, the dilemma may raise considerations of principle as much as pragmatics. Can the accused be sure that she is acting reasonably in relying on the advice of the solicitor? What is the benefit of legal advice, after all, if the accused must second-guess her solicitor?[156] Writing in 1998, Easton highlighted the challenges lawyers face in determining the appropriate advice to give to clients who are subject to inference-drawing procedures:

> 'Lawyers may be called on to give evidence at the client's trial regarding advice given earlier. Notes must be kept of any requests made by the police, whether the client appears to understand the significance of speaking or remaining silent, how the caution was worded and the reasons why the lawyer advised the client to speak or refrain from speaking. The legal adviser needs to be clear that the client understands the implications of silence. The lawyer also needs to assess carefully the relevant facts of the case and its strength to consider whether to advise

[153] *R v Hoare & Pierce* [2005] 1 WLR 1804, [2005] 1 Cr App R 22, [2004] EWCA Crim 784.

[154] *R v Hoare & Pierce* [2005] 1 WLR 1804, para 55.

[155] Easton, 'Legal Advice, Common Sense and the Right to Silence' (1998) 2 E & P 109 at 114. Easton argues that it is the weaknesses of common-sense thinking that render clear judicial guidance so important.

[156] Cooper, 'Legal Advice and Pre-Trial Silence – Unreasonable Developments' (2006) 10 E & P 60 at 67 ('There would seem to be little point, if any, in insisting that a suspect receives (or at least has the opportunity to receive) legal advice in the police station if the jury might then conclude that it effectively amounts to an admission by conduct to accept a solicitor's advice to remain silent').

> silence in those circumstances, and whether speaking is more hazardous than silence, notwithstanding the risk of adverse inferences.'[157]

It is generally acknowledged that a test based on 'genuineness' alone could open the door to the pro forma giving of legal advice to remain silent as a means of circumventing the drawing of inferences. Commenting on the English experience, Malik makes the point that 'it is *solicitors*, not *defendants*, who should be penalised for conduct of his sort'.[158]

[11.69] The consistency of this line of English authority with European jurisprudence has been called into question.[159] The drawing of inferences under s 34 was addressed in *Condron.* The court found fault with the direction to the jury in so far as the trial judge had left the jurors free to draw an adverse inference even if they considered it plausible that the applicants had remained silent because of legal advice. The applicants had been deprived of a fair trial because the jury should have been directed that it could draw an adverse inference only if satisfied that the applicants' silence could be attributed to their having no answer or no answer that would survive cross-examination.[160] The fact that the cross-examination of the applicants trespassed on the legal advice they had received in confidence was not in itself incompatible with the Convention because the applicants had effectively waived legal professional privilege by making the legal advice an overt aspect of their defence.[161]

[11.70] The issue was revisited in *Beckles v United Kingdom*,[162] where the court found that art 6(1) had been violated because, as in *Condron*, the trial judge had misdirected the jury. The applicant had been convicted of robbery, false imprisonment and attempted murder. He made two off-the-cuff statements to the police on arrest. However, during the first of two custodial interviews, he remained silent on the basis of legal advice. The applicant was interviewed a second time several months later and on this occasion he answered questions put to him by the police and gave an account consistent with his evidence at trial. In language reminiscent of *Condron* (and, indeed, *Betts and Hall)*, the European Court criticised the trial judge's failure to direct the jury to consider the applicant's reliance on legal advice in these circumstances:

> '[T]he Court considers that the trial judge failed to give appropriate weight in his direction to the applicant's explanation for his silence at the police interview and

---

157 Easton, 'Legal Advice, Common Sense and the Right to Silence' (1998) 2 E & P 109 at 120–121.

158 Malik, 'Silence on Legal Advice: Clarity But Not Justice?: *R v Beckles*' (2005) 9 E & P 211 at 216.

159 Choo & Jennings, 'Silence on Legal Advice Revisited: *R v Howell*' (2003) 7 E & P 185 at 188–189.

160 *Condron v United Kingdom* (2001) 31 EHRR 1, para 61.

161 *Condron v United Kingdom* (2001) 31 EHRR 1, para 60.

162 *Beckles v United Kingdom* (2002) 36 EHRR 132.

left the jury at liberty to draw an adverse inference from the applicant's silence notwithstanding that it may have been satisfied as to the plausibility of the explanation given by him ... [H]e invited the jury to reflect on whether the applicant's reason for his silence was a 'good one' without also emphasising that it must be consistent only with guilt.'[163]

[11.71] It was the view of the European Court that the jury should have been told that if they were satisfied that the applicant's silence could not sensibly be attributed to his having no case to answer or none that would stand up to police questioning it should not draw an adverse inference.[164] The Criminal Cases Review Commission subsequently referred the case to the Court of Appeal which quashed the applicant's convictions and ordered a retrial.[165] The court found that the trial judge had omitted reference in his direction to the genuineness and reasonableness of the applicant's reliance on legal advice and that, based on this misdirection, the jury may have drawn adverse inferences.[166] Approving *Hoare & Pierce*, the court affirmed that reasonableness is the touchstone for assessing an accused's decision to remain silent on the basis of legal advice. Lord Woolf CJ couched the test in the following terms:

> 'If the jury consider that the defendant genuinely relied on the advice, that is not necessarily the end of the matter. It may still not have been reasonable for him to rely on the advice, or the advice may not have been the true explanation for his silence.'[167]

In summary, this is now the prevailing position in England on the drawing of adverse inferences from silence based on legal advice.

[11.72] For the purposes of the present discussion, the most pertinent aspect of the English experience concerns the impact of inference-drawing procedures on legal professional privilege. In *Condron*, the European Court of Human Rights held that judicial scrutiny of legal advice was compatible with art 6 because the applicants had essentially waived their entitlement to legal professional privilege:

> 'The court would observe at this juncture that the fact that the applicants were subjected to cross-examination on the content of their solicitor's advice cannot be said to raise an issue of fairness under Article 6 of the Convention. They were

[163] *Beckles v United Kingdom* (2002) 36 EHRR 132, para 64.

[164] *Beckles v United Kingdom* (2002) 36 EHRR 132, para 64.

[165] *R v Beckles (No2)* [2005] 1 WLR 2829, [2005] 1 Cr App R 23, [2005] 1 All ER 705.

[166] For analysis of the decision of the Court of Appeal see Malik, 'Silence on Legal Advice: Clarity But Not Justice? *R v Beckles*' (2005) 9 E & P 211.

[167] *R v Beckles (No 2)* (2005) 1 WLR 2829 at 2844. This standard has been incorporated into a specimen direction issued by the Judicial Studies Board: JSB Crown Court Bench Book Specimen Directions, s IV 40, 'Defendant's Failure to Mention Facts when Questioned or Charged, s.34 CJPOA 1994', posted at www.jsboard.co.uk.

under no compulsion to disclose the advice given, other than the indirect compulsion to avoid the reason for their silence remaining at the level of a bare explanation. The applicants chose to make the content of their solicitor's advice a live issue as part of their defence. For that reason they cannot complain that the scheme of section 34 of the 1994 Act is such as to override the confidentiality of their discussions with their solicitor.'[168]

[11.73] Thus, reliance on legal advice to remain silent is one of the relevant factors to which a national court must give appropriate weight.[169] Yet, by proffering legal advice as an explanation for silence, a suspect necessarily puts the substance of the legal advice in issue. She may be deemed to have waived legal professional privilege with the consequence that the prosecution may cross-examine her about the advice without imperilling the fairness of the trial. Lord Woolf recognised the conundrum in *R v Beckles (No 2)*:

> 'Where the reason put forward by a defendant for not answering questions is that he is acting on legal advice, the position is singularly delicate. On the one hand the Courts have not unreasonably wanted to avoid defendants driving a coach and horses through section 34 and by so doing defeating the statutory objective. Such an explanation is very easy for a defendant to advance and difficult to investigate because of legal professional privilege. On the other hand, it is of the greatest importance that defendants should be able to be advised by their lawyer without having to reveal the terms of that advice if they act in accordance with that advice.'[170]

The implications for the defence are particularly profound because once privilege has been waived, then any aspect of the discussions between solicitor and client are open to disclosure. Daly contends that this state of affairs threatens 'the continued existence of a meaningful legal professional privilege' and, in turn, 'the quality of legal advice which can be provided to suspects detained for questioning by the police'.[171]

[11.74] The wording of the new s 19A inserted into the Criminal Justice Act 1984 differs from the English s 34 in an important respect. Doubtless wary of the English experience, the parliamentary draftsman has avoided use of the term 'reasonably' and opted instead for the formula of a suspect failing to mention 'a fact which in the circumstances existing at the time clearly called for an explanation'. It is by no means clear, however, that this wording will remove the need for courts to probe into confidential legal advice where that advice is cited

168 *Condron v United Kingdom* (2000) 31 EHRR 1, para 60.

169 *Condron v United Kingdom* (2000) 31 EHRR 1, para 60. This approach to waiver is consistent with that of the Irish courts.

170 *R v Beckles (No 2)* [2005] 1 WLR 2829 at 2843.

171 Daly, 'Silence and Solicitors: Lessons Learned from England and Wales?' (2007) 17(2) ICLJ 2 at pp 6–7.

as the reason for a suspect remaining silent during garda questioning. It is worth recalling that not every reference to legal advice will necessarily be construed as a waiver of privilege.[172] However, the English case law suggests that solicitors acting for suspects should be mindful of the likelihood of waiver when advising clients and making representations to the gardaí.[173]

---

[172] See, eg, *R v Bowden* [1999] 1 WLR 823 (mere statement that the defendant declined to answer question on legal advice did not amount to waiver).

[173] A pointed noted by McGillicuddy, 'Restrictions on the Right to Silence under the Criminal Justice Act 2007 – Part 1' (2008) 18(3) ICLJ 77 at 86.

Index

All references are to paranumbers